Classroom Management

Classroom Management

Creating a Successful K–12 Learning Community

Third Edition

Paul R. Burden
Kansas State University

WILEY

John Wiley & Sons, Inc.

Photo Credits

Page 1	Will & Deni McIntyre/Photo Researchers, Inc.
Page 15	Will Hart/PhotoEdit
Page 40	Bill Freeman/PhotoEdit
Page 63	Bob Daemmrich/The Image Works
Page 83	Cindy Charles/PhotoEdit
Page 97	Elizabeth Crews/The Image Works
Page 120	Tom Stewart/Corbis Images
Page 146	Jeff Greenberg/The Image Works
Page 167	Jeff Greenberg/The Image Works
Page 188	Bob Daemmrich/The Image Works
Page 214	Mary Kate Denny/PhotoEdit
Page 236	Richard Hutchings/PhotoEdit

ACQUISITIONS EDITOR	Christopher Johnson
EDITORIAL ASSISTANT	Lindsay Lovier
SENIOR PRODUCTION EDITOR	Valerie A. Vargas
SENIOR MARKETING MANAGER	Jeffrey Rucker
MEDIA EDITOR	Sasha Giacoppo
SENIOR DESIGNER	Madelyn Lesure
PHOTO EDITOR	Lisa Gee
PRODUCTION MANAGEMENT	Ingrao Associates
COVER CREDIT	©Gabe Palmer/CORBIS

This book was set in 10/12 Times Roman by Laserwords Private Limited, Chennai, India and printed and bound by RR Donnelley. The cover was printed by Phoenix Color, Inc.

The book is printed on acid-free paper.∞

To order books or for customer service, please call 1-800-CALL WILEY (225-5945).

Library of Congress Cataloging-in-Publication Data:

Burden, Paul R.
    Classroom management : creating a successful K–12 learning community / Paul R. Burden.—3rd ed.
        p. cm.
    Includes bibliographical references and index.
    ISBN : 978-0-471-71073-8 (pbk. : alk. paper)
        1. Classroom management—United States. 2. School discipline—United States. I. Title.
LB3013.B873 2005
371.102′4—dc22

2005054654

Printed in the United States of America

10 9 8 7 6 5

Contents

6. Maintaining Appropriate Student Behavior   97

7. Motivating Students to Learn   120

8. Addressing Issues of Diversity   146

9. Helping Students with Special Needs   167

10. Planning and Conducting Instruction   188

Preface

This third edition of *Classroom Management* has been written to guide teachers and prospective teachers as they create a positive classroom community, with the involvement and cooperation of the students. Fundamental principles of classroom management and discipline are presented along with ways to involve students in the creation of their learning environment.

The book is a scholarly synthesis of the research base on classroom management and discipline, yet is written and formatted in a way that is easy to read, understand, and apply. It carries a practical, realistic view of teaching with the content being organized in a logical, sequential order. The content is applicable for teachers at all levels—elementary, middle level, and high school.

INTENDED AUDIENCE

This book is especially appropriate as the sole book for an undergraduate course on classroom management and discipline or for a seminar on student teaching or professional development. It may be used as a supplementary book to another textbook in educational psychology or teaching methods courses. Additionally, the book may be used in graduate classes, seminars, and staff development programs for in-service teachers. The book may be seen as a handbook for future reference due to its comprehensive coverage of the issues and its use of lists, tables, and figures for recommended practice. The information provides a foundation for decision making.

RELATING THIS BOOK TO STANDARDS

Content in this book relates to the professional standards of many agencies. Standards are used to guide the development of new teachers, help in-service teachers improve their performance, and assess both teacher preparation and teacher performance. Many teacher education programs are designed around the INTASC standards. Many states require a passing score on the Principles of Teaching and Learning test (Praxis II) before granting a teaching license. The Praxis III standards and the NBPTS standards are used to assess and improve the teaching of in-service teachers. A brief description of the standards is provided here, and tables of those standards follow the preface.

INTASC Standards

The Interstate New Teacher Assessment and Support Consortium (INTASC), created in 1987, is a consortium of state education agencies and national educational organizations dedicated to the reform of the preparation, licensing, and ongoing professional development of teachers. INTASC's primary constituency is state education agencies responsible for teacher licensing, program approval, and professional development. Its work is guided by one basic premise: *An effective teacher must be able to integrate content knowledge with the specific strengths and needs of students to assure that all students learn and perform at high levels*. More information can be found at this Web site: www.ccsso.org/projects/Interstate_New_Teacher_Assessment_and_Support_Consortium/.

Praxis Series

The Praxis Series is a set of tests developed and disseminated by the Educational Testing Service (ETS) for assessing skills and knowledge of each stage of a beginning teacher's career, from entry into teacher education to actual classroom performance. More information about the Praxis Series can be found at this Web site: http://ets.org/praxis/index.html. There are three parts of the Praxis Series:

- **Praxis I**: Pre-Professional Skills Tests (PPST). These academic skills tests are designed to be taken early in a student's college career to measure reading, writing, and mathematics skills.
- **Praxis II**: Subject Assessments. There are several assessments available in the Praxis II series, and they measure a teacher candidate's knowledge of the subjects they will teach, as well as general and subject-specific pedagogical skills and knowledge.
- **Praxis III**: Classroom Performance Assessments. These assessments are conducted for beginning teachers in classroom settings. Assessment of teaching practice is through direct observation of classroom practice, a review of documentation prepared by the teacher, and semistructured interviews. The framework for knowledge and skills for these assessments consist of 19 assessment criteria organized within four categories: planning and preparation, the classroom environment, instruction, and professional responsibilities.

This *Classroom Management* book is not intended to address the preprofessional skills of reading, writing, and mathematics in Praxis I. However, it is designed to address the Praxis II test on Principles of Teaching and Learning and the Praxis III classroom performance criteria areas.

NBPTS Standards

The National Board of Professional Teaching Standards (NBPTS) has established standards for highly accomplished teaching, with the standards based on five core propositions. NBPTS has a national voluntary system of certifying teachers who meet the standards in their teaching performance. Teachers meeting all the standards are certified National Board Certified Teachers. More information about the NBPTS standards can be found at this Web site: http://www.nbpts.org/.

NEW TO THIS EDITION

A number of significant changes were made in this third edition, including the following:

- A new chapter on Helping Students with Special Needs (Chapter 9)
- A new feature in each chapter on Developing Your Management Plan, leading readers to write their own plan

- A list of annotated Further Readings at the end of each chapter.
- New sections in several chapters, including the following:

  Chapter 1—a section on principles for working with students and preventing misbehavior

  Chapter 1—a section on what classroom management accomplishes

  Chapter 2—a section on Spencer Kagan's win–win discipline model

  Chapter 2—a section on determining your management plan

  Chapter 3—a section on managing assessment, record keeping, and reporting

  Chapter 6—a section on having a mental set for management

  Chapter 6—a section on building positive teacher–student relationships

  Chapter 6—a section on managing whole-group instruction

  Chapter 8—a section on classroom management implications for diverse classrooms

  Chapter 10—a section on managing student work

  Chapter 11—a section on dealing with chronic misbehaviors

  Chapter 12—a section on teaching students alternatives to disruption and violence

- Tables to indicate how this book addresses professional standards from INTASC, Praxis II Principles of Teaching and Learning, Praxis III, and NBPTS
- Sixteen new teacher testimonials in the Voices from the Classroom feature

SPECIAL FEATURES

Classroom Management: Creating a Successful K–12 Learning Community has several important features that make it both instructor and reader friendly.

- *Outline of Chapter Headings and Subheadings.* Each chapter begins with an outline of headings and subheadings to serve as an advance organizer for the chapter content.

- *A List of Chapter Objectives.* Each chapter begins with a list of objectives to identify expected reader outcomes.

- *Voices from the Classroom.* Several of these features are included in each chapter to provide descriptions by real elementary, middle school, and high school teachers about ways they deal with particular topics addressed in the chapter. These teachers come from all parts of the country and all different community sizes. There are 19 at the elementary level, 9 at the middle, and 15 at the high school level. Sixteen of these are new in this edition.

- *Developing Your Management Plan.* Each chapter has this feature, and it asks the readers to make decisions and write about their own management plan concerning the chapter topics. By the end of the book, readers will have made decisions and wrote about all of the key components of a classroom management plan for their own classroom.

- *What Would you Decide?* Several of these features are placed in each chapter to engage the reader in the content. Each one includes several sentences describing a classroom situation concerning an issue in the chapter followed by a few questions asking the reader to make decisions about the application of the concepts.

- *A List of Main Points.* At the end of each chapter, a list of major concepts is provided to serve as a summary of the significant issues.

- *Discussion/Reflective Questions.* Several questions are included at the end of each chapter to promote discussion in a seminar, classroom, or workshop where a number of people are considering the chapter's content.

- *Suggested Activities.* Supplemental activities are suggested at the end of each chapter to enable the reader to investigate and apply issues addressed in the chapter.

- *Further Reading.* Two to four books are suggested at the end of each chapter for more in-depth background about the chapter topics.

- *References.* All citations made in the book are included in a reference section at the end of the book to show the source of the research base.

ACKNOWLEDGMENTS

Many people provided support and guidance as I prepared this book. A very special acknowledgment goes to my wife Jennie and children Andy, Kathryn, and Alex. Their support kept my spirits up when deadlines were pressing, and their understanding during my absences while preparing the content enabled me to complete the project.

The editors and staff at Wiley facilitated the preparation and refinement of this book. A number of classroom teachers provided descriptions of their professional practice, which are included in the Voices from the Classroom features in each chapter. The experiences that these teachers share help illustrate the issues and bring life to the content.

Sandi Faulconer provided valuable assistance at Kansas State University in preparing several tables and helping coordinate a number of activities. Finally, I would like to extend my gratitude to the following reviewers who provided thoughtful, constructive feedback on the manuscript:

Philip DiMattia, Boston College
J'Anne Ellsworth, North Arizona University
Thomas J. Lasley, University of Dayton
Michael A. Morehead, New Mexico State University
Merrill Oaks, Washington State University
Cecilia M. Pierce, University of Alabama at Birmingham
Patricia Ann Popp, The College of William and Mary
Karen Samuelson, University of Massachusetts at Boston
Donna H. Schumacher-Douglas, University of Northern Iowa
Robert L. Shearer, Miami University
Marlys Vaughn, Millsaps College

Paul Burden

Standards

PRAXIS II: STANDARDS FOR PRINCIPLES OF TEACHING AND LEARNING

The table below indicates how the Praxis II standards for the Principles of Teaching and Learning are addressed in this book.

PRAXIS II Standard	Chapter Coverage
1. Students as Learners Student development and the learning process Students as diverse learners Student motivation and the learning environment	2, 3, 5, 6, 7, 8, 9
2. Instruction and Assessment Instructional strategies Planning instruction Assessment strategies	2, 3, 7, 8, 9, 10
3. Communication Techniques Basic, effective verbal and nonverbal communication techniques Effect of cultural and gender differences on communications in the classroom Types of communications and interactions that can stimulate discussion in different ways for particular purposes	2, 6, 7, 8, 10, 11, 12
4. Profession and Community The reflective practitioner The larger community	1, 2, 4

PRAXIS III: STANDARDS FOR CLASSROOM PERFORMANCE ASSESSMENTS

The table below indicates how the Praxis III standards are addressed in this book.

PRAXIS III Standard	Chapter Coverage
1. Planning and Preparation	1, 2, 3, 7, 8, 9
Demonstrating knowledge of content and pedagogy	
Demonstrating knowledge of students	
Selecting instructional goals	
Demonstrating knowledge of resources	
Designing coherent instruction	
Assessing student learning	
2. The Classroom Environment	1, 2, 3, 4, 5, 6, 10, 11, 12
Creating an environment of respect and rapport	
Establishing a culture for learning	
Managing classroom procedures	
Managing student behavior	
Organizing physical space	
3. Instruction	7, 8, 9, 10
Communicating clearly and accurately	
Using questioning and discussion techniques	
Engaging students in learning	
Providing feedback to students	
Demonstrating flexibility and responsiveness	
4. Professional Responsibilities	1, 2, 3, 4, 5, 10, 11, 12
Reflecting on teaching	
Maintaining accurate records	
Communicating with families	
Contributing to the school and district	
Growing and developing professionally	
Showing professionalism	

NBPTS PROPOSITIONS

The table below indicates how the National Board of Professional Teaching Standards (NBPTS) core propositions are addressed in this book.

NBPTS Propositions	Chapter Coverage
1. Teachers are committed to students and their learning.	1, 2, 3, 6, 7, 8, 9
Teachers recognize individual differences in their students and adjust their practice accordingly.	
Teachers have an understanding of how students develop and learn.	
Teachers treat students equitably.	
Teachers' mission extends beyond developing the cognitive capacity of their students.	
2. Teachers know the subjects they teach and how to teach those subjects to students.	3, 7, 10
Teachers appreciate how knowledge in their subjects is created, organized, and linked to other disciplines.	
Teachers command specialized knowledge of how to convey a subject to students.	
Teachers generate multiple paths to knowledge.	
3. Teachers are responsible for managing and monitoring student learning.	1, 2, 3, 5, 6, 7, 10, 11, 12
Teachers call on multiple methods to meet their goals.	
Teachers orchestrate learning in group settings.	
Teachers place a premium on student engagement	
Teachers regularly assess student progress.	
Teachers are mindful of their principal objectives.	
4. Teachers think systematically about their practice and learn from experience.	1, 2, 12
Teachers are continually making difficult choices that test their judgment.	
Teachers seek the advice of others and draw on education research and scholarship to improve their practice.	
5. Teachers are members of learning communities.	4, 12
Teachers contribute to school effectiveness by collaborating with other professionals.	
Teachers work collaboratively with parents.	
Teachers take advantage of community resources.	

About the Author

Paul R. Burden is an assistant dean and professor in the College of Education at Kansas State University, Manhattan, where he has supervised student teachers and taught courses on teaching methods, classroom management and discipline, foundations of education, and instructional leadership. Previously, he was a middle-level science teacher in Buffalo, New York, and later earned his doctoral degree at the Ohio State University. He received the College of Education's Outstanding Undergraduate Teaching Award at Kansas State University in 1999.

His recent publications include *Methods for Effective Teaching* (Allyn & Bacon, 2007), *Countdown to the First Day of School* (2000, National Education Association), *Powerful Classroom Management Strategies: Motivating Students to Learn* (2000, Corwin Press), as well as *Establishing Career Ladders in Teaching* (1987, Charles C. Thomas Publishers). From 1986 to 1997, he served as the editor of the *Journal of Staff Development*, a quarterly journal sponsored by the National Staff Development Council, and has presented over 70 papers at regional and national educational conferences in addition to authoring 15 articles and four book chapters. He has been a presenter at over 40 staff development programs and currently serves as a reviewer for several journals.

Married with three children, Dr. Burden enjoys traveling with his family and working on genealogy. He can be contacted at Kansas State University, 261 Bluemont Hall, Manhattan, Kansas 66506; (785) 532-5550; burden@ksu.edu.

Chapter 1

Understanding Management and Discipline in the Classroom

CHAPTER OBJECTIVES

This chapter provides information that will help you:
- Describe the role of classroom management in creating a learning community.
- Determine what constitutes order in the classroom.
- Identify the areas of responsibility in classroom management and discipline.
- Describe the types and causes of student misbehavior.
- Identify principles for working with students to create a positive learning environment.

Classroom Management: Creating a Successful K-12 Learning Community/Third Edition, by Paul R. Burden
ISBN 0-471-71073-3   Copyright © 2006 John Wiley & Sons, Inc.

CHAPTER OUTLINE

What do award-winning teachers do that make them so popular and successful? Do they jazz up the curriculum in some way? Do they use especially creative instructional approaches? Do they warm up to the students as if they were their own children? Do they add some magic or sparkle to the classroom experience? The answer is probably a little of each of these suggestions. But it likely goes deeper than that.

Successful teachers are often very effective managers of the classroom environment. They create a positive learning community where students are actively involved in their own learning and the management of the classroom. They organize the physical environment, manage student behavior, create a respectful environment, facilitate instruction, promote safety and wellness, and interact with others when needed. All of these issues relate to classroom management. The main objective is to create a positive learning community, and then to take steps to maintain that positive environment by guiding and correcting student behavior.

A COMMUNITY OF LEARNERS

Over the years, the way teachers have gone about instruction has changed as more is known about the nature of teaching and learning. In recent years, more emphasis has been placed on building learning communities in the classroom because students appear to be most successful in that environment. Problems with student misbehavior are also minimized in an environment where students are actively involved in their classroom and their instruction.

A learning community is designed to help all students feel safe, respected, and valued in order to learn new skills. Anxiety, discomfort, and fear are incompatible with the learning process, and make teaching and learning difficult. Successful classrooms are those in which students feel supported in their learning, willing to take risks, challenged to become fully human with one another, and open to new possibilities.

With the increasing diversity in classrooms, the need to create supportive classroom communities becomes even more important. Teachers must identify community building as a high priority if we are to have classrooms that include diverse students and make them welcome, appreciated, and valued members of the classroom environment. Actions can be taken to build an inclusive classroom learning community (Baloche, 1998).

In *Because We Can Change the World*, Sapon-Shevin (1999) identified five characteristics of learning communities:

1. *Security.* A safe, secure community allows for growth and exploration. A nurturing community is a place where it is safe to be yourself, take risks, ask for help and support, and delight in accomplishments. A safe environment helps protect students from distractions and disruptions that interfere with the learning process.

2. *Open Communication.* In a cohesive environment, there is open communication. All forms of communication—oral, written, artistic, and nonverbal—are encouraged. In safe, accepting environments, students' individual differences and needs are openly acknowledged. Students share freely what is happening, what they need, and what they are worried about. Since all students have the right to feel safe, for example, open communication should be encouraged to address the concerns.

3. *Mutual Liking.* In supportive classroom communities, students are encouraged to know and like their classmates. Opportunities are provided for students to interact with one another, and students are given many chances and strategies for learning to see and say nice things about classmates.

4. *Shared Goals or Objectives.* Cooperative communities are those in which students work together to reach a shared goal or objective. This can be achieved with whole-class projects where students work toward a goal while interacting and supporting one another.

5. *Connectedness and Trust.* In learning communities, students feel a part of the whole. They know that they are needed, valued members of the group. They know others are depending on them to put forth their best effort. Trust and connectedness mean sharing the good things as well as any concerns or problems.

To create a learning community, teachers often plan lessons designed to involve students in cooperative learning activities. These activities seem to have three elements that are critical to their success: face-to-face interactions, a feeling of positive interdependence, and a feeling of individual accountability (Johnson, Johnson, & Holubec, 1994). In addition, it is necessary to teach students social skills and to process group functioning for these learning activities to be successful.

Teachers also need to arrange the physical environment for instruction, guide and correct behavior, and create a supportive classroom. All of these responsibilities for creating a learning community relate to classroom management.

WHAT IS CLASSROOM MANAGEMENT?

Classroom Management involves teacher actions to create a learning environment that encourages positive social interaction, active engagement in learning, and self-motivation.

Several key questions come to mind about classroom management. How can the physical environment be organized? How can the school year begin effectively? What rules and procedures are appropriate? How can students be held academically accountable? How can appropriate behavior be encouraged and supported? How might order be restored if there are disruptions? How can class time and instruction be managed effectively? How can the safety of students be assured? All of these issues are part of classroom management. Before discussing the areas of responsibility in classroom management, the issue of order in the classroom is examined.

Order in the Classroom

A learning community needs to have order for students to be successful. *Order* means that students are following the actions necessary for a particular classroom event to be successful; students are focused on the instructional tasks and are not misbehaving. Establishing and maintaining order is an important part of classroom management.

It is useful to distinguish the difference between off-task behavior and misbehavior. *Off-task behavior* includes student actions that are not focused on the instructional activities, yet would not be considered to be disruptive or be defined as misbehavior. Off-task behavior includes daydreaming, writing notes or doodling, or not paying attention.

Misbehavior includes behavior that interferes with your teaching, interferes with the rights of others to learn, is psychologically or physically unsafe, or destroys property (Levin & Nolan, 2004). Classroom order is threatened by misbehavior. *Discipline* is the act of responding to misbehaving students in an effort to restore order.

There are several important issues concerning order.

1. *A Minimal Level of Order is Necessary for Instruction to Occur.* Order can be established for instruction by actions such as selecting rules and procedures, encouraging and reinforcing appropriate behavior, reacting to misbehavior, and managing instructional tasks. With many students off task, instruction cannot occur.

2. *Student Involvement in Learning Tasks is Affected by Order in the Classroom.* An effective classroom manager places emphasis on managing the group rather than managing individual students. When there is order in the classroom, then individual students can become engaged in the instructional tasks.

3. *Student Cooperation is Necessary to Establish Order.* Order in classrooms is achieved *with* students and depends on their willingness to be part of the sequence of events. Students in a learning community want to cooperate because they see the benefits for them.

4. *Expectations for Order are Affected by a Number of Classroom Variables.* Teacher expectations for order may vary depending on factors such as the type of instructional activities, the maturity level of the students, the time of day, the time in the lesson, and the particular students involved. For example, a teacher may not enforce a certain rule at the end of a class period when students are gathering their books and materials in the same way as when a discussion is underway in the middle of the class period.

WHAT WOULD YOU DECIDE? *Managing Students in Small Groups*

Teachers often have special procedures and behavioral guidelines for times when students work in small groups or in a laboratory setting. Suppose that you are dividing your science class into small groups to examine and test a number of rock and mineral samples. You now need to decide about ways to provide directions and guidelines for the tasks and also about ways to monitor the students while they work together in their groups.

1. How might your decisions about guidelines to maintain control be affected by the age level and maturity of the students?

2. How might you need to monitor students differently to maintain control in small groups as compared to whole-class instruction?

Areas of Responsibility

There are several areas of responsibility in classroom management and discipline (see Table 1.1). An effective classroom manager handles the following seven areas of responsibility.

1. *Select a Philosophical Model of Classroom Management and Discipline.* A number of educators have proposed certain models of classroom management and discipline, such as teaching with love and logic, cooperative discipline, discipline with dignity, and assertive discipline (see Chapter 2). These models reflect various philosophical views of student development, teaching and learning, and classroom management. Viewing these proposed models on a continuum, they range from low teacher control to high teacher control.

These theoretical models are useful to teachers because they offer a basis for analyzing, understanding, and managing student and teacher behavior. With an understanding of these varied theoretical approaches, you can assess your position on these

Table 1.1   Areas of Responsibility in Classroom Management and Discipline

Classroom management involves teacher actions to create a learning environment that encourages positive social interaction, active engagement in learning, and self-motivation. An effective classroom manager handles these areas of responsibility:

1. Select a philosophical model of classroom management and discipline.
2. Organize the physical environment.
3. Manage student behavior.
4. Create a respectful, supportive learning environment.
5. Manage and facilitate instruction.
6. Promote classroom safety and wellness.
7. Interact with colleagues, parents, and others to achieve classroom management objectives.

issues and then select a philosophical model that is consistent with your beliefs. The techniques you use to manage student behavior should be consistent with your beliefs about how students learn and develop.

2. *Organize the Physical Environment.* The way the desks, tables, and other classroom materials are arranged affects instruction and has an influence on order in the classroom (see Chapter 3). To create an effective learning environment, you will need to organize several aspects of the physical space. First, you will need to arrange the floor space by the placement of student desks, the teacher's desk, bookcases, filing cabinets, tables, and activity centers. Second, you will need to decide how to store a number of materials, including textbooks and resource books, frequently used instructional materials, teacher supplies and instructional materials, equipment, and infrequently used materials. Finally, you will need to decide how to use bulletin boards and wall space. Decisions in all of these areas will determine how you will organize the physical environment for teaching and learning.

3. *Manage Student Behavior.* Guidelines are needed to promote order in the classroom and to provide a conducive learning environment (see Chapter 5). Rules and procedures support teaching and learning and provide students with clear expectations and well-defined norms. This, in turn, helps create a safe, secure atmosphere for learning.

Rules are general codes of conduct that are intended to guide individual student behavior in an attempt to promote positive interaction and avoid disruptive behavior. *Procedures* are approved ways to achieve specific tasks in the classroom, such as handing in completed work or sharpening a pencil.

When misbehavior occurs, teachers need to respond in an effort to get the student back on task and to maintain order in the classroom. A three-step response plan is discussed in Chapter 11, including providing assistance to get the student back on task as the first step, followed by the use of mild responses such as nonverbal and verbal signals, and then ending with moderate responses such as withdrawing privileges or changing the seat assignment. Special approaches are often needed to deal with challenging students (see Chapter 12).

To establish order, you must teach, demonstrate, establish, and enforce classroom procedures and routines at the start of the year. Successful classroom managers hover over activities at the beginning of the year and usher them along until students have learned the work system.

4. *Create a Respectful, Supportive Learning Environment.* There are many facets to creating a favorable learning environment, but it is vital for a positive learning community. First, teachers can take a number of actions to establish a cooperative, responsible classroom by developing positive teacher–student relationships, promoting students' self-esteem, and building group cohesiveness (see Chapter 6). These actions will help create an environment where students feel valued and comfortable, thus setting the stage for teaching and learning. Second, teachers can focus student attention on appropriate classroom behavior by helping students assume responsibility for their behavior, by maintaining student attention and involvement, and by reinforcing desired behaviors (see Chapter 6).

Third, a comprehensive plan can be developed to motivate students to learn, involving decisions about instructional tasks, feedback and evaluation, and academic and behavioral expectations (see Chapter 7). Finally, teachers can be most effective in creating a respectful, supportive learning environment when they have an understanding of the diverse learners in their classroom (see Chapter 8) and of students with special needs (see Chapter 9).

5. *Manage and Facilitate Instruction.* Certain factors in a lesson have a bearing on classroom order, and teachers need to take these factors into account when planning lessons (see Chapter 10). These include decisions about the degree of structure of the lesson, the type of instructional groups to use, and the means of holding the students academically accountable.

There are also certain actions that teachers often take at the beginning, middle, and end of a lesson that affect the order of the classroom. These include actions such as taking attendance, giving directions, distributing materials, handling transitions, summarizing the lesson, and preparing to leave. Collectively, these instructional management skills help manage and facilitate instruction while also influencing classroom order.

6. *Promote Classroom Safety and Wellness.* Students need to feel physically and emotionally safe before they can give their full attention to the instructional tasks. Strategies used to manage student behavior, create a supportive classroom, and manage and facilitate instruction all contribute to classroom safety and wellness. In addition, teachers sometimes need to take actions to solve problems and conflicts that threaten classroom order and the learning environment. For that reason, it is helpful to have a set of tools such as dealing with conflict resolution and anger management to solve problems (see Chapter 12).

Students who are considered difficult or challenging may threaten the sense of safety and wellness in the classroom. Their actions may cause other students to take guarded or even confrontational actions in response to difficult students. For that reason, teachers need to be prepared to deal with challenging students in constructive ways (Chapter 12).

7. *Interact with Colleagues, Parents, and Others to Achieve Classroom Management Objectives.* Working with parents is another means to help maintain order in the classroom (see Chapter 4). When the parents and teacher communicate and get along together, students are more likely to receive the needed guidance and support and will probably have more self-control in the classroom. In addition, teachers may need to consult and interact with colleagues and others when difficulties occur with classroom management and student behavior.

Developing Your Management Plan: *Reflecting on Your Experiences*

The seven areas of responsibility in classroom management (see Table 1.1) serve as an organizer for understanding the many issues related to classroom management and discipline. They also serve as a framework for decisions you need to make as you develop a management plan for your own classroom.

Each following chapter in this book addresses specific aspects of these areas of responsibility. Each chapter also includes a feature such as this one prompting you to think about the chapter topics and asking you to make decisions and write about your own management plan concerning those chapter topics. By the end of the book, you will have made

decisions and wrote about all of the key components of a classroom management plan for your own classroom.

As a preview of the decision areas in the following chapters, reflect on your educational experiences as a student concerning the seven areas of responsibility in classroom management.

1. How did your teachers successfully demonstrate the application of each area of responsibility?

2. Are there certain areas that appear more important to you? Why?

UNDERSTANDING MISBEHAVIOR

Even with an effective management system in place, students may lose interest in the lesson and get off task. You must be prepared to respond with appropriate strategies to restore order. To provide a context for your decision making in this area, you should first understand misbehavior in context, the types and causes of misbehavior, and the degree of severity that is exhibited.

It is important first to recognize that the best way to deal with discipline problems is to avoid them in the first place. You should develop challenging, interesting, and exciting lessons and treat students with dignity and respect. If misbehavior then occurs, you can consider the guidelines and principles presented in Chapter 11 for dealing with inappropriate behavior.

Misbehavior in Context

Students who are off task are not performing the planned instructional activity. They may be pausing to think about an issue, daydreaming, or doing other things that are nondisruptive but prohibit them from being engaged in the instructional activities. Students who are off task need to be addressed differently than students who are purposely misbehaving and interfering with the academic activities. In such cases, you may need to intervene to stop the misbehavior.

Recognize that your decisions about interventions are complex judgments about the act, the student, and the circumstances at a particular moment in classroom time. Some student actions are clearly misbehavior and require teacher intervention. In many cases, however, the situation is not quite so simple. The key to understanding misbehavior is to view what students do in the context of the classroom structure. Not every infraction of a rule is necessarily misbehavior. For instance, inattention in the last few minutes of a class session will often be tolerated because the lesson is coming to an end. However, you would most likely intervene when inattention is evident earlier in the class.

Misbehavior, then, needs to be seen as "action in context" (Mehan, Hertweck, Combs, & Flynn, 1982), and requires interpretation based on what the teacher knows about the likely configuration of events. You need to make reliable judgments about the probable consequences of students' actions in different situations. Consistency in your response does not mean that you need to behave in the same way every time, but rather that your judgments are reliable and consistent.

Types of Misbehavior

Misbehavior includes behavior that interferes with your teaching, interferes with the rights of others to learn, is psychologically or physically unsafe, or destroys property. This misbehavior may show up in the classroom in a number of ways, as indicated in the following categories:

- *Needless Talk* —talks during instructional time about topics unrelated to the lesson or talks when should be silent.
- *Annoying Others* —teases, calls names, or bothers others.
- *Moving Around the Room* —moving around the room without permission or going to areas where is not permitted.
- *Noncompliance* —does not do what is requested, breaks rules, argues, makes excuses, delays, does the opposite of what is asked.
- *Disruption* —talks or laughs inappropriately, hums or makes noises, gets into things, causes "accidents."
- *Aggressive Actions* —shows hostility toward others, pushes or fights, verbally abuses, is cruel to others, damages property, steals others' property.
- *Defiance of Authority* —talks back to the teacher, is hostile to comply with the teacher's requests.

Causes of Misbehavior

One way to understand classroom control is to determine why students misbehave. In some cases, the reasons are complex and personal and perhaps beyond your comprehension or control. However a number of causes of misbehavior can be addressed directly by the teacher.

1. *Health Factors.* Student behavior problems may be related to health factors. Lack of sleep, an allergy, illness, or an inadequate diet may greatly affect the student's ability to complete assignments or interact with others. For some children, sugar has an effect on their behavior and may result in hyperactivity. Physical impairments such as a vision or hearing loss, paralysis, or a severe physiological disorder may also contribute to behavior problems.

2. *Neurological Conditions.* Some students may have a mental disorder that affects their behavior in some way. For example, attention deficit disorder is a mental disorder in which the area of the brain that controls motor activity doesn't work as it should. This is among the most common childhood mental disorders and affects about four percent of school-age children, according to the National Institute of Mental Health. Such students may be inattentive (easily distracted, don't follow directions well, shift from one unfinished task to another, and seem not to be listening), hyperactive (talkative, fidget, and squirm), and impulsive (don't wait their turn, blurt out answers, and engage in dangerous activities without considering the consequences). Children born with fetal alcohol syndrome may be hyperactive or impulsive, and crack babies (children born to women who were using crack cocaine during pregnancy) may exhibit similar behaviors.

WHAT WOULD YOU DECIDE?   *Dealing with a Talking Student*

Let's assume that a student in your class regularly talks to nearby students when you have them doing independent work at their desks. The student is academically capable and seems to want to become friends with others.

1. What reasons might the student have for talking to the others at this time? What might be the motives?

2. What are some actions you might take to have the student stop talking in this setting?

---

3. *Medication or Drugs.* Medication or drugs, whether legal or illegal, may also be a factor. Over-the-counter medicine for nasal congestion, for example, may cause a student to be less alert than usual. Alcohol or drug abuse also may contribute to unusual behavior at school.

4. *Influences from the Home or Society.* Conditions in the student's home may be related to behavior problems. Student behavior problems may be associated with a lack of adequate clothing or housing, parental supervision and types of discipline, home routines, or significant events such as divorce or the death of a friend or relative. Factors in the community or in society also may contribute to student behavior problems. There has been considerable concern and debate over the effects of television on the beliefs and conduct of children. Violence on television is seen by some to influence students to be more aggressive.

5. *The Physical Environment.* The physical arrangement of the classroom, temperature, noise, and lighting may affect student behavior. Student crowding may also be involved. These factors may contribute to a students' lack of commitment to a lesson, and may lead to inattention and misbehavior.

6. *Poor Behavior Decisions by the Student.* The classroom is a complex environment for students as well as for teachers. Students are confronted with challenges, temptations, and circumstances that will cause them to make decisions about their own behavior. Their own personalities and habits come into play here. Given all of these factors, students will sometimes make poor decisions that lead to misbehavior.

7. *Other Students in the Classroom.* Some misbehavior results from students being provoked by other students in the classroom; the student may be drawn into an incident of misbehavior when another student does something inappropriate. In addition, peer pressure from other students may cause individual students to misbehave in ways they would not consider by themselves.

8. *Teacher Factors When Managing the Class.* Teachers sometimes needlessly create disciplinary problems by the way they manage and conduct their classes. Inappropriate teacher behaviors include being overly negative, maintaining an authoritarian climate, overreacting to situations, using mass punishment for all students, blaming students, lacking a clear instructional goal, repeating or reviewing already learned material, pausing too long during instruction, dealing with one student at length, and lacking recognition of student ability levels. While few teachers can avoid all of these behaviors all of the time, effective teachers recognize the potentially damaging effects of classroom order and discipline. Being aware of these characteristics is the first step to avoiding them. It is useful periodically to reflect on your own teaching behavior to determine if you are taking actions that are contributing to inattention or misbehavior.

9. *Teacher Factors Concerning Instruction.* Teachers make many decisions about the content and delivery of instruction. Students may lose interest in a lesson if the teacher presents uninteresting lessons, does not plan meaningful activities or engage students in the lessons, is ineffective in instructional delivery, or does not deliberately plan to incorporate motivational elements into the instruction. When students lose interest in a lesson, they are more likely to get off task and misbehave.

WHAT WOULD YOU DECIDE?   *Dealing with a Sleepy Student*

You have a student in your classroom who has difficulty paying attention in class and appears to be sleepy much of the time. One day during a classroom film, the student fell asleep. Many other days she does not complete her class work or homework.

1. What might be some reasons for the student's sleepiness and lack of attention in class?

2. What might you do to identify the actual cause of the sleepiness and inattention?

Degrees of Severity

Misbehavior ranges from mildly to severely disruptive behavior. Severely disruptive behavior and crime in schools may involve violence, vandalism, coercion, robbery, theft, and drug use. These behaviors typically occur outside the classroom in places such as the lunchroom, corridors, or outside the building. Moderate levels of misbehavior involve tardiness, cutting class, talking, calling out answers in class, mild forms of verbal and physical aggression, inattentiveness, and failure to bring supplies and books. Most misbehavior is comparatively mild and is related to attention, crowd control, and getting work accomplished in the classroom.

When selecting an appropriate response to misbehavior, it is important that you take into account the degree of severity of the misbehavior. You can evaluate severity by factors such as appropriateness, magnitude, intent, and extent to which a behavior differs from what is expected in a particular setting. The degree of your response should match the degree of severity of the misbehavior. Teachers often ignore certain minor misbehaviors because their intervention may be more disruptive than the misbehavior.

PRINCIPLES FOR WORKING WITH STUDENTS AND PREVENTING MISBEHAVIOR

Problem behaviors have a variety of causes, and evidence suggests that some factors are within the school and classroom environment (California, 2000; Charles, 2005; Mayer, 1995). To promote classrooms that are conducive to learning and to help prevent problem behaviors, teachers must address certain contextual factors within the classroom. Here are some basic principles for working with students in a manner that establishes a positive, productive classroom in which students learn and have a satisfying educational experience.

1. *Maintain Focus on Your Major Task in Teaching.* Your major task is to help students be successful in achieving educational objectives, to promote student learning, and to help students develop the knowledge and skills to be successful in your classroom and beyond.

2. *Understand Your Students' Needs and How to Meet Them.* Know your students' likes and dislikes, what motivates them, their needs and desires, and what influences their lives. Use that information to create an appropriate learning environment.

3. *Understand and Respect Ethnic or Cultural Differences.* With an understanding of the ethnic or cultural background of the students, teachers will be more prepared to facilitate learning and guide behavior.

4. *Know What Causes Misbehavior and How to Deal with Those Causes.* Take steps to reduce or remove the causes of misbehavior.

5. *Provide Clear Rules and Procedures to Guide Student Conduct.* Rules and procedures need to be clearly identified and taught so students understand the behavioral expectations.

6. *Have a Specific Plan for Responding to Misbehavior with a Hierarchy of Interventions.* Have a specific set of strategies to stop the misbehavior, keep students positively on track, and preserve good relations.

7. *Reduce the Use of Punitive Methods of Control.* Coercive or punitive environments may promote antisocial behavior. Other techniques that involve the students in creating a positive learning environment are more desirable.

8. *Take Actions to Establish a Cooperative, Responsible Classroom.* Use techniques to maintain attention and involvement, reinforce desired behaviors, promote student accountability and responsibility, and create a positive learning community.

9. *Involve Students Meaningfully in Making Decisions.* Decisions can involve things such as the selection of classroom rules and procedures, instructional activities and assessments, and curriculum materials. Student involvement generates commitment to the learning process and to the classroom environment.

10. *Teach Critical Social Skills.* Many students lack the social skills necessary to relate positively to peers and to do well academically. Teachers who help students develop these social skills help promote learning and successful classroom discipline.

11. *Involve Parents and Guardians to a Reasonable Degree.* Communicate with the parents regularly about what you are doing in the classroom and about the progress of their children. Make it clear that you want and need their support.

VOICES FROM THE CLASSROOM | *Establishing Rules for Controlling Conduct*

Beatrice Gilkes, High School Computer Science Teacher, Washington, D.C.

To help maintain control in the classroom, I ask my students to discuss realistic expectations for all persons in the classroom, including myself, that will help lead to the students being successful. Next, we discuss and select specific rules of behavior that affect maximum learning success in the classroom. Throughout this discussion, we emphasize three key words—love, respect, and commitment. We then commit ourselves to these rules, and their recommendations for penalties are included in the agreement. Students place this list of rules in their notebooks. This approach to getting a commitment from the students about classroom conduct has been effective for me in 40 years of teaching.

WHAT EFFECTIVE BEHAVIOR MANAGEMENT ACCOMPLISHES

An effective system of classroom management should be supportive and encouraging as a means to guide instruction and manage appropriate student behavior, and a learning community is created with this focus. An effective classroom management plan helps achieve the following purposes (Charles & Charles, 2004):

- *Maintains an Effective Environment for Learning.* Learning occurs best in environments that are reasonably well-ordered, free from threat, relatively free from disruptions, and encouraging of exploration and interaction.
- *Promotes Good Personal Relations.* Treat students with respect, accept them as worthwhile, and treat them with consideration. Guide students to adopt the same behaviors in their interactions.
- *Helps Students Develop Self-Control.* One of the purposes of behavior management is to help students develop the ability to control themselves and direct themselves in various situations.
- *Heightens Students' Sense of Purpose.* Effective behavior management helps students develop a clearer sense of purpose concerning what they wish to experience, what they want to learn, and how they want their lives to progress.
- *Fosters a Sense of Responsibility.* Effective behavior management heightens student initiative and choice but is always anchored in responsibility. Your

management plan should hold students accountable for their instructional and behavioral responsibilities.

MAIN POINTS

1. A learning community is designed to help all students feel safe, respected, and valued in order to learn new skills. Characteristics of a learning community include security, open communication, mutual liking, shared goals or objectives, and connectedness and trust.

2. Classroom management involves teacher actions to create a learning environment that encourages positive social interaction, active engagement in learning, and self-motivation.

3. Order means that students are following the actions necessary for a particular classroom event to be successful; students are focused on the instructional tasks and are not misbehaving.

4. Misbehavior includes behaviors that interfere with the act of teaching, interfere with the rights of others to learn, are psychologically or physically unsafe, or destroy property.

5. Off-task behavior includes student actions that are not focused on the instructional activities, yet are not considered disruptive or defined as misbehavior.

6. There are several areas of responsibility in classroom management and discipline (see Table 1.1).

7. Misbehavior ranges from mildly to severely disruptive behavior.

DISCUSSION/REFLECTIVE QUESTIONS

1. How would you describe a learning community? Identify some examples from your own schooling experience.

2. Give some examples of off-task behaviors and misbehaviors. Clarify the difference.

3. Of the seven areas of responsibility in classroom management (see Table 1.1), which are the three most important from your perspective? Why?

4. Why is it important to know the cause of the student's misbehavior?

5. What are some benefits and disadvantages of involving students in making decisions about issues such as the selection of rules and procedures, instructional activities and assessments, and curriculum materials?

SUGGESTED ACTIVITIES

1. One aspect of a learning community is having shared goals or objectives. Think of a unit you might teach and identify five ways that you could build shared goals into your plans.

2. Talk to several teachers to see what they consider to be mild, moderate, and severe misbehavior. Ask how

they respond to the misbehavior at each level. Ask if they have a systematic plan to address misbehavior.

3. What are four things you could do at the start of the school year to help you understand your students' needs and interests?

FURTHER READING

BALOCHE, LYNDA A. (1998). *The cooperative classroom: Empowering learning.* Upper Saddle River, NJ: Prentice-Hall/Merrill.
  Has two main sections with a K–12 focus: (1) developing the classroom as a learning community and (2) building small-group cooperation. Practical information and well researched.

SAPON-SHEVIN, MARA. (1999). *Because we can change the world: A practical guide to building cooperative, inclusive classroom communities.* Boston: Allyn & Bacon.
  Discusses techniques to develop a cohesive classroom community in pre-K through middle school classrooms. Emphasizes creating a caring, supportive classroom.

Chapter 2

Models of Discipline

CHAPTER OBJECTIVES

This chapter provides information that will help you:
- Identify the features of low, medium, and high control approaches to classroom management and discipline.
- Identify the characteristics of the specific discipline models proposed by educators who are representative of the low, medium, and high control approaches.
- Describe steps to be taken to clarify your own classroom management philosophy and management plan.

Classroom Management: Creating a Successful K-12 Learning Community/Third Edition, by Paul R. Burden
ISBN 0-471-71073-3   Copyright © 2006 John Wiley & Sons, Inc.

CHAPTER OUTLINE

Let's say that you want to take your dog out for a walk. You have one of those leashes in which you push a button to control how long or short the cord is on the leash. Would you use a short leash so the dog is by your side, or would you use a longer leash to allow your dog some freedom to walk around and explore? What reasons would you have for using a short or long leash? You see, you determine the degree of freedom the dog has.

In the classroom, you also determine the degree of freedom for your students as a means of creating a successful learning environment. How much freedom or control do you want to establish for your students? What are your purposes for insisting on this degree of control?

As a starting point, it is useful to see how other educators have dealt with this issue of freedom and control in the classroom. Some educators endorse many freedoms for students with limited controls, while other educators endorse stronger controls with limited freedoms. By seeing how other educators view the issue of control and order, you will gain a philosophical perspective about the range of possibilities for decisions that you might make. As you proceed through this book, you can see how the various ideas fit into the continuum of low to high control, and then decide on the strategies that you are most comfortable with. No single model is advocated or represented in this book.

This chapter provides a brief orientation to various discipline models, ranging from low to high teacher control. It is not intended to provide extensive information about each model to the point where you would be skilled enough to enact that model. For that purpose, more extensive summaries of these models are available from other sources (e.g., Charles, 2005; Edwards, 2004; Manning & Bucher, 2003; Wolfgang, 2005). Of course, the original sources mentioned in this chapter for the respective models provide even a fuller description.

THE DEGREE OF CONTROL

When deciding how to handle classroom management and discipline, you probably will take into account your views of child development, your educational philosophies, and other factors. These views can be categorized in various ways, but perhaps the most useful organizer is by the degree of control that you exert on the students and the classroom. A continuum showing a range of low to high teacher control can be used to illustrate the various educational views, and the various discipline models can be placed on the continuum. This continuum is based on the organizer that Wolfgang (2005) used when examining models of discipline.

A *model of discipline* is a set of cohesive approaches to deal with establishing, maintaining, and restoring order in the classroom that represent a certain philosophical perspective on a continuum of low to high teacher control. Table 2.1 provides a summary of the characteristics of various discipline models, ranging from low to high teacher control. Later in the chapter, Table 2.2 identifies representative authors for each of the three discipline models.

Your approach to freedom and control may fall into one particular part of the continuum, but this does not mean that you will follow this approach in every situation. You may branch out and use other strategies as the situation warrants. Now, let's look at the models at each point on the continuum.

LOW TEACHER CONTROL APPROACHES

Low control approaches are based on the philosophical belief that students have primary responsibility for controlling their own behavior and that they have the capability to make these decisions. Children are seen to have an inner potential, and opportunities to make decisions enable personal growth. The child's thoughts, feelings, ideas, and preferences are taken into account when dealing with instruction, classroom management, and discipline.

The teacher has the responsibility for structuring the classroom environment to facilitate the students' control over their own behavior. When determining classroom rules, for example, teachers guide the discussion and help students recognize appropriate behavior and select related rules and consequences. When misbehavior occurs, the teacher helps students see the problem and guides students in making an appropriate decision to resolve the problem. With these non-directive teacher actions, low teacher control approaches fall into the guiding model of discipline.

With this philosophical belief, students have a high degree of autonomy while the teacher exerts a low degree of control. This does not mean that the classroom is a chaotic place for learning. There are standards that the students will help develop, and the teacher is ultimately responsible for enforcing the standards to enable learning to take place in an orderly environment.

Table 2.1   Characteristics of Various Discipline Models

Descriptors	The Guiding Model	The Interacting Model	The Intervening Model
Degree of teacher control	Low	Medium	High
Degree of student control	High	Medium	Low
Degree of concern for the students' thoughts, feelings, and preferences	High	Medium	Low
Theoretical basis	Humanistic and Psychoanalytic Thought	Developmental and Social Psychology	Behaviorism
View of children	• Children develop primarily from inner forces. • Decision making enables personal growth. • Students are masters of their destiny.	• Children develop from both internal and external forces.	• Children develop primarily from external forces and conditions. • Children are molded and shaped by influences from their environment.
Main processes used	• Develop caring, self-directed students. • Build teacher–student relationships.	• Confront and contract with students when solving problems. • Counsel students.	• Establish the rules, and deliver the rewards and punishments.
Approaches used by teachers	• Structure the environment to facilitate students' control over their own behavior. • Help students see the problem and guide them into an appropriate decision to solve the problem. • Be an empathic listener. • Allow students to express their feelings.	• Interact with children to clarify and establish boundaries. • Enforce the boundaries. • Formulate mutually acceptable solutions to problems.	• Control the environment. • Select and use appropriate reinforcers and punishments.

Low control educators might use several types of non-directive approaches to create a supportive learning environment and to guide behavior. To illustrate these non-directive, low teacher control approaches, the discipline models from five representative authors are discussed in the following sections.

Congruent Communication: Haim Ginott

Haim Ginott (1922–1973) was a professor of psychology at New York University and at Adelphi University. Among educators, he is most known for his books that address relationships between adults and children. *Between Parent and Child* (1965) and *Between Parent and Teenager* (1969) offered ideas on how to communicate effectively with children. Ginott focused on how adults can build the self-concepts of children, especially emphasizing that adults should avoid attacks on the child's character and instead focus on the situation or actions. Later, Ginott carried these principles to educators in *Teacher and Child* (1972), proposing that teachers maintain a secure, humanitarian, and productive classroom through the use of congruent communication and appropriate use of praise.

Congruent communication is a harmonious and authentic way of talking in which teacher messages to students match the students' feelings about the situations and about themselves. In this way, teachers can avoid insulting and intimidating their students and instead express an attitude of helpfulness and acceptance while showing increased sensitivity to their needs and desires.

There are several ways that teachers can express congruent communication, all directed at protecting or building students' self-esteem.

- *Deliver Sane Messages.* Sane messages address situations rather than the students' characters. They acknowledge and accept student feelings. Too often, teachers may use language that blames, orders, admonishes, accuses, ridicules, belittles, or threatens children. This language does not promote children's self-esteem. Instead, Ginott proposes that teachers use language that focuses on the situation and the facts, not threatening that child's self-esteem.

- *Express Anger Appropriately.* Ginott points out that students can irritate and annoy teachers, making them angry. Anger is a genuine feeling, and teachers should express their anger in reasonable and appropriate ways that do not jeopardize the self-esteem of their students. An effective way is simply to say, "It makes me angry when . . ." or, "I am appalled when . . . ." In this way, the students hear what is upsetting the teacher without hearing put-down statements such as, "You are so irresponsible when you . . . ."

- *Invite Cooperation.* Provide opportunities for students to experience independence, thus accepting their capabilities. Give students a choice in matters that affect life in the classroom, including things such as seating arrangements and certain classroom procedures. Avoid long drawn-out directions, and instead give a brief statement and allow students to decide what their specific course of action should be. By inviting cooperation, you begin to break down students' dependency on yourself.

- *Accept and Acknowledge Student Feelings.* When a problem occurs, listen to students and accept the feelings they are expressing as real. Serve as a sounding board to help students clarify their feelings and let them know that such feelings are common.

- *Avoid Labeling the Student.* Ginott maintains there is no place for statements such as, "You are so irresponsible, unreliable." "You are such a disgrace to this class, this school, your family." When students hear these statements, they begin to believe them, and then they may start to develop a negative self-image. Avoid labeling, while striving to be helpful and encouraging.

- *Use Direction as a Means of Correction.* Instead of criticizing students when a problem occurs, Ginott proposes that teachers describe the situation to the students and offer guidance about what they should be doing. For example, when a student spills some supplies on the floor, offer some suggestions about ways to do the cleanup rather than criticize the student.

• *Avoid Harmful Questions*. Ginott points out that an enlightened teacher avoids asking questions and making comments that are likely to incite resentment and invite resistance. For example, don't ask "Why" questions such as, "Why can't you be good for a change?" "Why do you forget everything I tell you?" Instead, point out that there is a problem and invite the student to discuss ways to solve the problem.

• *Accept Students' Comments*. Students may ask questions or make statements that seem unrelated to the topic under discussion. Show respect and give the student credit for the question or comment because it may be important to the student in some way.

• *Do Not Use Sarcasm*. While you may use sarcasm as a way to be witty, it may sound clever only to yourself and not to the students receiving the comments. Students may end up with hurt feelings and damaged self-esteem.

• *Avoid Hurried Help*. When a problem arises, listen to the problem, rephrase it, clarify it, give the students credit for formulating it, and then ask, "What options are open to you?" In this way, you provide students with an opportunity to acquire competence in problem solving and confidence in themselves. Hurried responses to problems are less likely to achieve these purposes.

• *Be Brief When Dealing with Minor Mishaps*. Long, logical explanations are not needed when there is a lost paper, a broken pencil, or a forgotten assignment. Brief statements should be solution-oriented.

WHAT WOULD YOU DECIDE? *Ginott—Low Teacher Control*

Imagine that you have your students working in small groups on a project. Then one of the students begins to talk in an angry way to another group member, stands up, and tosses some papers aside.

1. How would you communicate with that student using Ginott's principles of congruent communication (e.g., to express sane messages, express anger appropriately, invite cooperation)?

2. How might your actions be affected if the student was of a different ethnic group from you?

Discipline as Self-Control: Thomas Gordon

Thomas Gordon, a clinical psychologist, is known for his pioneering of teaching communication skills and conflict resolution to teachers, parents, youth, and business leaders. In education, he is most known for T.E.T.:*Teacher Effectiveness Training* (1974) and *Discipline That Works: Promoting Self-Discipline in Children* (1991).Gordon maintains that effective discipline cannot be achieved through rewards and punishments, but rather through techniques to promote students' own self-control. He proposed approaches to help students make positive decisions, become more self-reliant, and control their own behavior. To help students make positive decisions, however, teachers must give up their controlling power.

Teachers guide and influence students and also take actions to create an environment where students can make decisions about their behavior. Several principles incorporate the essence of Gordon's concepts.

1. *Identify Who Owns the Problem.* Gordon used a device called a behavior window to determine who owns the problem. The student's behavior may cause a problem for the teacher or for the student, or there may be no problem. The person feeling the negative consequences of the behavior is said to own the problem, and this person is the one to take steps to solve the problem.

2. *Use Confrontive Skills When Teachers Own the Problem.* Teachers can modify the environment, recognize and respond to student feelings, word statements so they do not trigger the student's coping mechanism, shift gears, and use a no-lose method of conflict resolution. All of these approaches are intended to help guide and influence the students into effective interactions in the classroom.

3. *Use Helping Skills When the Student Owns the Problem.* When a student owns the problem, the student needs to take steps to solve it. Teachers can provide assistance through the use of helping skills. This can be done by using listening skills and by avoiding communication roadblocks.

4. *Use Preventive Skills When Neither the Student Nor Teacher Has A Problem with the Behavior.* As a means to avoid problems from occurring, teachers can use techniques such as collaboratively setting rules and using participative problem solving and decision making.

Teaching with Love and Logic: Jim Fay and David Funk

In *Teaching with Love and Logic* (1995), Jim Fay and David Funk describe how to create a classroom environment in which students can develop their own self-discipline and independent problem-solving skills. *Love and logic* is an approach to working with students that teaches students to think for themselves, raises the level of student responsibility, and prepares students to function effectively in society.

There are four basic principles of love and logic: (1) maintain the student's self-concept, (2) share control with the students, (3) balance the consequences with empathy, and (4) share the thinking by asking questions and modeling. With those principles as the foundation for the discipline plan, Fay and Funk selected three basic rules for their love and logic program: (1) use enforceable limits, (2) provide choices within the limits, and (3) apply consequences with empathy.

In describing various types of teaching styles, Fay and Funk (1995) describe teachers using the love and logic approach to discipline as being consultants. Consultant teachers do the following (pp. 197–198):

1. Set enforceable limits through enforceable statements.
2. Provide messages of personal worth, dignity, and strength through choices.
3. Provide consequences with empathy rather than punishment.
4. Demonstrate how to take good care of themselves and be responsible.
5. Share feelings about their personal performance and responsibilities.

6. Help people solve problems by exploring alternatives while allowing them to make their own decisions.

7. Provide latitude, within reasonable limits, for students to complete responsibilities.

8. Induce thinking through questions.

9. Use more actions than words to convey values.

10. Allow students to experience life's natural consequences, allow time to think through a problem, encourage shared thinking and shared control, and let them be teachers as well as students.

The love and logic approach gives students considerable credit for having the ability to solve their own problems, and teachers create an environment where students have the opportunity to make such decisions.

WHAT WOULD YOU DECIDE?   *Low Teacher Control*

Teachers adopting the low teacher control approach—the guiding model—to discipline intentionally exhibit a low degree of control when structuring the classroom environment and responding to misbehavior. Instead, they structure the environment to facilitate students' control over their environment and behavior.

1. If you adopted the guiding model, how would you approach the selection of rules and procedures at the start of the school year?

2. If you adopted the guiding model, how might you react to a student was talking out in class, disturbing others, and not getting her work done?

Inner Discipline: Barbara Coloroso

In *Kids Are Worth It! Giving Your Child the Gift of Inner Discipline* (2002), Barbara Coloroso emphasizes guiding students to make their own decisions and to take responsibility for their choices. To have good discipline, teachers must do three things: (1) treat students with respect and dignity; (2) give them a sense of power in their lives; and (3) give them opportunities to make decisions, take responsibility for their actions, and learn from their successes and mistakes. She believes that dealing with problems and accepting the consequences help students take charge of their lives.

Through these approaches, Coloroso believes that students will develop inner discipline. Her beliefs are humanistic and focused on promoting students' self-worth and dignity. With the guidance from adults, Coloroso believes that students can grow to like themselves and think for themselves. To enable students to develop inner discipline, teachers need to provide the appropriate degree of structure and support for students.

As a starting point, Coloroso says that teachers need to ask themselves, "What is my goal in teaching?" and, "What is my teaching philosophy?" The first question deals with what teachers hope to achieve, and the second with how they will approach the tasks. Because teachers act in accordance with their beliefs, it is important for them to clarify these beliefs concerning the degree of freedom and control they apply to their classrooms. Teachers who want to control students use rewards and punishments, but teachers who want to empower students to make decisions and to resolve their own problems will give students opportunities to think, act, and take responsibility.

The best way to teach students how to make good decisions is to put them in situations that call for decisions; ask them to make the decision, possibly with guidance from the teacher; and let them experience the results of their decision. Coloroso believes that teachers should not rescue students from bad decisions, but rather guide the student to new decisions that will solve the problem. When students are given ownership of problems and situations, this allows students to take responsibility for their decisions. She describes a six-step problem-solving strategy that students can use to identify and define the problem, list and evaluate possible solutions, and select, implement, and evaluate the preferred option.

From Discipline to Community: Alfie Kohn

Alfie Kohn is recognized as one of the most original thinkers in education today. A former teacher, he now is a full-time writer and lecturer. He has written five influential books, two of them linking to discipline models: *Punished by Rewards* (1999) and *Beyond Discipline: From Compliance to Community* (1996).

Kohn challenges traditional thinking by suggesting that our first question about children should not be, "How can we make them do what we want?" but rather, "What do they require in order to flourish, and how can we provide those things?" After reviewing a number of popular discipline programs, Kohn concludes that all are based on threat, reward, and punishment as the means to obtain student compliance. Kohn even views "consequences" as being punishments. Nothing useful comes from rewards and punishments because they cause students to mistrust their own judgment and stunt their becoming caring and self-reliant.

Instead, Kohn says teachers should focus on developing caring, supportive classrooms where students participate fully in solving problems, including problems with behavior. He advises teachers to develop a sense of community in their classrooms, where students feel safe and are continually brought into making decisions, expressing their opinions, and working cooperatively toward solutions that benefit the class.

When starting the school year, Kohn doesn't think rules are a good idea. When rules are used, Kohn is critical that students look for loopholes, teachers function as police officers, and punishment is used as a consequence. He maintains that students learn best when they have the opportunity to reflect on the proper way to conduct themselves. In this way, the teacher and students work together to identify how they want their classroom to be and how that can be made to happen. Students help create their own learning environment.

Kohn does not dismiss the value of structure and limits on student behavior. He presents criteria for determining how defensible a structure or limit is. Some of his criteria include purpose, restrictiveness, flexibility, developmental appropriateness, presentation style, and student involvement.

Classroom meetings are seen by Kohn as valuable tools to create a community and to address classroom problems and issues. Classroom meetings bring social and ethical benefits, foster intellectual development, motivate students to be more effective leaders, and greatly cut down on the need to deal with discipline problems. Kohn sees four focal points in these meetings: (1) sharing, such as talking about interesting events; (2) deciding about issues that affect the class, such as procedures for working on projects; (3) planning for various curricular or instructional issues; and (4) reflecting about issues such as what has been learned, what might have worked better, or what changes might improve the class.

All of these strategies will help create a community, which Kohn (1996) defines as a place in which students feel cared about and are encouraged to care about each other (pp. 101–102). Students then feel valued and respected, and the students matter to one another and the teacher. When students come to think in the plural, they feel connected to each other and feel physically and emotionally safe.

MEDIUM TEACHER CONTROL APPROACHES

Medium control approaches are based on the philosophical belief that development comes from a combination of innate and outer forces. Thus, the control of student behavior is a joint responsibility of the student and teacher. Medium control teachers accept the student-centered psychology that is reflected in the low control philosophy, but they also recognize that learning takes place in a group context. Therefore, the teacher promotes individual student control over behavior whenever possible, but places the needs of the group as a whole over the needs of individual students. The child's thoughts, feelings, ideas, and preferences are taken into account when dealing with instruction, classroom management, and discipline, but ultimately the teacher's primary focus is on behavior and meeting the academic needs of the group.

Students are given opportunities to control their behavior in an effort to develop the ability to make appropriate decisions, yet they may not initially recognize that some of their behavior might be a hindrance to their own growth and development. Students need to recognize the consequences of their behavior and make adjustments to reach more favorable results.

The teacher and students often develop rules and procedures jointly. Teachers may begin the discussion of rules by presenting one or two rules that must be followed, or the teacher may hold veto power over the rules that the students select. This represents a higher degree of control than is used by low control teachers. Medium control teachers then would be responsible for enforcing the rules and helping students recognize the consequences of their decisions and actions. Medium control educators might use logical consequences, cooperative discipline, noncoercive approaches, or other interactive approaches. These strategies fall into the interacting model of discipline.

Several educators have described cohesive approaches to deal with students that represent the medium teacher control approach when creating a supportive learning environment and guiding student behavior. The discipline models from several representative authors are discussed in the following sections.

WHAT WOULD YOU DECIDE? *Medium Teacher Control*

Teachers adopting the medium teacher control approach—the interacting model—to discipline want to involve students to some degree in establishing guidelines in the classroom and in dealing with misbehavior. The teachers may enforce the boundaries and work with the students to determine suitable solutions.

1. How might your selection of rules and consequences be influenced by this philosophical approach?

2. How might this philosophical approach to control also affect your decision making about aspects of curriculum and instruction, such as your choice of instructional activities and assessment techniques?

Logical Consequences: Rudolf Dreikurs

Rudolf Dreikurs (Dreikurs, Grunwald, & Pepper, 1982) based his strategies on the belief that students are motivated to get recognition and to belong with others. Students seek social acceptance from conforming to the group and making useful contributions to it. Dreikurs views his approaches as democratic in that teachers and students together decide on the rules and consequences, and they have joint responsibility for maintaining a positive classroom climate. This encourages students to become more responsibly self-governing.

To Dreikurs, discipline is not punishment; it is teaching students to impose limits on themselves. With his approaches, students are responsible for their own actions, have respect for themselves and others, have the responsibility to influence others to behave appropriately, and are responsible for knowing the classroom rules and consequences. Based on Dreikurs' ideas, there are several techniques that you can use to help misbehaving students behave appropriately without reliance on punishment.

First, identify the goal of the misbehavior. Examine the key signs of the misbehavior and also consider your feelings and reactions as a means to tentatively identify the goal of the student's misbehavior. The student's goal may be to gain attention, to seek power, to seek revenge, or to display inadequacy. Then disclose this goal to the student in a private session as a means to confirm the goal. This is a positive means of confronting a misbehaving student. Its purpose is to heighten the student's awareness of the motives for the misbehavior.

Second, alter your reactions to the misbehavior. Once the goal of misbehavior has been identified, first control your immediate reaction to misbehavior so that your response does not reinforce the misbehavior. For example, if the student's goal is to seek attention, never give immediate attention, but try to ignore the behavior whenever possible. Then, have a discussion with the student to identify a number of alternatives for changing the behavior.

Third, provide encouragement statements to students. Encouragement consists of words or actions that acknowledge student work and express confidence in them. Encouragement statements help students see what they did to lead to a positive result and also help students feel confident about their own abilities. For example, you might say, "I see that your extra studying for the test paid off because you did so well." The focus is on what the student did that led to the result obtained.

Most important, use logical consequences. Instead of using punishment, Dreikurs prefers to let students experience the consequences that flow from misbehavior. A *logical consequence* is an event that is arranged by the teacher that is directly and logically related to the misbehavior. For instance, if a student leaves paper on the classroom floor, the student must pick the paper off the floor. If a student breaks the rule of speaking out without raising his or her hand, the teacher ignores the response and calls on a student whose hand is up. If a student makes marks on the desk, the student is required to remove them.

Cooperative Discipline: Linda Albert

Based largely on the philosophy and psychology of Alfred Adler and Rudolf Dreikurs, Linda Albert (2003) developed a classroom management and discipline plan called cooperative discipline. Similar to Dreikurs' ideas, cooperative discipline is founded on three concepts of behavior: (a) students choose their behavior; (b) the ultimate goal of student behavior is to fulfill the need to belong; and (c) students misbehave to achieve one of four immediate goals (attention, power, revenge, and avoidance of failure).

Albert's main focus is on helping teachers meet student needs so that students choose to cooperate with the teacher and with each other. Her cooperative discipline includes five action steps: pinpoint and describe the student's behavior, identify the goal of the misbehavior, choose intervention techniques for the moment of misbehavior, select encouragement techniques to build self-esteem, and involve parents as partners. Albert's cooperative discipline program, therefore, is designed to establish positive classroom control through appropriate interventions and to build self-esteem through encouragement.

The building blocks of self-esteem are helping students feel capable, helping students connect (become involved and engaged in the classroom), and helping students contribute (discussed more fully in Chapter 6). To achieve the goals of cooperative discipline intervention and encouragement strategies, use democratic procedures and policies, implement cooperative learning strategies, conduct classroom guidance activities, and choose appropriate curriculum methods and materials.

Albert offers a number of strategies to implement her cooperative discipline plan. She presents intervention techniques when misbehavior occurs, ways to reinforce desirable behavior, approaches to create a cooperative classroom climate, and ways to avoid and defuse confrontations. Albert also proposes that teachers and students collaboratively develop a Classroom Code of Conduct as a means to involve students and foster their sense of responsibility to the group.

Janet Kulbiski, Kindergarten Teacher, Manhattan, Kansas

After reading Jane Nelsen's book *Positive Discipline in the Classroom* (2000), I changed my attitude about misbehavior and tried some different behavior management strategies in my classroom. I now see misbehavior as an opportunity for teaching appropriate action.

Several of Nelsen's techniques have been very helpful in my classroom. I use natural and logical consequences, allow students choices, and redirect misbehavior. Natural consequences occur without intervention from anyone, such as when a child does not wear his coat and then gets cold. Logical consequences, by contrast, require intervention connected in some logical way to what the child did. If a child draws a picture on the table, a logical consequence would be that the child cleans it up.

It is important to give students choices whenever possible. This gives them a sense of control and worth, but all choices must be acceptable to you. For example, "Please, put the toy on my desk or in your backpack." Redirecting student behavior involves reminding them of the expected behavior. For example, instead of saying, "Don't run," I say, "We always walk." Eliminating "don't" from my vocabulary has helped a lot.

When I deal with misbehavior, I try to always use the situation as an opportunity for the child to learn the expected behavior. My goal is to leave the child feeling good about himself or herself and equipped to handle the situation appropriately next time.

Positive Discipline: Jane Nelsen, Lynn Lott, and Stephen Glenn

Jane Nelsen has also adapted Rudolf Dreikurs' concepts into a program called positive discipline. In *Positive Discipline*, Nelsen (1996) identified kindness, respect, firmness, and encouragement as the main ingredients of this program for parents and teachers. There are several key elements to Nelsen's approach: (1) Use natural and logical consequences as a means to inspire a positive atmosphere for winning children over rather than winning over children. (2) Understand that children have four goals of misbehavior (attention, power, revenge, and assumed inadequacy). (3) Kindness and firmness need to be used at the same time when addressing misbehavior. (4) Adults and children must have mutual respect. (5) Family and class meetings can be effectively used to address misbehavior. (6) Use encouragement as a means of inspiring self-evaluation and focusing on the actions of the child.

Nelsen has described how positive discipline principles can be applied to the classroom through the use of classroom meetings. In *Positive Discipline in the Classroom*, Nelsen and colleagues (Nelson, Lott, & Glenn, 2000) provide detailed descriptions for ways to conduct effective classroom meetings. In addition to eliminating discipline problems, classroom meetings help students develop social, academic, and life skills, and help students feel that they are personally capable, significant, and can influence their own lives.

With positive discipline, teachers demonstrate caring by showing personal interest, talking with the students, offering encouragement, and providing opportunities to nurture important life skills. Nelsen and colleagues caution that it is easy is misuse logical consequences because they are often simply punishments. Instead, they maintain that teachers think in terms of solutions, rather than consequences. To do so, Nelsen suggests strategies such as involving students in solutions to problems, focusing on the future rather than the present, planning solutions carefully in advance, and making connections between opportunity, responsibility, and consequence.

Noncoercive Discipline: William Glasser

William Glasser, a psychiatrist, received national attention with the publication of *Reality Therapy* (1965), in which he proposed that treating behavioral problems should focus on present circumstances rather than antecedents of the inappropriate behavior. Glasser took his reality therapy message to educators in *Schools Without Failure* (1969). He noted that successful social relationships are basic human needs. Glasser maintained that students have a responsibility for making good choices about their behavior and that they must live with their choices.

When using reality therapy, teachers and students need to jointly establish classroom rules, and the teacher is to enforce the rules consistently without accepting excuses. When misbehavior occurs, the teacher should ask the student, "What are you doing? Is it helping you or the class? What could you do that would help?" The student is asked to make some value judgments about the behavior, and the teacher can suggest suitable alternatives. Together, they create a plan to eliminate the problem behavior. When necessary, the teacher needs to invoke appropriate consequences.

Over time, Glasser expanded his reality therapy concepts. With the development of control theory (1984, 1986), he added the needs of belonging and love, control, freedom, and fun. Without attention to those needs, students are bound to fail. Glasser maintained that discipline problems should be viewed as total behaviors, meaning that the entire context of the situation needs to be examined in an effort to seek a solution. For example, physical inactivity may contribute to student misbehavior, whereas this element might be overlooked if the situation were examined in a more confined way.

With control theory, you must recognize that students want to have their needs met. Students feel pleasure when these needs are met and frustration when they are not. You must create the conditions in which students feel a sense of belonging, have some power and control, have some freedom in the learning and schooling process, and have fun. Thus, students will not be frustrated and discipline problems should be limited.

More recently in *The Quality School* (1998a), Glasser described how to manage students without coercion. Glasser asserts that the nature of school management must be changed in order to meet students' needs and promote effective learning. In fact, he criticizes current school managers for accepting low-quality work. In *The Quality School Teacher* (1998b) and *Every Student Can Succeed* (2000), Glasser offers specific strategies for teachers to move to quality schools.

Discipline with Dignity: Richard Curwin and Allen Mendler

In *Discipline with Dignity* (1999), Richard Curwin and Allen Mendler point out that discipline problems may be caused by student boredom, feelings of powerlessness, unclear limits, a lack of acceptable outlets for feelings, and attacks on dignity. To deal with these causes and to create an effective learning environment, Curwin and Mendler have developed a three-dimensional discipline plan: (1) the *prevention dimension* focuses on what the teacher can do to actively prevent discipline problems and how to deal with the stress associated with classroom disruptions; (2) the *action dimension* deals with actions the teacher can take when misbehavior occurs; and (3) the *resolution dimension* addresses ways teachers can resolve problems with chronic rule breakers and more extreme, out-of-control students.

Curwin and Mendler's model of discipline involves working with the students to develop the discipline plan; they label this the "responsibility model." This model requires teachers to give up some of their power to involve students in decision making, which Curwin and Mendler maintain is far more consistent with current classroom emphasis on critical thinking and decision making. The main goal of the responsibility model is to teach students to make responsible choices, and students are expected to learn from the outcomes of these decisions. This model fosters critical thinking and promotes shared decision making. Students feel affirmed even though they don't always get their way. They understand that they have some control of the events that happen to them, and they get a chance to learn that teachers also have rights, power, knowledge, and leadership.

There are four principles of this discipline plan that uses discipline as a learning process rather than a system of retribution. (1) Dealing with student behavior is part of the job. (2) Always treat students with dignity. (3) Discipline works best when integrated with effective teaching practices. (4) Acting out is sometimes an act of sanity.

A social contract is a basic tool for discipline planning in the responsibility model. The *social contract* is an agreement between the teacher and students about the rules and consequences for classroom behavior. Curwin and Mendler identify the following as important aspects of designing the contract: involve students in the process; ensure that rules are clear; develop consequences, not punishments; develop predictable consequences; allow the contract to change with class needs; have safeguards to protect the dignity of all students; increase communication among teachers, students, administrators, and parents; and integrate discipline methodology with the teaching of content.

WHAT WOULD YOU DECIDE?   *Curwin and Mendler—Medium Teacher Control*

In *Discipline with Dignity*, Curwin and Mendler say that a social contract in the classroom is a vital part of their plan. This contract is an agreement between the teacher and the students about the rules and consequences for classroom behavior. Two parts of this plan are to have predictable consequences and to allow the contract to change with class needs.

1. From your perspective, what are some reasonable consequences that could be identified for minor misbehaviors? For moderate misbehaviors?

2. During the discussions to establish the social contract, what if the students don't accept your suggestions for consequences? What if you don't accept their suggestions for consequences?

Curwin and Mendler identify nine principles when delivering consequences: (1) Always implement a consequence when needed. (2) Simply state the rule and consequence. (3) Be physically close to the student when implementing a consequence. (4) Make direct eye contact when delivering a consequence. (5) Use a soft voice. (6) Catch a student being good. (7) Don't embarrass a student in front of his peers. (8) Be firm and anger-free when giving the consequence. (9) Do not accept excuses, bargaining, or whining.

Curwin and Mendler also recognize the relationship between discipline and the process of teaching. In doing so, they discuss motivation, learning styles, enthusiasm in instructional delivery, evaluation and grading, and competition. They further discuss the unique challenges in dealing with out-of-control students and students with special problems.

Win–Win Discipline: Spencer Kagan

Spencer Kagan is an educational consultant who specializes in researching and developing discipline strategies and life skills training. Along with Patricia Kyle and Sally Scott, Kagan developed a model of discipline called *Win–Win Discipline* (Kagan, Kyle, & Scott, 2004). The two purposes of this model are to help students meet their needs through responsible, nondisruptive behavior and to develop long-term life skills. To be on the same side in establishing good discipline, teachers and students treat discipline as a joint responsibility.

There are three pillars to win–win discipline: (1) Same Side: The teacher, students, and parents work together rather than at odds with each other toward building responsible behavior, (2) Collaboration: Teachers and students cocreate immediate and long-term solutions to behavior problems, and (3) Learned Responsibility: Teachers help students make responsible choices in how they conduct themselves. Any disruptive behavior that interrupts the learning process can become an important learning opportunity.

Kagan and colleagues identified four types of disruptive behavior—aggression, breaking rules, confrontation, and disengagement. Further, they proposed that disruptive behavior springs from students seeking attention, avoiding failure, being angry, seeking control, and being energetic, bored, or uninformed. Teacher responses are identified for each of these causes. Interventions are designed to help students meet their needs through responsible choices, and the interventions are tailored in accordance to the type of disruption and the reason for the misbehavior.

Heavy emphasis is placed on preventing disruptive behavior through attention to curriculum, instruction, and management. Win–win discipline enables teachers to work with students so that needs that might otherwise prompt disruptive behavior can be identified and satisfied in nondisruptive ways. Students do not often disrupt when engaged in a curriculum that is interesting and adequately challenging.

HIGH TEACHER CONTROL APPROACHES

High control approaches are based on the philosophical belief that students' growth and development are the result of external conditions. Children are seen as being

Table 2.2 Proponents of Various Discipline Models

The Guiding Model	The Interacting Model	The Intervening Model
Low Control Approaches	Medium Control Approaches	High Control Approaches
Congruent Communication *Haim Ginott* • Use sane messages • Invite student cooperation • Express helpfulness and acceptance	**Logical Consequences** *Rudolf Dreikurs* • Teach in a democratic manner • Identify and confront students' mistaken goals • Use logical consequences	**Behavior Modification** *B.F. Skinner* • Identify desired behaviors • Shape behavior through reinforcement • Use behavior modification systematically
Discipline as Self-Control (Teacher Effectiveness Training) *Thomas Gordon* • Identify problem ownership • Maximize communication • Use the power of influence	**Cooperative Discipline** *Linda Albert* • Establish a sense of belonging • Build student self-esteem • Promote cooperative relationships	**Assertive Discipline** *Lee and Marlene Canter* • Recognize classroom rights • Teach desired behavior • Establish consequences
Teaching with Love and Logic *Jim Fay and David Funk* • Share control with students • Maintain student self-concepts • Balance consequences with empathy	**Positive Classroom Discipline** *Jane Nelsen, Lynn Lott, and H. Stephen Glenn* • Use classroom meetings • Exhibit caring attitudes and behaviors • Use management skills	**Positive Discipline** *Fredric Jones* • Structure classrooms • Set limits and promote cooperation • Have back-up systems
Inner Discipline *Barbara Coloroso* • Enable students to solve problems • Provide support and structure • Treat students with dignity and respect	**Noncoercive Discipline** (Reality Therapy and Control Theory) *William Glasser* • Provide quality education • Help students make good decisions • Provide support and encouragement	
From Discipline to Community *Alfie Kohn* • Provide an engaging curriculum • Develop a caring community • Allow students to make choices	**Discipline with Dignity** *Richard Curwin and Allen Mendler* • Create a three-dimensional plan • Establish a social contract • Teach students to make responsible choices	
	Win-Win Discipline *Spencer Kagan* • Work with students to solve problems • Focus on short- and long-term solutions • Help students make responsible choices	

molded and shaped by influences from the environment; they are not seen as having an innate potential. Therefore, teachers and adults need to select desired student behaviors, reinforce appropriate behaviors, and take actions to extinguish inappropriate behaviors. Little attention is given to the thoughts, feelings, and preferences of the students since adults are more experienced in instructional matters and have the responsibility for choosing what is best for student development and behavior control.

Teachers using high control approaches believe that student behavior must be controlled because the students themselves are not able effectively to monitor and control their own behavior. The teachers select the rules and procedures for the classroom, commonly without student input. Teachers then reinforce desired behavior and take actions to have students stop inappropriate, undesired behavior. When misbehavior occurs, teachers take steps to stop the disruption quickly and redirect the student to more positive behavior. Behavior modification, behavioral contracting, and reinforcers are characteristic of high control approaches. Compared to the previous models, there is more emphasis on managing the behavior of the individuals than the group.

Several educators have described cohesive approaches to deal with students that represent the high teacher control approach to classroom control and order. These approaches are discussed in the following sections.

Behavior Modification: B. F. Skinner

B. F. Skinner (1902–1990) spent most of his academic career at Harvard University, where he conducted experimental studies in learning. In *Beyond Freedom and Dignity* (1971), Skinner challenged traditional views of freedom and dignity and instead claimed that our choices are determined by the environmental conditions under which we live and what has happened to us. The application of these ideas to classroom practice has been called *behavior modification*, a technique that uses reinforcement and punishment to shape behavior.

Behavior modification, as proposed by Skinner and others, has several distinguishing features. Behavior is shaped by its consequences and by what happens to the individual immediately afterward. The systematic use of reinforcers, or rewards, can shape behavior in desired directions. Behavior becomes weaker if it is not followed by reinforcement. Behavior is also weakened by punishment.

Behavior modification is applied in the classroom primarily in two ways: (a) when the teacher rewards the student after a desired act, the student tends to repeat the act; and (b) when the student performs an undesired act, the teacher either ignores the act or punishes the student; the misbehaving student then becomes less likely to repeat the act.

Several types of reinforcers can be used: (1) edible reinforcers, such as candy, cookies, gum, drinks, nuts, or various other snacks; (2) social reinforcers, such as words, gestures, stickers, certificates, and facial and bodily expressions of approval by the teacher; (3) material or tangible reinforcers, which are real objects that students can earn as rewards for desired behavior; (4) token reinforcers, including stars, points, buttons, or other items that can be accumulated by students for desired behavior and then "cashed in" for other material or tangible reinforcers; and (5) activity reinforcers, which include those activities that students prefer in school. Reinforcers are further discussed in Chapter 6.

Behavior modification works best when used in an organized, systematic, and consistent way. The various types of behavior modification systems seem to fit into five categories (Miltenberger, 2004). (1) The "catch them being good" approach involves making positive statements to students who are doing what is expected of them. For example, a teacher might thank a student for getting out class materials and being ready to start the class. (2) The rules–ignore–praise approach involves establishing a set of classroom rules, ignoring inappropriate behavior, and praising appropriate behavior. This approach works best in elementary grades and is less effective in secondary grades. (3) The rules–reward–punishment approach involves establishing classroom rules, rewarding appropriate behavior, and punishing inappropriate behavior. This system is quite appropriate for older students. (4) The contingency management approach is a system of tangible reinforcers where students earn tokens for appropriate behavior that can be exchanged at a later time for material rewards. (5) Contracting involves preparing a contract for an individual student who has chronic problems or is hard to manage.

Assertive Discipline: Lee and Marlene Canter

Lee Canter is an educator who first came into prominence in 1976 with the publication of *Assertive Discipline* (Canter & Canter, 2002), a take-charge approach for teachers to control their classrooms in a firm and positive manner. Since that time, he has created an organization called Canter and Associates that prepares a variety of materials concerning classroom discipline and conducts workshops and training programs for teachers, administrators, parents, and other educators.

Over the years, Canter has expanded and built on the basic behavior management principles from the assertive discipline book. Since today's teachers face even more complex situations, a more comprehensive model was developed. The revised edition of *Assertive Discipline* (2002) goes beyond the initial take-charge approach and includes additional classroom management procedures. In the revised *Assertive Discipline*, Canter discusses the assertive attitude necessary to deal with classroom management and discipline, the parts of a classroom discipline plan, aspects of teaching responsible behavior, and ways to deal with difficult students. The goal of assertive discipline is to teach students to choose responsible behavior and in doing so raise their self-esteem and increase their academic success.

Canter maintains that teachers have the right and responsibility to (a) establish rules and directions that clearly define the limits of acceptable and unacceptable student behavior; (b) teach these rules and directions; and (c) ask for assistance from parents and administrators when support is needed in handling the behavior of students. The manner in which teachers respond to student behavior affects students' self-esteem and success in school. Therefore, teachers must use an assertive response style to state expectations clearly and confidently to students and reinforce these words with actions.

A classroom discipline plan has three parts: (a) rules that students must follow at all times; (b) positive recognition that students will receive for following the rules; and (c) consequences that result when students choose not to follow the rules. Sample rules may be to follow directions, keep hands and feet to oneself, or be in the classroom and seated when the bell rings. Positive recognition may include various forms of praise, positive notes sent home to parents, positive notes to students, or special activities or privileges.

Consequences are delivered systematically with each occurrence of misbehavior. The first time a student breaks a rule, a warning is given. The second time, the student may lose a privilege, such as being last in line for lunch or staying in class one minute after the bell. The third time, the student loses additional privileges. The fourth time, the teacher calls the parents. The fifth time, the student is sent to the principal. In cases of severe misbehavior, these preliminary steps may be skipped and the student is sent to the principal.

Another part of Canter's assertive discipline plan is to teach responsible behavior. This includes determining and teaching specific directions (classroom procedures), using positive recognition to motivate students to behave, redirecting nondisruptive off-task behavior, and implementing consequences. Canter further emphasizes that successful teachers need to blend academic and behavior management efforts into a cohesive whole so that classroom management actions are not apparent.

Canter gives special attention to dealing with difficult students, who represent perhaps five to ten percent of the students you may encounter. In *Assertive Discipline* (Canter & Canter, 2002), recommendations are provided for conducting a one-to-one problem-solving conference with the teacher and the difficult student. The goal of the conference is to help the student gain insight into the problem and ultimately choose more responsible behavior. Guidelines are offered to provide positive support to build positive relationships with difficult students, and recommendations are made for developing an individualized behavior plan. Parents and administrators can offer additional support when dealing with difficult students. Canter and Canter have a separate book on this subject: *Succeeding with Difficult Students* (1993).

VOICES FROM THE CLASSROOM | *Positive Recognition in Assertive Discipline*

Cammie Fulk, Fifth-Grade Teacher, Fulks Run, Virginia

To provide positive recognition in my assertive discipline plan, I post a personal calendar for each student each month. If a student has behaved well and completed all of the work for the day, a stamp is placed on that date. If not, then the reason for not receiving the stamp is written on that date. When a student receives five stamps in a row, a reward is given. For ten stamps in a row, a free homework pass is provided. At the end of each month, the calendar is sent home to be signed by the parents and then returned to me. This personal calendar has become a strong motivator in my fifth grade classroom.

In addition to the personal calendars, I have a gem jar on my desk as a reward for the entire class. It is simply a clear coffee cup with three permanent levels marked on the side to indicate 5, 10, and 15 minutes of free time earned. As I observe the entire class on task, I place several gems in the jar. Gems may be marbles, bubble gum, candy corn, jelly beans, or other small items. Gems can be earned for a variety of behaviors such as good hall behavior, the entire class on task, the entire class completing homework, or other valued actions. The sound of the gems hitting the glass cup brings smiles to my fifth graders.

Positive Discipline: Fredric Jones

Fredric Jones is a psychologist who conducted research on classroom practices and developed training programs for improving teacher effectiveness in behavior management and instruction. In *Positive Classroom Discipline* (1987), Jones emphasized that teachers can help students support their own self-control. Jones' *Tools for Teaching* (2000) extends the discussion of these issues. Jones recommends that teachers use the following five strategies to enact positive discipline.

1. *Structure the Classroom.* Teachers need to consider various rules, routines, and standards; seating arrangements; and student–teacher relationships when structuring the classroom. Rules, procedures, routines, and classroom standards need to be taught to students so they understand the standards and expectations in the classroom. Jones points out that the arrangement of the classroom furniture can maximize teacher mobility and allow greater physical proximity to students on a moment-to-moment basis. While presenting several ways to arrange student desks in a classroom, Jones indicates that any arrangement that provides quick and easy access to all students is likely to be successful. Jones also prefers to have assigned seats for students to disperse the good students between the chronic disrupters.

2. *Maintain Control by Using Appropriate Instructional Strategies.* Jones maintains that teachers lose control of their classes when they spend too much time with each student, such as during seatwork. Teachers commonly spend time to find out where a student is having difficulty, to explain further the part the student doesn't understand, and to supply students with additional explanations and examples. Instead, Jones recommends that teachers use the three-step sequence of praise, prompt, and leave. In this sequence, teachers first praise students for what they have done correctly so far. Second, prompt students by telling them exactly what to do next and encourage them to do it. The teacher then leaves to let the student take the needed action and also to be available to help other students.

3. *Maintain Control with Limit-Setting Techniques.* Jones proposed a series of specific actions that can be taken when a student is getting off task. These techniques primarily involve the use of body language to convince the students that the teacher is in control. These steps involve being aware of and monitoring the behavior of all students; terminating instruction when necessary to deal with a student; turning, looking, and saying the student's name; moving to the edge of the student's desk; moving away from the student's desk when the student gets back to work; placing your palms on the desk and giving a short, direct verbal prompt if the student does not get back to work; moving closer over the desk; and finally moving next to the student behind the student's desk.

4. *Build Patterns of Cooperation.* Jones proposed an incentive system called preferred activity time (PAT) that can be used so students can earn certain benefits if they behave and cooperate. The PAT may be a variety of activities and privileges that are given to the class as a whole at the start of a predetermined time (a week's worth). When an individual student misbehaves, the teacher uses a stopwatch or timer to record the length of time of the infraction, and this amount of time is subtracted from the class's total time. On the other hand, students can earn bonus time for the class by cleaning up the classroom in a hurry, being in their seats in time, or some other desired behavior.

5. *Develop Appropriate Backup Systems in the Event of Misbehavior.* Backups are to be used systematically from lesser sanctions to more serious ones. Low-level sanctions involve issuing a warning; pulling a card with the student's name, address, and telephone number; and then sending a letter to the parents. (But first the student is given an opportunity to correct the behavior; if so, then the letter is not sent.) Mid-level sanctions include time-out, detention, loss of privileges, and a parent conference. High-level sanctions include in-school suspension, Saturday school, delivering the student to a parent at work, asking a parent to accompany the student in school, suspension, police intervention, and expulsion.

Developing Your Management Plan: *Examining Your Philosophical Beliefs*

To help form your philosophy of classroom management, answer the following questions to reflect your current beliefs. You may modify your responses over time as you explore more information about classroom management and discipline.

- What is the purpose of education?
- What is a good teacher, and what is good teaching?
- What should be the goals of a classroom management plan?

- What degree of control do I want to maintain in the classroom? Do I see myself as an autocratic or a democratic teacher, or somewhere in between?
- How do I want my degree of control to be evident in my instructional, management, and disciplinary practices in the classroom?
- Which model of discipline (shown in Table 2.1 and Table 2.2) appeals to me? Why?

DETERMINING YOUR MANAGEMENT PLAN

How do you develop a philosophy of classroom management and a management plan for your classroom? Bosch (1999) maintains that classroom management must reflect the personality and teaching style of the individual teacher and is a skill that must be learned, practiced, evaluated, and modified to fit the changing situations in classrooms. Further, teachers must be able to modify and adjust their management strategies as conditions warrant, just as they modify their teaching strategies to match students' needs and learning styles.

Your goals, values, and beliefs about classroom management, discipline, instruction, and child development will affect your management philosophy, and your philosophy, in turn, will affect how you select and enact the particular aspects of your management plan.

Your Management Philosophy

Before you determine your management plan, you must select a philosophical model for classroom management and discipline. This chapter provided a brief orientation to various models of discipline which went from low to high teacher control, representing a continuum of philosophical perspectives for control in the classroom. This discussion

Table 2.3 Clarifying Your Classroom Management Plan

The following categories provide a framework for you to clarify and write your classroom management plan. The rest of this book provides additional background information for your decision making as you write your plan.

Philosophy on Classroom Management and Discipline

First provide background information about your personality, teaching style, and philosophy of education to reveal the origins and foundation of your classroom management philosophy.

Next, describe your philosophy on classroom management and discipline for your own classroom. What are your purposes for an effective classroom management plan? To what degree do you plan to control the decision making and actions in the classroom? To what degree will you involve students?

The Classroom Arrangement

How will you arrange student seating, the teacher's desk, furniture arrangement, bulletin boards, technology placement, storage of materials, and the use of wall space? This could include a diagram to show the placement of these features.

Rules

What behavior will you expect of your students?

What rules will you display and use in your classroom?

Describe how you determined the rules. Would you involve students in identifying the rules? If so, to what degree? How will you communicate the rules to the students, parents, and administrators?

Responses to Misbehavior

What will you do when a student misbehaves and breaks a rule? Will you have a hierarchy of consequences to deal with mild, moderate, and severe misbehavior? Specifically, what is your plan?

Procedures

What procedures will you use in your classroom (e.g., distributing materials, collecting homework, transitions in and out of the room, providing students assistance)? How will you teach the procedures to the students?

Creating a Respectful, Supportive Learning Environment

What type of classroom atmosphere would you like to create? What specifically will you do to create that atmosphere? How can you maintain and reinforce appropriate student behavior? How can you promote cooperation?

Managing and Facilitating Instruction

How will your lessons be structured? How will you begin and end your lessons? How will you group your students for instruction? How will you manage lesson delivery? How will you make modifications for diverse learners? How will you integrate technology in instruction?

Motivating Students to Learn

How will you include motivational strategies in your instruction, evaluation, and feedback? How will you incorporate these motivational issues into all levels of your instructional planning?

Promoting Safety and Wellness

How will you provide a physically and emotionally safe environment for students in your classroom? How will you respond to disruptive or violent behavior in the classroom? How might you prevent it?

Interacting with Parents, Colleagues, and Others

What are the reasons for communicating and interacting with parents, colleagues, and others? How will you communicate with them? How frequently?

on control is a useful starting point as you consider your philosophical perspective on classroom management and discipline. Adapted from Manning and Bucher (2003), the chapter feature on "Developing Your Management Plan" lists several questions about additional educational issues to prompt your consideration of education, teaching and learning, management, and discipline to help you clarify your philosophical beliefs.

To what degree do you want to exercise control in your classroom? That is the fundamental question when deciding on your approach to classroom management and discipline. To answer that question, you will likely consider a number of factors, such as your views of educational philosophy, psychology, and child development. For example, when determining your approach to control, you will likely take into account your beliefs about what is the dominant influence on a child's development—inner forces, outer forces, or a combination of the two. You may want to review Table 2.1 on the characteristics of the discipline models and Table 2.2 on the proponents of various discipline models.

Your Management Plan

Your analysis of the philosophical views of classroom management and discipline will probably reveal whether you are inclined to use low, medium, or high control approaches, each representing a different philosophical perspective. After determining your relative placement on the teacher control continuum, decide whether you want to use a particular discipline model shown in Table 2.2, synthesize two or more models, or create your own approach. Even if you choose one model, you may find that the context of the classroom and the actual events cause you to shift from that model and use elements of other approaches. You don't have to accept the entire set of actions proposed by a certain model. When determining the relative merits of the different discipline models, it may be useful to establish criteria to compare the relative characteristics, strengths, and weaknesses of each model.

There is more to developing your management plan than selecting a particular discipline model. To enact your philosophical view of classroom management and discipline, you will need to make decisions about the seven domains of responsibility in classroom management and discipline outlined in Chapter 1. Those domains can serve as organizers for your decision making to create an effective learning community.

To facilitate your thinking and decisions concerning the seven domains, Table 2.3 includes a list of categories that could be included in your classroom management plan. Each category is discussed in this book, with some categories being addressed in an entire chapter. In each of the following chapters, there is a feature titled "Developing Your Management Plan," and you will be prompted to write your answers to this feature. By compiling your answers to this feature from each chapter, you will have written your management plan.

MAIN POINTS

1. A continuum showing a range of low to high teacher control can be used to illustrate the various educational views expressed by educators about classroom management and discipline.

2. Low control approaches are based on the philosophical belief that students have primary responsibility for controlling their own behavior and that they have the capability to make these decisions.

3. Educators representative of the low control approach are Haim Ginott, Thomas Gordon, Jim Fay, David Funk, Barbara Coloroso, and Alfie Kohn.

4. Medium control approaches are based on the philosophical belief that students develop from a combination of natural forces within the child and outer forces of the child's environment. Thus, the control of student behavior is a joint responsibility of the student and the teacher.

5. Educators representative of the medium control approach are Rudolf Dreikurs, Linda Albert, Jane Nelsen, William Glasser, Richard Curwin, Allen Mendler, and Spencer Kagan.

6. High control approaches are based on the philosophical belief that students' growth and development are the result of external conditions. Children are seen as molded and shaped by influences from the environment where they live.

7. Educators representative of the high control approach are B.F. Skinner, Lee Canter, and Fredric Jones.

8. When deciding on your approach to control, you will likely consider your views of educational philosophy, psychology, and child development. It may also be useful to identify whether you are inclined to use low, medium, or high control approaches on the teacher behavior continuum.

DISCUSSION/REFLECTIVE QUESTIONS

1. What are the merits and problems that might be associated with each of the three levels of teacher control?

2. Recall a favorite teacher you had. What level of control did that teacher use? What are the indicators of that level of control?

3. What are the possible benefits and problems of conducting classroom meetings as proposed by Alfie Kohn?

4. Curwin and Mendler identified nine principles when delivering consequences. Which four of those principles are the most important from your perspective? Why?

5. Why is the Fredric Jones model included in the high control category?

SUGGESTED ACTIVITIES

1. Think about your schooling experiences, and identify teachers you had who fell in the low, medium, and high control approaches. How positive were your experiences in those classes?

2. Talk with several teachers to learn about the degree of control they use when selecting rules and dealing with misbehavior. Identify which discipline model each teacher seems to reflect.

3. Prepare a list of purposes that you want served in any classroom and discipline plan you use in your teaching.

FURTHER READING

CHARLES, C.M. (2005). *Building classroom discipline* (8th ed.). Boston: Allyn & Bacon.
   In separate chapters, the book provides an overview of the discipline models of several educators. Also includes chapters examining the nature of misbehavior, working effectively with all students, and formalizing your personal system of discipline.

MANNING, M. LEE, & BUCHER, KATHERINE T. (2003). *Classroom management: Models, applications, and cases.* Upper Saddle River, NJ: Prentice-Hall/Merrill.
   In separate chapters, the book provides descriptions of the classroom management and discipline plans of several leading educators. Also includes chapters on understanding the need for classroom management and on building your own management plan.

Chapter 3

Preparing for the School Year

CHAPTER OBJECTIVES

This chapter provides information that will help you:
- Describe ways to establish and maintain order to promote a successful learning environment.
- Identify ways to prepare for the school year.
- Describe ways to organize your classroom and materials.

CHAPTER OUTLINE

Imagine that you are going to take a two-week vacation to see the numerous state and national parks in southern Utah and northern Arizona. You gather information about the parks and attractions from a variety of sources, and then you start to plan your itinerary. Next, you make motel reservations and list all of the things you need to take with you such as hiking shoes, water bottles, sunscreen, sunglasses, camera, and clothing. Soon before you leave on the trip, you stop your newspaper and mail delivery and make arrangements for your pets for the days you are gone. All of these arrangements, and probably more, are needed to have a fun, trouble-free vacation.

Starting the school year also requires this type of advance planning. Even before school starts, you can make a number of decisions about instructional and management preparations, plans to promote a positive learning climate, arrangements for assessments and record keeping, plans for the very first day of school, and arrangements for floor space, storage, and other aspects of classroom space. Early planning and decision making on these issues will help ensure a positive beginning to the school year. These classroom management issues are explored in this chapter.

PREPARING FOR THE SCHOOL YEAR

If you surveyed experienced teachers about the role of management at the beginning of the school year, you would undoubtedly hear comments about management and instructional preparations before school starts and about ways to plan for the first days of the school year. Studies on classroom management have verified that the first few days of the school year set the tone for the entire year (Emmer, Evertson, & Worsham, 2006; Evertson, Emmer, & Worsham, 2006; Marzano, 2003).

To prepare, you can make management preparations, make instructional preparations, plan to manage assessments and record keeping, establish a plan for misbehavior, and also prepare for the first day of school. When the school year finally begins, there are certain actions that are appropriate during the first day and over the following few days. A number of these issues are addressed in this section. There are a number of resources that provide more details than can be discussed in this chapter. Resources are available for the elementary grades (Bosch & Kersey, 2000; Canter & Associates,

1998; Jonson, 2002; Moran et al., 2000; Roberts, 2001; Williamson, 1998), secondary grades (Arnold, 2001; Wyatt & White, 2001), and grades K–12 (Schell & Burden, 2000; Marzano, 2003; Wong & Wong, 2004).

Making Management Preparations

It is important to consider carefully a variety of management issues such as your school environment, room and seating arrangements, materials, rules and procedures, communication with parents, and other issues. Based on a study of experienced teachers (Schell & Burden, 2000), you could direct your attention to the following classroom management issues.

1. *The School Environment.* The first step is to become thoroughly familiar with the total environment before school starts: the room, school, facilities, personnel, services, resources, policies and procedures, other teachers, children, and the community. You will then have more information on which to base decisions, will probably feel more confident about your job, and will not need to devote time in the first few weeks to gather this information.

2. *Gather Support Materials.* After examining the curriculum guide and the textbooks, you might have ideas about activities for a certain unit or lesson. Supplementary materials may be needed when the time comes to teach that lesson. This is the time to gather any additional support materials such as games and devices, pictures, cassette tapes, ideas for activities, charts, maps, and graphs. The school may have discretionary funds for the purchase of these types of resources. They may be obtained from school supply catalogs, a local teacher store, or even at garage sales.

3. *Organize Materials.* It is useful to set up a filing system for storing district and school communications and other important documents. Papers kept in a filing cabinet include the district's policy handbook; correspondence from the principal, superintendent, or other supervisors; correspondence from professional organizations; lesson plans; and items on curricular content. Some teachers use file folders. A separate file folder may be created for each course unit to hold pertinent notes and resource materials. Textbooks, resource books, manipulative materials, and other types of instructional supplies and materials also need to be organized and stored.

4. *Classroom Procedures.* You can follow various procedures to accomplish specific tasks. Procedures may be identified regarding handing in completed work, sharpening a pencil, using the restroom, or putting away supplies. Before school starts, identify actions or activities requiring procedures that would contribute to a smoothly running classroom, and then decide what those procedures should be.

5. *Classroom Helpers.* Teachers call on students at all grade levels as helpers to perform various classroom tasks. Make a list of tasks that need to be done and then decide which ones students could perform. Give attention to how task assignment will be rotated to give every student an opportunity to help. Roles are often held for one or two weeks before being reassigned. Depending on the grade level and circumstances, some tasks may include students as line leader, light switcher, pencil sharpener, paper collector, plant waterer, chalkboard eraser, window and blind opener, and supply manager.

6. *Class Lists and Rosters.* It is useful to plan a means to record whether students have returned their book orders, picture money, field trip permission forms, and so on. You can prepare a generic class roster listing the students' names in alphabetical order in the left column, with blank columns on the right to check off the action. It is helpful to input the list on a computer disk so that an updated sheet can be easily generated when the roster changes.

VOICES FROM THE CLASSROOM *Using a Class List for Various Purposes*

Marge McClintock, Fifth Grade Science and Social Studies Teacher, New Providence, New Jersey

As soon as I am given my class list of students for the year, I assign the students numbers in alphabetical order for each class. The students are told their numbers and are required to put their numbers on all of their work. This has several benefits. When homework or seatwork is handed in, I ask a student to put the papers in numerical order for me. I can see in an instant which numbers are missing and take whatever action is needed.

Another benefit is managing the students on class trips. Although I always carry a class list with me on the trips, it is much faster to have the students call out their numbers in order when they're back on the bus or whenever roll needs to be taken.

A third benefit is in dividing the class into groups. It can be as easy as evens and odds. Or I can require the students to use higher-order math skills by saying, "All the students whose number can be factored by 3, please come to the front of the class. All students whose number can be factored by 2 and who aren't in the '3' group, please go to the back of the room. All the rest, stay where you are."

---

7. *School/Home Communication.* Open communication with parents is vital. Before school starts, many teachers prepare an introductory letter to parents to welcome them and to inform them about the teacher, the curriculum, grading practices and standards, the homework policy, rules and procedures, and so on (discussed more fully in Chapter 4). This letter can be sent home with the students on the first day of school. Teachers can also make plans for other types of parental communication such as phone calls, progress reports, or a back-to-school night.

8. *Birthdays and Other Celebrations.* Depending on your grade level, you may want to recognize student birthdays. Most schools have very specific policies for celebrating major holidays, such as Halloween, Christmas, Hanukkah, Martin Luther King Day, and Easter. Inquire about these policies so you'll understand what is expected.

9. *Distributing Textbooks.* Sometime in the first few days of school, you will need to distribute textbooks. You need to obtain the textbooks and prepare an inventory form on which to record each book number, with a space in which to write the student's name. You need to think about when and how the textbooks will be distributed. Since the first day of school often necessitates many announcements and activities, you might want to wait until the second or third day before distributing textbooks, or distribute them just before they are needed for the first time. Attention might be given to the specific means of distribution. One way is to have students line up one row at a time and go to the table where the books are stacked. When giving the book to the student, you can record the student's name on the inventory form.

10. *Room Identification.* On the first day of school, students need to locate your classroom. Especially for students new to the building, it is important to have the room clearly labeled. A poster on the outside doorway should include the room number, the teacher's name, and the grade level and/or subject (e.g., Room 211, Mr. Wagner, World History). This information should be written on the chalkboard so students see that they are in the correct classroom. Some type of welcoming statement should also be placed on the chalkboard, such as, "Welcome, I'm glad you're here."

11. *Room Arrangement.* Room arrangement is an issue that can be decided before school starts. Take into account the fixed features in the room, instructional materials and supplies, traffic areas, work areas, boundaries for activity areas, visibility to see all students, and the purposes of various seating arrangements. Determine the arrangement in the classroom for your desk, the students' desks, tables, bookshelves, filing cabinets, and other furniture. The room arrangement you select should be consistent with your instructional goals and activities. Teacher-led instructional approaches such as presentations and demonstrations will require one type of room arrangement, whereas small-group work would require a different type of arrangement.

12. *Seat Selections and Arrangements.* One teacher may prefer to select each student's seat, while another lets the students select their seats. This decision should be made before school starts. In either case, be sure that there are enough seats for the number of students you expect. You might take the age level and maturity of the students into account as you select the manner of assigning seats. You might change the seating arrangements during the school year to accommodate work groups, to move students who need close supervision to more accessible seats, or simply to provide a change.

13. *Room Decoration.* It is important to make your classroom an attractive, comfortable place. Consider having some plants in the classroom, or even an aquarium. Displays of pictures, posters, charts, and maps also help cover the walls with informative and appealing materials. Attractive bulletin boards add color. You might prepare one bulletin board listing classroom information and use another one to display seasonal items. After school starts, you could have students prepare bulletin boards.

Making Instructional Preparations

Prior to the start of the school year, carefully consider a variety of instructional issues such as long-range plans, supplementary materials, student assessment, a folder for substitute teachers, a syllabus, and so on. Based on a study of experienced teachers (Schell & Burden, 2000), you could direct your attention to the following instructional issues.

1. *Long-Range Plans.* It is helpful to peruse the curriculum guides and other related materials so you can appreciate what should be covered by the end of the school year. Some tentative decisions need to be made on the amount of time to be spent on each particular unit. Some curriculum guides include recommendations for the number of weeks to spend on each unit.

You may want to solicit advice from other teachers, particularly from those who teach your same subject or grade level. To the extent possible, make your rough schedules conform to the school calendar by taking into account grading periods and holidays. Be careful not to overschedule yourself. Leave some time for review near the end of each unit or chapter, for reteaching as the situation warrants, and for unexpected occurrences such as school closings due to inclement weather.

WHAT WOULD YOU DECIDE?   *Long-range Planning*

Prior to the school year, you will need to make some long-range plans that will provide a framework for your daily and weekly plans. These general plans may be for the entire year, and then be broken down into semesters, grading periods, and units.

1. What curriculum guides and other materials will you need to gather to provide a basis for your long-range planning decisions?

2. How will you determine the amount of time to be spent on each unit for each course?

3. How will you keep of a record of your long-range plans?

---

2. *Supplementary Materials.* For each major curricular topic in your rough long-range plans, start an ongoing list of related supplementary materials or activities. It may include field trip locations, resource people, media, games, assignments, bulletin boards, and additional books. Inquire about library or media center resources, such as films or videotapes, and order and reserve them. You might prepare other supplementary materials to use during the first few weeks of school.

3. *Skeleton Plans.* A *skeleton plan* is a brief overview of intended accomplishments. It often includes a weekly list of expected accomplishments. Skeleton plans include more details than the long-range, yearly plans, but not the detail needed for daily lesson plans. Skeleton plans for the first three or four weeks serve as a guide for preparing the more detailed lesson plans.

4. *Weekly Time Schedules.* You should establish your weekly schedule before school starts and include a copy in a handy place such as in your lesson plan book. The weekly schedule is often displayed in a chart, with the weekdays listed at the top and the hours listed on the left-hand column. The principal or others probably will determine the class schedule for middle and secondary teachers in the school building, and the schedule will show what grade level and subject is taught during each class period.

5. *Daily Lesson Plans.* After you have completed the skeleton plans for the first three or four weeks, it is time to prepare the daily lesson plans for the first week of school. Lesson plan formats vary; one that is often used includes boxes for the days of the week and the subjects taught. In these boxes, notes may be included about objectives, a list of topics to be covered or activities to be conducted, materials, and means of assessment. Beginning and probationary teachers are often required to show the principal or assistant principal their weekly lesson plans for the coming week.

6. *Syllabus.* You need to give students information about each course at the start of the year. You could plan and prepare this information as well as any related materials before school starts. The course syllabus includes the course title, the title of the textbook and any other primary resource materials, a brief course description, a list of course objectives, a content outline, course requirements (e.g., tests, homework, projects), how grades will be calculated (e.g., the points for each requirement and the point total needed for certain grades), a description of the homework policy, the attendance and tardiness policy, and a listing of classroom rules and procedures.

7. *Policy Sheets.* The syllabus might include all related classroom policies and procedures, though some teachers do not include these items. Depending on the grade level and circumstances, some teachers do not provide a course syllabus. As a result, a teacher might prepare a separate policy sheet for the students which may state the classroom rules and procedures, the policy for attendance and tardiness, and the like. If a course syllabus is not used, this policy sheet might also state the grading policy.

8. *Tentative Student Assessment.* It is useful to make an initial assessment of the students' understanding and skills at the start of the school year so you can better recognize the abilities and differences within the class. These assessments could be conducted sometime during the first week of school, but you should think about how to plan for the assessment and then make any necessary arrangements before school starts. Assessment procedures might include worksheets, oral activities, observation checklists, pretests, or review lessons. After conducting these early assessments, you could then record the results on a class roster that was drawn up earlier.

9. *Homework.* Give careful consideration to how you will evaluate students and determine report card grades. One element of student evaluation often involves homework, and preparation for developing a homework policy can be done before school starts. Prepare a homework policy in the form of a letter that is sent to parents at the start of the school year (see Chapter 4). The homework policy should explain why homework is assigned, explain the types of homework you will assign, inform parents of the amount and frequency of homework, provide guidelines for when and how students are to complete homework, let parents know you will positively reinforce students who complete homework, explain what you will do when students do not complete homework, and clarify what is expected of the parent (Sarka & Shank, 1990).

10. *Backup Materials.* It is useful to have some backup materials available when instruction takes less time than anticipated, when a change of plans is necessary, or when students finish their activities early. These backup materials may be related to the particular topics being covered at the time. Many teachers have a collection of puzzles, educational games, discussion questions, brainteasers, creative writing, word searches, and riddles. You can gather these materials before school starts.

11. *Opening Class Routine.* Students often perform better when they know that a particular routine will be regularly followed at the start of class. You can decide on the particular actions to be taken. You may need to take attendance, make announcements, and attend to other tasks at the start of the class period. The purpose of having a routine is to provide an orderly transition as students enter the room and get ready for instruction. Some teachers have students review vocabulary words or other problems related to the curriculum while other tasks are performed.

12. *Folder for Substitute Teachers.* A substitute teacher will take your place when you are absent. It is important to prepare materials for substitute teachers to help support what they do, maximize the learning, and minimize any off-task behavior. Many teachers keep a folder for substitute teachers that includes important information. It can be kept on your desk with the plan book.

The type of material in a folder for substitute teachers varies, but the following information would be useful to include: a copy of the daily schedule, times of recess and lunch, a list of the classroom rules, a list of classroom procedures (e.g., morning opening, taking attendance, lunch count, lunch, dismissal, fire drills), a list of reliable students in each class period, hall pass procedures (to go to the rest room, library, or office), information on where to find certain items (e.g., lesson plans, audiovisual equipment, supplies), names of others to contact for information or help (e.g., a nearby teacher with room number), and a list and description of students with special needs. Much of this information can be collected before school starts, and additional information can be added as needed.

VOICES FROM THE CLASSROOM | *Planning for a Substitute Teacher*

Mary Pat Whiteside, Middle School Teacher, Palm Coast, Florida

Establishing procedures for times when you are absent helps avoid stress for you, your students, and your substitute teacher. The first step is to discuss with your students your expectations for their behavior when a substitute teacher is there. I start by having my students discuss their worst experiences with a substitute. Then I ask if they want substitutes to leave our school and go out to the community bearing tales of horror. Next, I tell students that my rule for them is to treat substitutes better than they treat me. Inappropriate behavior by them leads to punishment by me and a phone call home.

The second step is to plan for the substitute teacher. I have a folder labeled "Substitute" which includes seating charts, class attendance lists, clear plans designed for easy understanding, a folder of extra work, the location of my emergency lesson plans, and a substitute feedback sheet.

At the top of the feedback sheet, I ask that the classroom rules be enforced, and I ask for short notes from the substitute about each class's general behavior. I also ask the substitute to list any students who were uncooperative, disruptive, or tardy. I ask that the substitute not discipline my students, but leave me the information and I will handle any problems which arose when I return. This system works well for me, and I now look forward to returning to order instead of chaos.

Managing Assessment, Record Keeping, and Reporting

It is vital to give advance thought concerning how you will assess student achievement, record student progress and scores, and report the assessment information. Assessment always has been important in teaching, but the No Child Left Behind (2002) legislation and additional state and local accountability demands for ensuring student learning have placed a higher level of attention on assessment and reporting. Even before the school year starts, you should decide how you will assess student learning, keep records of student performance, and report the assessment data.

• *Assessment.* While there are many aspects to assessment, you will need to select the means of assessment. Teacher-made tests and quizzes are common. In addition, you may choose to have students demonstrate their learning through the use of performance-based measures with (a) *products* (e.g., portfolios, work samples, projects, lab reports) or (b) *performances* (e.g., oral presentations, presentations with media, demonstrations, debates, athletic demonstrations). For each of these assessment approaches, you will also need to determine how you will assess the level of student proficiency. This could be done through an answer key for a test, or with the use of rubrics or other rating forms for performance-based measures.

• *Record Keeping*. Once students have been assessed and you have scored their work, you must keep records in a gradebook. Gradebooks typically have a section for the daily attendance log, achievement scores, and conduct scores. All student assessment scores are placed in the gradebook, so prior thinking about your overall assessment plan will help you design the columns and labels in a useful manner. In addition to scores for performance on test items, portfolios, or other measuring techniques, some teachers have separate charts to record student proficiency for particular knowledge and skills related to the curriculum standards.

Entering the assessment scores in the gradebook is only part of your task. Then you must have a plan to translate all of the performance measures into a grade at the end of the report card period. For example in a given subject, will you have a weight of 20 percent for homework, 40 percent for tests, 20 percent for a portfolio, and 20 percent for cooperative group projects? Furthermore, what performance level constitutes an A or a B? You need to think about your grading system before the start of the school year and establish your plan.

• *Reporting*. Your school district will likely determine a number of aspects of what will be recorded on report cards and how the information will be reported. First, the district determines what achievement and nonachievement (e.g., conduct) progress will be reported. Also, it determines what grading system will be used (e.g., letter grades, pass/fail, checklists). There may be additional ways the district determines how grades are reported.

In addition to report cards, you can communicate student progress to parents in many ways, such as through parent–teacher conferences, newsletters, and open houses. During a parent–teacher conference, you may want to have a portfolio for each student ready to show representative work. For a newsletter, you may want to share information about the activities and the performance of the entire class. So you need to give advance thought about what information you will be reporting, and that will be a guide for the kind of data and materials you need to gather and report.

Establishing a Plan to Deal with Misbehavior

With an understanding of classroom management and discipline, you will need to develop a plan for dealing with misbehavior in the classroom. A seven-step plan is presented here that begins with the establishment of a system of rules and procedures. You need to provide a supportive environment during instruction and also provide situational assistance when students get off task. If the student does not get back on task, you need to move through advancing levels of consequences. If none of these actions work, you may need to involve other personnel.

You should deal with misbehavior in a way that is effective while also avoiding unnecessary disruptions. Researchers and educators have proposed movement from low to high intervention when developing a plan to address misbehavior (e.g., Charles, 2005; Levin & Nolan, 2004; Wolfgang, 2005). Once the rules and procedures and a supportive classroom environment are in place, the teacher moves from low to high interventions as described below.

1. *Establish Your System of Rules and Procedures.* Establish an appropriate system of rules and procedures as a foundation for dealing with discipline (discussed more fully in Chapter 5). It is vital that you select a system of rules and procedures appropriate to the situation. This system should incorporate reward or reinforcement for desirable behavior and the consequences of misbehavior. No single approach is best for all teachers and all teaching situations. For instance, rules and procedures for a tenth-grade English class would not be appropriate for a third-grade class. Furthermore, the system needs to be consistent with established school and district policies and with your own educational philosophy, personality, and preferences.

2. *Provide a Supportive Environment During Class Sessions.* Once the system of rules and procedures has been established at the start of the school year, you need to maintain a supportive environment. Actions taken in the normal course of instruction are for the purpose of guiding and reinforcing students for positive behavior (discussed more fully in Chapter 6).

Providing a supportive environment is accomplished primarily through cueing and reinforcing appropriate behavior, and getting and holding attention. Cueing and reinforcing involve stressing positive, desirable behaviors; recognizing and reinforcing desired behaviors; and praising effectively. Getting and holding attention necessitate focusing attention at the start of lessons; keeping lessons moving at a good pace; monitoring attention during lessons; stimulating attention periodically; maintaining accountability; and terminating lessons that have gone on too long. Treat students with dignity and respect, and offer challenging, interesting, and exciting classes.

3. *Provide Situational Assistance During Class Sessions.* Students may get off task during a lesson. This off-task behavior may be in the form of misbehavior or may simply be a lapse in attention. Either way, you need to promptly provide situational assistance. *Situational assistance* denotes actions that you take to get the student back on task with the least amount of intervention and disruption possible. Situational assistance can be provided by removing distracting objects, reinforcing appropriate behaviors, boosting student interest, providing cues, helping students over hurdles, redirecting the behavior, altering the lesson, and other approaches (discussed more fully in Chapter 11).

4. *Use Mild Responses.* If a student continues to be off task after situational assistance is provided, then you need to use mild responses to correct the student's behavior. These are not intended to be punitive. Mild responses may be nonverbal or verbal (see Chapter 11). Nonverbal responses include ignoring the behavior, using signal interference, using proximity control, or using touch control. Verbal responses include reinforcing peers, calling on the student during the lesson, using humor, giving a direct appeal or command, reminding the student of the rule, and several other approaches.

5. *Use Moderate Responses.* If students do not respond favorably to mild responses and continue to exhibit off-task behavior, you need to deliver moderate responses (see Chapter 11). These punitive responses deal with misbehavior by removing the desired stimulus so as to minimize the inappropriate behavior. Moderate responses include the use of logical consequences and various behavior modification techniques such as time-out and loss of privileges.

6. *Use Stronger Responses.* If moderate responses are insufficient, you need to move to a more intrusive type of intervention (see Chapter 11). These stronger responses are intended to be punitive, by adding aversive stimuli such as reprimands and overcorrection. The purpose of aversive stimuli is to decrease unwanted behavior.

7. *Involve Others When Necessary.* If all efforts have failed to get the student to behave properly, then you need to involve other persons in the process. This occurs most commonly with chronic or severe behaviors. You may consult or involve counselors, psychologists, principals and assistant principals, teaching colleagues, college personnel, mental health centers, school social workers, school nurses, supervisors and department heads, and parents (see Chapter 12). Their assistance and involvement will vary depending on their expertise.

Planning for the First Day

Starting the school year effectively is vitally important when establishing a system of classroom management. Marzano (2003) reports that a strong first day and an emphasis on classroom management in the first few days make a big difference in getting off to a good start. Several principles should guide your decisions about planning the start of the school year and your actions in the first few days (Emmer et al., 2006; Evertson et al., 2006; Good & Brophy, 2003).

1. *Plan to Clearly State Your Rules, Procedures, and Academic Expectations.* When students arrive in your class for the first time, they may have uncertainties. They will want to know your expectations for behavior and for academic work. They will want to know what the rules are for general behavior and also the consequences for adhering to or breaking them (discussed more fully in Chapter 5). They want to know what the procedures are for going to the restroom, turning in homework, sharpening their pencils, talking during seatwork, and other specific activities. They will be interested in finding out about course requirements, grading policies, standards for work, and other aspects of the academic program.

Your philosophical perspective about classroom management will likely affect your decisions. As discussed in Chapter 2 on the models of discipline, you need to consider the degree you want to involve students in identifying the rules and procedures. Some teachers like to determine the rules before school starts, while other teachers prefer to involve students in the discussion of the rules to develop a sense of ownership. Still other teachers let the students discuss and determine the rules themselves. You need to decide on your approach to the selection of rules and procedures prior to the start of school.

It is especially important to take the necessary time during the first few days of school to describe your expectations in detail about behavior and work. Emphasize and be explicit about desirable behavior. Combine learning about procedures, rules, and course requirements with your initial content activities to build a good foundation for the year.

2. *Plan Uncomplicated Lessons to Help Students be Successful.* Content activities and assignments during the first week should be designed to ensure maximum student success. Select relatively uncomplicated lessons at the start of the school year so that few students will likely need individual help. This allows you to focus on monitoring behavior and to respond to students in ways that shape and reinforce appropriate behavior. It provides you with opportunities to reinforce students for their academic work and to begin to develop positive relationships with students.

3. *Keep a Whole-Class Focus.* Plan activities for the first week that have a whole-class focus, rather than small-group activities. Whole-class activities make it easier to monitor student behavior and performance. In this way, you can focus on reinforcing appropriate behavior and preventing inappropriate behavior.

4. *Be Available, Visible, and in Charge.* You must be in charge of students at all times. Move around and be physically near the students, and maintain a good field of vision to see all students wherever you stand. Move around during seatwork to check on student progress.

5. *Plan Strategies to Deal with Potential Problems.* Unexpected events can develop when you meet your students for the first time. These might include interruptions by parents, office staff, custodians, or others; late arrivals on the first day; one or more students being assigned to your class after the first day; and an insufficient number of textbooks or necessary materials. You can give advance thought to how you would deal with common, unplanned events should they occur. Treat each unexpected situation in a calm, professional manner. This will serve as a good model for your students when they confront unexpected or challenging events. Treat students respectfully and deal with some of the needed details later. For example, you can ask a late enrolling student to take a seat and begin work, and then you could handle the particular enrollment procedures later.

WHAT WOULD YOU DECIDE?   *Potential Problems*

On the first day, there may be some unplanned and unexpected events, such as a student arriving late, students going to the wrong classroom, or disturbances between students.

1. What are some things that might happen on the first day of school that are unplanned?
2. How might you deal with each of those unplanned events that you identified?

---

6. *Closely Monitor Student Compliance with Rules and Procedures.* By closely monitoring students, you can provide cues and reinforcement for appropriate behavior. Better classroom managers monitor their students' compliance with rules consistently, intervene to correct inappropriate behavior whenever necessary, and mention rules or describe desirable behavior when giving feedback. Effective managers stress specific corrective feedback rather than criticism or threat of punishment when students fail to comply with rules and procedures.

7. *Quickly Stop Inappropriate Behavior.* Inappropriate or disruptive behavior should be handled quickly and consistently. Minor misbehavior that is not corrected often increases in intensity or is taken up by other students. Quickly respond to inappropriate behavior to maximize on-task behavior. Act in a professional manner to settle the difficulty and preserve the student's dignity in front of the other students.

8. *Organize Instruction on the Basis of Ability Levels.* The cumulative record folders will indicate students' prior academic performance in reading, math, and other subjects. Select instructional content and activities to meet the ability levels of your students.

9. *Hold Students Academically Accountable.* Develop procedures that keep students accountable for their academic work. This may include papers to be turned in at the end of class, homework, in-class activities, or other means. Return the completed papers promptly and with feedback. Some teachers give a weekly assignment sheet to each student. This sheet is completed by the student, checked by the parent, and returned to the teacher daily.

10. *Be Clear When Communicating Information.* Effective teachers clearly and explicitly present information, give directions, and state objectives. When discussing complex tasks, break them down into step-by-step procedures.

11. *Maintain Students' Attention.* Arrange seating so all students can easily face the area where their main attention needs to be held. Get everyone's focused attention before starting a lesson. Monitor students for signs of confusion or inattention, and be sensitive to student concerns.

12. *Organize the Flow of Lesson Activities.* Effective classroom managers waste little time getting the students organized for the lesson. They maximize student attention and task engagement during activities by maintaining momentum and providing signals and cues. They successfully deal with more than one thing at a time (e.g., talking with one student but also keeping an eye on the rest of the class).

Developing Your Management Plan: *Preparing for the School Year*

You can make decisions and plans about a number of issues prior to the start of the school year. This early decision making greatly influences the opening days. Each major section in this chapter addressed a series of issues needing attention. Begin to list the specific plans and decisions for your own classroom for each of the following areas. You may want to look at the numbered lists in this chapter under each of these major sections to provide a framework for the recording of your decisions and plans.

- Management Preparations
- Instructional Preparations
- Assessment, Record Keeping, and Reporting
- A Plan to Deal with Misbehavior
- Planning and Conducting the First Day
- Organizing Your Classroom and Materials

Conducting the First Day

The first day of school is often a time of nervousness for teachers and students. Fortunately, you can do a number of things on the first day to address student concerns, as discussed below.

1. *Greet the Students.* Stand by the classroom door before class begins. When students are about to enter your classroom, greet them with a smile and a handshake. As you do this, tell them your name, your room number, the subject or period, if needed; the grade level and anything else appropriate, such as the student's seating assignment (Wong & Wong, 2004). Your name, room number, section or period, and grade level or subject should be posted outside your door and on the chalkboard.

2. *Tell Students About their Seat Assignment.* There are various ways to handle seat assignments for students. Some teachers prefer to let students select their seats while other teachers prefer to assign seats. Either way, students should be told what to do as they enter the classroom for the first time. If you determine the seating assignment, there are several possible ways to inform students of their seat assignment as they enter the room. You might have a transparency showing on an overhead projector indicating the seating arrangement. A different transparency would be used for each of your class sections. Also have a copy of the seating chart in hand as the students are greeted at the door.

3. *Correct Improper Room Entry.* Observe students as they enter the room and take their seats. Some students may not go directly to their seats or may behave inappropriately. It is important to ask a student who enters the room inappropriately to return to the door and enter properly. Be calm, but firm; tell the student why this is being done, give specific directions, check for understanding, and acknowledge the understanding (Wong & Wong, 2004). The communication might be something like this:

> *Todd, please come back to the door.*
>
> *I am sorry, but that is not the way you enter our classroom every day. You were noisy, you did not go to your seat, and you pushed Ann.*
>
> *When you enter this classroom, you walk in quietly, go directly to your seat, and get to work immediately on the assignment that is posted.*
>
> *Are there any questions?*
>
> *Thank you, Todd. Now show me that you can go to your seat properly.*

During the interaction, be sure to use the student's name and be polite with a "please" and "thank you."

4. *Handle Administrative Tasks.* Taking attendance is one of the first administrative tasks to be done at the start of the class period. Have the students raise their hands when called to indicate that they are present and to give you an opportunity to see the face that goes with the name. As you call each name, ask the student whether you pronounced it correctly. After the first day of school, some teachers prefer not to take attendance at the start of class. Instead, they give an assignment that the students are to begin as soon as they enter the classroom. After the students are underway, the teacher can take attendance by visually scanning the room; the names do not need to be called. This approach, or one similar to it, takes very little time and allows students to move quickly into the academic work.

5. *Make Introductions.* Students appreciate knowing something about the teacher. At the start of the class period, tell the students your name and some personal information, such as the number of years you have been teaching, professional development activities, family, personal interests and activities, hobbies, and other background information. This helps the students know you as a person and may be informative and comforting to them. This is also the time to let the students know that you are enthusiastic about working with them and that you will be reasonable and fair with them. Some teachers like to use this opening time to have the students briefly introduce themselves. Some get-acquainted activities for students could be included on the first day to help promote good feelings.

6. *Discuss Classroom Rules and Procedures.* All classrooms need rules and procedures if they are to run smoothly and efficiently. Rules should be taught on the first day of class to establish the general code of conduct (discussed more fully in Chapter 5). Post the rules in a conspicuous place in the classroom. If a letter has been prepared for parents that describes the rules and procedures, this should be given to the students so they can take it home.

Some classroom procedures may be taught on the first day of school, but many teachers prefer to teach procedures (e.g., distributing materials, getting ready to leave the classroom, handing in papers) over the next several school days instead. Procedures can be taught when the need for them first occurs. For example, when it is time to collect papers at the end of an activity, you could teach students the appropriate procedure.

7. *Present Course Requirements.* Before school started, you would have prepared the course requirements and syllabus. On the first day, students want to know what content will be covered and what is expected of them concerning grading. Take time to discuss the course content and some of the activities planned for the year. If you have prepared a syllabus, hand it out. Discuss the grading requirements concerning tests, homework, projects, and the like and indicate what levels are needed for the various letter grades.

WHAT WOULD YOU DECIDE? *Planning an Initial Activity*

On the first day or two of class, many teachers plan an initial activity which focuses on some aspect of the curriculum. These activities are intended provide some content review from the prior year and to provide an opportunity to teach procedures and to get acquainted.

1. What purposes would you have for an initial activity?

2. How might you provide variations of that activity based on the varied ability levels or learning styles of the students?

3. How might you relate the content to various cultural backgrounds of your students?

8. *Conduct an Initial Activity.* Depending on the amount of time available on the first day, many teachers plan an initial activity related to the curriculum. It should provide a review of some material that students had in the previous year, or may be a preview of content to be covered. Either way, the activity should be designed so that the students can complete it without much assistance and with much success. This leaves you free to monitor the students during the activity, to provide assistance when necessary, and to take corrective action on off-task behavior.

9. *End the Class Period.* A routine to end the class period is needed, and this must be taught to students. Procedures need to be established and time saved for actions such as returning books and supplies, disposing of scrap paper and cleaning up the classroom, and putting away books and other materials in preparation for leaving the classroom.

ORGANIZING YOUR CLASSROOM AND MATERIALS

Decisions about room arrangement must be made before students arrive on the first day of school. Before arranging the classroom, consider (a) the movement patterns of students throughout the classroom; (b) the need for students to obtain a variety of materials, texts, reference books, equipment, and supplies; and (c) the need for students to see the instructional presentations and display materials. Arrange and decorate your room in a manner that supports effective classroom management (Marzano, 2003). Good room arrangement can help teachers cope with the complex demands of teaching by minimizing interruptions, delays, and dead times. Based on studies of effective classroom managers, there are five keys to good room arrangement (Emmer et al., 2006; Evertson et al., 2006).

1. *Use a Room Arrangement Consistent with Your Instructional Goals and Activities.* You will need to think about the main types of instructional activities that will be used in your classes and then organize the seating, materials, and equipment compatibly. Teacher-led presentations, demonstrations, or recitations will require students to be seated so they can see the instructional area. In contrast, small-group work will require very different room arrangements.

2. *Keep High Traffic Areas Free of Congestion.* High traffic areas include the space around doorways, the pencil sharpener and trash can, group work areas, certain bookshelves and supply areas, the teacher's desk, and student desks. High traffic areas should be kept away from each other, have plenty of space, and be easily accessible. For example, try not to seat a student next to the pencil sharpener because of the heavy traffic and the possibility of inappropriate behavior.

3. *Be Sure Students Are Easily Seen by the Teacher.* It is important that teachers easily see students to identify when a student needs assistance or to prevent task avoidance or disruption. Clear lines of sight must be maintained between student work areas and areas of the room that the teacher will frequent.

4. *Keep Frequently Used Teaching Materials and Student Supplies Readily Accessible.* By having easy access and efficient storage of these materials, activities are more likely to begin and end promptly, and time spent on getting ready and cleaning up will be minimized. Establishing regulated storage areas can help reduce the occurrence of students leaving materials in their desks or taking them out of the room.

5. ***Be Certain Students Can Easily See Instructional Presentations and Displays.*** The seating arrangement should allow all students to see the chalkboard or the multimedia screen without moving their chairs, turning their desks around, or craning their necks. Place the primary instructional area in a prominent location to help students pay attention and to facilitate note taking.

VOICES FROM THE CLASSROOM   *Using a Make-Up Work Center*

Susan Lovelace, High School Teacher, Sebastian, Florida

I realized that I was spending much time with students before and after class who wanted to know what they missed when they were absent. As a result, I organized an area for make-up work information in the back of the classroom. I purchased a dry-erase board and six pocket folders, each with a different color for each of the classes I teach. Above that board, I put a sign that reads "What Did I Miss?"

At the end of the day, I write the assignment or activities that we covered in class that day on the dry-erase board. For each folder under the dry-erase board, I put any handouts, worksheets, or returned work in the labeled pocket folder for each class. For example, my first-period class knows they have the blue folder, so students know where to look.

Now my students know to go directly to the make-up work center to find out what they missed, and I am not using valuable time repeating make-up work information several times a day.

Floor Space

A classroom typically contains many items such as student desks, the teacher's desk, bookcases, tables, and activity centers that take up floor space. When determining how to arrange the classroom, you need to consider the functions of the space and the various factors mentioned earlier in an effort to facilitate learning and to minimize interruptions and delays.

A good starting point in planning the floor plan is to decide where you will conduct whole-group instruction. Examine the room and identify where you will stand or work when you address the entire class to conduct lessons or give directions. This area should have a chalkboard, an overhead projector screen, a table on which to place the overhead projector, a small table to hold items needed during instruction, and an electrical outlet. Consider the following items:

• ***Student Desks.*** Even if other arrangements are to be used later in the year, you might start the year with student desks in rows facing the major instructional area, since it is easier to manage students with this pattern. Be sure all students can see the major instructional area without having their backs to the area and without having to get out of their seats. It is important to keep student desks away from high traffic areas. Avoid placing their desks near the door, pencil sharpener, trash can, and supply areas. Leave ample aisles between the desks to enable easy movement of students and

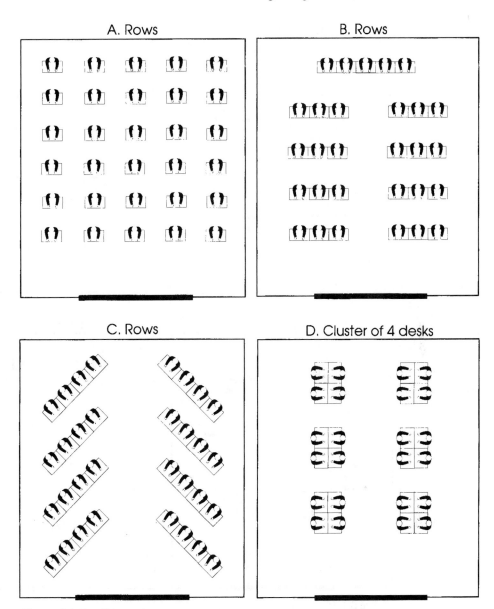

Figure 3.1 Possible seating arrangements

yourself when monitoring seatwork. Figure 3.1 shows a number of possible seating arrangements.

  • *The Teacher's Desk.* Your desk should be situated so that you can see the students, but it is not essential that the desk be at the front of the room. Placement of your desk at the rear of the room, in fact, may help when monitoring students during independent work. Students facing away from you cannot discern when you

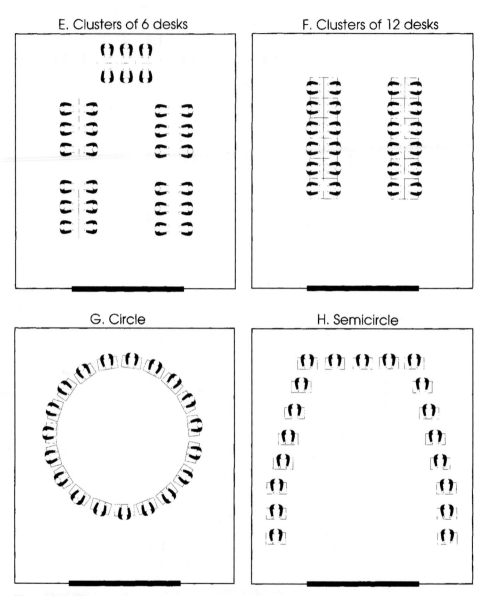

Figure 3.1 (*Continued*)

are looking at them unless they turn around. This tends to encourage students to stay at their assigned tasks. Instead of sitting at their desk during independent work, many teachers prefer to move around the room to monitor and assist students.

• ***Bookcases and Filing Cabinets.*** Other items should be placed so students' visibility of chalkboards or relevant displays is not obstructed. They also should not prevent your monitoring. If a bookcase contains frequently used items such as resource books, dictionaries, or supplies, then it should be conveniently located and monitored.

If it contains seldom-used items, an out-of-the-way place is best. If there is only one bookcase, it is helpful to use it for frequently used items.

• *Activity Centers or Work Areas.* An activity center is an area where one or more students come to work on a special activity. It may be in the form of a learning center or a computer work area. One or more tables commonly serve as the work surfaces. When you select the placement of tables for this area, be sure that you can see all students in the work area, keep traffic lanes clear, and avoid congested areas. A center often will have special equipment such as tape recorders with headphones, a computer, a filmstrip projector, or other materials and supplies. Enough table and work space must be provided for students to work efficiently. It is useful to place the work area at the side or the back of the room and to the backs of other students.

Storage Space

Teachers and students use a wide variety of instructional materials. All of these materials are not used every day and must be stored when not in use. Therefore, storage space must be provided for textbooks and resource books, frequently used instructional materials, teacher's supplies and instructional materials, equipment, and infrequently used materials.

1. *Textbooks and Resource Books.* Some textbooks are not retained by students and thus must be stored in the classroom for easy access. Resource books obtained from the school library, public library, or other sources may be available for student use. All of these books should be stored in a bookcase that enables easy access.

2. *Instructional Materials.* Instructional materials that students need will vary with the subject area that you teach. These may include rulers, scissors, special paper, pencils, staplers, tape, glue, and other supplies. As with textbooks and resource books, a storage location should be selected to enable easy access to the materials. Clearly labeled containers for each of the supply items are often very helpful in maintaining an orderly supply area. These materials may be stored on shelves of a bookcase or cabinet, or on a counter.

3. *Teacher Supplies.* Supplies that only you would use should be kept in your desk or in storage areas used only by you. These supplies include items such as hall passes, attendance and lunch count forms, ditto masters, computer disks, computer programs, lesson plan book, tablets, file folders, and chalk. These items should be placed in secure places so students don't have access to them.

4. *Equipment.* Items like an overhead projector, tape recorders, computers, or other instructional media may not be used every day. Therefore, these items must be stored when not in use.

5. *Infrequently Used Items.* Some instructional materials are used only once a year. These include seasonal decorations (e.g., Halloween, Thanksgiving), bulletin board displays, or special project materials. Certain instructional materials may be used for only one unit, as in the case of a model of the human eye for a science class. Some teachers prefer to keep seasonal decorations or other infrequently used materials at their homes.

VOICES FROM THE CLASSROOM *Space for Supplies and Assignments*

Sheila Shelby, Fifth-Grade Teacher, Columbia, South Carolina

It is important for me and my students to have the necessary supplies and materials when needed. As a result, I have designated a spot in the classroom as the student work station which holds supplies such as a stapler, a tape dispenser, paper clips, pencils, a three-hole punch, and other materials.

In addition, I have a mail sorter box, which is labeled by subject areas, for students to turn in assignments. This box keeps papers organized and secure, and it is especially helpful when I have a substitute teacher in the classroom.

My teacher's desk is located at the back of the classroom and becomes the place where I keep lesson plans and all the important things I need to review or file at the end of the school day. By providing space just for students and a place to house assignments, my desk can be used just for my purposes.

Bulletin Boards and Wall Space

Constructive use of bulletin boards and wall space can contribute to a positive classroom environment. This can be achieved by displaying relevant instructional material, assignments, rules, schedules, student work, and other items of interest. Many teachers involve students in the selection of content and the preparation of bulletin boards and the use of wall space. One approach is to select a different group of students to plan and prepare a bulletin board each month.

Some teachers prefer to dedicate each bulletin board to a certain purpose. For example, one bulletin board could be used to post classroom rules, a daily or weekly schedule, classroom helpers, lunch menus, a school map, emergency information, or any other procedural information. Another bulletin board could be used to display student work. A third type of bulletin board could be simply for decoration, with seasonal, motivational, or artistic items. Other bulletin boards can be used to post information and news articles about school or community events. In addition, bulletin boards can also be used to post content-related news articles, posters, or information.

Some of the material commonly placed on bulletin boards, such a listing of classroom rules, can be placed on posters and displayed on the walls of the classroom if the content will not likely change during the school year. On the other hand, designated areas of the chalkboard can be used to display student assignments or special announcements because this information is likely to change daily.

MAIN POINTS

1. Many management and instructional preparations can be completed prior to the start of the school year.

2. Plans for dealing with misbehavior, assessment, record keeping, and reporting should be made prior to the start of the school year.

3. Early planning and decision making about classroom management issues will help ensure a positive beginning to the school year.

4. Organizing your classroom and materials includes attention to seating, floor space, storage space, bulletin boards, and wall space.

5. Room arrangements can enhance the learning environment and also help reduce traffic congestion.

DISCUSSION/REFLECTIVE QUESTIONS

1. In what ways might you use students as classroom helpers? How might this affect the learning environment?

2. What are the benefits of planning uncomplicated lessons at the start of the school year? What might happen if the lessons are too challenging?

3. What are the merits of having a plan for systematically dealing with misbehavior?

4. What are the merits and disadvantages for placing students' seats in rows?

5. When planning to organize your classroom and materials, what are important issues that you would take into account as you make your decisions?

SUGGESTED ACTIVITIES

1. Think about how you will record your instructional plans (lesson plans, weekly plans, and long-range plans). Will this information be on forms or on the computer? How will you plan to store and retrieve these plans for future use?

2. Talk with several teachers to find out how they do long-range planning for the school year, each semester, each marking period, and each unit.

3. For your grade level or subject area, sketch the physical layout of a classroom that would help promote learning yet minimize disruption and congestion.

4. Select several ways to organize students' seats and evaluate the merits and the problems associated with each seating pattern.

FURTHER READING

K–12

GUILLAUME, ANDREA M. (2004). *K–12 Classroom Teaching: A Primer for New Professionals* (2nd ed.). Upper Saddle River NJ: Prentice-Hall/Merrill.
Provides a very practical overview to many aspects of teaching, including issues needing attention at the start of the school year.

KRONOWITZ, ELLEN L. (2004). *Your First Year of Teaching and Beyond* (4th ed.). Boston: Allyn & Bacon.
Provides an introduction to many aspects of teaching with chapters on topics such as classroom organization and management, discipline, parents, materials, curriculum planning, and the first day.

THOMPSON, JULIA G. (2002). *First-Year Teacher's Survival Kit* San Francisco: Jossey-Bass.
Provides an excellent, thorough, yet practical guide to all aspects of starting your school year. Many useful charts and specific guides. Covers planning for behavior, curriculum, and instruction.

WONG, HARRY K., & WONG, ROSEMARY T. (2004). *The First Days of School: How to be an Effective Teacher* (3rd ed.). Mountain View, CA: Harry Wong Publications.
Is a highly popular guide for beginning teachers. Loaded with very practical guidelines on positive expectations, classroom management, lesson mastery, and other vital topics.

Elementary

COUGHLIN, DEBORAH. (2002). *How to plan for the school year: The elementary teacher's essential guidebook*. Portsmouth, NH: Heinemann.
Is a reader-friendly guide to plan for preparing your instructional plans, setting up the classroom, organizing your classroom management system, and teaching. Includes many useful forms to be used by the teacher.

JONSON, KATHLEEN F. (2002). *The new elementary teacher's handbook: Flourishing in your first year* (2nd ed.) Thousand Oaks CA: Corwin Press.
Provides thorough, practical advice on topics such as organizing the classroom, managing the classroom, preparing instructional plans, dealing with discipline, assessing student work, and working with parents.

LINDBERG, JILL A., & SWICK, APRIL M. (2002). *Common-sense classroom management: Surviving September and beyond in the elementary classroom*. Thousand Oaks CA: Corwin Press.
Includes many specific suggestions on organization, planning, classroom atmosphere, discipline, and instruction.

MURRAY, BONNIE P. (2002). *The new teacher's complete sourcebook: Grades K–4*. New York: Scholastic Professional Books.
Is packed with tips on topics such as setting up your classroom, preparing lessons, determining your classroom

management system, managing paperwork, and working with parents.

Middle and Secondary

ARNOLD, HARRIETT. (2001). *Succeeding in the secondary classroom: Strategies for middle and high school teachers.* Thousand Oaks, CA: Corwin Press.

Provides practical suggestions for preparing for the first day, instructional planning, record keeping, classroom management and discipline, and working with colleagues and parents.

CUSHMAN, KATHLEEN. (2003). *Fires in the bathroom: Advice for teachers from high school students.* New York: The New Press.

Based on the candid discussions and recommendations from a number of urban high school students, insightful and practical recommendations are provided about topics such as knowing your students, respect and fairness, classroom behavior, a culture of success, motivation, teaching difficult academic work, and when things go wrong. Sensitive and profound.

THOMPSON, JULIA G. (2002). *Discipline survival guide for the secondary teacher.* San Francisco: Jossey-Bass.

Provides an excellent, thorough, yet practical guide to all aspects classroom behavior and discipline. Considers issues such as rules and expectations, class time, cooperation, and preventing and solving discipline problems. Many useful charts and specific guides.

WYATT, ROBERT L., & WHITE, J. ELAINE. (2001). *Making your first year a success: The secondary teacher's survival guide.* Thousand Oaks, CA: Corwin Press.

Is a brief guidebook with suggestions about issues such as starting the school year, classroom management, lesson plans, assessment, and working with parents.

Chapter 4

Planning to Work with Parents

CHAPTER OBJECTIVES

This chapter provides information that will help you:
- Identify the reasons for contacting and interacting with parents.
- Describe reasons why some parents resist involvement.
- Determine ways that a parental support system can be developed.
- Identify when to contact parents.
- Determine ways to communicate with parents.

Classroom Management: Creating a Successful K-12 Learning Community/Third Edition, by Paul R. Burden
ISBN 0-471-71073-3   Copyright © 2006 John Wiley & Sons, Inc.

CHAPTER OUTLINE

Imagine that you are a parent and that you and your family just moved into a new community during the summer. You have one child in third grade and another in seventh grade. Because you moved from another state, you are concerned that the curriculum might be quite different in this new district, and you wonder how your children will adjust to the new community and their new school and teacher. Wouldn't you want to talk to the teachers to share some of these issues? Wouldn't you like to hear about the curriculum and how the teachers will handle instruction? Wouldn't you like to maintain ongoing contact throughout the school year? Yes, of course!

Good communication with parents should be a priority because it keeps teachers and parents informed about what is happening. It also builds trust so that there can be a working partnership in the event there are difficulties with the students. Although a teacher's primary responsibility is to work with students, it is important to communicate and interact with the students' parents throughout the school year. The reason for the communication will often determine the timing of the contact and the means by which the contact will be made.

At the start, we must recognize that children come from many types of family settings. Some come from a "traditional" family with one stay-at-home parent, some are from two-career families, or from blended families. In addition, there are single-parent families, gay and lesbian families, families raising grandchildren, families with adopted children, families with foster children, families with children with special needs, and even homeless families (Diffily, 2004). As a result of these various family settings, the term *parent* is used in this chapter in a broad sense to represent the adult or adults who have parental responsibility. Thus this definition of a parent could include the biological parents, foster or stepparents, a grandparent, an aunt or uncle, an older sibling, or a guardian.

What are the reasons for working with parents? Why is it important to understand the parents and their point of view? When should parents be contacted? What are the ways that teachers might communicate with parents? We will examine these questions in this chapter.

REASONS FOR WORKING WITH PARENTS

Students ultimately benefit from good communication and effective working relationships between the school and home. Parental involvement in their children's schooling has been associated with better attendance, more positive student attitudes and behavior, greater willingness to do homework, and higher academic achievement (Henderson & Berla, 1995). There are several reasons why you would want to communicate with parents.

1. *To Create Open, Two-Way Communication and to Establish Friendly Relations.* Positive contacts with parents early in the year help establish positive, friendly relations. In this way, parents and teachers see each other not as adversaries but as allies in helping the student be successful. Two-way communication can be fostered, and that will result in appropriate school–community relations that will benefit everyone involved.

2. *To Understand the Student's Home Condition.* Information about a student's home setting can help you decide on an appropriate course of action with the student. You may learn the parents are having marital problems, have limited ability to read or speak English, exert excessive pressure for the child to excel academically, or tend to be abusive to the student when there are problems at school. Such factors can be important as you decide how best to help each student academically and behaviorally.

3. *To Inform Parents of Academic Expectations and Events As Well As Student Performance.* Parents appreciate knowing your policy concerning homework, late papers, and grading guidelines. Informing parents at the start of the school year helps prevent misunderstandings about your expectations. Parents also like to know what content will be covered, when the quizzes or tests are scheduled, and what special events are scheduled. Introductory letters or a back-to-school night are helpful, as are newsletters devoted to special events, units to be covered, or the academic schedule. Finally, parents want to know how their children are doing. Report cards and conferences provide information periodically, but parents appreciate learning about early indications of academic difficulties.

4. *To Enlist Parents' Help with Academic Issues.* Teachers often seek help from parents at the start of the year. They may send a list of needed classroom and instructional supplies home to the parents to supplement purchases made by the school district. You may want to identify parents who might be available to serve as classroom aides or chaperones for regular or special events. This assistance may include preparing materials for bulletin boards, assisting during a field trip, and the like.

5. *To Inform Parents of Disciplinary Expectations and Actions.* At the start of the year, teachers often inform parents of their disciplinary policy and their expectations for student conduct. As with the academic information at the start of the year, this communication is often accomplished through an introductory letter or a newsletter, or at the back-to-school night. If a student misbehaves, you may need to inform the parents of the situation.

6. *To Enlist the Parents' Help in Dealing with Their Children.* When students have difficulties, the parents should be contacted to identify ways they might help. When students misbehave, the parents should be contacted so that you can work together to help the student stay on task and be successful. Parents exert much influence on their children, and they can cooperate and support your actions. You and the parents may agree on strategies to help the child and to build the child's cooperation and commitment to address any problems.

UNDERSTANDING PARENTS

Parents want their children to succeed in school and generally appreciate teachers' efforts to keep them informed and involved about academic and behavioral issues (Berger, 2004). Parental reactions to problems vary widely. Reactions are largely determined by individual experiences, life experiences, education and training, expectations, socioeconomic circumstances, and other factors. The reactions of the child, the teacher, and others also have a bearing on how the problem will be handled (Walker, Shae, & Bauer, 2004).

It is important to listen carefully to parents to identify their concerns and suggestions. Trust is developed when parents know that their ideas are recognized and understood. The full benefits of parent–school relationships are not realized without this interaction and collaboration.

VOICES FROM THE CLASSROOM *Understanding the Parents*

Debbie McLean, First-Grade Teacher, Mobile, Alabama

I have taught in inner city schools for about 25 years. For most of those years, I have been repeatedly surprised at the parent's reaction and follow-up to behavior problems that occur with their child at school. For example, one little girl had chronic behavior problems and was suspended. Her mother was horrified and spanked the child when they got home. But the very next day, the mother took off work and took the girl shopping. The girl returned to school with a new hairdo, new clothes, shoes, and a book bag. I just didn't understand.

I recently received some training about poverty based on Ruby Payne's work (*A Framework for Understanding Poverty*, 2001). In poverty, one believes that one is fated or destined to do certain things, and thus there is nothing you can do to change your behavior. Your goal is to not get caught, and to deny it if you are caught. If your denial doesn't work, you will be punished. But with punishment comes forgiveness. In poverty, discipline is all about penance and forgiveness. In middle class, discipline is about changing behavior.

Why Some Parents Resist Involvement

As much as you would like the cooperation and support of parents when dealing with a student with academic or behavioral difficulties, you may find parents apathetic or resistant to involvement (McEwan, 2005). There are several possible reasons for parental resistance.

• As students, some adults may have had unhappy experiences. They may view schools as being oppressive and not a place of hope for their children. These parents may consider it unlikely that school personnel can solve the problems.

• Parents of children who have a history of misbehavior may adopt coping mechanisms in an effort to deal emotionally with the problems (Walker, Shae, & Bauer, 2004).

Their responses may point to self doubt, denial, withdrawal, hostility, and frustration. These parents may resist involvement with all school personnel.

- Some parents view teachers, principals, counselors, and other school personnel as the experts in addressing issues such as misbehavior (Turnbull, Turnbull, Erwin, & Soodak, 2006). Consequently, they may resist involvement because they do not want to interfere with the actions taken by the teacher or other officials.

- Some parents are threatened by the school itself and by the bureaucracy. They may be intimidated by the size of the school, the need to report to the school office when visiting the school, the busy nature of the school, the lack of private areas for discussion, and other physical aspects of the school. As a result, those parents may resist involvement because they have a sense of discomfort about the school.

- Diversity among the parent population and the sense of being different from school personnel may make parents uncomfortable in seeking contact with teachers or administrators (Swap, 1993). For example, Asian immigrant parents may think that communication with teachers is considered to be "checking up on them" and an expression of disrespect (Yao, 1988). Members of other ethnic groups, likewise, may feel out of place.

- Some parents don't know what is expected of them or how they might contribute to their child's education. They may withdraw or become angry or frustrated when the school seems to be failing to meet their child's needs. They do not realize that the school would value their involvement.

- Some parents don't become involved with the school for practical reasons. They may not speak English or may have limited competency in English. They may not drive a car, or they may have limited access to transportation. They may not have access to a babysitter or cannot afford one. Or they may simply be too tired after long days at work themselves.

Building a Parental Support System

It is helpful to identify ways you can build a parent support system so that you can communicate effectively with the parents and enlist their help when the need warrants. Joyce Epstein, a leading advocate of comprehensive parental involvement, identified six types of parental involvement (Epstein et al., 2003):

1. *Parenting.* Help all families establish home environments to support learning.
2. *Communicating.* Design more effective forms of communication to reach parents.
3. *Volunteering.* Recruit and organize parent help and support.
4. *Learning at Home.* Provide ideas to parents on how to help the child at home with homework and other curriculum-related activities.
5. *Decision Making.* Include parents in school decisions, developing parent leaders and representatives.
6. *Collaborating with Community.* Identify and integrate resources and services from the community to strengthen school programs, family practices, and student learning and development.

It is important to counteract parental resistance. Recognizing that there are varying degrees of parental support and involvement, you will most likely try to build a support system by focusing on communicating with parents and by seeking parent volunteers to help in various ways with academic issues. Other aspects of parental involvement are considered in other sources (Barbour, & Scully, 2005; Diffily, 2004; Epstein, 1991; National PTA, 2000, 2004; Swap, 1993; Warner, 2001).

WHAT WOULD YOU DECIDE? *Back-to-School Night*

Let's assume that you teach in a school that has much ethnic diversity, and that some parents do not attend the back-to-school night or the parent–teacher conferences at the end of the report card periods.

1. How might you find out why the parents did not attend?

2. How could you communicate to those parents that it is acceptable to attend such sessions and that their child would ultimately benefit from their attendance?

3. What are some alternative ways that you can communicate important information to the parents who do not attend these events?

CONTACTING AND COMMUNICATING WITH PARENTS

As discussed previously, there are several reasons for working with parents. The timing of the contact will depend on the reason for it. There are three points to consider when contacting parents.

1. *Initial Contact with All Parents* would occur at the start of the year. These contacts would be designed to inform parents about the academic program, grading guidelines, the homework policy, rules and procedures, and other academic and behavioral expectations. Requests for additional classroom supplies and for parent volunteers for activities are generally made at this time. You could make these contacts through an introductory letter, a newsletter, a back-to-school night, or other means.

2. *Ongoing Contact with All Parents* occurs throughout the year to provide information about content being covered in class, the schedule for tests or other evaluation requirements, field trips, the progress of the students, and so on. You may need additional parent volunteers throughout the year and may contact parents at various times as the need arises. These ongoing contacts could be made through a newsletter or information sheet, an open house, report cards, or other means.

3. *Contact with Selected Parents* needs to occur to inform them about unique concerns about their child's progress. These contacts may occur when there is both positive and negative news to report. You will often contact parents when there is a problem, yet it is easy to overlook contacting parents when there is good news to report. Parents especially appreciate reports of good news; if a problem arises later, parents are often more willing to support and cooperate with the teacher.

Ways to Communicate with Parents

There are many ways to communicate with parents, and the method may be affected by its purpose. To discuss a serious act of misbehavior, for example, you would probably not wait for a parent–teacher conference scheduled at the end of a report card period to contact the parents but would likely call the parents immediately.

Much communication with parents occurs at the start of the year in the form of an introductory letter, a letter about classroom management and discipline, a back-to-school night, and information sheets. Ongoing communication may be through an open house, newsletters, notes and letters, phone calls, special events and informal contacts, sending home student work, report cards, and parent–teacher conferences. To contact parents about their child's academic work or behavior, you could call them or arrange for a special conference.

Introductory Letter

Teachers sometimes send an introductory letter home with the students to give to their parents during the first week of school prior to the back-to-school night. This letter is intended to serve as a brief welcome to the new year, include some basic information about the class, and invite the parents to the back-to-school night that will soon follow.

The letter may include some information classroom and school policies such as the schedule, homework, absences, and the curriculum. You may mention in the letter that more will be said about these and other issues at the Back-to-School Night. A sample introductory letter to parents is displayed in Figure 4.1. You can adapt this letter for your particular situation.

Letter About Classroom Management and Discipline

You need to share your plan for classroom management and discipline with the parents and the principal. If you expect them to be involved when you need them, they need to know that you have a plan and to be aware of your rationale for rules, positive recognition, and consequences.

At the start of the school year, you need to discuss rules, consequences, and other aspects of management with the students. A copy of this information sheet should be given to the students to take home to their parents. The letter should provide details of the classroom management and discipline plan and explain why it is important. Ask the parents to discuss the plan with their children, sign the plan, and return the signature portion to you. A sample letter to parents about classroom management and discipline is displayed in Figure 4.2. You may adapt that letter for your particular situation.

If the back-to-school night is scheduled early in the year, you may ask the parents to return the signature portion at that time. Or you may prefer to wait and present the letter to the parents at the back-to-school night and get the signatures at that time. Letters can then be sent home to parents who did not attend that evening.

Back-to-School Night

Many schools schedule a back-to-school night or family night during the first or second week so parents can receive information about the academic program, grading

September 4

Dear Parents:

Now that the school year has begun, I'd like to introduce myself. I am Melissa Riley, and I am your child's ninth-grade algebra teacher this year. I have taught in this school district for 14 years, and have taught pre-algebra, algebra, geometry, and trigonometry. I completed my undergraduate work at the University of Illinois and my master's degree at Kansas State University.

I want this to be a successful school year for you and your child. To ensure this success, it is important that we maintain open communication. Please do not hesitate to contact me if you have any questions or concerns. You could call me at school after dismissal between 3:30 and 4:30 p.m. at 555-7308. Or you could call anytime during the day and leave a message for me to call you back. My e-mail address is mriley@hotmail.com.

At various times throughout the school year, I will be sending a newsletter home with your child to provide information about classroom activities and special events. On a regular basis, your child will bring home graded assignments for you to look at. I also look forward to seeing you at the conference session that we schedule at the end of each report card period.

The annual Back-to-School Night for this school is scheduled for next Thursday, September 12, from 7:30 to 9:15 p.m. On that evening, you will have the opportunity go through your child's schedule of classes in shortened 10-minute class periods. When you meet me during algebra class, I will share information about the curriculum, my approach to instruction, my academic expectations and procedures, my policy on discipline, and other issues. The books and materials that we will be using this year will also be on display. I encourage you to attend Back-to-School Night because it will give you an opportunity to understand the mathematics program and become better acquainted with me.

By working together and keeping in good contact, I'm confident that this will be an exciting and successful school year. I look forward to meeting you at Back-to-School Night.

Sincerely,

Melissa Riley

Figure 4.1 Sample introductory letter to parents

guidelines, homework policy, rules and procedures, and other expectations. Requests for additional classroom supplies and for parent volunteers for activities are generally made at this time.

Some schools do not schedule a back-to-school night or, if they do, it comes later than the first or second week of school. As a result, you may find other ways to communicate with parents since it is important to establish contact as early as possible. For example, a letter about classroom management and discipline might be expanded to include information that is commonly covered at a back-to-school night.

Dear Parents:

Now that the school year has begun, I'd like to introduce myself and give you some information about how I conduct my classes. My name is Keith McKinsey, and I am your child's fifth-grade teacher. I have taught in this school district for eight years. I completed my undergraduate work at Florida State University and my master's degree at Kansas State University.

To maintain an appropriate learning environment, I have established the following classroom rules that all students are expected to follow:

1. Follow the teacher's directions.

2. Keep your hands, feet, and objects to yourself.

3. Do not swear or tease.

To encourage students to follow the rules, I will recognize appropriate behavior with praise, various types of reinforcement, and notes or calls home to you. If students choose to break the rules, I have established an escalating series of responses ranging from gentle prompts and reminders, to the use of logical consequences, and to detention. In class, we have discussed these rules, the reinforcement for following the rules, and the consequences if the students choose to break the rules. My goal is to ensure success for your child. Working together, I'm confident that it will be an enjoyable and productive school year.

Please indicate that you understand this discipline plan by signing your name below and indicate the phone numbers where you can be reached during the day and evening. You might also discuss the rules to make sure your child understands them.

Please do not hesitate to contact me if you have any questions or concerns. You could call me at school after dismissal between 3:30 and 4:30 p.m. at 555-6188. Or you could call anytime during the day and leave a message for me to call you back. My e-mail address is Kkeith@hotmail.com.

Sincerely,

Keith McKinsey

(Please tear off the bottom part and return it to Mr. McKinsey.)

I have read and understand the classroom management plan in Mr. McKinsey's classroom, and I have discussed it with my child.

Parent/Guardian

Signature _____ Date _____

Comments:

Figure 4.2 Sample letter to parents about classroom management and discipline

The scheduling of the back-to-school night is handled in different ways. For middle, junior high, and senior high schools, parents are often given their child's schedule, and they follow it just as the student would, but in shortened class sessions of 10–15 minutes. In this way, the parents see every teacher in the way that their child would during the school day. Teachers often use this time to present information to the parents about academic and behavioral guidelines and expectations.

Preparing for Back-to-School Night   A back-to-school night is often your first contact with the parents, so thorough preparation is necessary. There are many ways to prepare for this evening.

 • ***Prepare Your Own Introductory Letter to Parents about the Back to School Night in Your Classroom.*** (see the sample introductory letter in Figure 4.1). Do not rely only on notices that the school sends home. Some teachers like to have their students prepare special invitations for their own families.

 • ***Make Sure the Classroom Looks Attractive and Neat.*** Post your name and room number prominently on the door and the front chalkboard. Display samples of work by all students. Display copies of the textbooks and other instructional materials.

 • ***Prepare a List of any Instructional Supplies or Materials That Parents Might Be Able to Provide.*** This list will vary depending on the subject and grade level. It may include such items as rulers, buttons, a box of facial tissues, or other supplies. Have enough copies of the list to give to all parents.

 • ***Prepare Separate Sign up Sheets for Parents.*** These may concern the need for a private, follow up conference about their child; volunteers to help at special events such as field trips; volunteers such as guest speakers in class; or volunteers to provide various instructional supplies requested by the teacher.

 • ***Plan a Well-Organized, Succinct Presentation.*** Parents want to hear about your background and experience, behavioral and academic expectations, procedures for issues such as homework and absences, and other policies. Be sure to plan for time at the end of the presentation for questions.

 • ***Prepare Handouts for Your Presentation.*** Parents will receive the handouts at the back to school night. Have enough copies of this material to give to all parents. A sample content outline of the presentation is shown in Table 4.1; your handout should include details about issues such as those listed in that table. On the front page of the handout, include your name, the school phone number, and the times at which you can be reached at that phone number. Attach other related materials to this handout; these materials may include a sheet showing the daily or weekly class schedule, a sheet of needed instructional materials and supplies, or a sheet concerning the classroom management and discipline policy. To simplify distribution, staple all the handouts together as one set of materials sequenced in the order that you will cover the material during the presentation.

Conducting the Back-to-School Night   Several guidelines should be taken into account when conducting the back-to-school night. Since your presentation is usually limited, possibly to only 10–15 minutes, it is important to plan how to conduct yourself. Greet parents at the door, introduce yourself, and ask them to be seated.

Table 4.1   Sample Content Outline for Your Back-to-School Night Presentation

---

1. Background about yourself
   a. College training and degrees earned
   b. Professional experience, including length of teaching service, grade levels taught, where taught
   c. Personal information (e.g., family, hobbies, special interests or experiences)
2. The curriculum, academic goals, and activities
   a. Overview of the curriculum and the topics to be covered (refer to the textbooks and related instructional materials on display in the room)
   b. Your approach to instruction
   c. Instructional activities and any special events such as field trips or unique programs
3. Academic expectations and procedures
   a. Grading guidelines and procedures (how grades are determined)
   b. Grading requirements (e.g., tests, quizzes, homework, projects)
   c. Homework (purposes, how often, make-up policy, absences)
   d. When report cards are delivered
   e. Parent–teacher conferences
4. Discipline
   a. Classroom rules
   b. Positive rewards
   c. Consequences for breaking the rules
   d. Incremental steps taken when misbehavior continues
   e. When parents will be contacted
   f. Parents need to sign the sheet concerning the classroom management and discipline policy
5. Ask parents to sign up for selected issues
   a. For a private, follow-up conference about their child
   b. For parent volunteers for providing instructional materials and supplies
   c. For parent volunteers to help at special events such as field trips
   d. For parent volunteers such as guest speakers in class
6. Express an interest in hearing any ideas and concerns from parents at any time
7. Time for questions at the end of the session (save several minutes if possible)

Begin your presentation using the handout that you previously prepared concerning your background, the daily and weekly schedule, the curriculum, academic goals and activities, academic expectations and procedures, discipline, and other issues. At the start, give a copy of the handout to each parent.

Have parents sign up for individual follow-up conferences if they want to talk with you at length about their child. Back-to-school night is not intended to deal with concerns about individual students. Allow time for parents to ask questions. This will be an opportunity for you to provide clarification about issues and to hear the concerns of parents.

Information Sheets

Not all schools schedule a back-to-school night, and not all parents attend a scheduled night. As a result, you can prepare a packet to send home that provides information about the curriculum, grading expectations and requirements, rules and procedures, the discipline plan, and other matters. The sheets may be the same as those given to parents who attend the back-to-school night, or a shortened version.

Open House

Once or twice a year, most schools schedule an open house for parents to visit the classrooms during a particular evening to see their child's teacher, observe the classroom and samples of student work, and learn about books and materials being used. Some districts do not have a back-to-school night but instead schedule the first open house in mid- to late September. At open house, teachers may give a formal presentation about the program. Or schools may allow parents to drop in at any time during open house to discuss issues informally with the teacher.

Since open houses are conducted well into the school year, materials and projects that students have prepared can be displayed. Science fairs, for example, may be scheduled at the same time as an open house to provide an opportunity for parents to see students' science displays. Since some parents attending the open house may not have attended the back-to-school night, it is often useful to have extra copies of the handout provided at the back-to-school night to describe your policies.

Newsletters

A newsletter periodically sent to all parents contains information about special events, content to be covered in the curriculum, tests or quizzes that are coming up, student projects, or other issues. Newsletters may be as brief as one page, or may be longer according to need. You can report accomplishments of the class and of individual students. Students could prepare the newsletter as a group or class project, under suitable circumstances.

Assignment Sheets

Another way to communicate with parents is through an assignment sheet that describes the assignments for the next week or two. The student is asked to show it to the

---

VOICES FROM THE CLASSROOM   *Assignment Sheets*

Kathy Sublett, Eighth-Grade History and Language Arts Teacher, Anderson, California

It is important for students to know where they stand in their grades on a weekly basis. To give this weekly feedback, I provide students and their parents with an assignment sheet that shows the assignments that have been made, the ones the student turned in, and the ones due next. I inform parents about this at the back-to-school night and also in a memo that I send home.

There are two purposes of the assignment sheet. First, it helps remind students that they are responsible for their assignments. They only have to look at the sheet to see which assignments they are missing. Second, it is self-protection against irate parents who are amazed when they receive a deficiency notice for their child. I simply ask the parents to look at their child's assignment sheet to see what has not been turned in. The assignment sheets have helped defuse many tense situations. I can then ask the parents for their support in getting students to focus on their work.

parents. Some teachers may prefer that the parents sign the sheet and have it returned to school. This ensures that the students are fully aware of what needs to be turned in for evaluation, and they can make needed arrangements in their schedules; also the parents are aware of what is happening.

Individual Notes and Letters

Notes and letters are written to individual parents to discuss some particular issue about their child. You can use them to request that a conference be arranged with you, to invite parents to class functions, to inform parents about their child's work, or to offer suggestions. Notes should be carefully written. They should be free of errors in spelling, grammar, and sentence structure. Furthermore, they should be brief, clear, honest, and factual. Educational jargon should not be used. Notes and letters are especially useful for contacting parents who are hard to reach by telephone.

Make sure that you address the letter correctly since the parent and child may not have the same last name. If the parents do not read English, try to take needed steps to write the letter or note in their native language. Avoid writing a letter when you are upset about a classroom event; calm down first. Try to end with a positive statement about working together for the benefit of the child.

Be cautious about sending notes home to parents only when there is bad news to deliver. Certainly there are times when such notes need to be sent. You should also send notes home to parents with good news about the child's academic work or behavior. Brief, positive notes take only a few minutes to write to express pleasure about the child's performance. By systematically writing one or two notes to different parents each day, you will provide good news and help build positive relationships with the parents. Parents will usually talk with their child about the note, and the child may come to school the next day with a more positive attitude.

WHAT WOULD YOU DECIDE?   *Sending Notes or Letters Home*

Sending notes or letters home to parents is one way to communicate with the parents about classroom issues or their child's performance.

1. What types of information might you convey in the notes or letters?

2. What guidelines will you establish for yourself about the content, the writing form, the frequency, and other factors for the notes or letters?

3. How might you need to vary these guidelines if you were teaching in the second, eighth, and twelfth grades?

Phone Calls

Like notes and letters, telephone calls are made to parents to discuss a particular issue. The phone calls could request that a conference be arranged with you, invite parents to class functions, inform parents about their child's work, or offer suggestions. As with notes and letters, be cautious about calling parents only when you have bad news. Also call parents when there is good news to report.

Phone calls can be quite brief because you only need to have two or three positive statements to share. They are not intended to be a lengthy discussion about the student. The parents should be asked to tell the child about the phone call.

There are times when you need to contact parents about the child's misbehavior. You need to plan ahead before making the call. The call should begin with a statement of concern such as, "Mrs. Erickson, I care about Kristina and I feel that her behavior in the classroom is not in her best interest." You then should describe the specific problem and present any pertinent documentation. You go on to describe what you are doing and have done to deal with the misbehavior. At this point, it is helpful to invite parental input by asking questions such as, "Has Kristina had similar problems in the past? Why do you feel she is having these problems at school? Is there something going on at home that could be affecting her behavior?"

It is then useful to get parental input about how to solve the problem. State what you will do to help solve the problem and explain what you want the parent to do. Before ending the telephone conversation, you should let the parent know that you are confident that the problems can be worked out and tell the parent that there will be follow-up contact from you. Then recap the conversation.

VOICES FROM THE CLASSROOM   *Constructive Phone Calls to Parents*

Kathryn Tallerico, High School English Teacher, Thornton, Colorado

As a tenth grader, Rudy was a bright student who had a history of being hostile, pouty, and downright rude. My two interdisciplinary teammates and I had a series of problems with her last year, and we eventually had a conference with her father.

This year, Rudy showed up in my Creative Writing class. I had to work hard to face her without prejudice and to assume that she would cooperate and succeed. Well, she did. Whether it was the class, the maturation process, or both, I'm not sure, but she had become a delight to teach.

After three months of bliss, I called her father and was able to sincerely praise her turnaround. I told her father how difficult it had been to like her the previous year. He simply said, "I know, I know. That's what she was like at home, too." Then he shared a bit about his personal hurt, and thanked me profusely for taking the time to bring my observations to his attention. I could hear the pride in his voice. I hung up glowing with the rare satisfaction of having

witnessed a major growth within the short time I got to spend with an adolescent.

The next day at school, Rudy thanked me too. She said her dad let her know how much it meant to him. She added that it was very important to her that he know how much she had truly changed. Then I thanked her, and we hugged.

In retrospect, I sincerely believe that careful, honest discussion at all stages had laid the groundwork for Rudy's dramatic growth. I use four guidelines for myself when communicating with parents: (1) keep accurate records of the facts and rely on these when speaking to parents, (2) always have at least one truly kind or complimentary remark to make about the student, (3) record notes about the conversation and place a memo in a planner for a week or two ahead to provide the parent with follow-up information, and (4) ask the parent for information, help, and advice—communication must be two-way to be effective.

Web Sites and E-Mail

Many schools have Web sites, and these may include links to a Web site for each teacher in the school. In these cases, teachers can place information on the Web site to communicate to students and parents about homework, class projects, grading policies, and many other issues.

As computer use becomes more common, many families have e-mail capability. Teachers can provide students and parents with their e-mail address to open this type of communication. Parents can contact the teacher with questions or comments through e-mail, and teachers can report student progress and other information to parents through e-mail.

Special Events and Informal Contacts

Throughout the year, teachers and parents may attend many special events. These may include sporting events, concerts, plays, carnivals, craft displays, and others. Contacts with parents at these events may provide brief opportunities to share a few words about their child's work. These contacts are especially useful as progress reports and as a means of discussing a particular issue. You might say something about the student's interests, such as, "Josh's work during our unit on Australia focuses on the animal life. He is very interested in animal life in all of our studies."

Sending Home Student Work

You can inform parents about their child's academic progress by sending home completed and graded student work. Parents can see what you have covered, the child's work, and any notes or remarks you have made.

Sending home only completed worksheets may not be very enlightening to the parents. It is useful to send home a variety of materials including worksheets, tests, quizzes, homework, projects, lab reports, writing samples, artwork, or other types of student products. Be sensitive about notes or remarks you place on the papers. These notes are evaluative statements, but they should also include comments about good points and improvement as well about areas still needing attention.

Papers that are sent home with students to show their parents may not even get home or all the papers may not be shown to the parents. To overcome these problems, you might devise various ways to have parents sign a sheet to indicate that they have seen the material. For example, a parent response sheet might list the material being sent home, with a blank space for parents to sign and date indicating that they discussed the piece with their child. The form also could include space for the parents to write any comments. The student then returns the response sheet to you.

WHAT WOULD YOU DECIDE?   *Sending Student Papers Home*

Sending graded student papers home for parents to see is one important means of communication. However, it useful to plan ahead about several aspects of this.

1. What guidelines will you establish for yourself concerning comments you place on the student papers, the type of papers sent home, and the ways to confirm that parents did actually receive the papers?

2. How might you modify your procedures if a number of the parents have limited English proficiency or if there are several ethnic groups represented?

Report Cards

Parents are informed of their child's academic performance when report cards are distributed. Most report cards have an area where you can either write a statement or indicate a code for a statement concerning effort and citizenship. As with notes, letters, and phone calls, you should avoid making only negative notes on report cards. Deserving students should receive positive notes.

When warranted, include notes on the report card to indicate the need to improve and the actions needed to improve the situation. Parents may call teachers shortly after report cards have been delivered if they have any questions about them. Have documentation ready to justify what you have noted.

Parent–Teacher Conferences

Another important way of communicating with parents is through parent–teacher conferences to report information about progress, academic performance, or behavior. Many school districts schedule a day or two at the end of each report card period for parent–teacher conferences so parents can meet individually with the teachers. Conference days are typically scheduled only for elementary grades; all parents are invited to attend these individually scheduled conferences.

Many middle schools, junior high schools, and high schools do not schedule parent–teacher conferences, but instead arrange for a block of time on one day at the end of the report card period for parents to visit with each teacher on a drop-in basis. The ways to prepare for and conduct this session will be somewhat different than those used at the elementary level, but the general principles discussed here for preparing for this parental contact still apply.

In addition to the conferences conducted at the end of report card periods, parent–teacher conferences are held with particular parents as the need warrants. When a student persistently misbehaves or has academic problems, you may ask the parents

Table 4.2   14 Ways to Communicate with Parents

1. An Introductory Letter
2. A Letter about Classroom Management and Discipline
3. Back-to-School Night
4. Information Sheets
5. Open House
6. Newsletters
7. Assignment Sheets
8. Individual Notes and Letters
9. Phone Calls
10. Web Sites and E-Mail
11. Special Events and Informal Contacts
12. Sending Home Student Work
13. Report Cards
14. Parent–Teacher Conferences

of that child to come to the school for a conference. Prior to having such a conference, you may want to meet with the student to work out a plan to address the problem. If this meeting with the student does not lead to resolution, then a meeting with the parents is warranted, and the student may be asked to also attend.

To have effective parent–teacher conferences, teachers should thoroughly prepare for the conference, take certain actions when conducting the conference, and provide appropriate follow-up. Guidelines discussed in the following sections center primarily on parent–teacher conferences to address academic issues. These guidelines would need to be adapted somewhat to address individually scheduled parent–teacher conferences concerning academic or disciplinary issues.

Preparing for the Conference

Preparation for a drop-in conference with parents at the end of the report card period will be different from preparation for an individually scheduled parent–teacher conference. Administrators in middle schools, junior high schools, and high schools commonly take steps to inform parents about the day and time for the drop-in conferences at the end of the report card periods. Since these teachers have responsibility for many students, it is usually not feasible to have sample materials available for all students. Instead, teachers often have the grade book on hand along with sample tests, quizzes, homework, and projects that students completed throughout the marking period.

If an individual parent–teacher conference is needed, the teacher often calls the parents to select a day and time. Before the conference, the teacher may gather pertinent materials about the student and the situation. If it is an academic issue, the teacher may collect the grade book and a sample of work done by the student, including tests, projects, and homework to be shown to the parents during the conference. If it is a behavioral issue, anecdotal record sheets and other documentation may be gathered.

Whether for a drop-in conference at the end of the report card period or for an individually scheduled conference, the physical environment needs to be prepared for the session. You can arrange for these materials: (1) a table for the conference; (2) three or four adult-sized chairs for the table; and (3) a clean, tidy room.

Developing Your Management Plan: *Communicating with Parents*

Fourteen ways to communicate with parents were discussed in this chapter, as summarized in Table 4.2. As the next part of your management system, list the 14 ways to communicate with parents and then identify your specific intentions to use each in your own classroom.

For example, will you prepare information sheets describing the curriculum, grading expectations and requirements, rules and procedures, and other aspects of your classroom? What specific content will you include in these sheets? How will you make these sheets available to students and parents?

Also, what are your plans to telephone the parents? When will you call them and under what circumstances? What guidelines will you establish for yourself in these calls? How will you keep a record of these calls?

For each of the 14 ways to communicate with parents, you can ask yourself questions similar to those shown above to provide a description of your intentions in your own classroom.

Conducting the Conference

Discussion and questions in the conference should be sequenced to develop rapport, obtain information from parents, provide information to parents, and summarize and follow up. There are several guidelines to consider.

The following guidelines include a technique to "sandwich" your main messages in between good news or positive statements at the start and at the end of the conference. The parents who hear good comments at the start are then in a comfortable frame of mind. As the conference comes to a close, it is useful to summarize your main points and then conclude with additional positive statements.

1. *Begin the Conference in a Positive Manner.* Walk up to the parents, introduce yourself, and welcome them into the room. Start the conference with a positive statement about the student, such as, "Emily really enjoys providing leadership for students in her small group when working on projects."

2. *Present the Student's Strong Points Before Describing the Matters Needing Improvement.* Highlight the student's strengths as you move into a discussion about his or her performance. Show samples of the student's work to the parents. Later, identify matters that need further improvement.

3. *Encourage Parents to Participate and Share Information.* Allow opportunities to ask questions and share information about the student. Pose questions to parents at various points of the conference to encourage their input.

4. *Plan a Course of Action Cooperatively.* If the student needs to work on a particular issue, discuss the possible actions that you and the parents could take. Come to agreement about the course of action that each of you will take.

5. *End the Conference with a Positive Comment.* Thank the parents for coming and say something positive about the student at the end of the conference.

6. *Use Good Human Relations Skills During the Conference.* To be effective, you should be friendly and informal, positive in your approach, willing to explain in understandable terms, willing to listen, willing to accept parents' feelings, and careful about giving advice. You should avoid the following: arguing and getting angry; asking embarrassing questions; talking about other students, teachers, or parents; bluffing if you do not know an answer; rejecting parents' suggestions; and being a "know-it-all" with pat answers (Linn & Miller, 2005).

Handling Conference Follow-Up

During the conferences, it is useful to make a list of follow-up actions. These actions may include providing more thorough feedback to the student during the next marking period, recommending additional readings to some students, providing certain parents with periodic updates on their child's performance, or a host of other actions. It is important to follow up in the ways that were identified during the parent–teacher conference.

MAIN POINTS

1. Teachers work with parents to (a) understand the student's home setting; (b) inform parents of academic expectations and events as well as student performance; (c) enlist parents' help with academic issues; (d) inform parents of disciplinary expectations and actions; and (e) enlist parents' help in dealing with their children.

2. Parental resistance may be due to (a) the parents' unhappy experiences when they were students; (b) parental coping mechanisms in dealing with ongoing problems with their children; (c) the parents' view that educators are the experts; or (d) the parents' perception of the intimidation and bureaucracy of the school.

3. The individual classroom teacher will most likely try to build a parental support system primarily by communicating to reach parents and by seeking parent volunteers to help in various ways with school-related issues.

4. The timing of the contact with the parents will be determined by the reason for the contact. The three main times of parental contact are (a) initial contacts with all parents at the start of the school year; (b) ongoing contacts with all parents throughout the school year; and (c) contact with selected parents concerning their child's academic or behavioral progress.

5. Initial communication with parents occurs at the start of the school year in the form of an introductory letter, a letter about classroom management and discipline, a back-to-school night, and information sheets.

6. Ongoing communication throughout the school year may occur with an open house, newsletters, assignment sheets, notes and letters, phone calls, Web sites and e-mail, special events, informal contacts, sending home student work, report cards, and parent–teacher conferences.

DISCUSSION/REFLECTIVE QUESTIONS

1. How might information about a student's home setting help you as a teacher decide on an appropriate course of action with the student? How might this information create some problems for you?

2. Based on your experiences and observations, why might some parents resist involvement with their child's teacher(s)?

3. When is an appropriate point to contact parents if a student is exhibiting mild misbehavior? Moderate misbehavior?

4. In what ways did your teachers in the middle and secondary grades contact and interact with your parents? When and how did this communication occur?

5. What are some ways that teachers can communicate with parents about academic expectations and events?

SUGGESTED ACTIVITIES

1. Prepare an introductory letter that you might send to parents at the start of the school year.

2. Prepare a letter that you might send to parents prior to a parent–teacher conference.

3. Ask several teachers to describe the ways that they prepare for and conduct the back-to-school night. What

recommendations do they have to aid your preparation?

4. Think about the reasons that parents may not attend parent–teacher conferences. Identify ways that you might communicate to those particular parents.

FURTHER READING

DIFFILY, DEBORAH. (2004). *Teachers and families working together*. Boston: Allyn & Bacon.

Is a concise resource that examines different perspectives of family involvement, barriers and benefits, and strategies to communicate with and involve families.

HUGHES, MELISSA; OAKES, KRISTEN; LENZO, CAROLINE; & CARPAS, JACKIE. (2001). *The elementary teacher's guide to conferences and open houses*. Greensboro, NC: Carson-Dellosa Publishing Co.

Discusses guidelines for general conferences and open houses. Offers specific suggestions for traditional and alternative conferences and open houses. Has many forms and checklists.

McEWAN, ELAINE K. (2005). *How to deal with parents who are angry, troubled, afraid, or just plain crazy* (2nd ed.). Thousand Oaks, CA: Corwin Press.

Discusses why many parents are angry or upset, offers suggestions to defuse or disarm out-of-control parents, and suggests ways to solve related problems and to create a nurturing school.

National PTA. (2000). *Building successful partnerships: A guide for developing parent and family involvement programs*. Bloomington, IN: Solution Tree.

A practical resource that provides a blueprint for developing quality parent involvement programs. Includes discussion of issues such as communicating, parenting, student learning, and volunteering.

Chapter 5

Choosing Rules and Procedures

CHAPTER OBJECTIVES

This chapter provides information that will help you:
- Examine the need for classroom rules.
- Identify guidelines for selecting rules and procedures.
- Identify ways to teach and review the rules.
- Examine the need for classroom procedures.
- Identify guidelines for ways to select, teach, and review procedures.

Classroom Management: Creating a Successful K-12 Learning Community/Third Edition, by Paul R. Burden
ISBN 0-471-71073-3   Copyright © 2006 John Wiley & Sons, Inc.

CHAPTER OUTLINE

RULES IN THE CLASSROOM
Examine the Need for Rules
Select the Rules
Teach and Review the Rules
Obtain Commitments

PROCEDURES IN THE CLASSROOM
Examine the Need for Procedures
Select the Procedures
Teach and Review the Procedures

Think about all the traffic laws that govern the use of motor vehicles. Guidelines are set for ways to signal, turn, yield the right of way, pass other vehicles, and numerous other aspects of driving. These laws have been established in each state to ensure the safety of the driver and others. In a similar way, guidelines are also needed in the classroom to govern how the teacher and the students conduct themselves so that the learning objectives are achieved and everyone is successful.

Rules and procedures are used to guide and govern student behavior in classrooms. Even in positive learning communities where students are actively involved in arranging their learning environment, rules and procedures are necessary to guide behavior. Teachers need to consider carefully what rules and procedures are needed in order to manage the class effectively.

Your philosophical perspective on the models of discipline will greatly influence how you select rules and procedures. As discussed in Chapter 2, teachers using the intervening model (high teacher control) would likely select rules and procedures without consulting students. Teachers using the interacting model (medium teacher control) would likely have a discussion with the students and then collaboratively decide on the rules and procedures. Teachers using the guiding model (low teacher control) would likely turn the discussion over to the students and let them determine the rules and procedures.

Many educators who have written about creating a learning community endorse student involvement in some classroom decision making, including the selection of rules and procedures. Alfie Kohn (1996), for example, maintains that teachers should create classroom learning communities by moving away from discipline through the use of student involvement. He would allow students to make choices, and says that teachers need to develop a caring community and provide an engaging curriculum. Kohn's principles are consistent with the guiding model (low teacher control). Some degree of student involvement in the selection of rules and procedures helps build ownership and commitment (Marzano, 2003).

As you consider the information on rules and procedures, reflect on your philosophical perspective concerning discipline and classroom management. One model may represent your beliefs about child development and management of student behavior. That, in turn, will give you a perspective about the degree of control you would want to take when determining rules and procedures.

Basing your classroom decisions on the principles of freedom, justice, and equality helps students look beyond their own individual cultural needs and interests and into the realm of common societal values (Landau, 2004). Your rules and procedures should respect the individual nature of each student. At the same time, all students need and deserve information about classroom expectations so that they can equally participate in protecting the common welfare needs of the group.

RULES IN THE CLASSROOM

Rules refer to general behavioral standards or expectations that are to be followed in the classroom. They are general codes of conduct that are intended to guide individual behavior in an attempt to promote positive interaction and avoid disruptive behavior. Rules guide the way students interact with each other, prepare for class, and conduct themselves during class. They are commonly stated in positive terms. In addition to general rules, teachers sometime state rules for specific situations (e.g., gum chewing is not allowed).

The effective use of rules involves several actions. You should examine the need for certain rules in the classroom, select appropriate rules, select the consequences, teach the rules to the students, obtain a commitment from the students about the rules, and then periodically review the rules throughout the school year.

Examine the Need for Rules

Rules provide guidelines for appropriate behaviors so that teaching and learning can take place. They should be directed at organizing the learning environment to ensure the continuity and quality of teaching and learning and not simply be focused on exerting control over students.

VOICES FROM THE CLASSROOM   *Promoting Polite Behavior*

David Young, Third-Grade Teacher, Silverdale, Washington

During the first weeks of school, I work hard to create a positive atmosphere in my classroom and teach basic, polite behavior. As a class, we brainstorm and discuss what polite things students might do at school and in class. We then come up with a short list of things such as saying please and thank you, waiting your turn patiently, and putting away someone else's things without even being asked.

After we have created our list, I try to catch students doing any of these polite behaviors, quickly get the class's attention, share the behavior I observed, and compliment the student. This quick celebration of polite behavior reinforces the behavior. As the year goes on, I cut back on these celebrations, but still do this occasionally. As a result, my classes have been better behaved and more polite, and I have been able to spend more time on teaching and less dealing with inappropriate behavior.

Rules are necessary to have teaching and learning take place, and they need to be realistic, fair, and reasonable. Rules that are selected should meet the following purposes: (a) the teacher's right to teach is protected; (b) the students' rights to learning are protected; (c) the students' psychological and physical safety are protected; and (d) property is protected (Levin & Nolan, 2004).

You need to examine the way you teach and the type of classroom environment you would like to maintain when considering rules. A number of factors should be considered, including your educational philosophy, the age and maturity of the students, school rules and expectations, the type of classroom climate to be developed, and the rationale for a particular rule.

Select the Rules

After considering the need for classroom rules, you are ready to select rules that are appropriate for your classroom. Sample rules include these: (a) follow the teacher's directions; (b) obey all school rules; (c) speak politely to all people; and (d) keep your hands, feet, and objects to yourself. These rules are probably appropriate for all grade levels (K–12).

Due to differences in student maturity and developmental levels, some rules may be needed for certain grade levels. For example, students in the primary grades (K–3) often need direct guidance on many matters. Some additional rules may be appropriate for these grades: (a) follow directions the first time they are given; (b) raise your hand and wait to be called on; (c) stay in your seat unless you have permission to get up; or (d) do not leave the room without permission.

For departmentalized settings and grade levels, some rules about materials and starting class are often used. For example, rules might include these: (a) bring all needed materials to class, and (b) be in your seat and ready to work when the bell rings at the start of the period. A number of guidelines for selecting classroom rules are displayed in Table 5.1. Below are listed guidelines to consider when selecting classroom rules.

1. *Make Classroom Rules Consistent with School Rules.* Before you identify classroom rules, you must become familiar with school rules and recognize your

Table 5.1 Eight Guidelines for Selecting Classroom Rules

---

1. Make classroom rules consistent with school rules.

2. Involve students in making the rules to the degree that you are comfortable and to the degree that the students' age level and sophistication permit.

3. Identify appropriate behaviors and translate them into positively stated classroom rules.

4. Focus on important behavior.

5. Keep the number of rules to a minimum (four to six).

6. Keep the wording of each rule simple and short.

7. Have rules address behaviors that can be observed.

8. Identify rewards when students follow the rules and consequences when they break them.

---

responsibilities to them. For instance, school rules may identify behaviors that are specifically forbidden (e.g., no running in the halls) or specifically required (e.g., a student needs a hall pass when out of the classroom during class time).

2. *Involve Students in Making the Rules to the Degree That You Are Comfortable and to the Degree That the Students' Age Level and Sophistication Permit.* Among other things, student involvement in selecting rules will be affected by your philosophical perspective. Many teachers do not provide for student choice in rule setting; they may clearly present the rules and discuss the rationale for them. Other teachers find that students feel greater commitment and are more likely to adhere to the rules if they help formulate the rules and consequences. You can be an effective manager whether or not you involve students in identifying classroom rules.

If students are involved in selecting classroom rules, you can exert different degrees of direction during the discussion of them. You may begin with a general discussion of rules used in everyday life. Rich discussions can be prompted by questions such as: What is the purpose of traffic lights? Why do people need to pass a written test about laws and a driving test to obtain a driver's license? Why were rules established for sports such as basketball and football? What would a basketball game be like without the rules?

This can be followed by a guided discussion about appropriate rules to guide students' actions. Since students may not select all areas that you consider important, you may need to prompt the discussion at times. Teachers often guide students into selecting about five rules as a means to focus on important behavior. The degree of formality in managing the acceptance of the rules varies; you may want the class to vote on the list or you may prefer to handle approval by consensus.

VOICES FROM THE CLASSROOM   *Involve Students in Selecting the Rules*

Laurie Robben, Fourth-Grade Teacher, Greenwich, Connecticut

When we discuss the rules on the first day of school, I begin with a discussion of what the lunchroom would be like with no rules. (No assigned tables, no order to buying lunch, no criteria for throwing away garbage.) Fourth graders are quick to surmise that lunch would be chaos. It might be fun for a while, but their lunch would soon become an unpleasant experience.

I then carry this discussion into the classroom. We brainstorm why we need rules. What problems would we face? They often say that everyone would talk at once, there would be little or no learning, and that it would be as loud as a gym. We then create a rule to avoid each possible negative outcome. We first list all possible rules and then restate the rules that are finally selected into positive statements.

Finally, I put the class into groups of four or five and have them illustrate a rule of their choice. While they perform this task, I neatly write the rules on a poster, which is displayed throughout the year.

---

3. *Identify Appropriate Behaviors and Translate Them into Positively Stated Classroom Rules.* Since rules are a general code of conduct, they should focus on the conduct desired. Students respond better when the rule is stated in a way that expresses the desired behavior. To the extent possible, try to state rules positively. Instead of "No fighting," state the rule as "Keep your hands and feet to yourself."

Instead of "No teasing, swearing, or yelling," state the rule as "Speak politely to all people."

4. *Focus on Important Behavior.* When identifying appropriate student behavior, you could make a list of student actions for various settings. Rules should focus on important behavior that meets one of the purposes of rules mentioned earlier. If you had a rule for every type of behavior, major and minor, you would have a very extensive list. Rules should focus only on important behavior.

5. *Keep the Number of Rules to a Minimum (Four to Six).* By focusing on important behavior, the number of rules can be limited. Four to six rules is a good number for important behaviors. The rules can be written in broad enough language so they encompass related behaviors. For example, a rule about "Follow the teacher's directions" covers important behavior and is broad enough to cover a number of circumstances. By selecting rules with that degree of generality, the number can be limited to between four and six.

6. *Keep the Wording of Each Rule Simple and Short.* A rule that has several conditions and qualifiers in its wording may be confusing. It is better to keep the wording simple and short so the meaning is clear and recognizable.

7. *Have Rules Address Behaviors That Can Be Observed.* Sometimes rules focus on an attitude, such as "Be kind to others." However, what constitutes being kind is open to many interpretations. A certain action might be viewed by one student as being unkind, whereas another student might not see it that way. To avoid problems of this nature, it is preferable that the rule address behaviors that can be observed. In this way, the behavior did or did not occur, and there is no gray area of interpretation.

8. *Identify Rewards When Students Follow the Rules and Consequences When Students Break the Rules.* Students need to know what will happen to them if they break the rules. They may then choose to follow the rule rather than incur the consequence. If the student chooses to break the rule, then that student chooses the consequence. Rewards may include a variety of reinforcers such as social reinforcers, activities and privileges, tangible reinforcers, and token reinforcers (discussed more thoroughly in Chapter 6). Students need to be told that these reinforcers will be delivered if they follow the rules.

WHAT WOULD YOU DECIDE? *Selecting Classroom Rules*

Some teachers select classroom rules themselves while other teachers involve students to varying degrees in identifying the rules. If students are involved, teachers may have an open discussion, may provide one or two "must" rules as a starting point, or may take a variety of approaches from being completely open to being somewhat directive when determining the rules.

1. Do you intend to involve students in identifying rules? If so, how involved will you allow the students to be in the process?

2. How will you determine the consequences for the rules that are identified? Should students be involved in selecting consequences?

Similarly, students need to be told what consequences will be delivered if they choose to break a rule. When a student gets off task, first provide situational assistance in an effort to get the student back to work. If the student stays off task, then you should deliver mild responses such as nonverbal and verbal actions. If that doesn't work, you can move on to logical consequences and other actions (discussed in Chapter 11).

Teach and Review the Rules

After the classroom rules have been identified, rules should be taught in the first class session as if they were subject matter content. This discussion should include an explanation of the rules, rehearsal, feedback, and reteaching. It is important that the students recognize the rationale for the rules and are provided with specific expectations for each rule. Specific guidelines for teaching and reviewing classroom rules are displayed in Table 5.2.

Presentation and discussion of the rules are intended to help students understand the rules, recognize their responsibilities in relation to them, and build a commitment to follow them. Below are listed a number of guidelines to consider when teaching and reviewing classroom rules.

1. *Discuss the Rules in the First Class Session.* When making plans for the first day of school, include time to discuss the classroom rules in the first class session in which teachers meet the students. Students need to know the rules from the very start.

You should teach the classroom rules as if they were subject matter content; this could include a handout, a transparency, discussion, practice, and even a quiz about the rules. This discussion should include an explanation of the rules, rehearsal, feedback, and repeat teaching. If different rules apply for various activities (e.g., large-group work, small-group work, labs, independent work), these should also be clarified at this time.

Table 5.2   Nine Guidelines for Teaching and Reviewing Classroom Rules

---

1. Plan to discuss and teach the rules in the first class session.

2. Discuss the reasons for the rules.

3. Identify specific expectations relevant to each rule; provide examples and emphasize the positive side of the rules.

4. Inform students of the consequences when rules are followed and also when they are broken.

5. Verify understanding.

6. Send a copy of your discipline policy home to parents and to the principal.

7. Post the rules in a prominent location.

8. Remind the class of the rules at times other than when someone has just broken a rule.

9. Review the rules regularly.

---

2. *Discuss the Reasons for the Rules.* It is important the students recognize the rationale for the rules because it can build their understanding of and commitment to them. If there is a sound rationale for a rule, students are more likely to follow the rule and not challenge it. As mentioned earlier, this can start out as a general discussion about the need for rules in all aspects of life (e.g., for driving a car, for playing in a softball game). This discussion can then lead into the need for rules in the classroom to help teaching and learning.

3. *Identify Specific Expectations Relevant to Each Rule. Provide Examples and Emphasize the Positive Side of the Rules.* Examples of specific behaviors that meet or break a rule should be identified. This will help clarify your expectations. Since the wording of the rules is often brief and somewhat general, this discussion allows you to clarify what will be acceptable or unacceptable behavior for each rule.

4. *Inform Students of the Consequences When Rules Are Followed and also When They Are Broken.* Point out to the students that you are helping them make good decisions about their behavior. When the students make good decisions about their behavior, positive results will occur. When students don't make good decisions, results will be negative. Appropriate decisions are rewarded; inappropriate decisions are not. After discussing the general reasons for providing consequences, you should discuss the specific consequences that will be used.

5. *Verify Understanding.* As in any subject matter lesson, student understanding of the rules and consequences must be verified. This may take the form of questions, a game format, or even a quiz. If there is evidence that students do not fully understand the rules and consequences, repeat teaching may be needed.

6. *Send a Copy of Your Discipline Policy Home to Parents and to the Principal.* It is helpful to send a copy of the classroom rules and consequences to the parents. Include a form for the parents to sign indicating that they have read the discipline policy and have reviewed it with their child. This process helps develop understanding and commitment to the policy. The form could include space for the parents to write questions or comments. This signed form should be returned to you. It is helpful to provide the principal with a copy of your policy.

7. *Post the Rules in a Prominent Location.* The rules should then be written on a poster and displayed in a prominent place in the classroom, perhaps on a side wall where students will easily see them. This display is a constant reminder that the rules exist to guide behavior.

8. *Remind the Class of the Rules at Times Other Than When Someone Has Just Broken a Rule.* Rather than waiting for a rule to be broken to remind the students about a particular rule, it is better to select a time when there have been no problems to remind students about the rules. It is helpful to anticipate potential problems and remind students of the rules before the problems occur. For example, before an activity that requires students to move around the classroom, it is a good idea to remind students about the rule "Keep your hands and feet to yourselves." You alert the students about the rule and the appropriate behavior, and this presumably will minimize poking and shoving during the activity.

9. *Review the Rules Regularly.* At all grade levels, it is important to review the rules frequently for several weeks at the start of the school year. Daily review during the first week, three times a week during the second week, and once a month thereafter is a good approach. In the first few weeks, it may be useful for the students to evaluate their behavior and consider whether improvement is needed. Periodic review throughout the school year is then appropriate, especially right after a holiday or after the winter or spring break. Review classroom rules with each new student who might transfer into the class after the start of the school year. In that case, it is often helpful to talk to the new student yourself and also assign him or her to a student who knows and follows the rules to help explain them to the new student.

VOICES FROM THE CLASSROOM   *Rules and Consequences*

Margaret Shields, High School Mathematics Teacher, Pittsburgh, Pennsylvania

I select four rules that are stated positively, identifying what students are expected to do rather than what they shouldn't do. These rules are (1) Do not disrupt the learning of others, (2) Be prompt, (3) Be ready (physically and mentally), and (4) Be seated. I emphatically state that students do not have the right to interfere with anyone else's learning.

Consequences are essential to the rules. They should be hierarchical and, more importantly, be things that are under control of the teacher. For example, do not include a one-day suspension as a consequence if you do not have the authority to suspend students. My consequences are (1) a warning, (2) detention after school, (3) a phone call to the student's home, and (4) a referral to the office.

Don't make idle threats. Students know from others whether you really call the students' homes. Respect from students is essential in a well-managed classroom. Respect is earned, it is not automatic. Many inexperienced teachers demand respect before they have earned it. Be patient. If you are fair and consistent, respect will follow.

Obtain Commitments

After initially teaching the rules to the students, you should have your students express their understanding of the rules and indicate their intention to follow the rules. While this can be done in a variety of ways, one of the most effective is to have students sign a copy of the paper that lists the rules and includes a statement such as, "I am aware of these rules and understand them." Each student thus affirms understanding of the rules. You can keep these signed sheets. An extra copy of the rules could be given to students for placement in their desk or in a notebook.

As discussed earlier, sending the discipline policy home to the parents is another means of obtaining a commitment to the policy. In this way, parents are informed of the policy at the start of the school year. Parents can contact you if they have any concerns or questions about the discipline policy. If not, the parents are asked to sign and return a form that states that they are aware of the rules and understand them (similar to the form their child could sign at school).

PROCEDURES IN THE CLASSROOM

Procedures are approved ways to achieve specific tasks in the classroom. They are intended to help students accomplish a particular task, rather than prevent inappropriate behavior as in the case of rules. Procedures may be identified to direct activities such as handing in completed work, sharpening a pencil, using the restroom, or putting away supplies. The use of procedures, or routines, has several advantages (Leinhardt, Weidman, & Hammond, 1987): they increase the shared understanding of an activity between you and students, reduce the complexity of the classroom environment to a predictable structure, and allow for efficient use of time.

Some procedures may be sufficiently complex or critical, such as safety procedures for a laboratory or student notebook requirements, that you should provide students with printed copies of the procedures. Many procedures, however, are not written because they are very simple or their specificity and frequency of use allow students to learn them rapidly. Just as with rules, it is important to clearly state the procedures, discuss the rationale for them, and provide opportunities for practice and feedback, where appropriate.

Examine the Need for Procedures

As a first step, you must examine the need for procedures in your classroom. What activities or actions would benefit from having a procedure that would regularize student conduct in the performance of that action? To answer this key question, you might think about all the actions that take place in the classroom and identify those that would benefit from having an associated procedure.

Fortunately, you do not need to start from scratch in doing this assessment because research studies of classroom management in elementary and secondary classrooms have resulted in a framework that can be used to examine and identify typical classroom procedures. A number of the specific areas that might need classroom procedures are displayed in Table 5.3, some of which are adapted from Emmer et al. (2006), Evertson et al. (2006), Jones and Jones (2004), and Weinstein and Mignano (2003).

Select the Procedures

When examining the items in Table 5.3, you need to consider the unique circumstances in your classroom. The grade level, maturity of the students, your preference for order and regularity, and other factors may be taken into account when deciding which items will need a procedure. It may turn out that you will select many items from the table because these items involve fairly standard actions in many classrooms.

After selecting the items needing a procedure, decide specifically what each procedure will be. You could draw on your own experiences when deciding on the specific procedures. You might recollect your own schooling experiences, your observations of other classrooms, your conversations with other teachers, and your own teaching experience when determining what specific procedures would be appropriate and efficient.

Table 5.3 Areas Needing Classroom Procedures

1. Room Use Procedures
   a. Teacher's desk and storage areas
   b. Student desks and storage for belongings
   c. Storage for class materials used by all students
   d. Pencil sharpener, wastebasket, sink, drinking fountain
   e. Restroom
   f. Learning stations, computer areas, equipment areas, centers, and display areas
2. Transitions In and Out of the Classroom
   a. Beginning the school day
   b. Leaving the room
   c. Returning to the room
   d. Ending the school day
3. Out-of-Room Procedures
   a. Restroom, drinking fountain
   b. Library, resource room
   c. School office
   d. School grounds
   e. Cafeteria
   f. Lockers
   g. Fire or disaster drills
4. Procedures for Whole-Class Activities and Instruction, and Seatwork
   a. Student participation
   b. Signals for student attention
   c. Talk among students
   d. Making assignments
   e. Distributing books, supplies, and materials
   f. Obtaining help
   g. Handing back assignments
   h. Tasks after work is completed
   i. Make-up work
   j. Out-of-seat procedures
5. Procedures During Small Group Work
   a. Getting the class ready
   b. Taking materials to groups
   c. Student movement in and out of groups
   d. Expected behavior in groups
   e. Expected behavior out of groups
6. Beginning the Class Period
   a. Attendance check
   b. Previously absent students
   c. Late students
   d. Expected student behavior
   e. What to bring to class
   f. Movement of student desks
7. Ending the Class Period
   a. Summarizing content
   b. Putting away supplies and materials
   c. Getting ready to leave
8. Other Procedures
   a. Classroom helpers
   b. Behavior during delays or interruptions
   c. Split lunch period

Developing Your Management Plan: *Selecting Rules and Procedures*

The following outline provides a framework for your thinking and decision making about rules and procedures. Determine how you will enact the specific action for each part of the outline and write this into your management plan. For example, how will you obtain commitments from the students once the rules have been selected?

Rules

- Examine the Need for Rules

- Select the Rules
- Teach and Review the Rules
- Obtain Commitments

Procedures

- Examine the Need for Procedures
- Select the Procedures
- Teach and Review the Procedures

Teach and Review the Procedures

Students should not have to guess if they need to raise their hands during a discussion or interpret subtle signals from you to determine what you want them to do. From the very first day of school, teach and review the various procedures that are needed. Leinhardt et al. (1987) found that effective teachers spend more time during the first four days of school on management tasks than on academic tasks. Several steps serve as guides when teaching and reviewing classroom procedures.

   1. *Explain the Procedure Immediately Prior to the First Time the Activity Will Take Place.* Rather than explain procedures for many activities and actions on the first day, plan to space out your explanation over the first several days. It is often useful to wait for a situation to arise that provides an opportunity to explain the procedure. Some procedures will likely be taught early, such as asking to go to the restroom, while others, such as where to go during a fire drill, could be taught a few days later or just prior to the event.

   2. *Demonstrate the Procedure.* After the explanation, it is often useful to demonstrate what you want the students to do. For example, you could demonstrate how students are expected to use the pencil sharpener or how to get extra supplies. This will show students what actions are expected of them.

   3. *Practice and Check for Understanding.* After your explanation and demonstration, students could then be asked to practice the procedure. They might be asked to line up in the manner explained to proceed to the next class. In this way, students actually go through the physical motions of the procedure. It is also useful to ask students about the procedures to see if they understand when and how the procedures need to be used.

   4. *Give Feedback.* As the students are practicing the procedure, observe carefully to determine whether they do it properly. If so, provide reinforcement. If there are some problems, constructively point this out and indicate how the procedure should be done.

VOICES FROM THE CLASSROOM   *Procedures to Help Students Keep Track of Assignments*

Destin Mehess, Middle School Science Teacher, Pueblo, Colorado

I teach my students at the beginning of the school year to be responsible for their homework and assignments, and I show them the designated area where assignments are to be turned in. Each of my classes has an assignment box to place their homework and an assignment chart where the student is to check off when submitting an assignment. This chart is a visual aid that helps students keep track of what has or has not been turned in.

Students who are absent are held responsible for getting their assignments. As a result, I have an absent box which provides information about the assignments and a calendar showing the date when an assignment was given and when it is due.

The assignment box and absent box help students keep track and be responsible for their assignments. Students do not come to class and hand me assignments or come to me after an absence asking about new assignments. They know what is expected from the first day.

---

5. ***Reteach As Needed.*** If a number of students have difficulty during the practice of the procedure, it may be necessary to reteach the procedure and perhaps explain it in a different way. It would then be useful to demonstrate the procedure once again and give the students another opportunity for practice.

6. ***Review the Procedures with the Students Prior to Each Situation for the First Few Weeks.*** Rather than go through an activity and notice a student not following the procedure properly, it is better to remind students of the details of needed actions just before they are asked to perform them. At the end of class, for instance, you could remind students of the procedure for turning in their completed work just before you ask them to turn it in. Students appreciate the reminders instead of the criticism they might receive for not following the procedure. These reminders can be given for the first few weeks until the students have adopted the procedures.

7. ***Review the Procedures After Long Holidays.*** After being away from school for many days, some students may forget some particular procedures. Therefore, reviewing the procedures after a long holiday is a useful step to reinforce them.

MAIN POINTS

1. Rules are general codes of conduct that are intended to guide individual behavior in an attempt to promote positive interaction and avoid disruptive behavior.

2. Rules that are selected should meet the following purposes: (a) the teacher's right to teach is protected; (b) the students' rights to learning are protected; (c) the students' psychological and physical safety are protected; and (d) property is protected.

3. To promote student commitment to their learning environment, involve students in making the rules to the extent that the students' age level and sophistication permit.

4. Procedures are approved ways to achieve specific tasks in the classroom.

5. Teachers must first select tasks that would benefit from procedures and then determine the particular actions that students will follow.

6. A number of guidelines can be considered when selecting, teaching, and reviewing classroom rules and procedures.

DISCUSSION/REFLECTIVE QUESTIONS

1. What are the advantages and disadvantages of involving students in the selection of classroom rules?

2. How might your teaching style and educational philosophy influence the way that you select your classroom rules? How might you need to alter these rules if you were using cooperative learning groups?

3. How could you develop student commitment to the classroom rules and procedures as a means to promote a positive learning environment?

4. What are the benefits and potential problems of having many very specific classroom procedures?

5. How might the grade level and subject area affect your selection of rules and procedures?

SUGGESTED ACTIVITIES

1. For your grade level or subject area, select the classroom rules that you prefer to use. Next, develop a plan for teaching these rules to the students on the first day of class.

2. Prepare a letter that you might send to parents describing your classroom discipline policy.

3. Talk to two or more teachers to determine what rules and specific procedures they use. Obtain any printed guidelines that they provide students.

4. Identify tasks you would like to have performed by classroom helpers. Establish a procedure for showing the students what to do in these roles. Establish a procedure for rotating these roles to other students every week or two.

FURTHER READING

THOMPSON, JULIA G. (2002). *Discipline survival guide for the secondary teacher*. San Francisco: Jossey-Bass.
Provides an excellent, thorough, yet practical guide to all aspects classroom behavior and discipline. Considers issues such as rules and expectations, class time, cooperation, preventing and solving discipline problems. Many useful charts and specific guides.

THOMPSON, JULIA G. (2002). *First-year teacher's survival kit*. San Francisco: Jossey-Bass.
Provides an excellent, thorough, yet practical guide to all aspects of starting your school year. Many useful charts and specific guides. Covers planning for behavior, curriculum, and instruction.

WONG, HARRY K., & WONG, ROSEMARY T. (2004). *The first days of school: How to be an effective teacher* (3rd ed.). Mountain View, CA: Harry Wong Publications.
Is a highly popular guide for beginning teachers. Loaded with very practical guidelines on positive expectations, classroom management, lesson mastery, and other vital topics.

Chapter 6

Maintaining Appropriate Student Behavior

CHAPTER OBJECTIVES

This chapter provides information that will help you:
- Have a mental set for classroom management.
- Identify ways to build positive teacher–student relationships.
- Determine techniques to manage whole-group instruction.
- Identify ways to help students assume responsibility for their behavior.
- Identify techniques to maintain student attention throughout a lesson.
- Determine ways to reinforce students effectively.

Classroom Management: Creating a Successful K-12 Learning Community/Third Edition, by Paul R. Burden
ISBN 0-471-71073-3   Copyright © 2006 John Wiley & Sons, Inc.

CHAPTER OUTLINE

When you walk into a classroom where students are actively engaged in learning and are cooperating with the teacher and others, you can almost feel the good vibrations given off by the class. Students want to be involved and productive, and they enjoy working together. This type of classroom, however, doesn't happen by chance. Teachers take deliberate actions to establish a cooperative, responsible classroom so that students choose to cooperate and make efforts to be academically successful. Students need to feel that they are expected to be orderly, cooperative, and responsible. Developing a positive classroom climate is one of the most important ways to establish and maintain student cooperation and responsibility.

Classroom climate is the atmosphere or mood in which you and the students interact. This feeling is a composite of attitudes, emotions, values, and relationships. Climate probably has as much to do with learning, productive work, and self-concept as anything else in the educational program.

A poor classroom climate may be either chaotic and disorganized or cold, unfriendly, and threatening. A general lack of humor prevails, and there may be sarcasm and animosity. A threatening environment may cause students to work under duress, making them dislike both the teacher and school. If coldly and rigidly controlled, students may fear to make errors. They obey the rules for fear of reprisals.

In contrast, a good classroom climate is warm, supportive, and pleasant. It has an air of friendliness, good nature, and acceptance. It is encouraging and helpful, with low levels of threats. Such a climate encourages work and promotes a sense of enjoyment and accomplishment for everyone (Charles, 2005).

This chapter examines how you can develop a positive classroom climate and thus help maintain appropriate student behavior. First, you must develop a mental set for management. You also must build positive teacher–student relationships, manage whole-group instruction, help students assume responsibility for their behavior, maintain student attention and involvement, and improve classroom climate with reinforcers.

HAVING A MENTAL SET FOR MANAGEMENT

A review of research studies on classroom management verified the importance and effectiveness of having a mental set about managing student behavior (Marzano, 2003). In relation to classroom management, a *mental set* is a teacher's heightened awareness of one's surroundings and involves a conscious effort to control one's thoughts and behaviors in that setting. That sounds pretty fancy, but it translates into the following actions that you can take in the classroom when attending to student behavior.

Withitness

Use specific techniques to be aware of the actions of students in your classroom (withitness). Jacob Kounin (1970) is considered the first researcher to systematically study the characteristics of effective classroom managers. He coined the term *withitness* to describe a teacher's disposition (or mental set) to look at all parts of the classroom at all times to be aware of what is happening and then to demonstrate this withitness to students by quickly and accurately intervening when there is inappropriate behavior. Reflecting on the old adage, teachers who are "with-it" seem to have "eyes in the back of their heads."

1. *Monitor Regularly and React Immediately.* To exhibit withitness, you should periodically and systematically scan your classroom, note the behaviors of individual students or groups of students, and respond quickly to inappropriate actions. When engaged in whole-group instruction, here are some specific techniques you can use to monitor students in the classroom (Marzano, 2003):

- Walk around the room, making sure you spend some time in each quadrant.
- Periodically scan the faces of the students in the class, making eye contact with each student if possible.
- As you scan the classroom, pay particular attention to incidents or behaviors that look like they could turn into problems.
- Make eye contact with those students involved in the incident or who are exhibiting the behavior.
- If this doesn't work, move toward the students. Say something to the students, if necessary.

2. *Foresee Problems.* Another aspect of withitness is the ability to foresee potential problems and make needed adjustments to minimize behavior problems. You should mentally review what might go wrong with specific students in specific classes and consider the way you might address these potential problems.

When planning certain classroom activities, for example, you might recognize possible confusion or disruption when supplies are being distributed. With this advance thought, you could either modify the way you distribute the materials or take certain precautions when the materials are passed out. Also, you might know that specific students act in certain ways under particular conditions, such as a hyperactive student having difficulty focusing on tasks immediately after lunch. In these cases, you can give advance thought to ways to head off the potential problem behavior.

VOICES FROM THE CLASSROOM   *A Rubric for Participation to Guide Behavior*

Lind Williams, High School English Teacher, Provo, Utah

At the start of each year, I teach my students about appropriate classroom behavior. To do this, I created a rubric that displays a scale between mature and immature behaviors—I call this my *Participation Grade Rubric*. The rubric helps clarify what I view as active, on-task, appropriate behavior for students in class, and the rubric helps students understand what appropriate and inappropriate behavior looks like. For each behavioral indicator on the rubric, a description is included to show a high range, a mid range, and a low range of the behavior.

Students invariably chuckle at the descriptors in the low range of the rubric because the inappropriateness of the behavior is pretty obvious. I give examples or model some of the behaviors such as laying heads on desks, putting unfinished work away when there is still class time, saying comments that ruin or derail class discussions, and conversational etiquette.

I present these behavioral expectations at the start of the school year, but it takes time for students to be fully independent and self-managed in their conduct. The rubric provides some guidance about appropriate behaviors and helps the students grow in that direction.

Students are assessed with this rubric throughout the school year. When I conference with a student with problem behaviors, we can read the descriptions to see where his or her behavior lies on the rubric.

Emotional Objectivity

Use specific techniques to be emotionally objective with your students. When students misbehave, you may get upset and emotional to some degree. It is important that your disciplinary actions are not seen as an attack on the students involved, and you should try to be as objective as possible. *Emotional objectivity* is the ability to interact with students in a businesslike, matter-of-fact manner even though you might be experiencing strong emotions. This is particularly important when you are carrying out negative consequences for inappropriate behavior.

Your feelings of anger and frustration are only natural when dealing with misbehavior, but it is not useful to display these emotions when delivering consequences. Here are some techniques that you can use to help maintain a sense of emotional objectivity with students.

1. *Look for Reasons for the Misbehavior.* Maintaining emotional objectivity is much easier if you don't personalize student misbehavior. Simply trying to understand the reasons for the misbehavior can help you maintain your businesslike manner.

2. *Monitor Your Own Thoughts.* Take time to monitor your attitudes about specific students. When your attitude about specific students is positive, it is fairly easy to interact with them. However, you might not be aware of the extent that negative

attitudes about some students may get in the way of interacting with them. To help avoid any negative bias, before class each day you could: (1) mentally review your students, noting those who you anticipate having problems; (2) try to imagine these problem students succeeding or engaging in positive classroom behavior; and (3) when you interact with these students, try to keep in mind your positive expectations.

BUILDING POSITIVE TEACHER–STUDENT RELATIONSHIPS

Research studies on classroom management highlight the importance of having positive teacher–student relationships in promoting appropriate student behavior (Marzano, 2003). The level of dominance and cooperation established by the teacher is an important factor in forming good relationships. An optimal teacher–student relationship consists of equal parts of dominance and cooperation.

Level of Dominance

Effective classroom managers use specific techniques to establish an appropriate level of dominance in the classroom. High dominance is characterized by clarity of purpose and strong guidance in both academic and behavioral aspects of the classroom. Thus, the teacher provides guidance about the content to be addressed and the behavior expectations in the class. A moderate to high level of dominance and a moderate to high level of cooperation (addressed later) provide the optimal teacher–student relationship for learning (Marzano, 2003). You can express dominance in the following ways.

1. *Establish Rules and Procedures.* The rules and procedures that you determine go a long way in establishing your dominance in the classroom (discussed in Chapter 5).

2. *Use Disciplinary Interventions.* When misbehavior occurs, you must follow with interventions to stop the inappropriate behavior. Your use of interventions is another expression of your dominance in the classroom (discussed in Chapter 11).

3. *Exhibit Assertive Behavior.* One of the best ways to communicate a proper level of dominance is to exhibit assertive behavior. *Assertive behavior* is the ability to stand up for one's legitimate rights in ways that make it less likely that others will ignore or circumvent them. There are three primary ways that you can exert constructive, assertive behavior:

- Use assertive body language. This includes making and keeping eye contact, maintaining an erect posture, facing the student but not too close, and having your facial expression match the content of your message.
- Use an appropriate tone of voice. This includes speaking clearly and deliberately, using a pitch slightly elevated from normal classroom use, and avoiding emotion in the voice.
- Persist until the appropriate behavior is displayed. This includes not ignoring an inappropriate behavior; not being diverted by a student denying, arguing, or blaming; and listening to legitimate explanations.

4. *Establish Clear Learning Goals.* Another way to express a proper level of dominance is to be very clear about the learning goals that are to be addressed in a unit, a quarter, or semester. Clear learning goals can be communicated when you do the following:

- Establish learning goals at the beginning of a unit of instruction.
- Provide feedback on those goals.
- Continuously and systematically revisit the goals.
- Provide summative feedback regarding the goals.

VOICES FROM THE CLASSROOM   *The Support of the "Home Court"*

Merilee Dauster, Elementary Physical Education and Health Teacher, Ellisville, Missouri

There are many ways to set your classroom tone and expectations. I start the year by discussing the "home court" advantage, which is the atmosphere set by fans at their home field. When a sports team is in their home court, the fans cheer and support the players. This makes the players feel good and want to do their best for their fans. A team's fans show their support by being friendly, saying kind things, and applauding.

In my class, we talk about how our room is our "home court" and that students should feel that their classmates are supportive of them. When they try something new, the students know that their classmates will not laugh or make them feel embarrassed. Having this classroom tone allows the students to excel and have greater achievement.

Level of Cooperation

Effective classroom managers use specific behaviors that communicate an appropriate level of cooperation. High cooperation is characterized by a concern for the needs and opinions of others and a desire to function as a member of a team as opposed to an individual. A moderate to high level of dominance and a moderate to high level of cooperation provide the optimal teacher–student relationship for learning (Marzano, 2003). You can promote cooperation in the following ways.

1. *Provide Flexible Learning Goals.* While you would determine the learning goals for each lesson and unit, you could provide some flexibility by allowing students to set some of their own learning goals at the beginning of a unit or by asking students what they would like to learn. This conveys a sense of cooperation.

2. *Take a Personal Interest in Students.* All students appreciate the personal attention of the teacher, and anything that you do to show interest in students as individuals has an impact on their learning. Here are some behaviors that communicate personal interest (Marzano, 2003):

- Talk informally with students before, during, and after class about their interests.
- Greet students outside of school, at extracurricular events, or at stores.
- Single out a few students each day in the lunchroom and talk with them.
- Comment on important events in their lives, such as participation in sports, drama, or other activities.
- Compliment students on important achievements in and outside of school.

- Meet students at the door as they come into class and say hello to each student.

3. *Use Equitable and Positive Classroom Behaviors.* Teachers should ensure that their behaviors are equal and equitable for all students, thus creating an atmosphere in which all students feel accepted. These behaviors also foster positive teacher–student relationships. This can be done in many ways, such as the following:

- Make eye contact with each student in the room; freely move about all sections of the room.
- Over the course of a class period, deliberately move toward and be close to each student.
- Allow and encourage all students to be part of class discussions and interactions.
- Provide appropriate "wait time" for all students.

4. *Respond Appropriately to Students' Incorrect Responses.* When students respond incorrectly or make no response at all to a question you have posed, they are particularly vulnerable. Your appropriate actions at these critical points go a long way toward establishing a positive teacher–student relationship. Useful behaviors in these situations include the following (Marzano, 2003):

- Emphasize what was right. Give credit to aspects of the incorrect response that are correct.
- Encourage collaboration. Allow students time to seek help from peers.
- Restate the question. Ask the question a second time and allow time for the student to think before expecting a response.
- Rephrase the question. Ask the question in a different way or from a different perspective.
- Give hints or cues. Provide enough guidance so that students gradually come up with the answer.
- Provide the answer and then ask for elaboration. If the student cannot come up with the answer, state the answer yourself and then ask the student to say it in his own words.
- Respect the student's option to pass, when appropriate.

Types of Students

To promote positive relationships with your students, be aware of the needs of different types of students. Many factors contributing to student diversity are discussed in Chapter 8, including differences due to factors such as academic ability, language, culture, disabilities, and socioeconomic status. Consider those characteristics and take steps to connect to your students in an effort to create positive teacher–student relationships.

You may need to make a special effort to build positive relationships with high-need students, such as the special needs students discussed in Chapter 9 and the challenging students discussed in Chapter 12. Students who are considered high-risk and who face challenging circumstances in their lives often come to school resistant to adult intervention. Consequently, you may need to consult with school counselors and others as you determine ways to create a supportive environment and promote positive relationships with those students.

VOICES FROM THE CLASSROOM   *Helping All Students Feel Capable*

Terri Jenkins, Eighth-Grade Middle School Language-Arts Teacher, Hephzibah, Georgia

Four years ago, I was teaching in an inner city school with 99 percent minority enrollment. From the beginning, I was convinced that all of these children could learn. My goal each day was to provide material and present it in such a way that ensured every student would experience some degree of success. I will never forget one particular series of lessons.

We began reading "The Graduation" by Maya Angelou, which recounts her own graduation and valedictory address. We then learned the Negro spiritual "We Shall Overcome." The story and song were inspirational, but they weren't enough. I wanted to make the entire experience personal. I told the class that one day someone sitting in that very classroom would be responsible for giving a valedictory address at his or her own graduation, and that their next assignment was to prepare a speech and present it in class. The speeches were wonderful as I introduced each and every one of them as the valedictorian of that year. As they spoke, I could hear a new determination in their voices; I could see a new pride in their posture.

Three weeks ago, there was a soft tap on my classroom door and a welcomed face appeared.

Immediately I recognized Carol, one of those students who had given her valedictory address in my eighth-grade classroom almost five years ago. After a big smile and a warm hug, she quietly spoke. "I just had to come by and personally invite you to my graduation on June 5. I'll be giving the valedictory address, and I want you to be there." With that, an irrepressible smile burst across her face. After much earned congratulations, she looked at the tears in my eyes and said, "I did it just for you." Carol had become a believer in her dreams, a believer in herself.

Self-esteem and belief in oneself are essential. I firmly believe that self-esteem must be built through real achievement. I still strive to provide lessons designed to maximize student success and ensure achievement, and I continually verbalize my own convictions that they all can be winners. I make every effort to personalize success in the classroom. I realize that I cannot assure success for every student in my classroom, but I now know that I truly can make a difference.

Interacting with Students

A significant body of research indicates that academic achievement and student behavior are influenced by the quality of the teacher–student relationship (Jones & Jones, 2004). Students prefer teachers who are warm and friendly. Students who feel liked by their teachers reportedly have higher academic achievement and more productive classroom behavior than students who feel their teachers hold them in low regard. This research suggests that you need to learn and conscientiously apply skills in relating more positively to students. The guidelines listed below will help you build positive relationships (Charles, 2000; Good & Brophy, 2003; Jones & Jones, 2004).

1. *Use Positive Human Relations Skills.* When learning to manage the classroom climate, appropriate human relations skills are needed. There are four general human relations skills that apply to almost everyone in all situations: friendliness, positive attitude, the ability to listen, and the ability to compliment genuinely

(Charles, 2000). When working with students, also give regular attention, use reinforcement, show continual willingness to help, and model courtesy and good manners.

   2. *Enable Success*. Students need to experience success. Successful experiences are instrumental in developing feelings of self-worth and confidence toward new activities, and this in turn positively affects the teacher–student relationship. Students need to be provided with opportunities to achieve true accomplishments and to realize significant improvements (Charles, 2000). Student learning is increased when they experience high rates of success in completing tasks (Jones & Jones, 2004). Students tend to raise their expectations and set higher goals, whereas failure is met with lowered aspirations.

   To establish moderate-to-high rates of success: (a) establish unit and lesson content that reflect prior learning; (b) correct partially correct, correct but hesitant, and incorrect answers; (c) divide instructional stimuli into small segments at the learners' current level of functioning; (d) change instructional stimuli gradually; and (e) vary the instructional pace or tempo to create momentum (Borich, 2004).

   3. *Communicate Basic Attitudes and Expectations to Students and Model them in Your Behavior*. Students tend to conform not so much to what teachers say as to what they actually expect. You must think through what you really expect from your students and then see that your own behavior is consistent with those expectations. If you expect students to be polite to each other, for example, you should treat your students in the same manner.

   4. *Communicate High Expectations*. Teacher behaviors that create positive expectations almost always enhance the teacher–student relationship, and behaviors that create negative expectations result in poor relationships and poor student self-concepts, and thus reduce learning. For example, students often put forth a solid effort when you say that work may be hard but also express confidence that the students will be able to do it.

   5. *Be Fair and Consistent*. Students want to be treated fairly, not preferentially. Your credibility is established largely by making sure that words and actions coincide and by pointing this out to the class when necessary. If students can depend on what you say, they will be less likely to test you constantly.

   6. *Show Respect and Affection to Students*. You must like your students and respect them as individuals. Your enjoyment of students and concern for their welfare will come through in tone of voice, facial expressions, and other routine behavior. Middle and secondary teachers should make efforts to get to know students personally. Students who like and respect their teachers will want to please them and will be more likely to imitate their behavior and attitudes.

   7. *Create Opportunities for Personal Discussions and Interactions*. Other than through day-to-day activities, teachers often find it helpful to set time aside to get to know their students. Some possible approaches include these: (a) talk with students before and after class; (b) demonstrate your interest in students' activities; (c) arrange for interviews with students; (d) send letters and notes to students; (e) use a suggestion box; and (f) join in school and community events (Jones & Jones, 2004).

WHAT WOULD YOU DECIDE? *Sharing Personal Information*

Teachers vary in the degree that they share personal information and opinions with students in their classes. Suppose that you have traveled extensively in the United States and that you are responsible for teaching American history.

1. In your everyday interactions with your students, how personal will you be with your

students and what factors will you take into account when deciding on this?

2. To what extent will you relate personal experiences to the curriculum?

3. How might the grade level and ethnic diversity of your students affect your decisions?

MANAGING WHOLE-GROUP INSTRUCTION

In his widely respected book *Discipline and Group Management in Classrooms* (1970), Jacob Kounin reported how instructional techniques contribute to classroom management. The implications from his research can be organized into three areas: preventing misbehavior, managing movement through the lesson, and maintaining group focus.

Preventing Misbehavior

When approaching whole-group instruction, teachers can take a number of actions to prevent misbehavior based on Kounin's work.

1. *Exhibit Withitness.* As discussed earlier in this chapter, a teacher who has withitness knows what is going on in the classroom at all times, notices who is misbehaving, and responds to the misbehavior in an appropriate and prompt manner. Systematic and periodic monitoring of each student in the class is a key part of withitness because it will help prevent misbehavior from occurring.

2. *Use Overlapping.* Overlapping refers to teachers supervising or handling more than one group or activity at a time. For example, a teacher working with one group of students can notice and simultaneously address a behavior incident in another part of the classroom. Teachers who are skilled at overlapping are more aware of what is going on, thus they have good withitness as well. As a result, teachers who overlap can effectively monitor classroom behavior and intervene when needed to keep students on task. When students know their teacher has withitness and is able to overlap, they are less inclined to get off task.

3. *Use Desists.* Desists are statements by teachers to stop an inappropriate action or a misbehavior by asking or telling a student what to do. To be effective, desist statements should be specific and spoken clearly. A desist might be in the form of an appeal, such as "Shanae, please put away the comb and continue with the class assignment." Or it could be in the form of a command such as, "Wayne, stop talking with your friends and continue with your calculations in the lab activity." Effective use of desists helps keep students on task and minimizes disorder and misbehavior.

4. *Avoid Satiation.* Satiation occurs when the teacher asks the students to stay on a learning task too long, and then the students begin to lose interest and enthusiasm, make more mistakes, and misbehave. This can also occur if a certain type of activity or instructional approach is used over and over again. Teachers can prevent misbehavior by avoiding satiation and thus maintaining student interest and engagement. Satiation can be minimized by (1) highlighting progress and providing feedback; (2) providing variety in the content, group structure, level of difficulty, and instructional materials and activities: and (3) offering a challenging activity to promote a greater sense of purpose and accomplishment.

Managing Movement Through the Lesson

To minimize misbehavior and to promote learning, teachers need to have the lesson progress at a reasonable pace and avoid having the lesson go astray with abrupt changes or shifts. Kounin (1970) described the movement of the lesson in terms of momentum and smoothness, as described below. Some problems with maintaining movement through a lesson are outlined in Table 6.1.

1. *Momentum.* Momentum refers to teachers starting lessons with dispatch, keeping lessons moving ahead, making transitions among activities efficiently, and bringing lessons to a satisfactory close. Momentum deals primarily with the pacing of the lesson, and the teacher needs to avoid slowdowns in the progression through the lesson. For example, one problem in momentum is jerkiness, where the teacher fails to develop a consistent flow of instruction, going too fast at some times and too slow at others.

Table 6.1   Problems in Maintaining Movement Through a Lesson

These are terms that Kounin (1970) used to describe problems in momentum and smoothness when progressing through a lesson.

Dangle: Occurs when a teacher leaves a topic or activity "dangling" before completion to do something else or to insert some new material. Later, the teacher may resume the first activity (also see *truncation*).

Flip-flop: The teacher is engaged in one activity and then returns to a previous activity that the students thought they had finished.

Jerkiness: The teacher fails to develop a consistent flow of instruction, thus causing students to feel jerks in the lesson momentum, from slow to fast (also see *thrust*).

Slowdown: When teaching, the teacher moves too slowly or stops instruction too often. Thus, students lose interest or learning momentum. Fragmentation and overdwelling are two types of slowdowns.

- **Fragmentation:** This is a type of slowdown where the teacher breaks down an activity into subparts that could be taught as a single concept; all the subdivisions are unnecessary and slow down instruction.
- **Overdwelling:** This is a type of slowdown where the teacher dwells on an issue and engages in a stream of talk that clearly lasts longer than the time needed for students' understanding.

Stimulus bound: The teacher is distracted by some outside stimulus and draws the students' attention to it and away from the lesson.

Thrust: The teacher inserts some new information at a point where students are involved in another activity, and the new material seems irrelevant to them.

Truncation: The teacher engages in a dangle, yet fails to resume the original activity (also see *dangle*).

2. *Smoothness.* Smoothness refers to staying on task in the lesson without abrupt changes, digressions, or divergences. Kounin described several problems when trying to maintain a smooth, continuous flow of activities throughout a lesson. Some of these problems include shifting from one topic to another, shifting back to earlier activities or content, or injecting unrelated information into a lesson.

Maintaining a Group Focus

Group focus occurs when a teacher makes a conscious effort to keep the attention of all students at all times. When this occurs, the teacher maintains efficient classroom control and reduces student misbehavior (Kounin, 1970). Group focus includes group alerting, group accountability, and high participation formats.

1. *Use Group Alerting.* Group alerting refers to taking actions to engage the attention of the whole class when only individuals are responding. This includes a teacher's attempts to involve all students in learning tasks, maintain their attention, and to keep them "on their toes." With group alerting, teachers create suspense before calling on a student to answer a question, keep students in suspense regarding who will be called on next, call on different students to answer questions, and alert nonperformers that they might be called on next.

2. *Maintain Group Accountability.* Group accountability takes place when the teacher lets the students know that their performance in class will be observed and evaluated in some manner. This assessment does not necessarily mean a grade will be recorded, only that the students' performance will be gauged. For example, the teacher might use record-keeping devices such as checklists and task cards. Other strategies include asking students to raise their hands in response to certain questions, asking students to take notes and then checking them, or asking students to write answers and then using various techniques to check them during the class session. Student misbehavior decreases when students know they are held accountable for their learning and behavior and that the teacher knows each student's progress.

3. *Use High Participation Formats.* High participation formats are lessons that have all students performing in some way even though they may not be involved in answering a teacher's question. High participation formats occur when each student is expected to manipulate materials, solve problems, read along, write answers, or perform a concurrent task. In this way, students do not simply sit when others are answering questions; they are actively engaged as well.

HELPING STUDENTS ASSUME RESPONSIBILITY FOR THEIR BEHAVIOR

Students should be given the message that they are responsible for their own behavior, and teachers should provide students with strategies and training to realize that control. Research on the impact of teaching strategies geared toward personal responsibility is strong (Marzano, 2003). Positive benefits for using self-regulatory techniques include increasing competence in specific academic areas, increasing classroom participation, and reducing behavioral problems. Several approaches for helping students assume responsibility for their behavior are presented here.

1. *Use General Classroom Procedures That Enhance Student Responsibility.* Without providing students with special training, teachers can enhance student responsibility with classroom meetings, the use of a language of responsibility, written statements of beliefs, and self-analyses.

- *Classroom Meetings.* Classroom meetings can be used for a variety of purposes such as deciding about issues affecting the class, planning for various curricular or instructional issues, and reflecting on what has been learned. In relation to classroom management, these meetings can address causes and consequences of misbehavior, and can lead to discussion, reflection, and resolution of problems. It is important to identify ground rules for the meetings to ensure that they achieve their intended purposes.

- *Teach Students the Words Concerning Responsibility.* Certain words can be used to discuss classroom management and discipline issues, such as responsibility, rights, freedoms, and equality. To help students develop responsibility for their behavior, they need to know the vocabulary to explore and to discuss the concepts.

- *Written Statements of Belief.* Some teachers have their students discuss and identify a classroom theme for the school year, such as "All students have a right to be treated with respect." When we take time to articulate our beliefs, we are forced to be specific about those beliefs. The class may include a narrative description in addition to the theme. Teachers also may have the class prepare a classroom constitution to outline rights and responsibilities.

- *Written Self-Analyses of Behavioral Incidents.* When misbehavior occurs, it is helpful to use a prescribed form to record the student's analysis of the behavioral incident. Information may include the date of the incident, location, others involved, and the nature of the incident. In addition, the form may have questions prompting the student's self-analysis and reflection of the incident with questions about how they believe they contributed to the incident, how it should be resolved, and how the student could stop this from happening again.

2. *Provide Students with Self-Monitoring and Control Strategies.* Self-monitoring and control techniques are those in which students are taught to observe their own behavior, record it in some way, compare it with some predetermined criterion, and then acknowledge and reward their own successes. This is *not* a strategy to be used with an entire class. Rather, this strategy should be used with specific students for whom general management techniques are not working. This procedure involves record keeping of behavioral incidents, contingency management, monitoring, meetings, and often involvement of the parents. It follows many of the principles of behavior modification.

Some students in your class may not regularly have behavioral difficulties, but they may benefit from your suggestions about self-control. One approach is to have students ask themselves questions when they are tempted to violate the rules or if they feel they are about to lose control. Students might ask themselves, "Is this worth the trouble it will cause me?" "Is this what I want to happen?" By pausing to question themselves, students will have an opportunity to assess the situation as well as calm down.

3. *Provide Students with Social Skills Training and Problem-Solving Strategies.* Some students may violate classroom rules or procedures out of frustration due to poor social interactions with other students. Other students may have difficulty with challenging situations and consequently may misbehave. The steps in social skills training and in problem solving strategies are similar:

- When you feel like you might do something harmful or inappropriate, stop and think.
- What are some other things you can do?
- What will happen if you do them?
- Pick the best choice.

MAINTAINING STUDENT ATTENTION AND INVOLVEMENT

To manage a group of students effectively, you need to capture and hold student attention and encourage ongoing involvement. *Attention* means focusing on certain stimuli while screening out others. General guidelines and specific techniques for maintaining student attention and involvement are offered below.

Securing and maintaining attention is an important responsibility. If students are not engaged in the learning process, it is unlikely that they will learn the material and it is possible that they will get off task and disrupt order. Preventive steps therefore need to be taken. In addition to techniques that promote student attention to class activities, you may consider motivational strategies (discussed in Chapter 7).

Recommendations for ways to maintain student attention and involvement come from a number of sources (Eggen & Kauchak, 2004; Good & Brophy, 2003; Jones & Jones, 2004); some of the following guidelines come from these sources.

1. *Use Attention-Getting Strategies.* You can use certain strategies to capture students' attention at the start of a lesson. These attention-getting strategies can be used throughout the lesson to maintain student interest, and they fall into four categories (Eggen & Kauchak, 2004): physical, provocative, emotional, and emphatic. Overuse of any one approach, however, reduces its ability to arouse and maintain attention.

- *Physical.* Attention-getters deal with any stimulus that attracts one or more of the senses (sight, sound, touch, taste). Pictures, maps, the chalkboard, music, and manipulative objects are examples. Even your movement and vocal expression can be considered to be physical stimuli.
- *Provocative.* Attention-getters involve the use of unique or discrepant events. To create them, you could introduce contrasting information, play the devil's advocate, and be unpredictable to the degree that the students enjoy the spontaneity.
- *Emotional.* Attention-getters are approaches aimed at involving students emotionally. This may be something as simple as calling the students by name.
- *Emphatic.* Attention-getters place emphasis on a particular issue or event. For example, you might cue students to an issue by saying, "Pay careful attention now. The next two items are very important."

WHAT WOULD YOU DECIDE?   *Maintaining Attention in Unique Ways*

To maintain student attention, you may deliberately create disequilibrium by introducing contrasting information, playing the devil's advocate, or being unpredictable.

1. If you were teaching a social studies class, how might you create disequilibrium when discussing the role of the Supreme Court throughout the history of the United States?

2. As a means to be provocative, how might you approach a discussion about the consequences of the *absence* of a Supreme Court in U.S. government?

3. How might student differences in learning styles affect the way you approach this topic while simultaneously giving consideration to maintaining order?

2. *Arrange the Classroom So That Students Do Not Have Their Backs to the Speaker.* When presenting material during a lesson, students should be seated so that everyone is facing the presenter (who may be you, a student, or a guest). This may seem like a simple task, but too often classrooms are arranged so that students do not have a complete view of the presenter and the instructional medium. Not only is the presenter unable to see all of the students, but also the students are not able to observe all of the presenter's nonverbal behaviors.

You may prefer to have all the student seats facing the area where you spend most of your time in direct instruction, such as by the chalkboard or by the overhead projector. Or you may prefer to have them work in cooperative groups much of the time and thus arrange the desks in clusters. In that case, students can be asked to turn or move their chairs when you want their undivided attention.

3. *Select a Seating Arrangement That Does Not Discriminate Against Some Students.* Some teachers may spend as much as 70 percent of their time in front of the classroom. As a result, students at the back of the classroom contribute less to class discussions and are less attentive and less on task than those near the front. Involvement is more evenly distributed when high- and low-achieving students are interspersed throughout the room. You can enhance on-task behavior by carefully arranging the seating and moving around the room. You should experiment with seating arrangements to promote student attention and involvement.

4. *Monitor Attention During Lessons and Provide Situational Assistance as Necessary.* Students are much more likely to pay attention if they know you regularly watch them, both to see if they are paying attention and to note signs of confusion or difficulty. Regularly scan the class or group throughout the lesson.

When students show signs of losing interest or getting frustrated, you should provide *situational assistance*—teacher actions designed to help students cope with the instructional situation and to keep students on task, or to get them back on task before problems become more serious. Situational assistance may include actions such as removing distracting objects, providing support with routines, boosting student interest, helping students over hurdles, altering the lesson, or even modifying the classroom environment.

5. *Keep Lessons Moving at a Good Pace.* Delays in a lesson may be caused by actions such as spending too much time on minor points, causing everyone to wait while students respond individually, passing out equipment individually, and so forth. Attention will wander while students are waiting or when something they clearly understand is being discussed needlessly (as in lengthy review lessons). You need to recognize what causes delays and minimize them in an effort to keep the lesson moving at a good pace.

6. *Vary Instructional Media and Methods.* Monotony breeds inattentiveness, and the repeated and perhaps exclusive use of one approach to instruction will soon result in a classroom of bored students. Moreover, student achievement is increased when a variety of instructional materials and techniques are used (Good & Brophy, 2003). Varying media by using an overhead projector, chalkboards, videotapes, and slides provides a more interesting approach to teaching any lesson.

You should use a variety of teaching methods to solicit students' attention through the use of demonstrations, small and large groups, lectures, discussions, field trips, and the like. Using a variety of instructional techniques helps. For example, lectures can be mixed with demonstrations, group responses with individual responses, and short factual questions with thought-provoking questions. You should periodically review your instructional approaches to avoid falling into a dull routine. Not only does variability decrease boredom in students but it also appeals to the different student learning styles. On the other hand, you need to be cautious about having too much variety because it may distract students from the content and may decrease achievement. A happy balance must be struck.

7. *Stimulate Attention Periodically.* Student attention wanders when instruction becomes predictable and repetitive. You can promote continual attention as a lesson or an activity progresses. You can stimulate attention by cueing students through transitional signals that a new section of the lesson is coming up. For example, you might say, "We have just spent the last fifteen minutes considering what running water erosion is. Now let's look at the ways that farmers and other people try to stop this erosion." Or you can use challenging statements such as, "Now, here's a really difficult (or tricky or interesting) question—let's see if you can figure it out."

8. *Show Enthusiasm.* Your own enthusiasm is another factor in maintaining student attention. Enthusiasm can be expressed through vocal delivery, eyes, gestures, body movement, facial expressions, word selection, and acceptance of ideas and feelings. Teacher enthusiasm has been related to higher student achievement (Good & Brophy, 2003). Students often learn more from lessons that are presented with enthusiasm and expressiveness than from dry lectures.

You do not need to express a high degree of enthusiasm all of the time. Depending on the circumstances of the lesson, you may vary the degree of enthusiasm being expressed. For example, there may be times during a lesson when you might be very animated and vocally expressive. Other times, you may choose to be very mild-mannered.

9. *Use Humor.* Students appreciate a certain amount of humor in the classroom, and it can help maintain student attention. You may enjoy making silly statements or sharing funny experiences with your students. Be cautious that jokes are not used to

Table 6.2   Eight Questioning Tips to Maintain Attention

1. Use random selection when calling on students.
2. Use variety and unpredictability in asking questions.
3. Ask the question before calling on a student.
4. Wait at least five seconds after asking the question before calling on a student.
5. Have students respond to classmates' answers.
6. Do not consistently repeat questions.
7. Ask questions that relate to students' own lives.
8. Vary the type of questions being asked.

tease or demean any student, even if expressed in a funny way, because the student may interpret these statements as being serious.

   10. *Use Questions Effectively to Maintain Attention.* You can use questions to achieve various academic objectives. To maintain attention and encourage ongoing involvement, there are several guidelines for you to consider about questions (see Table 6.2).

   11. *Maintain Individual Accountability.* Students should be accountable for being involved in lessons and learning all of the material. It is helpful to ask a question or require the student periodically to make some kind of response (Good & Brophy, 2003). An unpredictable pattern in the way you handle questions or responses helps maintain individual accountability and causes students to be mentally engaged in the lesson and to be more attentive.

WHAT WOULD YOU DECIDE?   *Holding Students Accountable*

Let's assume that you are teaching a math lesson and that you are having five students complete sample problems at the chalkboard while the rest of the students remain in their seats.

1. For those who are still in their seats, how might you hold them academically accountable for the material?

2. How could you provide feedback to the students at the board as well as to those still in their seats?

3. How might the lack of a procedure for academic accountability in this setting contribute to a loss of order in the classroom?

---

   12. *Pay Close Attention When Students Talk and Answer Questions.* Use active listening skills. This often entails using nonverbal skills that indicate that you are interested in what students are saying. If you do not give attention and show interest when students answer questions, you communicate to them that what they have to say is not very important, which, in turn, will discourage involvement. Nonverbal expressions of your interest might include nodding, moving toward the student, leaning forward, maintaining eye contact with the student, and showing interest in your facial expression. Verbal expressions of interest may include statements such as, "Uh huh," "I see," "That's a thoughtful answer," or "I appreciate your thorough, insightful answer."

13. *Reinforce Students' Efforts and Maintain a High Ratio of Positive to Negative Verbal Statements.* Students attend more fully if a positive learning environment has been created. One of the best means for accomplishing this is to respond positively to their efforts. Positive and encouraging statements are very important for all students, and they can be motivated by positive reinforcement. On the other hand, a teacher who consistently belittles students' efforts will create a negative learning environment that will likely lead to inattention and off-task behavior. Make many more positive and encouraging statements than negative statements. Think about it from the students' point of view; would you like to be in a classroom where you hear mostly negative statements or positive statements?

14. *Terminate Lessons That Have Gone On Too Long.* When the group is having difficulty maintaining attention, it is better to end the lesson than to struggle through it. This is especially important for younger students whose attention spans are limited. Nevertheless, some teachers continue lessons in order to maintain a certain schedule. This can be counterproductive since students may not learn under certain conditions and in any case will have to be taught again. It is always helpful to give advance thought to a back-up activity for each lesson. For example, you may select a different instructional technique for covering the same lesson objectives.

Developing Your Management Plan: *Maintaining Appropriate Student Behavior*

There are many different ways to organize strategies that teachers could use to maintain appropriate student behavior. The content in this chapter, however, was organized around categories supported by research studies on this topic.

As a starting point, it is useful for you to provide a general description for ways you intend to maintain appropriate student behavior within the categories used in this chapter, as shown below. This written plan will then provide a framework for your more specific plan when you have a teaching assignment.

Having a Mental Set for Management

Building Positive Teacher–Student Relationships

Managing Whole-Group Instruction

Helping Students Assume Responsibility for Their Behavior

Maintaining Student Attention and Involvement

Using Reinforcers

IMPROVING CLASSROOM CLIMATE WITH REINFORCERS

A *reinforcer* is an event or consequence that increases the strength or future probability of the behavior it follows. Reinforcement is used to strengthen behaviors that are valued and to motivate students to do things that will benefit them. This section includes a review of various types of reinforcers along with guidelines for their effective use.

It is important to recognize that the awarding of reinforcers must be contingent on the student's behavior. If a student does what is expected, then an appropriate reinforcer can be awarded. Students are thus reinforced for their appropriate actions and that behavior is strengthened. In the absence of the needed behavior, students do not receive reinforcers.

Types of Reinforcers

Several techniques of reinforcement are available, including recognition, activities and privileges, tangible reinforcers, and token reinforcers. Many of these reinforcers can be used with both individual students and the entire class.

Recognition

Recognition is a social reinforcer serving as a positive consequence to appropriate behavior. Social reinforcers may be expressed by verbal or written expressions, nonverbal facial or bodily expressions, nonverbal proximity, and nonverbal physical contact. Social reinforcers are especially valued by students when given by people important to them. Social forms of approval are especially useful when reinforcing student behavior if you and the students have a good relationship. Praise is an expression of approval by the teacher after the student has attained something, and social reinforcers are often used to express this praise.

Most recognition should be done privately with the student, but some may be done publicly. You need to consider carefully student characteristics when deciding how to deliver praise. A seventh grader, for example, might be somewhat embarrassed by being praised in front of the class.

Recognition should always be contingent on performance of appropriate behavior. You should be specific about the behavior that resulted in the praise and the reasons for giving it. With verbal expressions, the terms used, the inflection, and degree of enthusiasm should vary. Also, the type of praise (private, indirect, or public) should change. Social reinforcers should always be paired with other reinforcers. Systematic and appropriate reinforcement improves student behavior. It helps students know that their efforts and progress are recognized and appreciated.

VOICES FROM THE CLASSROOM | *Complimenting Students*

Saralee Wittmer, Second-Grade Teacher, Amarillo, Texas

I use a "Compliment Train" to build a positive classroom community. My students earn a Unifix cube each time they receive a class compliment. A compliment can come from other teachers, the principal, the janitor, parents, and other students. Once the class has five cubes, they have made a Compliment Train and have earned a special treat.

The class votes on how they want to celebrate with this special treat. We might do things such as read all day, eat donuts for breakfast snack, play games, enjoy extra recess time, or watch a movie. The Compliment Train grows longer all year long, and students love to see how many times they have celebrations.

Activities and Privileges

Activity reinforcers include privileges and preferred activities. After students complete desired activities or behave in appropriate ways, you can then reinforce them with various activities and privileges. Some of these reinforcers could be various jobs as a classroom helper. Activity reinforcers are often very effective for reinforcing the entire class. A list of sample activities and privileges that can be used as reinforcers is provided in Table 6.3.

It is important to verify that certain behaviors are desirable. When you and the student are on good terms, just performing certain tasks such as straightening the room or cleaning the chalkboards with you can be rewarding. Many other activities and privileges have an intrinsic value that doesn't depend on the student's relationship to you. Running errands, studying with a friend, going to the library, being first in line, or choosing an activity are each likely to be a positive incentive that produces satisfaction in its own right. You may have students fill out a sheet at the beginning of the school year to identify activities and reinforcers that they would appreciate.

Table 6.3   Examples of Activity and Privilege Reinforcers

Privileges
   Playing a game
   Helping the teacher
   Going to the library
   Decorating a bulletin board
   Working or studying with a friend
   Reading for pleasure
   Using the computer
   Writing on the chalkboard
   Earning extra recess time

Classroom Jobs
   Distributing or collecting papers and materials
   Taking attendance
   Adjusting the window shades
   Taking a note to the office
   Watering the plants
   Stapling papers together
   Erasing the chalkboard
   Operating the overhead projector
   Cleaning the erasers

Tangible Reinforcers

Tangible or material reinforcers are objects that are valued in and of themselves: certificates, awards, stars, buttons, bookmarkers, book covers, posters, ribbons, plaques, and report cards. Food also may serve as a tangible reinforcer: cookies, sugarless gum, popcorn, jellybeans, peanuts, candy, or raisins. If you are interested in using food (m & m's, cookies, etc.), recognize some cautions. Some parents may object to certain foods (such as those high in sugar), and there may be cultural differences related to food. Students may be allergic to certain foods, and there may be health and state regulations governing dispensing food in schools.

Since tangible reinforcers serve as external or extrinsic reinforcement, their use should be limited. Other types of reinforcers are generally more available and more reinforcing in natural settings than tangible reinforcers. When you give awards, it is a good idea to distribute them so as to include a good number of the students. Don't give awards only for outstanding achievement; award for improvement, excellent effort, good conduct, creativity, and so on.

For example, you may select one or more students each week to receive awards for something of value that they have done. Awards may be in the form of a certificate accompanied by a pencil, poster, trading card, book, or other item. You may have students select their prize from a reward box that includes jewelry, magazines, cups, and other items students would value. This can also be done by teachers who are departmentalized and who work as a team with a larger group of students. While at first review, this may seem too juvenile for middle and secondary students, it can be successful if the students value the awards.

Some schools have a student-of-the-month program, with the selection criteria being the most improved grade point average or other valued behavior. Members of the student council could select the winner, who might receive a T-shirt, a pin, a poster, or some other valued prize.

Token Reinforcers

A token reinforcer is a tangible item that can be exchanged for a desired object, activity, or social reinforcer at a later time. Tokens may be chips, points, stars, tickets, buttons, play money, metal washers, happy faces, or stickers. The backup reinforcer is the reward for which tokens can be exchanged. Token reinforcement is useful when praise and attention have not worked. Tokens are accumulated and cashed in for the reinforcer.

Using Reinforcers Effectively

It is important to recognize the general principle of reinforcement: behaviors that are reinforced will be retained; behaviors that are not reinforced will be extinguished. You need to consider carefully whom to reinforce, under what conditions, and with what kinds of reinforcement. Reinforcement is likely to be effective only to the extent that

(a) the consequences used for reinforcers are experienced as reinforcers by the student; (b) they are contingent on the student achieving specific performance objectives; and (c) they are awarded in a way that complements rather than undermines the development of intrinsic motivation and other natural outcomes of behavior (Good & Brophy, 2003).

MAIN POINTS

1. Classroom climate is the atmosphere or mood in which interactions between teacher and students take place. The feeling is a composite of attitudes, emotions, values, and relationships.

2. Effective classroom managers have a mental set for management in which they consciously have high awareness of the actions in the classroom and respond quickly when misbehavior occurs.

3. An optimal teacher–student relationship consists of equal parts of dominance and cooperation.

4. Positive teacher–student relationships can be developed by taking actions to create an appropriate level of dominance and cooperation, address diverse students, and use various strategies to interact with students.

5. Successful management of whole-group instruction can be achieved by deliberate actions to prevent misbehavior, manage movement through the lesson, and maintain a group focus.

6. Helping students assume responsibility for their behavior can be achieved by using selected general classroom procedures, written self-monitoring strategies, and social skills and problem solving training.

7. A variety of approaches can be used that cause students to pay attention to the class activities at all times.

8. A reinforcer is an event or consequence that increases the strength or future probability of the behavior it follows. Reinforcement is used to strengthen behaviors that are valued and to motivate students to do things that will benefit them.

9. Recognition, activities and privileges, tangible reinforcers, and token reinforcers can be used to reinforce desired student behavior.

DISCUSSION/REFLECTIVE QUESTIONS

1. From your experiences and observations, what are the characteristics of a positive classroom climate?

2. When considering the teacher–student relationship, give some examples of high and low dominance by a teacher. Also give some examples for high and low cooperation.

3. Describe some examples where a teacher does not have good momentum and smoothness when proceeding through a lesson.

4. Discuss how regular classroom meetings might help promote student on-task behavior. What guidelines would you establish for discussions in the meetings?

5. Why would attention-getting strategies promote student involvement? What precautions could you identify for their use?

6. How might your selection and use of reinforcers be affected by grade level or subject area?

SUGGESTED ACTIVITIES

1. Prepare a written plan for what you will do to maintain withitness in your classroom. What guidelines or reminders will you create for yourself?

2. List some guidelines for yourself as you take actions to create an appropriate level of dominance and cooperation in the classroom.

3. Identify several techniques that you can use to maintain group accountability in your class.

4. Reflect on your schooling experiences and identify some strategies that your teachers used to successfully capture and maintain students' interest.

5. Talk with several teachers to see what they do to keep students on task and maintain appropriate behavior.

FURTHER READING

BURKE, K. (2000). *What to do with the kid who ...: Developing cooperation, self-discipline, and responsibility in the classroom* (2nd ed.). Thousand Oaks, CA: Corwin Press.

Examines ways to provide positive guidance for students for their behavior. Discusses setting the classroom climate, teaching social skills, teaching responsible behavior, and dealing with students with behavior problems or special needs. Includes useful lists and graphics.

CUSHMAN, KATHLEEN. (2003). *Fires in the bathroom: Advice for teachers from high school students*. New York: The New Press.

Based on the candid discussions and recommendations from a number of urban high school students, insightful and practical recommendations are provided about topics such as knowing your students, respect and fairness, classroom behavior, a culture of success, motivation, teaching difficult academic work, and when things go wrong.

Chapter 7

Motivating Students to Learn

CHAPTER OBJECTIVES

This chapter provides information that will help you:
- Adopt a comprehensive approach when incorporating motivational strategies in all levels of instructional planning.
- Apply motivational strategies in instruction through the instructional strategies you select, the tasks you ask students to complete, and the way that you interact with students during lessons.
- Apply motivational strategies in the ways that you evaluate students and provide feedback.

CHAPTER OUTLINE

PLANNING FOR MOTIVATION

MOTIVATIONAL STRATEGIES FOR INSTRUCTION

MOTIVATIONAL STRATEGIES FOR EVALUATION AND FEEDBACK

Imagine that one of your students doesn't seem interested in the subject matter of your course. The student exerts minimal effort on classroom activities, seatwork, projects, homework, and tests. The student gets off task easily, bothers other students, and disturbs classroom order. It may be that there are many students like this in your classroom, and you are searching for ways to get these students interested and engaged in the lesson.

This is where motivation ties in. If you can motivate students, they are more likely to participate in activities and less likely to get off task and contribute to disorder. An effective classroom manager deliberately plans for ways to motivate students. Motivation is one important part of effective classroom management. However, it involves more than simply praising a student. Student motivation will be affected by your selection of instructional content, the instructional strategies, the tasks that you ask the students to complete, the way you provide feedback, the means of assessment, and other issues.

Many educators use the word *motivation* to describe those processes that can arouse and initiate student behavior, give direction and purpose to behavior, help behavior to persist, and help the student choose a particular behavior. Of course, teachers are interested in a particular kind of motivation in their students—the motivation to learn. Teachers who ask questions such as, "How can I help my students get started?" or "What can I do to keep them going?" are dealing with issues of motivation.

Keller (1983) suggested that there are four dimensions of motivation: interest, relevance, expectancy, and satisfaction. *Interest* refers to whether the student's curiosity is aroused and sustained over time. *Relevance* refers to whether the students see instruction as satisfying personal needs or goals. *Expectancy* refers to whether students have a sense that they can be successful in the lesson through their personal control. *Satisfaction* refers to the student's intrinsic motivations and their responses to extrinsic rewards.

Some teachers are distressed by the apparent lack of motivation in their students. This may be more apparent at the high school level where students may have experienced years of challenges in their lives and in school. Getting to know the thoughts, needs, characteristics, and feelings of your students is an important first step. This information will help guide your decisions when planning for motivation. With a deliberate plan for incorporating motivational aspects into instruction and assessment, perhaps you can help your students overcome a lack of motivation to learn.

PLANNING FOR MOTIVATION

Before examining specific motivational strategies, it is important to consider three aspects of planning for motivation.

1. *Develop a Comprehensive Approach to Motivation.* The message about motivation from research and best practice is clear—develop a comprehensive approach to motivate students to learn instead of looking at one or two classroom variables in isolation. Much of the information about motivation addresses important topics such as needs, satisfactions, authority, and recognition. These issues should not be considered in isolation, and the ways teachers address these issues show up in their decisions about instructional tasks, evaluation, recognition, and other areas.

2. *Adjust Motivational Strategies to Your Instructional Situation.* Motivational strategies discussed in this chapter come from research and best practice, and thus they provide a framework for classroom decisions. It is likely, however, that you will need to evaluate your own situation—grade level, subject area, student characteristics—to determine which strategies are most appropriate in your context. Some strategies might need to be modified to work successfully in your classroom. Some strategies might be used a great deal while others might not be used at all. Your professional assessment of your situation will guide the selection and use of the motivational strategies.

3. *Build Motivational Issues into All Levels of Your Instructional Planning.* Your instructional planning actually includes many time frames: the course, the semester, the marking period, each unit, each week, and each lesson.

As you consider how to incorporate the motivation concept of relevance, for example, into your instruction, you would think about ways to apply that concept in each time frame listed here. How might you help students see the relevance of the entire course, and how might that be reflected in your course syllabus and introduction to the course? How might you highlight the relevance of the content during each

---

VOICES FROM THE CLASSROOM   *Planning for Motivation and Opportunities to Learn*

Janet Roesner, Elementary Teacher, Baltimore, Maryland

It is important to identify the learning goals and the indicators of learning for each unit—this provides a clear focus when planning the unit. Next, a teacher needs to determine the skills and type of thinking the students will need in order to be successful in the lesson. These acquired skills then become strategies for success and can be applied to all areas of learning.

One important question to ask when planning a unit is, "How will this learning be meaningful?" Making meaningful connections to the students'

background knowledge, experiences, and interests is key to motivating the learners. Giving students opportunities to decide on real-life assessments that are clearly related to the learning goals is very motivating. In this way, interest peaks, application of knowledge soars, and students succeed.

Each lesson in a unit must make meaningful connections to the learning goal. In this way, students begin to learn for understanding rather than for just completing the work.

marking period and each unit? Similarly, students would appreciate seeing the relevance of the content that is covered in each week and in each lesson.

You need to think globally to help students see the big picture as well as the importance of each smaller piece of content. Your long-range planning should take the topic of relevance into account, and the relevance should be apparent in each unit and lesson. Therefore, your planning for motivation needs to be conducted for all levels of planning.

MOTIVATIONAL STRATEGIES FOR INSTRUCTION

The instructional strategies that you use, the tasks that you ask the students to complete, and the way that you interact with students during instruction all influence students' motivation to learn. As you prepare your plans, try to incorporate the following 12 motivational strategies into your instruction. Table 7.1 summarizes the motivational strategies for instruction.

Capture Student Interest in the Subject Matter

One of the first tasks in motivating students to learn is to arouse their curiosity and sustain this interest over time. Useful techniques for capturing student interest address the inner need to know or to satisfy curiosity; thus the techniques are intrinsically satisfying. Try to incorporate the approaches described below, especially at the start of the lessons. These approaches are especially useful when introducing new material. Teachers need to model interest in the subject matter.

• *Take Time to Understand What Students Perceive As Important and Interesting.* To capture student interest in the subject matter, it is useful first to recognize what the students' interests are. Listen to your students. You can then adapt the content and select instructional activities that address these interests. You can identify these interests through various approaches. As you near the start of a new unit, you might briefly describe to the students what issues and activities you are currently planning. They might then be asked to indicate topics or activities they are especially interested in and to offer additional suggestions. This interaction could be in the form of an informal discussion.

You may prefer to draw a "web" of these issues on the chalkboard. To do so, write the main topic in the center of a circle; then draw lines out from the circle and write the related issue on each line. As additional lines are drawn to represent the related topics, the diagram will look like a spider's web. Still more connecting lines may be drawn.

Another way to identify student interests is through a questionnaire about the unit topics and proposed activities. You may also devise your own ways to gather this student input. The key thing is to identify student interests in the subject matter and the possible instructional strategies, and take them into account in your planning decisions. With this information, you will be able to make better decisions to capture student attention throughout all sessions.

- ***Select Topics and Tasks That Interest Students.*** Whenever possible, incorporate topics that the students will find enjoyable and exciting into the lesson. Relating some current event is often a useful way to connect student interests. When considering tasks for a lesson, choose one that enables students to select and explore their interests in the topic while achieving the lesson objective. Students often appreciate a choice of tasks that relate to their preferred learning style.

- ***Set the Stage At the Start of the Lesson.*** You can set the stage for learning by providing a brief initial activity at the beginning of the lesson that is used to induce students to a state of wanting to learn. This is sometimes referred to as a *set induction*. Effective set induction activities should get students interested in what is to be taught during the lesson, must be connected to the content of the lesson that is to follow, must help students understand the material, and should be related to the students' lives or to a previous lesson.

  For example, a health lesson on the topic of first aid might begin with the reading of a newspaper report about a recent fire or accident. After reading the article, you could ask the students what they would do if they were the first ones to arrive after the accident. A number of ideas are likely to be generated in this discussion. Then you could bring that opening discussion to a close by saying that today's lesson will be about that exact topic—what type of first aid to administer for various conditions. Then you would move into the first part of the lesson. This set induction activity helps create interest in the lesson in a way that students could relate to their own lives.

- ***State Learning Objectives and Expectations At the Start of the Lesson.*** Students need to know exactly what they are supposed to do, how they will be evaluated, and what the consequences of success will be. Avoid confusion by clearly communicating learning objectives and expectations. At the start of a class, for example, you might list the five main issues to be considered in the next unit and explain that today's lesson deals with the first issue. In this way, the students have a conceptual picture in which to organize the content.

  Your description of learning objectives and expectations also serves as an advance organizer for the students so they understand what will happen in class. This introduction should also include a description of the value of the subject matter to be examined and the related tasks. In this way, students can better appreciate the material and have a reason to be motivated. Advance organizers help students by focusing their attention on the subject being considered, informing them where the lesson is going, relating new material to content already understood, and providing structure for the subsequent lesson.

- ***Use Questions and Activities to Capture Student Interest in the Subject Matter.*** As part of the advance organizer or soon after the beginning of a lesson, stimulate curiosity by posing interesting questions or problems. Students will feel the need to resolve an ambiguity or obtain more information about a topic. For example, you might ask students to speculate or make predictions about what they will be learning, or raise questions that successful completion of the activity will enable them to answer. Hook the students with key questions. In the study of presidents, for example, you might ask, "What are the characteristics of effective leaders?"

  You may use these questions and activities as a means to induce curiosity or suspense. Divergent questions that allow several possible acceptable answers are useful (e.g., "What do you think the author was trying to express in the first eight lines of this poem?"). Provide opportunities for students to express opinions or make other responses about the subject matter.

• *Introduce the Course and Each Topic in an Interesting, Informative, and Challenging Way.* When introducing the course and each topic, highlight the tasks to be accomplished, pique the students' interest, challenge their views, and even hint at inconsistencies to be resolved. The enthusiasm and interest in the subject that you express will carry over to the students.

WHAT WOULD YOU DECIDE? *Learning About Student Interests*

It is important to take student interests into account when making planning decisions about content, instructional strategies, and performance requirements.

1. How could you gather information from your students to determine their interests?

2. How might your information gathering approaches differ for students at different grade levels?

Highlight the Relevance of the Subject Matter

Another important motivational task is to help students understand that the subject matter is related to their personal needs or goals. Actions taken to achieve this purpose can also arouse student curiosity and sustain this interest over time. You might take the following actions as a means of highlighting the relevance of the subject matter.

• *Select Meaningful Learning Objectives and Activities.* Students will be motivated to learn only if they see the relevance of their learning. Select academic objectives that include some knowledge or skill that is clearly worth learning, either in its own right or as a step to some greater objective. Avoid planning continued practice on skills that have already been mastered, memorizing lists for no good reason, looking up and copying definitions of terms that are never meaningfully used, and other activities that do not directly relate to the learning objective.

• *Directly Address the Importance of Each New Topic Examined.* Students are more likely to appreciate the relevance of the subject matter if you discuss the ways it would be useful to them, both in school and outside. They need to see the connections between the concepts and the real world. Discuss the reason why the learning objective is important—in its own right or as a step to additional useful objectives. Relate the subject matter to today's situation and everyday life. Call students' attention to the usefulness of the knowledge and skills taught in schools to their outside lives.

You could have your students think about the topics or activities in relation to their own interests. This helps students understand that motivation to learn must come from within, that it is a property of the learner rather than a task to be learned. You might ask them, for example, to identify questions about the topic that they would like to have answered.

- *Adapt Instruction to Students' Knowledge, Understanding, and Personal Experience.* The content will be more relevant to the students if you relate it to the students' personal experiences and needs and to prior knowledge. You might begin a lesson on geography by listing several state or national parks and asking students if they have visited them. You then could ask why people are interested in visiting these parks. The mountains, lakes, or other geographical features often make these parks appealing. Through this discussion, students will see the importance of the content and will more likely become actively engaged in the lesson.

- *Have Students Use What They Previously Learned.* Another way to demonstrate the relevance of the subject matter is to have students use what they previously learned. This may be easy to do since one learning objective often provides the foundation for the next. For example, when discussing the reasons for the Civil War, you could ask the students if their earlier study of the U.S. Constitution and the Bill of Rights points to the reasons. In this way, you reinforce the previous learning and highlight the importance of each learning objective. You demonstrate to the students that each learning objective will have some subsequent use. Whenever possible, call for previously acquired facts and concepts.

- *Illustrate the Subject Matter with Anecdotes and Concrete Examples to Show Relevance.* Students may find little meaning in definitions, principles, or other general or abstract content unless the material can be made more concrete or visual. Promote personal identification with the content by relating experiences or telling anecdotes illustrating how the content applies to the lives of particular individuals. An initial lesson on fractions, for example, might include a discussion of how the students divide a pizza at home. This helps students see application of the content in the real world.

Vary Your Instructional Strategies to Maintain Interest

Students often become bored if they are asked to do the same thing throughout the lesson. Student interest is maintained and even heightened if you vary your instructional approach throughout the lesson.

- *Use Several Instructional Approaches Throughout the Lesson.* After capturing student interest at the start of a lesson, maintain interest by using varied approaches such as lectures, demonstrations, recitations, practice and drills, reviews, panels and debates, group projects, inquiry approaches, discovery learning and problem solving, role playing and simulation, gaming, and computer assisted instruction. These varied approaches help link to the students' learning style preferences.

As effective as a strategy may be, students will lose interest if it is used too often or too routinely. Vary your strategies over time and try not to use the same one throughout an entire class period. Try to make sure something about each task is new to the students, or at least different from what they have been doing. Call attention to the new element, whether it is new content, media involved, or the type of responses required.

- *Use Games, Simulations, or Other Fun Features.* Activities that students find entertaining and fun can be used to capture their attention in the subject matter. Students find these intrinsically satisfying. An instructional game is an activity in which students

Mike Edmondson, High School Chemistry and Physics Teacher, Columbus, Georgia

Students learn best when they are actively involved in the learning process, so I plan a variety of ways to get students engaged in my chemistry and physics classes, including some "offbeat" activities.

I have had my classes identify and research ecological issues, and then debate them in front of audiences and even write editorials for the local newspaper. My chemistry students have designed a mural-sized periodic table and various wall murals on other topics. They have used computer software to study the content, designed crossword puzzles about course content, written essays for science contests, and even participated in a cooking contest in which students designed and cooked their own recipes and then related the processes to chemistry.

My physics students have used toys to explain physical principles, built kites to study aerodynamics, and designed and built mobiles based on physics principles. We visited a large community theater to study how pulleys and counterweights are used to move sets and scenery. After reading about quantum theory, students presented skits in groups to illustrate the fundamental principles. We have used electric trains to determine velocity and acceleration, and we include art and music in the design of many projects. In addition, the students have served as tutors in elementary classrooms.

follow prescribed rules unlike those of reality as they strive to attain a challenging goal. Games can be used to help students learn facts and evaluate choices. Many games can be used as a drill and practice method of learning.

An instructional simulation recreates or represents an actual event or situation that causes the student to act, react, and make decisions. Simulations provide a framework for using the discovery method, the inquiry approach, experiential learning, and inductive approaches to instruction. Simulations help students practice decision making, make choices, receive results, and evaluate decisions.

Games, simulations, and other activities with fun features motivate students, promote interaction, present relevant aspects of real life situations, and make possible direct involvement in the learning process. Games and simulations are commercially available, with many now designed for use on computers. You can also devise your own games and simulations for use in the classroom.

• ***Occasionally Do the Unexpected.*** Another way to maintain student interest and to get their attention is by doing something unexpected. Note what usually goes on and then do the opposite. If you normally have a reserved presentation style, occasionally include some dramatic elements. Instead of preparing a worksheet for the class, have the students prepare it. If your discussions in social studies have been about the effects of certain events on the United States, focus your discussion on the effects on your community. An occasional departure from what the students have come to expect adds some fun and novelty to your instruction and helps maintain student interest. You might even change some of your classroom routines to add some variation.

Plan for Active Student Involvement

Rather than passively writing notes and preparing worksheets, students appreciate the opportunity to be more actively involved. As you consider ways to arrange for this student involvement, take into account the students' learning and cognitive styles.

• *Try to Make Study of the Subject Matter As Active, Investigative, Adventurous, and Social As Possible.* Students will find the subject matter more intrinsically interesting if they are actively involved in the lesson. You can capture their interest in the lesson if the activities that you select have built in appeal. The students' first learning experience with a new topic should incorporate these characteristics. Whenever possible, provide opportunities for students to move and be physically active.

Students might manipulate objects at their desks or move around the room for an activity. They might be allowed to investigate topics through activities that are part of an activity center or through cooperative learning tasks. Students might conduct a debate concerning a controversial issue, prepare some product as a result of a group project, or conduct a survey in the class or beyond the classroom. In addition to independent work, students need opportunities for social interaction through pairing or small groups.

• *Vary the Type of Involvement When Considering the Students' Learning and Cognitive Styles.* Information about multiple intelligences and brain hemisphericity can be used to plan various types of student involvement. Gardner and Hatch (1989) believe that all people have multiple intelligences. They identified eight independent intelligences—linguistic, musical, logical–mathematical, naturalist, spatial, bodily kinesthetic, interpersonal, and intrapersonal. In an effort to address the various intelligences of your students, you might plan for some activities that involve movement, student discussion, outlining, charting, organizing, and so on. A number of good sources are available offering suggestions for ways to incorporate the multiple intelligences into your teaching (e.g., Campbell, Campbell, & Dickinson, 2004; Chapman, 1993; Fogarty, 1997; Lazear, 2003).

Recognize that students' learning and cognitive styles determine their level of comfort and challenge in learning tasks. Students need times when they are comfortable with the tasks but also times when they are challenged by strategies outside their preferred learning or cognitive styles. You might allow students to choose from a menu of activities, for example, but also have them complete certain activities.

Select Strategies That Capture Students' Curiosity

If students are curious about the content, they are more likely to be interested in participating in the lesson. You can capture students' curiosity in various ways outlined here.

• *Select Tasks That Capitalize on the Arousal Value of Suspense, Discovery, Curiosity, Exploration, and Fantasy.* Stimuli that are novel, surprising, complex, incongruous, or ambiguous help lead to cognitive arousal. When their curiosity is aroused, students are motivated to find ways to understand the novel stimulus. This is especially important at the start of a learning experience when you are trying to capture students' attention.

Curiosity can be aroused through (a) surprise; (b) doubt, or conflict between belief and disbelief; (c) perplexity, or uncertainty; (d) bafflement, or facing conflicting demands; (e) contradiction; and (f) fantasy (Lepper & Hodell, 1989). With these strategies, a conceptual conflict is aroused. The motivation lasts until the conflict is resolved or until the students give up. If they cannot resolve the conflict, they will become bored or frustrated, so the activity should lead to resolution of the conflict to capture and maintain student interest.

• *Use Anecdotes or Other Devices to Include a Personal, Emotional Element in the Content.* When students feel they have some personal or emotional connection to the content, their curiosity and interest will be enhanced. Therefore, try to link to students' emotions and personal experiences whenever possible. When examining civil rights, for example, you might ask your students if they have experienced any situation where they have been treated unfairly due to gender, ethnicity, or other factor. In this way, students have an emotional connection to the content.

VOICES FROM THE CLASSROOM   *Hook Students on Confusion*

Nancy Kawecki Nega, Middle School Science Teacher, Elmhurst, Illinois

One of the best ways to interest students in a topic is to introduce it in a way that confuses or astounds them. Using a demonstration of a discrepant event is sure to capture and hold student interest. Making the demonstration interactive and involving as many students as possible increases the chances of success.

For example, when introducing the idea of air pressure, I use a two-liter plastic bottle. I pour a small amount of very warm water into it, swirl it around, pour it out, and immediately cap the bottle. I set the bottle where the whole class can see it, and then continue talking. Within a few minutes, the class notices that the bottle has started to cave in. I have them write in their notebooks what they observe and what they think is causing it. Soon, the bottle is completely caved in. They are in awe of what they see, and can understand the idea of a higher pressure being "stronger" than a lower pressure. Demonstrations like this make an impression on the students, raise their curiosity, and start the investigation of a topic in a positive, interesting, and challenging way.

Select Strategies and Present Material with an Appropriate Degree of Challenge and Difficulty

Students are motivated when the learning tasks are challenging and interesting. You should monitor the difficulty of the learning tasks, break down difficult tasks into smaller parts, and select higher-level outcomes whenever possible.

• *Assign Moderately Difficult Tasks That Can Be Completed with Reasonable Effort.* Students lose interest rapidly if they are not able to succeed because the work is too hard, or if they are able to succeed too easily when the work is not challenging enough. Activities should be at a moderate level of difficulty to maintain student interest and involvement.

Assessments conducted before instruction determine what your students already know and thus help you decide on the appropriate degree of difficulty for the work at hand. Also, carefully observe students at work to see if there is an appropriate level of difficulty. You might provide students with a menu of tasks to be completed in a unit: some tasks might be required, and some may be optional. The optional list should include some moderately difficult and some challenging tasks, allowing students to choose those that are moderately challenging to them.

• *Divide Difficult Tasks into Smaller Parts That Are Achievable Without Requiring Excessive Effort.* When difficult content or tasks are scheduled, break the activities down into smaller parts so that each part is challenging yet manageable for students to complete. Once each part is completed, the students can look back with pride at their accomplishments with difficult content.

• *Focus on Higher Order Learning Outcomes.* Higher level outcomes are often more intrinsically challenging and interesting to students. The lower levels of the cognitive domain include knowledge, comprehension, and application, and important curricular content is addressed at those levels. The higher levels of the cognitive domain include analysis, synthesis, and evaluation. These levels require students to do something with the knowledge—to differentiate, relate, categorize, explain, reorganize, appraise, compare, justify, and so on. These higher level outcomes often involve a higher level of difficulty and require students to be engaged in a variety of learning activities that would be seen as interesting and challenging.

• *Monitor the Level of Difficulty of Assignments and Tests.* Students' expectations for success erode quickly when teachers repeatedly give assignments and tests that are very difficult. Continuously check to see that your assignments and tests are at a reasonable level of difficulty and that students have a good opportunity to be successful. Also, help your students learn from their errors. You could retest students to the point where they reach mastery.

Group Students for Tasks

Arranging for various ways to group students can have a positive effect on student motivation. Grouping students promotes cooperation and teamwork.

• *Plan to Use a Variety of Individual, Cooperative, and Competitive Activities.* The types of activities you want your students to complete will affect the way that you group students. Interest is maintained when there is variety in the way the learning activities are structured. Some activities, such as seatwork, may be completed individually. Other projects can be completed in cooperative learning groups with four to six students in each group. Competitive activities also can be used to provide excitement and rewards. Students can compete either as individuals or as teams, depending on the game or competition used. Team approaches may be more desirable because they can be structured so students cooperate with members of their team. Make use of group competitive situations that stress fun rather than winning.

• *Promote Cooperation and Teamwork.* To satisfy students' needs for affiliation, provide opportunities for no risk, cooperative interaction. As you form groups, take into account such factors as the size of the group, the ability of group members, and gender and ethnic composition. Cooperative learning activities enable students to work together, thus minimizing individual fears of failure and competition among students. Each student in a group, however, must be held accountable for his or her contribution to the group. This could be achieved by participation points or other approaches.

Design the Lesson to Promote Student Success

Motivation to learn is enhanced when students are interested in the subject matter and expect to be successful. The lesson should be designed to accomplish these ends. The following techniques are intended to achieve those purposes through both intrinsic and extrinsic motivation.

- *Design Activities That Lead to Student Success.* Students are motivated to learn when they expect to be successful. Therefore, make sure that they fairly consistently achieve success at their early level of understanding, and then help them move ahead in small steps, preparing them for each step so that they can adjust to the new step without confusion or frustration. Pace students through activities as briskly as possible while thoroughly preparing them for new activities.

- *Adapt the Tasks to Match the Motivational Needs of the Students.* Individual differences in ability, background, and attitudes toward school and specific subjects should be considered as you make decisions about motivational strategies. Some students need more structure than others. Other students need more reinforcement and praise. Some students are more motivated to learn than others. You will need to select motivational strategies that are most effective for your students and adjust the frequency and intensity of their use depending on individual needs.

- *Communicate Desirable Expectations and Attributes.* If you treat your students as if they already are eager learners, they are more likely to become eager learners. Let them know that you expect them to be curious, to want to learn facts and understand principles, to master skills, and to recognize what they are learning as meaningful and applicable to their everyday lives. Encourage questions and inquiry. Through these means, you communicate desirable expectations and attributes.

- *Establish a Supportive Environment.* Be encouraging and patient in an effort to make students comfortable about learning activities and to support their learning efforts. Establish a businesslike yet relaxed and supportive classroom atmosphere. Reinforce students' involvement with the subject matter and eliminate any unpleasant consequences. Organize and manage your classroom to establish an effective learning environment.

- *Use Familiar Material for Initial Examples, but Provide Unique and Unexpected Contexts When Applying Concepts and Principles.* When you want to build interest, involve the familiar. For applications once learning has been achieved, however, it is unique and unexpected examples that keep interest high and help students

---

VOICES FROM THE CLASSROOM   *Positive Expectations Motivate Students*

Elizabeth Rogovoy, Fifth-Grade Teacher, Rockville, Maryland

Your expectations of your students will influence their classroom achievements. A good teacher will make the students feel like they can do anything. If my students struggle with a concept, I work with them, sometimes one-on-one, to help them be successful. This shows each student that I am not willing to give up on them and that they should not give up on themselves either.

Not all students are going to be successful all the time. However, if they feel that they can do anything, they will learn to focus on their prior positive outcomes and not dwell on negative experiences. We want to ensure academic success and also create happy, well-rounded human beings.

transfer what they have learned. For example, when teaching students about the classification system for plants and animals, you might begin by classifying different kinds of dogs to illustrate classification. You could then have them develop a classification system for music sold on compact disks at a local music store or for DVDs rented at a video store.

• *Minimize Performance Anxiety*. To motivate students to learn, they need to believe that they will be successful in their efforts. If you establish situations that cause tension, pressure, and anxiety, your students will likely choose safety and remain uninvolved for fear of failure. On the other hand, if you minimize risks and make learning seem exciting and worthwhile, most students will join in. One way to reduce anxiety is to make clear the separations between instruction or practice activities designed to promote learning and tests designed to evaluate student performance. Most classroom activities should be structured as learning experiences rather than tests. You might say, for example, "Let's assess our progress and learn from our mistakes."

Allow Students Some Control over the Lessons

Allowing students some control over the lessons helps them develop responsibility and independence. It also provides students with opportunities to develop self-management skills and to feel that they have some authority in the instructional situation. To the extent possible, allow students choices concerning instruction, but be sure to monitor their choices so the students are still able to be successful.

• *Promote Feelings of Control by Allowing Students a Voice in Decision Making*. To the extent possible, allow students a degree of control over their learning. Students who feel they can control the situation for learning (where, when, how) and the outcomes for learning (seeking the level they want to achieve) are more intrinsically motivated (Lepper & Hodell, 1989). This will help students feel that they can be successful in their learning.

Depending on your situation, the range of choices that you give students may be limited or broad. The degree of control you permit will be affected by the students' age and maturity, among other factors. Students appreciate even a limited degree of choice. For example, you might let students select the instructional activities from a menu of choices, the order in which they must be completed, when they are due, or how they should be completed. Then, students are more likely to have expectations for success.

• *Monitor the Difficulty of the Goals and Tasks That Students Choose for Themselves*. When choices are available, students should be counseled to select moderately difficult goals that they can reasonably expect to achieve. If they do not establish suitable goals, you can help them determine what to do to achieve such goals. When you include help sessions, study sheets, review sessions, or even training on study skills, students are more likely to feel that even moderately difficult goals can be achieved.

Express Interest in the Content and Project Enthusiasm

To be motivated to learn, students need to be interested in the subject matter and see its relevance (Keller, 1983). By expressing interest in the content yourself and projecting enthusiasm, you address these motivational issues.

Table 7.1   Motivational Strategies for Instruction

1. Capture Student Interest in the Subject Matter
   a. Take time to understand what students perceive as important and interesting.
   b. Select topics and tasks that interest students.
   c. Set the stage at the start of the lesson.
   d. State learning objectives and expectations at the start of the lesson.
   e. Use questions and activities to capture student interest in the subject matter.
   f. Introduce the course and each topic in an interesting, informative, and challenging way.
2. Highlight the Relevance of the Subject Matter
   a. Select meaningful learning objectives and activities.
   b. Directly address the importance of each new topic examined.
   c. Adapt instruction to students' knowledge, understanding, and personal experience.
   d. Have students use what they previously learned.
   e. Illustrate the subject matter with anecdotes and concrete examples to show relevance.
3. Vary Your Instructional Strategies throughout the Lesson to Maintain Interest
   a. Use several instructional approaches throughout the lesson.
   b. Use games, simulations, or other fun features.
   c. Occasionally do the unexpected.
4. Plan for Active Student Involvement
   a. Try to make study of the subject matter as active, investigative, adventurous, and social as possible.
   b. Vary the type of involvement when considering the students' learning and cognitive styles.
5. Select Strategies That Capture Students' Curiosity
   a. Capitalize on the arousal value of suspense, discovery, curiosity, exploration, and fantasy.
   b. Use anecdotes or other devices to include a personal, emotional element in the content.
6. Select Strategies and Present Material with an Appropriate Degree of Challenge and Difficulty
   a. Assign moderately difficult tasks that can be completed with reasonable effort.
   b. Divide difficult tasks into smaller parts that are achievable without requiring excessive effort.
   c. Focus on higher-order learning outcomes.
   d. Monitor the level of difficulty of assignments and tests.
7. Group Students for Tasks
   a. Plan to use a variety of individual, cooperative, and competitive activities.
   b. Promote cooperation and teamwork.
8. Design the Lesson to Promote Student Success
   a. Design activities that lead to student success.
   b. Adapt the tasks to match the motivational needs of the students.
   c. Communicate desirable expectations and attributes.
   d. Establish a supportive environment.
   e. Use familiar material for initial examples, but provide unique and unexpected contexts when applying concepts and principles.
   f. Minimize performance anxiety.

(Continued)

Table 7.1 (*Continued*)

9. Allow Students Some Control over the Lessons
    a. Promote feelings of control by allowing students a voice in decision making.
    b. Monitor the difficulty of the goals and tasks that students choose for themselves.
10. Express Interest in the Content and Project Enthusiasm
    a. Model interest and enthusiasm in the topic and in learning.
    b. Project enthusiasm.
    c. Introduce tasks in a positive, enthusiastic manner.
    d. Expect interest, not boredom, from the students.
11. Provide Opportunities to Learn
    a. Focus lessons around mid-level concepts that are substantive but not overwhelming to students.
    b. Make the main ideas evident in presentations, demonstrations, discussions, and assignments.
    c. Present concrete illustrations of the content and relate unfamiliar information to your students' personal knowledge.
    d. Make explicit connections between new information and content that students had learned previously, and point out relationships among new ideas by stressing similarities and differences.
    e. Elaborate extensively on textbook readings rather than allowing the book to carry the lesson.
    f. Guide students' thinking when posing high-level questions.
    g. Ask students to summarize, make comparisons between related concepts, and apply the information they were learning.
12. Support Students' Attempts to Understand
    a. Model thinking and problem solving, and work with students to solve problems when the students have difficulty.
    b. Keep the procedures in instructional tasks simple.
    c. Encourage collaborative efforts by requiring all students to make contributions to the group.

• *Model Interest and Enthusiasm in the Topic and in Learning.* Let your students see that you value learning as a rewarding, self actualizing activity that produces personal satisfaction and enriches your life. Furthermore, share your thinking about learning and provide examples for its application. In this way, students see how an educated person uses information in everyday life. For example, a social studies teacher might relate how her understanding of community, state, and national events helped her make informed decisions when voting for candidates during political elections. If you display a scholarly attitude while teaching and seem genuinely interested in achieving understanding, then your students are more likely to display these values.

• *Project Enthusiasm.* Everything that you say should communicate in both tone and manner that the subject matter is important. If you model appropriate attitudes and beliefs about topics and assignments, the students will pick up on these cues. Use timing, nonverbal expressions and gestures, and cueing and other verbal techniques to project a level of intensity and enthusiasm that tells the students that the material is important and deserves close attention.

- *Introduce Tasks in a Positive, Enthusiastic Manner.* It is especially important to be positive and enthusiastic when introducing tasks that you expect students to complete. Introducing new tasks involves actions such as providing clear directions, discussing the importance of the material, going over examples, and responding to student questions. Your positive manner will likely affect the attitude your students carry as they complete the tasks.

- *Expect Interest, Not Boredom, from the Students.* If you think the students will find the material boring, then students typically react with indifference and boredom. However, if you treat students as active, motivated learners who care about their learning and who are trying to understand, then positive motivation is much more likely to occur. Students will typically rise to the expectations of their instructor.

WHAT WOULD YOU DECIDE? *Teacher Enthusiasm*

Students often like a teacher to show enthusiasm, and even be animated and excited at times. Having a high degree of enthusiasm all the time may present some problems; some variation is desirable.

1. How might you show your enthusiasm in your voice, gestures, body movements, and other ways?

2. What might result if you showed low enthusiasm or high enthusiasm all the time?

3. How can you determine what is an appropriate degree of enthusiasm for you to exhibit in your classroom?

Provide Opportunities to Learn

Student motivation is enhanced when you take specific actions to provide students with opportunities to learn. These actions include the following.

- *Focus Lessons Around Mid-Level Concepts That Are Substantive but Not Overwhelming to Students.* Mid-level concepts are likely to be challenging but achievable. New material is presented, and most students should be able to learn it successfully.

- *Make the Main Ideas Evident in Presentations, Demonstrations, Discussions, and Assignments.* Obscure facts and insignificant information are not emphasized. Instead, make the main concepts apparent in every aspect of the lesson—in the introduction at the start of the lesson, the notes and instructional materials, the assignments, and the evaluation.

- *Present Concrete Illustrations of the Content and Relate Unfamiliar Information to Your Students' Personal Knowledge.* When new content is introduced, specific examples should be provided to enhance student learning. Especially in cases where students may be totally unfamiliar with the content, it is useful to relate the content to some aspect of the students' personal experiences. For example, when considering the types of cadence in several lines of poetry, you might provide an example of the cadence in a popular song which the students know.

• *Make Explicit Connections between New Information and Content That Students Had Learned Previously, and Point Out Relationships among New Ideas By Stressing Similarities and Differences.* By deliberately referring back to related content previously covered, you repeat and reinforce some of the content, which will enhance understanding. You also can show how the content previously covered and the new content are connected. In a U.S. history class, for example, you might refer back to the causes of World War I when examining the causes of World War II. In doing so, you can show any similarities and differences. Students are likely to leave with a better understanding of both wars.

• *Elaborate Extensively on Textbook Readings Rather Than Allowing the Book to Carry the Lesson.* By supplementing the textbook, you can bring in contemporary information, real life examples, and unique extra resources that enrich your students' understanding of the textbook content. Furthermore, your elaborations and supplements make the class more interesting to the students.

• *Guide Students' Thinking When Posing High-Level Questions.* High level questions may require students to analyze, synthesize, and evaluate the content in some meaningful way, and some students may have difficulty with this. You may need to guide your students' thinking by carefully sequencing the questions so the students are better able to answer correctly. Or you may need to provide clues or some type of assistance when dealing with high level questions.

• *Ask Students to Summarize, Make Comparisons Between Related Concepts, and Apply the Information They were Learning.* After learning new content, it is important to provide an opportunity for the students to summarize and process their learning in some way before moving ahead with new material. The summary helps students organize their learning and demonstrate their understanding. Advance organizers used earlier in the lesson may help students understand the concepts and apply the information.

Support Students' Attempts to Understand

Student motivation is enhanced when you take extra steps to support students' attempts to understand the material. These actions include the following.

• *Model Thinking and Problem Solving, and Work with Students to Solve Problems When the Students Have Difficulty* (instead of just providing the correct answers). Make deliberate efforts to help students understand. You might describe how you organize and remember the content in *your* mind. You might suggest various types of memory strategies for the students. When students have difficulty, guide them through the problem so they will know how to deal with it the next time. You could "think out loud" as you demonstrate to students how they might approach an issue or problem.

• *Keep the Procedures in Instructional Tasks Simple.* Sometimes the procedures used in instructional tasks get in the way of student learning. To overcome this problem, keep the procedures as simple as possible. To help students with the procedures, you could demonstrate the procedures, highlight problems, provide examples, or allow for sufficient time for work completion.

- *Encourage Collaborative Efforts By Requiring all Students to Make Contributions to the Group.* Students may better understand the content when interacting with other students in some way about the content. Provide opportunities for students to work together to share and process the content.

MOTIVATIONAL STRATEGIES FOR EVALUATION AND FEEDBACK

The way that you evaluate student performance and provide recognition and feedback influences students' motivation to learn. Consider the following seven motivational strategies as they relate to assessment and feedback. Table 7.2 summarizes the motivational strategies for evaluation and feedback.

Establish Evaluation Expectations and Criteria

Student learning can be fostered when the evaluation expectations and criteria are consistent with motivational principles (Ames, 1992; Blumenfeld, Puro, & Mergendoller, 1992; Stipek, 2002). The evaluation and reward system should focus on effort, improvement, and mastery. Factors that students have control over should be emphasized, and competition should be minimized.

- *Develop an Evaluation System That Focuses on Effort, Individual Improvement, and Mastery Rather Than on Work Completion, Getting the Right Answer, or Comparisons to Others.* In an evaluation with these focal points, learning goals will be fostered and student attention will be directed to their own achievement.

- *Make Rewards Contingent on Effort, Improvement, and Good Performance.* If your evaluation system focuses on effort, improvement, and good performance, then any rewards provided students should be contingent on those same features. Recognize that there is a range of ability levels in the classroom and all students should be expected to demonstrate good performance for their ability, even high ability students.

- *Avoid Norm Referenced Grading Systems.* When teachers grade on a curve, they ensure that some students will have a failing grade. This grading system reinforces negative expectations, promotes competition among students, and limits the number of students who receive positive reinforcement. Criterion referenced grading systems are preferred.

- *Describe Evaluations As Feedback to Show How Well Students Are Doing.* Consistent with the focus of your evaluation system, students need to see that feedback given to them will serve as feedback on their performance. Any feedback needs to be balanced, specific, and given in a timely way. Some teachers use a three to one rule—three positive statements to one negative statement—when giving feedback.

- *Emphasize the Factors That Students Have Control Over As Affecting their Performance.* Factors that students have control over include effort, note taking, persistence, preparation, and other issues. Minimize reference to uncontrollable factors such as mood, luck, ease or difficulty of the unit, poor test items, or other factors.

- *Minimize the Use of Competition and Comparisons to Others when Evaluating Students.* Competition can be used to prompt students to apply more effort, but it has drawbacks. Competition focuses students' attention on winning, often at the expense of valuing the new content being addressed. Failure in a competitive situation also undermines self esteem and prompts students to blame their failure on lack of ability rather than on lack of effort. To avoid these difficulties, minimize your use of competition and stress the cooperative nature of learning.

• *If Competition Is Used, Make Sure All Students Have an Equal Chance of "Winning".* Don't use the highest score as the only criterion when determining the winner in any classroom competition. Depending on the activity, your winning criterion might focus on the most creative, most unusual, most insightful, most decorative, or a host of other possibilities.

• *Avoid Unnecessary Differential Treatment of High and Low Achievers.* Criteria and feedback to students should be consistent whether the students are high or low achievers. Teachers sometimes expect less of low achievers and then provide positive statements when their performance is not necessarily praiseworthy.

Select Procedures for Monitoring and Judging

Student motivation to learn can be enhanced by taking intrinsic motivation and learning goals into account when selecting procedures for monitoring and judging student performance (Ames, 1992; Stipek, 2002). To be satisfied about their work, students need to receive feedback about their progress.

• *Use Several Approaches to Evaluation to Give Students Information About Their Accomplishments.* Rather than relying on one means of evaluating students, use several approaches to provide students with information about their performance. Tests, homework, projects, drill and practice, recitation, board work, and seatwork often measure different types of knowledge and skills. Multiple approaches provide students with a broader base of information, as well as providing several means for students to demonstrate their knowledge and skills. In addition, active response opportunities can occur through projects, experiments, role plays, simulations, or other creative applications of what has been learned.

• *Provide Frequent Opportunities for Students to Respond and to Receive Feedback About Their Academic Work.* Frequent feedback is needed throughout the grading period to provide students with reinforcement about their successes and to indicate areas that need improvement. This helps students feel satisfied about their work, and it can be a tool to fuel extra effort and commitment in the event of dissatisfaction.

Give many short tests rather than a few major tests. This gives students more opportunities to correct poor performance. Students should realize that a single poor performance will not do irreversible damage to their grades. Preparing for a short evaluation is also more manageable for students. Since students need frequent feedback, plan to use several evaluation approaches for students to demonstrate their competence.

• *Provide Immediate Feedback About Student Performance Whenever Possible.* Students also need to receive immediate feedback that can be used to guide subsequent responses. Drill, recitation, board work, and seatwork can be used to provide immediate feedback. For example, you might have five students at a time work on math problems at the chalkboard while you and the rest of the class watch them. You then could offer the students feedback about their work and discuss how to overcome the difficulties they had in arriving at a solution. Students profit from this feedback, which guides them in solving future problems.

    • *Limit Practices That Focus Students' Attention on Extrinsic Reasons for Engaging in Tasks* (e.g., close monitoring, deadlines, threats of punishment, competition). While it may be necessary to monitor student progress closely and have deadlines, students' attention should be directed to their own progress and mastery of the content rather than on the extrinsic reasons for completing the tasks.

    • *Make Evaluation Private, Not Public.* Evaluation information is personal and should be given privately to the student. If this information were made public, students would feel that it is a competitive situation, which you do not want to emphasize.

Developing Your Management Plan: *Motivating Students to Learn*

Most of this chapter is devoted to the numerous ways that motivational strategies can be incorporated into instruction, evaluation, and feedback. That content is summarized in Table 7.1 and Table 7,2. When developing your management plan, however, you should give most of your attention to the section at the start of the chapter on planning for motivation. For each of the following items that were in that planning section, think about and write your intentions for

planning for motivation. Your answers will provide a framework for your instructional planning.

First Develop a comprehensive approach to motivation.

Adjust motivational strategies to your instructional situation.

Last Build motivational issues into all levels of your instructional planning.

Decide When to Give Feedback and Rewards

Students need to reach a point of satisfaction with what they are doing and what they are achieving. You can help students be satisfied by providing feedback and rewards for their performance.

    • *Give Some Rewards Early in the Learning Experience.* By providing some type of reward early in the learning experience, students will likely put forth more effort to receive additional rewards. The reward may simply be praise or an opportunity for a special activity. Ultimately, students will feel satisfied, which is a motivator to learn.

    Select easy tasks in the early steps of the learning activity. This offers you opportunities to deliver praise and rewards, which in turn help influence subsequent student behavior. Every student should be able to receive some type of positive reinforcement early in the lesson. For example, you might select fairly simple sentence translations in the first part of a French class, but then gradually lead to more difficult translations later in the class. This gives you an opportunity to reward and reinforce students at an early point.

    • *Use Motivating Feedback Following Correct Responses to Encourage Continued Student Performance.* Students need to receive the satisfaction of receiving recognition for their successful performance, and this extrinsically reinforces students for their actions. Students are then more likely to continue performing the instructional tasks.

• *Provide Corrective Feedback When It Will Be Immediately Useful to Improve the Quality of Performance.* Corrective feedback can be given just before the next opportunity to practice. In this way, students receive feedback before they are expected to perform the next activity. If students had been making errors in math class, for example, you could give corrective suggestions to students just before they begin working on sample problems in class.

Select the Types of Feedback and Rewards

Feedback and rewards for students can come in various forms. Praise, informative feedback, and rewards are satisfying to students and can affect the quantity and quality of student performance.

• *Use Verbal Praise and Informative Feedback.* Rather than using threats or close monitoring, intrinsic satisfaction with instruction can be enhanced with verbal praise and other types of informative feedback. In this way, students receive satisfaction for the progress they have made. However, too much verbal praise may become ineffective. Specific praise statements should focus on the student's behavior.

• *Offer Rewards As Incentives, But Only When Necessary.* Rewards motivate many students to put forth effort, especially if they are offered in advance as incentives for reaching a certain level of performance. To ensure that rewards act as incentives for everyone and not just those of high ability, see that all students have reasonable opportunities to receive rewards.

When students receive consequences that they value, they become satisfied with themselves. This helps motivate students to continue working in ways that lead to success. Rewards can be delivered in various ways, including: (a) grades; (b) spoken and written praise; (c) activity rewards and special privileges (opportunities to play games, use special equipment, or engage in special activities); (d) symbolic rewards (honor roll, posting good papers); (e) material rewards (prizes, trinkets); and (f) teacher rewards (opportunities to do things with the teacher). Be cautious about relying too heavily on extrinsic rewards since this may become counterproductive.

• *Make Rewards Contingent on Mastery or a Performance Level That Each Student Can Achieve with Effort.* Through this approach, students receive positive information about competence, and it is intrinsically satisfying that they reached the mastery level.

• *Provide Substantive, Informative Evaluation That Is Based on Mastery Rather than on Social Norms.* Feedback about performance is intrinsically satisfying for students. In contrast, feedback about how the student performed in relation to other students may promote feelings of competition, which is not so satisfying.

Help Students Feel Satisfied with Their Learning Outcomes

An important part of motivating students to learn is to help students to feel satisfied with their learning outcomes. This can be done by drawing attention to successes they have experienced and by helping students recognize their efforts and improvements over time.

- *Draw Attention to the Successes That Students Have Achieved.* Displays and announcements about the work of individual students or groups would draw attention to the successes that students have experienced. In addition, you can make statements about class progress toward achieving the goals and about their overall performance.

- *Help Students Attribute Achievement to Effort.* For students to obtain feelings of satisfaction about their academic work, they must actually be successful in various ways. Success doesn't just happen—students must put forth effort. They need to see that their effort is related to their achievements and their feelings of success.

You can help students recognize that achievement is related to effort by drawing attention to the effort they exert in certain tasks. For example, when a student has achieved a better report card grade, you could say, "Gina, coming in for extra help and putting in extra study time really paid off during this grading period. You raised your grade by 14 points. Congratulations!"

- *Help Students Recognize That Knowledge and Skill Development Are Incremental.* Students may not see that each small step they take helps them become more knowledgeable and skilled. If they recognize the importance of each small step, they will realize that their learning is incremental, and they will have more feelings of success and satisfaction.

To help students recognize this, show how their understanding of each part of the subject matter contributes to their understanding of the whole. For example, when teaching students how to do a lay up in basketball, help them recognize and practice each important part of the action—dribbling, dribbling while running, raising the proper foot and arm when releasing the ball, and so on. Students realize that their skill development is incremental, and they can feel satisfaction as they successfully perform each step of the process. Even reading a novel to elementary students one chapter a day shows students that information is incremental.

Use Mistakes and Redoing Work As Learning Opportunities

Students need to see that their errors are a normal part of learning and that they can improve their thinking and understanding by examining their errors (Ames, 1992; Blumenfeld et al., 1992; Stipek, 2002). You can provide opportunities for students to improve their academic work and to redo assignments as a way to motivate students to learn and to foster learning goals.

- *Treat Errors and Mistakes As a Normal Part of Learning.* Your response to student errors and mistakes can set the tone for the students. If you treat mistakes as a normal part of learning and see them as a way to improve understanding, then students will likely adopt the same perspective. This takes the pressure off students, and it reinforces the concept that learning is incremental.

- *Use Mistakes as a Way to Help Students Check Their Thinking.* Instead of just seeing how many questions they got wrong, students should be given the opportunity to examine their mistakes and to identify the errors in their understanding. This process will help lead to improved student learning.

- *Provide Opportunities for Improvement or for Redoing Assignments.* After examining their mistakes, students should have opportunities to correct their mistakes

Table 7.2 Motivational Strategies for Evaluation and Feedback

1. Establish Evaluation Expectations and Criteria
   a. Develop an evaluation system that focuses on effort, individual improvement, and mastery rather than on work completion, getting the right answer, or comparisons to others.
   b. Make rewards contingent on effort, improvement, and good performance.
   c. Avoid norm-referenced grading systems.
   d. Describe evaluations as feedback to show how well students are doing.
   e. Emphasize the factors that students have control over as affecting their performance.
   f. Minimize the use of competition and comparisons to others when evaluating students.
   g. If competition is used, make sure all students have an equal chance of "winning."
   h. Avoid unnecessary differential treatment of high and low achievers.
2. Select Procedures for Monitoring and Judging
   a. Use several approaches to evaluation to give students information about their accomplishments.
   b. Provide frequent opportunities for students to respond and to receive feedback about their academic work.
   c. Provide immediate feedback about student performance whenever possible.
   d. Limit practices that focus students' attention on extrinsic reasons for engaging in tasks (e.g., close monitoring, deadlines, threats of punishment, competition).
   e. Make evaluation private, not public.
3. Decide When to Give Feedback and Rewards
   a. Give some rewards early in the learning experience.
   b. Use motivating feedback following correct responses to encourage continued student performance.
   c. Provide corrective feedback when it will be immediately useful to improve the quality of performance.
4. Select the Types of Feedback and Rewards
   a. Use verbal praise and informative feedback.
   b. Offer rewards as incentives, but only when necessary.
   c. Make rewards contingent on mastery or a performance level that each student can achieve with effort.
   d. Provide substantive, informative evaluation that is based on mastery rather than on social norms.
5. Help Students Feel Satisfied with Their Learning Outcomes
   a. Draw attention to the successes that students have achieved.
   b. Help students attribute achievement to effort.
   c. Help students recognize that knowledge and skill development are incremental.
6. Use Mistakes and Redoing Work as Learning Opportunities
   a. Treat errors and mistakes as a normal part of learning.
   b. Use mistakes as a way to help students check their thinking.
   c. Provide opportunities for improvement and for redoing assignments.
7. Press Students to Think
   a. Require students to explain and justify their answers.
   b. Prompt, reframe the question, or break it into smaller parts when students are unsure, and probe students when their understanding is unclear.
   c. Monitor for comprehension rather than procedural correctness during activities.
   d. Encourage responses from all students.
   e. Supplement short answer assignments in commercial workbooks with questions that require higher levels of student thinking.

and to improve their performance. In this way, student learning is fostered. You may provide students with the chance to redo assignments or retake quizzes as a means of promoting understanding. You might ask students to show something they learned from an error, perhaps through a reflection sheet.

VOICES FROM THE CLASSROOM *Using the "Ding" Option to Improve Classroom Climate*

Susan Lovelace, High School Teacher, Sebastian, Florida

I teach English in advanced courses where expectations are high and students often feel pressured to perform at their best. To alleviate some of the pressure, I offer my students the "Ding" option on their assignments. If a student feels that a paper that they prepared is far below his or her usual quality for whatever reason, they may "Ding" the paper before it is submitted. Students simply write DING at the top of their paper before turning it in to me. Then, they have 24 hours to submit another paper for that same assignment to replace the original paper.

I have a few simple rules about this. First, the original paper must be a complete paper. I don't permit Dings for incomplete work or a blank paper. This is not to be used as an excuse for not really making an effort or for forgetting about an assignment. Second, I require that the DING be written at the top of the paper when it is submitted, not after they have the paper returned with a low grade.

Third, the revised assignment must be submitted to me within 24 hours from when the Dinged assignment was submitted; this saves me from having to evaluate many papers at the end of the grading period. Finally, I permit two Dings per student for each grading period. This makes them more careful about their choices and saves me from grading second copies of all assignments. I have found that the Ding option has alleviated student stress and has contributed to a positive atmosphere in highly competitive courses.

Press Students to Think

Students need feedback to help improve their thinking and understanding of the content. You can press students to think during the lessons through your feedback and expectations for lesson participation.

- *Require Students to Explain and Justify Their Answers.* Teachers ask many questions for students to answer during instruction. Rather than accepting a brief answer to a question, you can ask students to explain their reasoning for their answers and to justify their answers. In addition, you might ask higher order questions that require students to apply, analyze, synthesize, or evaluate the concepts, rather than asking only questions that require students to repeat the facts.

- *Prompt, Reframe the Question, or Break It into Smaller Parts When Students Are Unsure, and Probe Students When Their Understanding Is Unclear.* Many adjustments in your lesson delivery may be needed depending on the students' ability to understand the content. If students seem to be unsure in their understanding, you may need to provide some prompts or clues, reframe the question, or present it in a different way. Especially if the content is complex, you may need to break it down into smaller parts to facilitate student understanding. When student understanding is unclear, it is best to probe their understanding with questions to be sure they understand or to identify the areas they don't understand.

• *Monitor for Comprehension Rather Than Procedural Correctness During Activities.* Rather than a work orientation in your classroom, have a learning orientation where you focus on student understanding. Less importance should be placed on whether students followed the project procedures precisely, and more importance should be placed on whether students understand the content for which the project was designed.

• *Encourage Responses from All Students.* Rather than allowing a small number of students to dominate the lessons, try to actively involve all students in the lesson. This could be done by asking students to vote on issues, to compare their responses, or to debate the merits of the issue under consideration. These and other approaches encourage active participation in the lesson and promote student thinking.

• *Supplement Short Answer Assignments in Commercial Workbooks with Questions That Require Higher Levels of Student Thinking.* Teachers often use worksheets from commercial workbooks for student seatwork or homework. The questions in these worksheets, however, often require the students to report back facts. As a result, it is important to supplement commercial worksheets with questions that require higher levels of student thinking—thinking involving application, analysis, synthesis, or evaluation of the concepts.

MAIN POINTS

1. Motivation describes those processes that can arouse and initiate student behavior, give direction and purpose to behavior, help behavior to persist, and help the student choose a particular behavior.

2. There are four dimensions of motivation: interest, relevance, expectancy, and satisfaction.

3. A comprehensive approach to motivate students to learn is needed since classroom factors are mutually dependent on one another and interact with one another.

4. Planning for motivation needs to be conducted at all levels of planning (the course, the semester, the marking period, each unit, each week, and each lesson).

5. The instructional strategies that you use, the tasks that you ask the students to complete, and the way that you interact with students during instruction all influence students' motivation to learn.

6. The way that you evaluate student performance and provide recognition and feedback influences students' motivation to learn.

DISCUSSION/REFLECTIVE QUESTIONS

1. Reflect on your own K–12 schooling and through your experiences in classrooms. For your most effective teachers, what did they do that successfully motivated you to learn?

2. What are the merits and disadvantages of offering students choices in instructional tasks and requirements?

3. What are some factors to consider when determining the degree of control you will give your students in decision making about content, activities, and assignments?

4. Describe several ways that review can be conducted at the end of a lesson to give students a sense of competence about what they just learned.

5. How might you adapt evaluation and recognition for a student with low abilities without lowering your standards?

SUGGESTED ACTIVITIES

1. Examine lesson plans that you previously prepared and critique them in relation to the motivational strategies for instruction listed in Table 7.1. What did you learn from this critique?

2. Talk with other teachers at your grade level or in your subject area to see how they motivate students or how they apply the motivational strategies in Tables 7.1 and 7.2.

3. Select a unit in a subject area of your choice. Identify the ways that you could highlight the relevance of that subject matter for your students in each lesson and throughout the unit.

4. Critique your system of evaluation and feedback in relation to the motivational strategies in Table 7.2. How might your system be changed to enhance students' motivation to learn?

FURTHER READING

BROPHY, J.E. (2004). *Motivating students to learn.* (2nd ed.). Mahwah, NJ: Lawrence Erlbaum Associates.
Offers strategies and principles to use in motivating students to learn. Identifies parts of the literature that are the most relevant to teachers, summarizes research in everyday language, and provides helpful examples with an eye toward the complexities of the classroom setting.

BURDEN, P.R. (2000). *Powerful classroom management strategies: Motivating students to learn.* Thousand Oaks, CA: Corwin Press.
In a reader-friendly style, the book provides a framework for planning for motivating students, examines the learning orientation of activities and assignments, describes numerous specific motivational strategies, and addresses working with hard-to-reach students.

STIPEK, D. (2002). *Motivation to learn: Integrating theory and practice* (4th ed.). Boston: Allyn & Bacon.
Provides an academic review of motivational issues including topics such as theories of motivation, goals, values, anxiety, and expectations.

Chapter 8

Addressing Issues of Diversity

CHAPTER OBJECTIVES

This chapter provides information that will help you:
- Describe multiple ways in which diversity is exhibited in student characteristics.
- Select instructional approaches and ways to interact with students that take into account their characteristics to promote student learning.
- Create a supportive, caring classroom.
- Offer a responsive curriculum and vary your instruction with student characteristics in mind.

Classroom Management: Creating a Successful K-12 Learning Community/Third Edition, by Paul R. Burden
ISBN 0-471-71073-3   Copyright © 2006 John Wiley & Sons, Inc.

CHAPTER OUTLINE

CLASSROOM MANAGEMENT IMPLICATIONS FOR DIVERSE CLASSROOMS

SOURCES OF STUDENT DIVERSITY
    Cognitive Area
    Affective Area
    Physical Area
    Learning Styles
    Creative Potential
    Gender
    Language
    Cultural Diversity
    Disabilities
    Students at Risk
    Socioeconomic Status

CREATING AN INCLUSIVE, MULTICULTURAL CLASSROOM
    Create a Supportive, Caring Environment
    Offer a Responsive Curriculum
    Vary Your Instruction
    Provide Assistance When Needed

Just think about the diversity apparent in a typical urban classroom. There may be a wide range of student cognitive and physical abilities. Students may have different degrees of English proficiency, and some may have a disabling condition such as a hearing disorder. A wide range of ethnic characteristics may be evident, and various socioeconomic levels are likely to be represented. The students may prefer to learn in different ways, such as in pairs, small groups, or independently. Some may prefer written work; others may learn best when performing an activity.

People differ in countless ways, and it is helpful to examine variables that account for human differences. Variables include human characteristics that differ or vary from one person to the next. For example, height, weight, and measured intelligence are variables. Gender, race, socioeconomic status, and age also are variables. Less observable but equally important variables include self-esteem, confidence, anxiety, and learning style.

These examples are just a few of the human variables that create a wide range of individual differences and needs in classrooms. Individual differences need to be taken into account when instructional methods and procedures are selected for classroom management and discipline. What are the sources of student diversity? How can our understanding of these student characteristics help teachers to create an inclusive, multicultural classroom? These issues are explored in this chapter.

CLASSROOM MANAGEMENT IMPLICATIONS FOR DIVERSE CLASSROOMS

Students who are in the classroom affect classroom management. America's schools are very diverse and have students from different economic, cultural, ethnic, and linguistic backgrounds. In addition, you may find that your classroom has a range of ability levels or achievement, groups of students with skills below grade level, and students with special needs. All of these factors contribute to the diversity in your classroom.

For you and your students to be successful, you may need to make adjustments in instructional and management practices to meet the needs of different groups of students in your class. For example, you may find a wide variety of academic ability in your classroom and consequently may need to vary your curriculum, instruction, and assessments due to that variety. You also may have several students whose primary language is not English, and similar adjustments may need to be enacted. You job is to enhance student learning, and adjustments based on student characteristics will be necessary.

As discussed in Chapter 1, there are several domains of responsibility for classroom management. Your understanding of your students will likely influence your decisions about ways that you will organize the physical environment, manage student behavior, create a supportive learning environment, facilitate instruction, and promote safety and wellness. To be an effective classroom manager in a diverse classroom, you should make a commitment to:

- Get to know all of your students.
- Create an inclusive classroom by making instructional and management modifications based on an understanding of your students.
- Create a classroom environment that promotes positive behavior and enhances student learning.

SOURCES OF STUDENT DIVERSITY

Individual differences abound, and adapting instruction to student differences is one of the most challenging aspects of teaching. The first step in planning to address the diversity of students is to recognize those differences. This section explores differences in cognitive, affective, and physical areas; differences due to gender, ethnicity, learning style, language, or creative potential; differences due to exceptionalities and at-risk characteristics; and others. In the classroom, students rarely fall cleanly into one category or another, and may exhibit characteristics from several categories.

Cognitive Area

Cognitive ability includes information processing, problem solving, using mental strategies for tasks, and continuous learning. Children in a classroom will differ in their cognitive abilities to perform these tasks. Thus, there may be a range of low academic ability to high academic ability students in a classroom. Intelligence involves the capacity to apprehend facts and their relations and to reason about them; it is an indicator of cognitive ability. Two of the most prominent contemporary researchers in intelligence are Howard Gardner and Robert Sternberg.

Gardner and Hatch (1989) believe that all people have multiple intelligences. They identified eight independent intelligences: logical–mathematical, linguistic, musical, naturalist, spatial, bodily kinesthetic, interpersonal, and intrapersonal. According to this theory, a person may be gifted in any one of the intelligences without being exceptional in the others. Gardner (1985) proposes more adjustment of curriculum and instruction to individuals' combinations of aptitudes. His vision of appropriate education is clear: Do not expect each student to have the same interests and abilities or to learn in the same ways. Sternberg (1997) calls for greater understanding of what people do when they solve problems so they can be helped to behave in more intelligent ways. He describes three types of intellectual activity: analytical, practical, and creative.

The work of Gardner, Sternberg, and other cognitive psychologists provide ideas for teachers when selecting instructional techniques. When considering the cognitive differences of your students, you should:

1. Expect students to be different.
2. Spend the time and effort to look for potential.
3. Realize that student needs are not only in deficit areas. Development of potential is a need, too.
4. Be familiar with past records of achievement.
5. Be aware of previous experiences that have shaped a student's way of thinking.
6. Challenge students with varied assignments, and note the results.
7. Use a variety of ways of grading and evaluating.
8. Keep changing the conditions for learning to bring out hidden potential.
9. Challenge students occasionally beyond what is expected.
10. Look for something unique that each student can do.

There are many useful resource guides available about addressing the diversity of students by applying the multiple intelligences concept to lesson activities (e.g., Campbell et al., 2004; Chapman, 1993; Fogarty, 1997; Lazear, 2003).

Struggling Learners

A student who is considered a struggling learner cannot learn at an average rate from the instructional resources, texts, workbooks, and materials that are designated for the majority of students in the classroom (Bloom, 1982). These students often have limited attention spans and deficiencies in basic skills such as reading, writing, and mathematics. They need frequent feedback, corrective instruction, special instructional pacing, instructional variety, and perhaps modified materials.

For the struggling learners in your class, you should: (a) frequently vary your instructional technique; (b) develop lessons around students' interests, needs, and experiences; (c) provide an encouraging, supportive environment; (d) use cooperative learning and peer tutors for students needing remediation; (e) provide study aids; (f) teach content in small sequential steps with frequent checks for comprehension; (g) use individualized materials and individualized instruction whenever possible; (h) use audio and visual materials for instruction; and (i) take steps to develop the

The actual petition shown below was handed to the middle-level math teacher by an identified gifted student who had become frustrated with his math class. The student attended a large middle school in a small city in the midwest. Twenty other students also signed the petition before it was given to the teacher.

WANTED: WORK

    I, as a concerned and bored student, am protesting against you underestimating our abilities. I'm sorry to say that I'm writing this in class, but what we do in here is really not worth working on. Review, review, that's all that we do. This class is no challenge. If I've learned anything in this class, it would be boredom. I want work. We want work. I have no intention to do anything in this class except twiddle my thumbs. I've found no enjoyment in sitting here listening to my teacher repeat things I've learned in fifth grade. I'm sure others feel the way I do. Please, we want a challenge!

Sincerely,
Bob

Figure 8.1 A petition to be challenged

student's self-concept (e.g., assign a task where the student can showcase a particular skill).

Gifted or Talented Learners

Gifted or talented students are those with above average abilities, and they need special instructional consideration. Unfortunately, some teachers do not challenge high ability students, and these students just "mark time" in school. Unchallenged, they may develop poor attention and study habits, negative attitudes toward school and learning, and waste academic learning time. This problem is illustrated in Figure 8.1, which reproduces a real note that a middle school teacher received concerning the need to challenge the class.

    For these students, you should: (a) not require that they repeat material they already have mastered; (b) present instruction at a flexible pace, allowing those who are able to progress at a productive rate; (c) condense curriculum by removing unneeded assignments to make time for extending activities; (d) encourage students to be self-directing and self-evaluating in their work; (e) use grading procedures that will not discourage students from intellectual risk-taking or penalize them for choosing complex learning activities; (f) provide resources beyond basal textbooks; (g) provide horizontal and vertical curriculum enrichment; (h) encourage supplementary reading and writing; and (i) encourage the development of hobbies and interests.

Affective Area

Education in the affective area focuses on feelings and attitudes. Emotional growth is not easily facilitated, yet the student's feelings about personal skills or the subject being studied are at least as important as the information in the lesson (Slavin, 2006). Self-esteem, time management, confidence, and self-direction are typical affective education goals. While affective goals have generally played a secondary role to cognitive goals in school, they should be given an important place when planning and carrying out instruction. Love of learning, confidence in learning, and cooperative attitudes are important objectives that teachers should foster. You may find a range of affective characteristics exhibited in the classroom—from low to high self-esteem, confidence, cooperation, self-direction, and the like. To encourage affective development, you should:

1. Identify students by name as early as possible.

2. Accept the student as he or she is, for each has interesting, valuable qualities.

3. Be aware of previous experiences that have helped shape the student's feelings.

4. Observe students; notice moods and reactions from day to day.

5. Make observations over time, noting trends.

6. Observe changes, or stability, under different conditions.

Physical Area

Perhaps the best place to observe the wide range of physical differences among students is the hallway of any middle school. Tall and short, skinny and heavy, muscular and frail, dark and fair, active and quiet describe just a few of the extremes one can see there. Physical (psychomotor) differences among students have sometimes been overlooked by teachers who are not involved in physical education (Woolfolk-Hoy, 2005). Psychomotor skills involve gross motor skills and fine motor skills, such as dribbling a basketball or drawing a fine line. These skills are integral parts of most learning activities. Indeed, psychomotor and affective objectives often overlap.

Physical demands on learning are obvious in areas of handwriting, industrial arts, sewing, typing, art, and driver education. However, they must not be minimized in less obvious areas such as science labs, computer classes, speech and drama, and music. Vision and hearing deficiencies also contribute to individual differences. You should recognize the importance of physical skills in the total learning program and explore the possibilities for including psychomotor development activities in classroom objectives. You should:

1. Remember that students come in many different sizes, shapes, colors, and physical states.

2. Be aware of previous experiences that have shaped physical performance and self-expression.

3. Know what the normal physical pattern is for each age level and note any extreme variations.

4. Provide materials for manipulation and observe carefully to see what skills emerge or are lacking.

5. Observe student responses to different environmental factors and different kinds of physical activities.

6. Give students a chance to express themselves physically.

Learning Styles

A learning style is an individual's preferences for the conditions of the learning process that can affect one's learning (Woolfolk-Hoy, 2005), including where, when, and how learning takes place and with what materials. These styles may play an integral role in determining how the student perceives the learning environment and responds to it. Therefore, knowledge about learning styles could help you provide options in the classroom that would enhance students' learning.

Theories and research studies about learning styles are tentative and ongoing, though several promising areas of instructional assistance have emerged. These include cognitive style, brain hemisphericity, and sensory modalities.

VOICES FROM THE CLASSROOM *Learning Styles*

Loraine Chapman, High School English Teacher, Tucson, Arizona

Shortly after I began teaching, I noticed that students react differently to learning tasks. For example, Kelly stated that unless she can hear the words she reads, she has difficulty comprehending. Delila needs complete silence when she reads and will even put her fingers in her ears when reading to make it quieter. When given the option, some students will always select a partner for work while others will work alone.

After gathering more information about learning styles, I began to incorporate that information into my lesson plans and developed strategies to take into account the various cognitive learning styles of my students. For example, sometimes I let students choose from a list of activities that all fulfill the lesson's objectives, but each activity involves a different type of learning experience reflecting the various learning styles.

I also believe that students need to learn to stretch and use all learning styles. So within a class, or over a few days or a week, tasks using all learning styles will be incorporated into the lessons and each student must complete each activity, no matter what the learning style.

Cognitive Style

Cognitive style should be considered in planning. Cognitive style refers to the way people process information and use strategies in responding to tasks. Conceptual tempo and field-dependence/field-independence are two categories of cognitive style that educators may consider when planning instruction.

First, conceptual tempo concerns students being impulsive or reflective when selecting from two or more alternatives. For example, impulsive students look at alternatives only briefly and select one quickly. They may make many errors because they do not take time to consider all the alternatives. However, not all cognitively impulsive students are fast and inaccurate. On the other hand, reflective students deliberate among the alternatives and respond more slowly.

Second, field-dependence/field-independence deals with the extent to which individuals can overcome effects of distracting background elements (the field) when trying to differentiate among relevant aspects of a particular situation. You could expect field-dependent students to be more people-oriented, to work best in groups, and to prefer subjects such as history and literature. Field-independent students would prefer science, problem-solving tasks, and instructional approaches requiring little social interaction

(Slavin, 2006). Field-dependent students respond more to verbal praise and extrinsic motivation, while field-independent students tend to pursue their own goals and respond best to intrinsic motivation (Good & Brophy, 1995).

Brain Hemisphericity

Brain hemisphericity is another aspect of student preferences for learning environments. The two halves of the brain appear to serve different functions even though they are connected by a network that orchestrates their teamwork. Each side is dominant in certain respects. Left-brain dominant people tend to be more analytical in orientation, being generally logical, concrete, and sequential. Right-brain dominant people tend to be more visually and spatially oriented and more holistic in thinking.

Teacher presentations focusing on left hemisphere activity include lecture, discussion, giving verbal clues, explaining rules, and asking yes–no and either–or questions in content areas. Useful materials include texts, word lists, workbook exercises, readings, and drill tapes. To develop left-hemisphere functions, you could: (a) introduce and teach some material in a linear manner; (b) sequence the learning for meaning and retention; (c) conduct question-and-answer periods; (d) emphasize the meaning of words and sentences; and (e) increase student proficiency with information processing skills such as note taking, memorization, and recall.

Teacher presentations featuring right hemisphere activity involve demonstration, experiences, open-ended questions, giving nonverbal clues, manipulations, and divergent thinking activity. Useful materials for these activities include flashcards, maps, films, audiotapes for main ideas, drawings, and manipulatives. To develop right-hemisphere functions, you could: (a) encourage intuitive thinking and "guesstimating"; (b) allow for testing of ideas and principles; (c) introduce some material in the visual/spatial mode; (d) use some nonsequential modes for instruction; and (e) integrate techniques from art, music, and physical education into social science, science, and language arts disciplines.

Sensory Modalities

Sensory modality is a third factor in students' preferences for a learning environment. A sensory modality is a system of interacting with the environment through one or more of the basic senses—sight, hearing, touch, smell, or taste. For teachers, the most important sensory modalities are the visual, auditory, and kinesthetic. Information to be learned is first received through one of the senses. The information is either forgotten after a few seconds or, after initial processing, is placed in short-term or long-term memory. Learning may be enhanced when the information is received through a preferred sensory modality. Use a variety of instructional approaches that enable the students to receive the content through one or more of the basis senses.

Creative Potential

Creativity is defined by Torrance and Sisk (1997) as the process of creating ideas or hypotheses concerning these ideas, testing the hypotheses, modifying and retesting the hypotheses, and communicating the results. Highly creative individuals sometimes demonstrate characteristics that are not always liked by others, such as independence of thought and judgment, courage of convictions, skepticism toward the voice of authority, and displays of nonconformity.

Creative students process information differently and react to the world in ways unlike their peers. Teachers and parents say they want children to be creative, but they too often set up constraints to prevent a truly creative child from "getting out of hand." Highly creative children tend to be estranged from their peers and misunderstood by their teachers, who reward students exhibiting conforming behavior. Too many teachers suppress individualism and creativity. You might show examples of work done by former students that reflect creativity. This leads to a discussion of the value of creativity and can encourage creative potential.

You can nurture creativity in your students by learning about creative personalities and developing ability for divergent production. In this regard, you should:

1. Listen for creative (unconventional) responses.

2. Reward creative responses by asking students to elaborate on those ideas.

3. Provide some learning activities in which students may be creative, not conforming.

4. Allow some work to be open-ended, perhaps messy, and ungraded, to encourage exploration, guessing, and playing with the material.

5. Set up flexible learning environments in which students are free to make choices and pursue areas of personal interest.

WHAT WOULD YOU DECIDE?   *Learning Styles with the Senses*

You might use a variety of instructional approaches to take into account your students varied learning styles and instructional preferences.

When planning a series of lessons, let's say that you want to deliberately incorporate the use of the senses—sight, hearing, touch, smell, and taste. Pick a unit that you might teach and think of the planning implications.

1. What advantages or disadvantages might occur due to including the senses in your instruction?

2. Identify some specific activities in which you could have the students use these senses as they perform the activities and learn the content.

Gender

The difference in learning between males and females is hard for psychologists and educators to understand. Researchers acknowledge that many descriptions of gender difference reflect social and political influences and previous experiences. At the same time, a strong case has been made for differences in neurological makeup between the sexes that lead them to think and learn differently.

Good and Brophy (1995) believe that the gender roles to which children are socialized will interact with the student roles stressed in schools and thus foster gender differences. They also believe that these roles influence how teachers respond to boys and to girls. Research suggests that boys are more active and assertive in class, so you should avoid self-defeating patterns of interaction with low-achieving, disruptive boys. You should guard against reinforcing obedience and conformity in girls, and work toward developing their intellectual assertiveness and efforts to achieve.

Current data on scholastic achievement of males and females fail to confirm some of the traditional assumptions about gender differences. Strategies can be used, however, that address gender issues and reduce gender bias (Grossman & Grossman, 1994). In addressing gender differences in your classroom, you should:

1. Remember that differences between boys and girls are not absolute, but a matter of degree.
2. Take care to provide equal opportunities for each sex; for example, encourage girls to explore math and science areas, and promote artistic sensitivity in boys.
3. Recognize that a student's gender is just one piece of information about that student.
4. Encourage all students to test the limits of learning and achievement.
5. Find ways of rearranging students for greater interaction and less gender-based distinction during learning activities.
6. Monitor your own teaching behaviors, and ask others to observe your sensitivity about sex bias in responding to students, giving instructions and assistance, leading discussions, encouraging students, or dealing with misbehaviors.

Language

Some students come from homes where English is not the primary language or is not spoken at all. They may have limited proficiency in English. In descending order, Spanish, French, German, Italian, and Chinese are the top five languages spoken in U.S. homes other than English. This fact has a bearing on teachers' decisions about management and work.

There are three types of bilingual education programs available to help children with limited proficiency in English (Romero, Mercado, & Vazquez-Raria, 1987): (a) transition programs that help students move into English as quickly as possible; (b) maintenance programs where both languages are maintained; and (c) enrichment programs where English-speaking students learn the language of the minority while language minority students learn English.

To address language differences, you should: (a) learn about the student's previous educational experiences, language ability, and achievement levels; (b) use alternative means of presenting material (e.g., tactile, visual, kinesthetic); (c) learn about the student's culture and be alert to cultural differences; (d) have the student work with someone who is bilingual in the same language; (e) use instructional materials that are at the proper reading level and include photos, illustrations, and content that will interest the student; and (f) share information from the student's culture and other cultures represented by your students.

Cultural Diversity

Several approaches can be taken to examine individual differences created by cultural diversity. Cultural pluralism and respect for cultural identity in the United States appear to be the dominant concepts. Cultural diversity is reflected in the wide variety of values, beliefs, attitudes, and rules that define regional, ethnic, religious, or other cultures. Minority populations wish their cultures to be recognized as unique and preserved for their children. The message from all cultural groups to schools is clear—make sure that each student from every cultural group succeeds in school.

Each cultural group teaches its members certain lessons. Differences exist in the conduct of interpersonal relationships, use of body language, cooperation with other group members, and acceptance of authority figures. You need to treat each student as an individual first because that student is the product of many influences. Many resources are available concerning cultural diversity (e.g., Banks, 2006; Gollnick & Chinn, 2006). As you consider individual differences due to cultural diversity, you should:

1. Examine your own values and beliefs for evidence of bias and stereotyping.

2. Read materials written by and about members of many cultural groups.

3. Invite members of various cultural groups to discuss the values and important beliefs within their culture, while remembering not to form perceptions based on only one member of a particular group. Wide variations exist in every group.

4. Regard students as individuals first, with membership in a cultural group as only one factor in understanding that individual.

5. Learn something about students' family and community relationships.

6. Consider nonstandard English and native languages as basic languages for students of culturally diverse populations, to support gradual but necessary instruction in the majority language.

7. Allow students to work in cross-cultural teams and facilitate cooperation while noting qualities and talents that emerge.

8. Use sociograms and other peer ratings to determine cross-cultural awareness and acceptance. A sociogram is a diagram created to show which students are interacting with other students.

9. Introduce global education content and materials into lessons.

10. Infuse the curriculum with regular emphasis on other cultures, not just one unit a year or a few isolated and stereotyped activities.

11. Take care not to assume that culturally diverse groups are deprived groups.

12. Select classroom routines that do not conflict with any cultural values.

WHAT WOULD YOU DECIDE? *Your Culture Is Different*

Many classrooms have students from a variety of ethnic and cultural backgrounds. It is possible that you will feel disconnected from your students because you have a different ethnicity or different cultural background from your students.

1. What could you do so that you and your students feel comfortable with one another?

2. What could you do so that the different backgrounds do not contribute to misunderstandings and off-task behavior?

Disabilities

Exceptional students include those with conditions considered disabilities. About 10 percent of students in the United States are identified as having disabling conditions that justify their placement in a special education program (Turnbull, Turnbull, Shank, & Smith, 2004). This figure increases to 15 percent when gifted children are counted as special education students. Categories for special education services include learning disabilities; speech or language impairment; mental retardation; emotional disturbances; other impairments of health; multiple disabilities; impairments in hearing, orthopedics, or sight; and deafness/blindness.

The Individuals with Disabilities Education Act (IDEA) of 1990 committed the nation to a policy of mainstreaming students who have disabilities by placing them in the least restrictive environment in which they can function successfully while having their special needs met. The degree to which they are treated differently is to be minimized. The least restrictive environment means that students with special needs are placed in special settings only if necessary and only for as long as necessary; the regular classroom is the preferred, least restrictive placement.

When considering the needs of these students, you should:

1. Concentrate on students' strengths, capitalizing on those strengths to overcome or circumvent deficits (e.g., consider allowing some work to be done orally if the student has limited writing skills).

2. Read about successful children and adults who have surmounted disabilities.

3. Communicate often with special education teachers and collaborate with them in providing appropriate programs for exceptional students' needs.

VOICES FROM THE CLASSROOM *Students with Learning Disabilities in the Regular Classroom*

Linda Innes, Seventh-Grade Language Arts Teacher, Kansas City, Missouri

I teach one class that is labeled a class-within-a-class, which means that students identified as being learning disabled (LD) are placed in the same class with regular middle school students. To help meet state standards required for LD students, the learning disability teacher coteaches the class with me. To meet the students' needs in this class, I do several things to be very clear and specific when teaching or giving directions.

First, I give directions in various ways. I have two or three other students repeat the directions that I just gave. Also, it is helpful to have the students write down the directions, especially if they are for homework.

Second, I give instruction thoroughly and slowly. When the students are taking notes, I speak in a slower manner, write out the notes word-for-word on the overhead projector, repeat what I have written and spoken several times, and monitor the room and the notes of the students to make sure that they are getting them copied down correctly. There are times when I or the LD teacher actually write the notes for some of the students or provide a photocopy due to the severe writing handicaps or slow processing skills.

Third, I place each LD student next to an academically strong student who can provide help whenever necessary. I have found that the stronger students benefit as well as the LD students. LD students get the personalized attention they require, and the regular student has the opportunity to explain the information and in the process learn it more thoroughly.

4. Hold appropriate expectations for exceptional students. Teachers sometimes expect too much; however, an even more debilitating practice for some exceptional students is to expect too little.

5. Model appropriate attitudes and behaviors for other students toward those with disabilities.

Students at Risk

Other environmental and personal influences may converge to place a student at risk. Students at risk are children and adolescents who are not able to acquire and/or use the skills necessary to develop their potential and become productive members of society (Dunn & Dunn, 1992a, 1992b). Conditions at home, support from the community, and personal and cultural background all affect student attitudes, behaviors, and propensity to profit from school experiences.

Students potentially at risk include children who face adverse conditions beyond their control, those who do not speak English as a first language, talented but unchallenged students, those with special problems, and many others. At-risk students often have academic difficulties and thus may be low achievers.

Students who are classified as at risk may include those in poverty, youth in stress, youth without a home, abused and neglected youth, academically disadvantaged youth, youth from dysfunctional families, youth with eating disorders, chemically abusive youth, sexually active youth, homosexual youth, youth with sexually transmitted diseases, pregnant youth and young parents, delinquent youth, youth in gangs, dropouts, suicidal youth, youth members of Satanic cults, overemployed youth, mentally ill youth, disabled and handicapped youth, and lonely and disengaged youth (Redick & Vail, 1991).

These students share some common characteristics. All of the following traits need not be present for a student to be identified as at risk. Based on a review of research and experience (Bhaerman & Kopp, 1988; Lehr & Harris, 1988), youth at risk tend to exhibit the following characteristics: academic difficulties, lack of structure (disorganized), inattentiveness, distractibility, short attention span, low self-esteem, health problems, excessive absenteeism and truancy, dependence, narrow range of interest, lack of social skills, inability to face pressure, fear of failure (feel threatened by learning), and lack of motivation.

A study of successful teachers of low-achieving students revealed a number of skills or competencies that can help these students (Lehr & Harris, 1988). The skills/competencies fell into five major areas: personal skills/competencies, professional skills/competencies, materials, methods, and learning environment. Over half of the teachers in the study listed the following skills/competencies needed to teach low-achieving, at-risk students:

1. Using a variety of techniques and methods.

2. Reteaching and giving students time to practice the skill.

3. Being positive.

4. Being patient.

5. Being caring, concerned, empathetic, loving, respecting, and humanistic.

6. Setting realistic goals and objectives (high expectations).

7. Being an effective communicator with students and parents.

8. Being a firm, consistent, and fair classroom manager.

9. Using a wide range and variety of materials.

Socioeconomic Status

Socioeconomic status (SES) is a measure of a family's relative position in a community, determined by a combination of parents' income, occupation, and level of education. There are many relationships between SES and school performance (Woolfolk-Hoy, 2005). SES is linked to intelligence, achievement test scores, grades, truancy, and dropout and suspension rates. The dropout rate for children from poor families is twice that of the general population, and for the poorest children, the rate exceeds 50 percent (Catterall & Cota-Robles, 1988).

Taking these factors into account, you should: (a) capitalize on students' interests; (b) make course content meaningful to the students and discuss the practical value of the material; (c) make directions clear and specific; (d) arrange to have each student experience some success; (e) be sure that expectations for work are realistic; and (f) include a variety of instructional approaches, such as provisions for movement and group work.

CREATING AN INCLUSIVE, MULTICULTURAL CLASSROOM

Understanding the sources of student diversity is not enough. You must use that information as the basis of many classroom decisions when creating a positive learning environment, selecting a responsive curriculum, determining instructional strategies, and providing assistance.

Create a Supportive, Caring Environment

How students feel about the classroom can make a big difference in the way they participate in the classroom. Your attitude toward the students and the curriculum can influence these student feelings. In an effort to create a supportive, caring environment, you can translate your attitude into the following actions.

1. *Celebrate Diversity.* Student diversity exists in many ways, as reviewed earlier in this chapter. Students don't want to be criticized because they have some characteristic that is different from others. Through your actions, recognize that each student contributes to the rich variety of ideas and actions in the classroom. Show that you appreciate and value the diversity that is reflected in the students in the classroom. In turn, students will feel appreciated rather than feeling different, and this will make them feel more comfortable in the classroom.

2. *Have High Expectations for Students, and Believe All Students Can Succeed.* Teachers may sometimes consider certain sources of student diversity—cognitive ability, language, disabilities, socioeconomic status, for example—as having a negative effect on student performance. Thus, teachers may lower expectations and adjust the content and activities accordingly. However, this is a disservice to the students when they are not given the opportunity to address meaningful and challenging content and to develop their knowledge and skills. It is important to hold high expectations for all students and to believe all students can succeed. Students appreciate the challenge and will find the classroom more stimulating and worthwhile than a classroom with lowered expectations.

3. *Give Encouragement to All Students.* Students who perform well academically often receive words of praise, reinforcement, and encouragement from teachers. There may be many students in a classroom who do not perform at the highest academic levels, but they would appreciate encouraging statements as well. Encouraging words and guiding suggestions will help all students feel that they are being supported in their efforts.

4. *Respond to all Students Enthusiastically.* When students see their teacher is welcoming and enthusiastic about each student, they feel more comfortable in the classroom and are more willing to participate fully. Warm greetings when students enter the classroom, conversations with individual students, and positive reactions when students contribute to classroom discussion are just a few ways that enthusiasm might be expressed. The main thing is that each student needs to feel valued, and they see this through enthusiastic teacher responses.

5. *Show Students that you Care About them.* When students know that you care for them and that you are looking out for them, it makes all the difference in the world. Students then feel valued, regardless of their characteristics, and are more likely to participate actively in the classroom. Even when the teacher needs to deal with a student concerning a problem, the student recognizes that the teacher's actions are well intended.

VOICES FROM THE CLASSROOM   *Celebrating the Diversity in Your Classroom*

Sandra Allen-Kearney, Fifth-Grade Teacher, Fort Pierce, Florida

Every year, I celebrate the diversity in my classroom during the winter holiday season in a big way. Students and parents work together to research their country of origin and create an oral report on the traditions of the winter holidays. In addition, each family creates a craft and/or food item to share with the class.

This has been a festive, educational way to bring the many cultures in our classroom together. We celebrate Christmas Around the World, Ramadan, Hanukkah, Diwali, la Posada, and Chinese New Year. We even celebrated a holiday I wasn't aware of called Junkanoo.

This was a very worthwhile celebration in my fifth-grade elementary classroom, but it has taken on a new level of meaning in my middle school ESOL class. My Chinese student, who has struggled to communicate with my Creole and Spanish-speaking students, was thrilled when the class dove into her fried rice, and she begged me to translate the fortune cookies. My Haitian and Mexican students found they had much in common when both groups brought in fried plantains, rice, and beans. A deeper understanding of the cultures in our room has gone a long way to bring an often-divided classroom together in diverse celebrations that aren't so different after all.

Offer a Responsive Curriculum

Students feel that they are valued when the curriculum is fair and relevant, and when the content and curriculum materials reflect the diversity of learners in the classroom.

1. *Use a Fair and Relevant Curriculum.* Teachers can make decisions to be sure the curriculum is inclusive, relevant, and free of bias. Using the district-approved curriculum guide as a starting point, teachers can select appropriate instructional content to demonstrate that their students are valued as people and that they offer a challenging, culturally relevant curriculum. This content may involve integrating subject areas from diverse traditions, and the content may even arise out of students' own questions so they can construct their own meaning.

2. *Consider Differentiating Curriculum Materials.* Curriculum materials must also reflect the diversity of learners in the classroom. Books and other instructional materials should be free of bias, and they should provide the voices and perspectives of diverse people.

Once appropriate curriculum materials are selected, teachers may allow students options in the use of these materials. Learning activity packets, task cards, and learning contracts are examples of differentiated materials that address individual differences by providing curriculum options. Learning centers, for example, include differentiated materials with several kinds and levels of goals and activities. Centers, packets, and cards can be made for a particular student's needs and then stored until another student has need of them. When prepared properly, the materials will accommodate different rates of learning and different cognitive styles.

While used more often at the elementary level, differentiated materials can be used at the middle, junior high, and high school levels with careful explanation, monitoring, and evaluation. Ample time must be allowed for follow-up of the activity and evaluation of the learning.

Developing Your Management Plan: *Addressing Issues of Diversity*

Many sources of student diversity were examined in this chapter. From one year to the next, you will not know ahead of time about the specific characteristics of your students. Your preparation in addressing issues of diversity, therefore, must rest in your overall plan to create an inclusive, multicultural classroom. The last section of this chapter has four subdivisions, as shown below. For each of the following items, think about and write your intentions for planning to create an inclusive classroom that recognizes and accommodates the diversity of all your students. This written plan will then provide a framework for your instructional planning.

- Create a supportive, caring environment
- Offer a responsive curriculum
- Vary your instruction
- Provide assistance when needed

Vary Your Instruction

To meet the needs of the diverse students, instruction cannot be one-dimensional. A variety of instructional approaches is needed to challenge all students and to meet their instructional needs. Useful resources include *The Differentiated Classroom* (Tomlinson, 1999), *How to Differentiate Instruction in Mixed-Ability Classrooms* (Tomlinson, 2001), *Differentiated Instructional Strategies* (Gregory & Chapman, 2002), and *So Each May Learn: Integrating Learning Styles and Multiple Intelligences* (Silver, Strong, & Perini, 2000). Several ways to vary your instruction are highlighted here.

1. *Challenge Students' Thinking and Abilities.* Students have various learning styles, and they may learn best with their preferred learning style. However, should teachers always try to match student preferences and instructional methods? Probably not. Sprinthall and colleagues (Sprinthall, Sprinthall, & Oja, 1998) point out that you should (a) start where the learner is (i.e., in concert with the pupil's level of development), (b) then begin to mismatch (i.e., use a different approach from what the student prefers) by shifting to a slightly more complex level of teaching to help the student develop in many areas, and (c) have faith that students have an intrinsic drive to learn. These practices complement the recommendations of Vygotsky, Kohlberg, and others to nudge students beyond comfort zones of learning into just enough cognitive dissonance to facilitate growth.

2. *Group Students for Instruction.* Grouping makes differentiation of instruction more efficient and practical. When each group is challenged and stimulated appropriately, students are motivated to work harder. Differentiated materials can be used more easily. On the other hand, labeling can be stigmatizing if grouping is based on variables such as ability or achievement. Grouping too much and changing groups too infrequently can obstruct student integration and cooperation.

With the proper planning, structure, and supervision, grouping is a useful way to provide for individual differences. When using grouping arrangements, you should:

- Reform groups often on the basis of students' current performance.
- Make liberal use of activities that mix group members frequently.
- Adjust the pace and level of work for each group to maximize achievement. Avoid having expectations that are too low for low groups. Students tend to live up or down to teachers' expectations.
- Provide opportunities for gifted students to work with peers at their own level by arranging cross age, between school, or community based experiences.
- Groups are composed of individuals, so remember that all do not have to do the same things at the same time in the same way. Retain individuality within the group.
- Form groups with care, giving attention to culture and gender.
- Structure the experience and supervise the students' actions.
- Prepare students with necessary skills for being effective group members, such as listening, helping, cooperating, and seeking assistance.
- Adjust methods when necessary. For example, expect to cover less content when using cooperative learning techniques, and supplement with reading assignments, handouts, or homework.

3. *Consider Differentiated Assignments.* Alternative or differentiated assignments can be provided by altering the length, difficulty, or time span of the assignment. Alternative assignments generally require alternative evaluation procedures.

Enrichment activities qualify as alternative assignments when directed toward the individual student's needs. There are three types of enrichment activities. First, relevant enrichment provides experiences that address the student's strengths, interests, or deficit areas. Second, cultural enrichment might be pleasurable and productive for the student even if not particularly relevant to his or her needs. An example would be an interdisciplinary study or a global awareness topic. Third, irrelevant enrichment might provide extra activity in a content area without really addressing student needs.

4. *Consider Individualized Study.* Individualized study can be implemented through learning contracts or independent studies as a means to address individual needs. Such plans are most effective when developed by the student with your assistance. Individualized study facilitates mastery of both content and processes. Not only can the student master a subject, but he or she can also master goal setting, time management, use of resources, self-direction, and self-assessment of achievement. Independent study is ideal for accommodating student learning styles. Individual ability is nurtured, and students often learn more than the project requires.

Independent study encourages creativity and develops problem-solving skills. It can be used in any school setting and all curricular areas. Most importantly, this method of learning approximates the way the student should continue to learn when no longer a student in school.

VOICES FROM THE CLASSROOM   *Individualized Study*

John Wolters, Sixth-Grade Teacher, Manhattan, Kansas

Getting away from dependence on the textbook is one way I've learned to provide for individual differences within my classroom. I decided to approach the unit on Mexico from an independent study format, allowing each student to choose the focus of his or her own study of the country. We began as a class by listing as many possible topics as we could. Then we listed resources that were available for our use. Each student was then free to choose his or her own topic(s) to study, learn the information, and present the content to the class.

One of my students, Steve, read 75–100 pages of information, made a timeline, drew three maps and a sketch book of Aztec people, and participated in a three-person panel discussion comparing the Aztecs, Incas, and Mayas. Not bad for a student who had finished only one book so far that school year, who struggled to keep on task during social studies discussions and work time, and who had a track record of turning in about 50% of his work.

What was the difference this time? Steve felt that he was in charge, and he thrived on this feeling. No one was telling him to answer the questions on page 232, to outline pages 56–60, or to be ready for the test on Thursday. Steve tasted success once he got into this project.

This format for covering material does not work in all subject areas all the time. It does, however, allow the students to choose relevant topics of their personal interest and create finished products that reflect their abilities. All of this results in increased motivation, creativity, and pride in the job they completed.

This method requires varied, plentiful resources, and it may not provide enough social interaction. The student may spend too long on the study, and parents may complain that nothing is being accomplished.

When considering individualized study, you should:

- Include the student in all phases of planning, studying, and evaluating.
- Encourage the student to ask higher order (analysis, synthesis, evaluation) questions as study goals.
- Encourage the student to develop a product as an outcome of the study.
- Provide the student with an opportunity to share the product with an interested audience.
- Emphasize learner responsibility and accountability.

5. *Have Students Participate in All Class Activities.* Regardless of the source of their diversity, all students like to participate in class activities such as discussions, projects, group activities, or computer-based activities. They enjoy the opportunity for involvement and interaction, and they seek the challenge. These activities also provide an opportunity for individual expression, and serve as a vehicle for recognition and appreciation.

6. *Give Opportunities for Students to Try Different Types of Activities.* While certain class activities and instructional strategies may seem well suited for a particular student, it is important to involve the student in many different types of activities in an effort to challenge the student and the student's thinking and understanding.

7. *Use Authentic and Culturally Relevant Pedagogies.* Each instructional strategy has particular strengths, and some of the strengths may match up well with students with particular needs. Direct instruction, for example, has been used effectively in teaching basic skills to students with special needs. Cooperative learning has been shown to be effective in urban classrooms with diverse student populations and in positively changing the attitudes of nondisabled students toward their peers who have disabilities.

Instructional approaches should be selected that develop classrooms that are multicultural and inclusive. Techniques can be used to anchor instruction in students' prior knowledge and help them learn the new content. Instructional approaches can be selected that are seen by the student as realistic and culturally relevant.

8. *Use Authentic and Fair Assessment Strategies.* Some students demonstrate their learning better through certain types of assessment. Since there are many types of students in classrooms, a variety of methods for evaluating student learning should be used. Using a variety of approaches, such as written or oral tests, reports or projects, interviews, portfolios, writing samples, and observations, will circumvent bias. In addition, evaluation of student learning should be at several levels—recall, comprehension, application, analysis, synthesis, and evaluation.

WHAT WOULD YOU DECIDE?   *Differentiated Materials*

Various types of materials can be used to meet the instructional objectives of a lesson and meet the learning interests of the students. Let's say that you are planning to teach a lesson on soil erosion.

1. How might you vary your instructional materials to accommodate individual differences?

2. How could you relate this topic to students' lives and make it interesting?

3. How might students' individual differences affect your planning decisions?

Provide Assistance When Needed

Many classrooms include students who could benefit from special assistance in their learning. When creating an inclusive, multicultural classroom, these students cannot be overlooked because they may not advance in their learning without such assistance.

1. *Provide Special Individualized Assistance to All Students.* Teachers often provide individualized assistance to students who have difficulty learning. This assistance can make a big difference in helping the student overcome hurdles, and can lead to better understanding. However, other students can benefit from this type of assistance as well. By providing assistance to all types of diverse learners, teachers express their interest in the student, provide support for student learning, and have the opportunity to challenge the learners in new directions.

2. *Work with Students with Special Needs.* As a first step, teachers need to know district policies concerning students with special needs and know what their responsibilities are for referrals, screening, and the preparation of individualized educational plans (IEP). Learning materials and activities can be prepared commensurate with the abilities of students with special needs. Positive expectations for student performance are a means to promote student learning.

MAIN POINTS

1. Individual differences need to be taken into account when instructional methods are selected and procedures are determined for classroom management.

2. Cognitive, affective, and physical differences are only part of the array of variables that account for student diversity.

3. Diversity can be due to influences of learning style, creative potential, gender, language, and cultural diversity.

4. Diversity can be affected by disabilities, conditions placing the student at risk, and socioeconomic factors.

5. Information about the sources of student diversity can be used as the basis of classroom decisions to create a supportive, caring learning environment.

6. Curriculum content and materials should reflect the diversity of learners in the classroom.

7. A variety of instructional approaches is needed to challenge all students and to meet their instructional needs.

DISCUSSION/REFLECTIVE QUESTIONS

1. What types of student diversity were evident in classrooms in your own K–12 schooling experience? In what ways did your teachers seem to take those student characteristics into account in the selection of content and the use of instructional approaches?

2. Are you enthusiastic or skeptical about the relevance of learning style theory and brain hemisphere research for classroom instruction? Why?

3. What are some challenges you might experience in dealing with students with limited English proficiency?

What could you do to overcome those challenges to promote student learning?

4. How might you recognize and celebrate the diversity of students in your own classroom, and even use this information to enhance instruction?

5. Should you have different expectations and evaluation standards to reflect the diverse students in your classroom? Why or why not?

SUGGESTED ACTIVITIES

1. Using the categories of differences addressed in this chapter as a guide, ask several teachers to describe individual differences they notice in their students. How do the teachers take these differences into account? What difficulties have they experienced?

2. Imagine that the students in your class have a wide range of academic abilities. Consider ways that you could be responsive to those differences and still help all students learn. Consider some curricular and instructional variations that you might use.

3. Examine textbooks and instructional materials in your major teaching area(s) and grade level and identify

ways in which they address individual differences and provide for individual needs.

4. Select a unit that you might teach, and identify specific ways that you could offer a responsive curriculum and also vary your instruction over a two-week unit when taking student diversity into account.

5. Ask several teachers about difficulties they have experienced when trying to provide for individual differences in the classroom. What could be done to help overcome these difficulties?

FURTHER READING

Gollnick, Donna M., & Chinn, Philip C. (2006). *Multicultural education in a pluralistic society* (7th ed.). Upper Saddle River, NJ: Prentice-Hall/Merrill.
 Provides descriptions of human differences due to class, ethnicity and race, gender, exceptionality, religion, language, and age. Discusses education that is multicultural.
Manning, M. Lee, & Baruth, Leroy G. (2004). *Multicultural education of children and adolescents* (4th ed.). Boston: Allyn & Bacon.

 Examines reasons for human differences, multicultural education, and implications for teaching and learning in a diverse society.
Marshall, Patricia L. (2002). *Cultural diversity in our schools*. Belmont, CA: Wadsworth.
 Examines diversity in schools and the implications for teachers. Includes separate chapters on various ethnic groups.

Chapter 9

Helping Students with Special Needs

CHAPTER OBJECTIVES

This chapter provides information that will help you:
- Identify the characteristics of disabilities and ways to assist students' instruction and behavior.
- Describe ways to modify instruction to help students with limited English proficiency learn.
- Recognize the characteristics of students who are troubled.
- Describe ways to seek out resources and to modify instruction and management due to the challenging troubles students are experiencing.

Classroom Management: Creating a Successful K-12 Learning Community/Third Edition, by Paul R. Burden
ISBN 0-471-71073-3   Copyright © 2006 John Wiley & Sons, Inc.

CHAPTER OUTLINE

You've probably seen this before as you waited in the checkout line at a store. The person in front of you has a special need or request, and the clerk does something different from the usual checkout procedure to address the person's needs. The clerk may need to call someone for a price check, arrange for another worker to carry a large item out to the car, or even deal with an angry customer due to mislabeling of a price. These are examples of things that a clerk would need to do differently from usual procedures based on the customer's needs.

In the classroom, you will have "customers with special needs" as well. You may have students with various types of disabilities that require you to make adjustments from your usual mode of operation due to the students' particular needs. Sometimes these adjustments will be only for those students, and other times you may need to make changes that affect the way you address the entire class. In addition, you may have students who have limited English language proficiency or students who are troubled in some way that require special considerations and adjustments in the way that you manage your classroom. These issues are explored in this chapter.

STUDENTS WITH DISABILITIES

According to the U.S. Department of Education, about 13 percent of the school population is enrolled in special education programs. The largest numbers among these students, in descending order, are categorized as having specific learning disabilities, speech impairments, mental retardation, emotional disturbance, health impairments, mobility impairments, hearing impairments, autism, and visual impairments. A number of these students will be included in regular classrooms. Several of these conditions are discussed here from a management and instructional perspective.

Students with Learning Disabilities

Students with learning disabilities make up 5 percent of the total student population. A *specific learning disability* is a disorder in one or more of the basic psychological processes involved in understanding or using spoken or written language. This disorder may appear as an impaired ability to listen, think, speak, read, write, spell, or do mathematical calculations. The term *learning disability* includes such conditions as perceptual handicaps, brain injury, minimal brain dysfunction, dyslexia, and developmental aphasia. It does not include learning problems that are the result of visual, hearing, or motor handicaps, mental retardation, emotional disturbance, or environmental, cultural, or economic disadvantage (Salend, 2005).

Many students with learning disabilities have average or above average intelligence, but they often fail to perform in line with their potential compared to their peers. Therefore, many of these students show a discrepancy between their ability and their actual performance in the classroom. Some students may have difficulty in one area while others may experience challenges in several areas, such as learning, language, perceptual, motor, social, and behavioral difficulties.

Students with learning disabilities may experience difficulties in four areas (Salend, 2005):

• *Learning and Academic Difficulties.* Many students with learning disabilities have memory, attention, and organizational difficulties that hinder their ability to learn and master academic content. They experience difficulties in perceiving, processing, remembering, and expressing information. Many of these students experience reading difficulties, and they consequently have trouble writing and expressing ideas in print.

• *Language and Communication Difficulties.* Many students with learning disabilities use immature speech patterns, experience language comprehension difficulties, and have trouble expressing themselves. In the classroom, they may have difficulty learning new vocabulary, following directions, understanding questions, pronouncing words, and expressing their needs.

• *Perceptual and Motor Difficulties.* Many students with learning disabilities may have difficulty recognizing, discriminating, and interpreting visual and auditory stimuli. For example, they may have trouble copying from the blackboard, following multiple-step directions, paying attention to relevant stimuli, and working on a task for a sustained period of time. They also may have difficulty with fine and gross motor movements.

• *Socio-Emotional and Behavioral Difficulties.* Students with learning difficulties may show signs of a poor self-concept, task avoidance, social withdrawal, loneliness, frustration, and anxiety. They may take actions that interfere with their learning and fail to predict consequences. Because of their poor social skills, they may fail to interpret social cues and make needed adjustments, thus resulting in difficulties in relating to and being accepted by their peers.

WHAT WOULD YOU DECIDE?   *Learning Disabilities*

Some students may appear to be off task or may misbehave when they really have some type of learning disability that interferes with their learning. Some students may deliberately do things to disguise or cover up their disability.

1. What could you do early in the school year to identify any students who have learning

disabilities? Who could you talk to? What records could you review? What could you do in your own classroom?

2. If two students in your class had language and communication difficulties, identify four changes that you would make in your instruction that would facilitate learning for these students.

The following strategies help students with learning disabilities to be academically successful and also promote appropriate behavior (Vaughn, Bos, & Schumm, 2003):

1. Control the difficulty of the task (e.g., teaching at the student's instructional level and sequencing examples and problems to maintain high levels of student success).

2. Teach students with learning disabilities in small interactive groups of six or fewer students.

3. Use a combination of direct instruction and cognitive strategy instruction.

4. Provide a framework for learning (e.g., with advance organizers about the content and the assignments)

5. Model processes and strategies using thinking aloud and instructional conversations (e.g., make learning visible with questions that illustrate steps in the thought process).

6. Teach self-regulation and self-monitoring (e.g., have the students ask themselves questions about their learning and performance, including self-monitoring and graphing of actions).

7. Provide opportunities for extended practice and application.

8. Use learning tools and aids (e.g., computers, calculators, spell checkers, tape recorders, and hand-held organizers).

9. Adjust workload and time (e.g., reducing the amount of work, providing time extension, and dividing work up into smaller sections or tasks).

10. Present content and have students demonstrate their learning in multiple ways.

11. Teach students to use memory strategies.

Students with Emotional or Behavioral Problems

Students with emotional and behavioral problems exhibit behaviors that are significantly different from the norm and persist over a long period of time. These behaviors are grouped into two broad categories: externalizing and internalizing. Externalizing behaviors are characterized by acting out, aggression, interfering, attention-getting, and conduct problems. Internalizing behaviors are viewed as more self-directed, such as being anxious, worried, and depressed.

There are seven main classifications of emotional and behavioral disorders (Vaughn et al., 2003). Some of these classifications fit the externalizing category, some fit the internalizing category, and some fit both.

- *Conduct Disorder.* Behaviors associated with conduct disorder and aggression include hitting, fighting, throwing, temper tantrums, teasing, acting defiant or disobedient, destroying property, bullying, being physically cruel to others, lying, and deceiving.

- *Hyperactivity.* This term refers to restless, overactive behavior. These students tend to be tense, unable to relax, and overly talkative; have difficulty being quiet; and run or move excessively.

- *Socialized Aggression.* This term refers to students who routinely engage in antisocial behavior. This may involve hanging around the wrong kinds of kids, displaying behaviors that are not typical of the age group, harassing others, and stealing and damaging property.

- *Pervasive Developmental Disorder.* This involves students expressing far-fetched, unusual, or unbelievable ideas. This may involve repetitive speech and unusual behaviors such as excessive rocking, nail biting, and head knocking.

- *Immaturity.* Behaviors associated with immaturity include lack of perseverance, failure to finish tasks, a short attention span, poor concentration, and frequent daydreaming or preoccupation. These students may show little interest in schoolwork and may need prodding to participate.

- *Depression.* Depression involves prolonged and persistent feelings of dejection that interfere with life functioning.

- *Anxiety–Withdrawal.* Anxiety refers to extreme worry, fearfulness, and concern (even when little reason for those feelings exists). Withdrawal describes the typical behavior of students who are anxious or depressed: they frequently withdraw from others and appear seclusive, preferring solitary activities.

To effectively address emotional and behavioral behaviors, you must establish an academic community and climate that promote learning and acceptance of all students, including students with the problems. No single approach to intervention works for all students with emotional or behavioral problems. However, a systematic, well-organized plan along with documentation of behavior changes will help you determine whether an intervention is working. Here are several strategies to help address students with these problem behaviors (Vaughn et al., 2003).

1. *Maintain an Organized Physical Environment.* Students with emotional and behavioral disorders work best in organized, structured environments in which materials, equipment, and personal items are well maintained, neatly arranged, and presented in a predictable way.

2. *Establish Positive Relationships.* Creating a positive classroom climate is important for all students, but especially so for students with emotional and behavior disorders. Develop trust by acting in a predictable way and doing what you say you will do. Exhibit caring and respectful behavior to all students, and create an emotionally supportive environment.

3. *Guide Changes in Student Behavior.* Establish reasonable classroom rules and procedures. Enforce them with consistency and supportive guidance.

4. *Resolve Conflicts and Promote Self-Control.* Consider having students prepare a conflict report when an incident occurs. This includes a description of the incident and decisions about ways to avoid the conflict in the future along with personal goal setting.

5. *Adapt Instruction.* Keep students occupied with purposeful activities. Provide instruction that allows all students to succeed. Also, group students in various ways to provide opportunities for students to learn academically and socially.

VOICES FROM THE CLASSROOM | *Calming an Emotionally Disturbed Student*

Jane Holzapfel, middle school computer literacy teacher, Houston, Texas

Emotionally disturbed students need a different approach to deal with misbehavior. By the time these students reach the middle school, every form of discipline has been tried on them.

I had one such student, Shantana, who was an eighth grader enrolled in my computer literacy class. On the first day, she entered my classroom on the offensive by announcing that she didn't belong in a class with any seventh graders. She demanded that I change her schedule and then was verbally abusive with the other students. She almost pulled one boy's pants down trying to take his chair away.

I needed something to calm Shantana whenever she came into the room upset. Talking with her only escalated her unacceptable behavior. I discovered that by gently putting some hand cream on her hands and stroking her hands slowly in mine, the tenseness of her body began to relax and so did her verbal mood. The stroking of her hands let her know that I cared and that she was accepted by me even though I did not always approve of her behavior.

Most days, she calmed down enough to make it possible for me to begin the lesson without her abusive language toward me or the other students. Sometimes she would resist the hand cream gesture, but I persisted and soon it became the ritual that redirected her behavior. Occasionally several other students would ask to join us for hand cream. Together we shared a minute or two of hand rubbing, and the class seemed to work even harder on those days.

Students with Attention Deficit and Hyperactivity Disorder (ADHD)

Attention deficit and hyperactivity disorder (ADHD) is a behavior syndrome involving poor attention span, hyperactivity, and weak impulse control. These traits generally inhibit learning and lead to misbehavior. It is estimated that 3 to 5 percent of school-age children in the United States have ADHD, with far more boys than girls affected (Wodrich, 2000).

Characteristics of ADHD are outlined in Table 9.1. Four conditions must be met for a positive diagnosis: (1) six or more symptoms must be present, (2) the symptoms have persisted for at least six months, (3) the symptoms originally appeared before the age of seven, and (4) the symptoms must result in impaired functioning in at least two settings (e.g., home and school).

Table 9.1   Symptoms of Attention Deficit and Hyperactivity Disorder (ADHD)

Inattention

Fails to give close attention or makes careless mistakes that are inconsistent with the student's developmental level

Fails to sustain attention to tasks or play

Fails to listen, even when spoken to directly

Fails to complete tasks

Has difficulty with organization

Resists working on tasks that require sustained attention

Loses materials and objects

Becomes easily distracted

Is forgetful

Hyperactivity

Fidgets or squirms

Has a difficult time remaining seated during class

Runs or climbs excessively when it is not appropriate

Has difficulty playing quietly

Acts as though he or she is "driven by a motor"

Talks too much

Impulsivity

Blurts out answers

Has difficulty waiting for his or her turn

Interrupts others or butts into activities

Here are some ways to work effectively with ADHD students (Attention Deficit Disorder Association, 2005; Hogan, 1997; McFarland, Kolstad, & Briggs, 1995; Stevens, 2000):

- *Maintain a Schedule and Have Consistent Daily Routines.* Post rules and schedules in the room and also on index cards on the students' desks.

- *Establish Clear Standards of Behavior.* State expectations and have realistic, predictable consequences for infractions.

- *Prepare Students for Transitions and Provide Support in Completing Transitions.* Alert students to an upcoming transition (e.g., "We'll be going to recess in three minutes. Finish what you are doing and put your materials away."). Continue with encouraging statements (e.g., "You have all your materials away. Now all you need to do is line up when I call your table.")

- *Assign Work That Is Within the Student's Capabilities.* The material may need to be broken into a series of smaller, shorter tasks.

- *Emphasize Time Limits.* Draw attention the amount of time students have for classroom activities and emphasize due dates.

- *Use Novelty in Instructions and Directions.* Highlight important instructions and key words with colored pens, highlight markers, or boldface print.

- *Be Brief and Clear*. Include only essential information in directions to be as clear and direct as possible, Break up lengthy directions into smaller segments.

- *Arrange the Environment to Facilitate Attention*. Carefully select the seating arrangement so ADHD students do not have distractions near them. Keep the room uncluttered and well organized to minimize distractions.

- *Allow for Movement and Postures Other Than Sitting*. Arrange activities so that they include movement as part of the activity, such as using manipulatives, drawing, or going to the board.

- *Provide Organizational Assistance*. Provide guidance for how students can organize their desks, materials, notebooks, and planners.

- *Provide Rewards Consistently and Often*. Positive feedback about performance and behavior is important for all students, but it should be increased for ADHD students. Use frequent reinforcement in the form of nods, smiles, pats on the back, and words of praise.

- *Avoid Fatigue, Stress, and Pressure*. These factors may overwhelm students' self-control and lead to inappropriate behavior. Provide opportunities for rest, relaxation, and movement.

- *Be Accepting of These Students' Limitations*. Much of their behavior is not intentional and cannot be completely eliminated.

Students with Speech and Language Disorders

Speech and language disorders are two types of communication disorders that require attention. Individuals with *speech disorders* have difficulty with the verbal means of communication. The major components of speech are articulation, fluency, and voice. Articulation has to do with the production of speech sounds, fluency refers to the flow and rhythm of language, and voice focuses on the quality of speech, including resonance, pitch, and intensity. *Language disorders* involve difficulties with content (the meaning of words and word combinations), form (the sounds of language, the rules of language, and grammar), and use of language in a social context (Vaughn et al., 2003).

Many students with speech or language disorders receive individual help outside the classroom, with the assistance of a speech teacher or a special education resource person. Within the classroom, potential negative consequences of speech and language disorders may affect the student's academic performance, self-concept, and relationship with peers. To minimize the negative consequences, the classroom teacher's role is to create a nonthreatening environment in which students can communicate through the use of strategies such as the following:

- Model appropriate language use at all times.
- Design instruction and select instructional strategies that promote language development.
- Give students many opportunities to speak without interruption or pressure.
- Ask open-ended questions and wait for responses.
- Listen attentively to what students have to say.
- Model acceptance for all students.

Students with Hearing Impairments

Students with hearing impairments may be deaf or may have partial hearing. Students with mild hearing impairments usually function well in the classroom, provided certain accommodations are made. Some students may need some type of sound amplification, such as with the use of a hearing aid. Other students may need interpreters or note takers; this person is often a paraprofessional.

Sometimes, accommodations must be individualized. However, the following strategies can be used by the regular classroom teacher to help students with hearing impairments (Vaughn et al., 2003):

- *Provide Preferential Seating.* Minimize the listening distance by having the student sit near you and away from high traffic, noisy areas.
- *Minimize Nonmeaningful Environmental Noise.* Use carpets or other sound-softening devices. Avoid unnecessary background noise such as hallway noise or music.
- *Use Visual Clues and Demonstrations.* Face students directly when you talk, use an overhead projector rather than the board whenever possible, provide demonstrations, and use pictures and diagrams.
- *Maximize the Use of Visual Media.* Provide access to computers and to closed-caption television.
- *Monitor the Student's Understanding.* Ask the student to repeat or rephrase important information or directions. Provide written directions and summaries.
- *Promote Cooperation and Collaboration.* Use peer and classroom tutors and note takers. Identify speakers in a group discussion. Inform interpreters of topics before class, and provide study guides or teaching notes.

VOICES FROM THE CLASSROOM   *Treat Students with Kindness*

Sandra Allen-Kearney, Fifth-Grade Teacher, Fort Pierce, Florida

At the beginning of every year, I always give all students a fresh slate when they enter my classroom, regardless of their past experiences. I treat all children with kindness, fairness, and consistency. I work very hard to help my at-risk, behaviorally challenged students feel loved and cared for, while setting the limits they desperately seek.

This philosophy has taken time and patience to nurture, but the rewards are tremendous. One day, I went to pick up my students from physical education, and I saw one of my most challenging students wearing his jacket backwards. I calmly asked him to put it on correctly, and he quickly complied.

At this, the physical education teacher's mouth dropped. She confronted the student in an angry voice, "I told you to put on your jacket properly in class several times, and you refused. I even put you in time-out for refusing to obey me, and you still wouldn't do it. Why did you put your jacket on the right way when Mrs. Kearney asked you to, when you wouldn't do it for me?"

His simple reply was, "Because she's nice to me." I will never forget that moment, or that young man, when all of my hard work paid off in that one sentence. As we walked back to class, I had to turn away and wipe my eyes when he wasn't looking.

Students with Visual Impairments

Students who are blind or who have limited vision can perform successfully in the regular classroom with some accommodations, supplementary aids, and services. Students with severe visual impairments may use a Braille machine, use a cane or guide dog, or have a paraprofessional who works with them throughout the day. You may need to make adjustments in the physical layout of the classroom to enable the use of this equipment and services.

The regular classroom teacher can make adjustments to help students with visual impairments be successful, such as the following.

- Have concrete examples students can touch.
- Provide sufficient lighting and avoid glare.
- Provide written copies of materials you place on the board or overhead projector.
- Allow a peer to take notes for the student.
- Provide opportunities for students to work in groups, especially when the assignment has a visual component.
- Modify writing activities as necessary by permitting students to dictate into a tape recorder.
- Describe the location of things in the room and remove clutter.
- Provide access to an electrical outlet for a tape recorder, lamp, or other electrical device.
- Ask the student what can be done to help him or her.

Students with Physical and Health Impairments

Students with significant physical disabilities and health impairments generally qualify for special education services under the Individuals with Disabilities Education Act (IDEA, 1997). *Orthopedic impairments* are skeletal and muscle problems that adversely affect a student's educational performance. These impairments may be caused by disease (e.g., polio, tuberculosis), might be congenital (such as clubfoot or absence of a limb), or be the result of a physical trauma such as amputations, fractures, burns, or cerebral palsy. *Health impairments* involve limited strength, vitality, or alertness due to chronic or acute health problems such as a heart condition, asthma, sickle-cell anemia, or epilepsy that affect a student's educational performance.

When accommodating students with physical and health impairments in your classroom, you should use others as resources, be flexible in your planning, and be ingenious and creative. Consider the following guidelines:

- *Use Resource People.* Resource people are typically available to provide guidance and assistance in the education of these students, including special education teachers, an occupational or physical therapist, or an adaptive physical education teacher.

- *Use Adaptive Technology.* Various types of electronic and mechanical equipment may be needed to provide a supportive environment for the impaired students.

• *Make Environmental Modifications.* Depending on the nature of the impairments, you may need to change the location of materials and equipment, make changes in work surfaces, modify objects (such as providing clips on a student's desk), and provide manipulation aids.

• *Educate Classmates.* Inform the classmates about the impaired student's condition in an effort to promote understanding, cooperation, realistic attitudes, and assistance.

• *Ask the Student What Could Be Done to Help.* Direct communication is often the best means to identify the most useful ways to make needed accommodations.

STUDENTS WITH LIMITED ENGLISH PROFICIENCY

There is tremendous language diversity in the United States, and it is not uncommon for a school district to have students representing numerous languages. According to the U.S. Census Bureau, in 2002, one in five U.S. residents aged five or older spoke a language other than English at home. The National Clearinghouse for English Language Acquisition reported in 2002 that about 4.4 million students have limited English proficiency. It has been estimated that about 7.3 percent of all public school students have limited English proficiency, and the great majority spends most or part of their time in English-only classrooms (Nieto, 2004).

Some students whose first language is not English may have acquired sufficient English language skills to perform in English-only classes. Others have not acquired sufficient skill in speaking, reading, or writing English and they need additional assistance. Schools have various types of programs to deliver assistance. If you have some students in your classroom who speak limited or no English, here are some strategies to use in communicating and teaching (Cary, 2000; Kottler & Kottler, 2002):

• Provide a safe environment for language risk taking.
• Increase time and opportunities for meaningful talk.
• Encourage English speaking while honoring students' first language and culture.
• Offer periodic summaries and paraphrases.
• Emphasize collaborative over individual work.
• Emphasize process over product, wholes over pieces.
• Think aloud and model a variety of reading comprehension strategies.
• Use a variety of reading supports such as text tours and picture walks (to preview the material), graphic organizers (story maps, character analyses), and text signposts (chapter headings, bold print).
• Encourage students to write about topics of their choice for real-world purposes.
• Use a variety of writing supports, such as group composing, graphic organizers, and drawing-based texts.
• Use sheltered instruction, which focuses on core curriculum content and uses a rich variety of techniques and materials such as artifacts, visuals, videos, movement, role-plays, and collaborative learning.

WHAT WOULD YOU DECIDE? *Limited English Proficiency*

It is possible that your next teaching assignment will include a number of students with limited English proficiency representing several languages. It is likely that you do not speak four languages and thus could not communicate directly with the students in their first language.

1. Where would you get resources for teaching students with limited English proficiency?

2. How might you use paraprofessionals, parent volunteers, and even the other students as assistants in your instruction of students with limited English proficiency?

STUDENTS WHO ARE TROUBLED

You may have students who have difficulty with their academic work and their behavior due to exceptionally challenging circumstances in their lives. Some students may have been the victims of circumstances beyond their control, such as having been abused or neglected, living in extreme poverty, or having parents who are abusing alcohol or drugs. Other students may do things that place themselves at risk, such as being prone to violence, abusing alcohol or drugs, having eating orders, or being depressed (cf., Frieman, 2001).

These are not your usual students, and the origins of their academic or behavioral problems initially may not be apparent. Significant deviations in a student's behavior may signal the presence of a problem. Some students exhibit those deviations from the first day they walk into your classroom.

When you notice atypical behavior, it is helpful to ask yourself a few questions to clarify the situation (Kottler & Kottler, 2000): What is unusual about this student's behavior? Is there a pattern to what I have observed? What additional information do I need to make an informed judgment? Whom might I contact to collect this background information? What are the risks of waiting longer to figure out what is going on? Does this student seem to be in any imminent danger? Whom can I consult about this case? These questions can provide guidance for analyzing the situation and deciding on a course of action. Now let's examine some of these circumstances that students find troublesome and challenging.

Substance Abuse

Substance abuse can profoundly affect the behavior of individuals. Students may be affected in two ways—they may be the children of substance abusing parents or the students themselves may be abusing drugs and alcohol.

Students Who Abuse Drugs and Alcohol

Just over 50 percent of high school students report they use alcohol at least once a month (Bosworth, 1997). The use of illicit drugs is almost as prevalent. About 40 percent of high school seniors admit they have used an illicit drug at least once, and 24 percent say they used drugs at least once a month. Illicit drugs include amphetamines, cocaine, inhalants, marijuana, and phencyclidine (PCP).

Students who abuse drugs and alcohol may exhibit a number of troublesome behaviors. They may not have regular school attendance, may often be tardy, be disruptive in class, and have academic problems. Your job is to identify students who have a problem and make sure they get professional help. Refer the student to the school counselor, nurse, or other appropriate support personnel.

Children of Substance Abusing Parents

According to the National Institute on Drug Abuse in 1998, 20 percent of children in the United States grow up in alcoholic families (Johnson, 2001). Alcoholic families exhibit greater levels of openly expressed anger and lower levels of warmth, cohesion, and direct communication than nonalcoholic families. Furthermore, alcohol is a significant factor in approximately 81 percent of child abuse cases (Johnson, 2001).

Children of substance abusers never experience what it is like to grow up in a normal family where parents are there to take care of them. These children face an array of troubling feelings, including guilt, anxiety, embarrassment, and depression. Their school performance is impaired. When they are older, they are more likely to drop out of school (McGrath, Watson, & Chassin, 1999; Post & Robinson, 1998).

Here are some things you can do to help children whose parents are substance abusers (Frieman, 2001):

- *Expect the Student to Perform at a High Level.* Do not prejudge, and expect the best.
- *Have a Consistent Learning Environment.* Provide a degree of regularity and structure with the schedule and routines. Have expectations for appropriate behavior, and enforce them in a consistent manner.
- *Keep in Control.* As the authority figure in the classroom, you control how the lessons are taught and how the students behave.
- *Hold Students Responsible for Their Own Behavior.* Frequently children of substance abusers have many responsibilities for caring for younger siblings and maintaining the household. You can help by involving them in projects where they are responsible only for their own behavior.
- *Set Limits When Necessary.* As much as you might feel compassion considering their home lives, you must still be consistent in monitoring and enforcing the classroom rules. Be sure to communicate the message that "I like you, but I don't like what you are doing."
- *Provide a Quiet Place to Work.* Children of substance abusers often have many disruptions at home and thus are not able to study and complete homework at home. You could provide a quiet area during school for the student to deal with schoolwork.

Students Who Have Been Abused or Neglected

Many children suffer from physical, emotional, or sexual abuse, and many more may be the victims of neglect by their parents or guardian. Teachers are among those required

Table 9.2 Recognizing Child Abuse and Neglect

Recognizing Child Abuse

The following signs in the child may signal the presence of child abuse or neglect.

- Shows sudden changes in behavior or school performance.
- Has not received help for physical or medical problems brought to the parents' attention.
- Has learning problems (or difficulty concentrating) that cannot be attributed to specific physical or psychological causes.
- Is always watchful, as though preparing for something bad to happen.
- Lacks adult supervision.
- Is overly compliant, passive, or withdrawn.
- Comes to school or other activities early, stays late, and does not want to go home.

Signs of Physical Abuse

Consider the possibility of physical abuse when the child:

- Has unexplained burns, bites, bruises, broken bones, or black eyes.
- Has fading bruises or other marks noticeable after an absence from school.
- Seems frightened of the parents and protests or cries when it is time to go home.
- Shrinks at the approach of adults.
- Reports injury by a parent or another adult caregiver.

Signs of Neglect

Consider the possibility of neglect when the child:

- Is frequently absent from school.
- Begs or steals food or money.
- Lacks needed medical or dental care, immunizations, or glasses.
- Is consistently dirty and has severe body odor.
- Lacks sufficient clothing for the weather.
- Abuses alcohol or other drugs.
- States that there is no one at home to provide care.

Signs of Sexual Abuse

Consider the possibility of sexual abuse when the child:

- Has difficulty walking or sitting.
- Suddenly refuses to change for gym or to participate in physical activities.
- Reports nightmares or bedwetting.
- Experiences a sudden change in appetite.
- Demonstrates bizarre, sophisticated, or unusual sexual knowledge or behavior.
- Becomes pregnant or contracts a venereal disease, particularly if under age 14.
- Runs away.
- Reports sexual abuse by a parent or another adult caregiver.

Signs of Emotional Maltreatment

Consider the possibility of emotional maltreatment when the child:

- Shows extremes in behavior, such as overly compliant or demanding behavior, extreme passivity, or aggression.
- Is either inappropriately adult (e.g., parenting other children) or inappropriately infantile (e.g., frequently rocking or head-banging).
- Is delayed in physical or emotional development.
- Has attempted suicide.
- Reports a lack of attachment to the parent.

---

by law to report suspected cases of child abuse or neglect. In 1974, Congress passed the Child Abuse Prevention and Treatment Act to provide financial support to states that implemented programs for identification, prevention, and treatment of child abuse and neglect.

During 2003, an estimated 2.9 million referrals alleging child abuse and neglect where received by child protective services for investigation. In that year, there were approximately 906,000 children who were determined to be victims of child abuse or neglect by the child protective service agencies (U.S. Department of Health and Human Services, 2005). Ways to recognize child abuse and neglect are outlined in Table 9.2, with content adapted from the National Clearinghouse on Child Abuse and Neglect Information (2003).

Students Prone to Violence, Vandalism, and Bullying

Violence and crime occur in communities, and that often shows up in schools to some degree. Some students seem prone to violent behavior, and they can cause considerable disturbance in schools. Some of these disruptive behaviors in schools are disturbing but not serious. A nationally representative survey of 2,270 public schools was conducted in 1999–2000, and the results were reported in *Crime and Safety in America's Public Schools* by the National Center for Education Statistics (NCES, 2004). For disorders in schools that were viewed as serious but not considered violent, student bullying (29 percent) was reported to be the most serious discipline problem, followed by students' acts of disrespect for teachers (19 percent), undesirable gang activities (19 percent), student verbal abuse of teachers (13 percent), and undesirable cult or extremist group activities (13 percent).

However, schools in that survey also reported serious violent incidents. These included rape, sexual battery other than rape, physical attacks or fights with a weapon, threats of physical attacks with a weapon, and robberies either with or without a weapon. In 1999–2000, 71 percent of public elementary and secondary schools experienced at least one violent incident. Approximately 1.5 million violent incidents occurred in 59,000 public schools that year. The most serious violence was experienced by a small percentage of schools.

Specific crimes reported by the public schools in that survey (NCES, 2004) included physical attacks or fights without a weapon (64 percent), threats of physical attack without a weapon (52 percent), vandalism (51 percent), theft or larceny (46 percent), possession of a knife or sharp object (43 percent), sexual harassment (36 percent), possession or use of alcohol or illegal drugs (27 percent), and distribution of illegal drugs (12 percent).

One approach to reducing the level of crime and violence in schools is to provide students with training intended to prevent certain behaviors. During the 1999–2000 school year, the most frequently reported program components were counseling, social work, psychological or therapeutic activity for the students (66 percent); behavioral or behavior modification intervention for students (66 percent); prevention training (65 percent); individual attention, mentoring, tutoring, or coaching (63 percent); and programs to promote a sense of community and social integration among students (57 percent) (NCES, 2004).

Students Living in Poverty

The 2004 federal poverty level for a family of four was $18,850. However, research by the National Center for Children in Poverty (NCCP, 2005) has shown that, on average, families of four need an income that is twice that amount (i.e., $37,700) to meet their most basic needs for food, clothing, shelter, health care, and child care; NCCP describes families below this level as being *low income*.

Here are the percentages and number of children in families in the United States related to the family incomes (NCCP, 2005). These figures show that 38 percent and about 27 million children in the United States are from low-income families.

17 percent of children—more than 11 million—live in poor families below the federal poverty level

21 percent of children—about 16 million—live in low-income families with incomes between the federal poverty level and twice the federal poverty level

62 percent of children—about 43 million—live in families above low income

Child poverty can be found in suburban, rural, and urban areas and across all races and ethnicities. However, there are variations by race and ethnicity. About 26 percent of white children are from low-income families, while 60 percent of black children and 62 percent of Latino children come from low-income families (NCCP, 2005). Furthermore, 35 percent of children of native-born parents are from low-income families while 58 percent of children of immigrant parents are from low-income families.

In *A Framework for Understanding Poverty*, Ruby Payne (2001) describes how there are different hidden rules of behavior depending on one's class and family income. She outlines how children from poverty, from the middle class, and from wealth think and behave differently about issues such as possessions, money, social emphasis, clothing, time, education, destiny, and language. Payne maintains that teachers must understand children of poverty to make decisions to effectively guide their education and behavior.

Payne (2001) points out that many of the behaviors that children of poverty bring to school are necessary to help them survive outside of the school. Children of poverty may laugh when disciplined, argue loudly with the teacher, have angry responses, use inappropriate or vulgar language, be disrespectful to teachers, be disorganized, and talk a great deal. Payne maintains that offering structure and choice in the classroom are two aspects of a discipline plan that will help students move toward self-governance.

Often children in low-income families, especially children of poverty, lag behind their more affluent peers in academic, physical, emotional, and social development. They may not have the going-to-school skills that many students have, and they will benefit from specific strategies and support from the teachers. Here are some suggestions (Frieman, 2001; Hargis, 1997):

- *Provide Free Learning Materials.* Seek out free resources or donations for extra instructional materials or special field trips or activities. Have extra supplies available in case some of your students don't have them.

- *Facilitate After-School Programs.* Schools may be the only safe place in the neighborhood, and many students may not want to leave at the end of the school day. Provide opportunities for activities or study after school.

- *Subsidize School Expenses.* Dances, sports, or other events can be expensive. Work with others in your school to find ways to keep costs low or to provide donations.
- *Treat Students with Respect.* Ensure that your classroom is emotionally and physically safe. Interact with your students in a respectful manner.
- *Teach Procedures in a Step-by-Step Manner to Clarify Expectations.* Point out expectations, describe why the procedure exists, and show how to complete the strategy.
- *Permit Students to Work Together.* This enables students to discuss problems and solutions together, and also allows students to help another student with something they do well.

Developing Your Management Plan: *Helping Students with Special Needs*

From one year to the next, you will not know ahead of time about the specific characteristics of your students. But you can count on the fact that some of your students will have special needs as discussed in this chapter. You will first need to meet your students and identify any special needs they might have, and then you would make plans to guide their instruction and behavior taking their special needs into consideration.

However, you can take some preliminary steps to be ready for any students with special needs in your classroom. Seek out the following information and keep copies of information in file folders for when you need to use it when working with your students. Consider how these issues will influence your overall plan for classroom management and discipline.

1. Identify resources in your school, district, and state that provide guidance to address students with particular special needs. These may include policy manuals, guidebooks with instructional tips, assessment information, and instructional materials.

2. Identify resources from professional organizations and government agencies that provide guidance, materials, and additional links to resources. A Web search, for example, on ADHD may result in useful instructional and behavior management strategies.

Students Facing Serious Challenges

The students already discussed in this chapter experience challenges due to their disability, their language, and other factors. However, some students face serious and exceptionally challenging situations in their lives that greatly influence their attendance and performance in school. While there are a number of these serious challenges, the issues of homelessness, eating disorders, depression, and suicide are addressed here.

Homelessness

Homeless children do not have a regular or adequate residence and may be living with others, in cars, motels, bus or train stations, campgrounds, or shelters (Council for Exceptional Children, 2003). Approximately 1.4 million children or 2 percent of the students in the United States are likely to become homeless during the school year (Bernstein, 2000).

When families become homeless, they are often forced to move frequently. Length-of-stay restrictions in shelters, short stays with friends or relatives, and relocation to seek employment make it difficult for homeless children to attend school regularly. In addition, guardianship requirements, delays in transfer of school records, lack of a permanent address, and/or lack of immunization records often prevent homeless children from enrolling in school. If they are able to enroll, they may not be able to get to school because of lack of transportation. Children who miss school frequently fall behind very quickly (National Coalition for the Homeless, 2001). Homeless students also may have few recreational opportunities; little privacy; and limited access to meals, books, school materials, and toys.

The McKinney Homeless Assistance Act, passed in 1987 and amended four times since, is a federal law that guarantees homeless children the right to a free, appropriate education in a mainstream school environment, and seeks to eliminate barriers to their attendance. Some school districts have developed strategies for educating homeless students (Holloway, 2003; Rafferty, 1998). These strategies include providing transportation to frequently changing residences, specialized instruction, and tutoring; meals, showers, school materials, and clothes; medical care, counseling, and other supportive services; and after-school and full-year programs to meet these students' basic and recreational needs.

In addition to provisions the school may make, classroom teachers can be powerful influences on the lives of children who are homeless. On a personal level, classroom teachers can listen and talk to the student to encourage healthy expression of emotions, recognize and accept emotions, be sensitive to different types of family situations in class discussions, and communicate with the parents to the extent possible.

Teachers also can provide academic assistance to children who are homeless in various ways such as the following:

- Partner students with classmates to serve as mentor or buddy concerning procedures in the classroom and the school.
- Find volunteers who can tutor the student at the school or at the student's shelter.
- Provide the student with needed supplies to do homework at the shelter.
- Check into services provided by the school or district for children who are homeless.
- Work with other counselors, special education teachers, or other resource people in the school to meet the needs of the children who are homeless.

Eating Disorders

Advertising, fashion, entertainment, and other factors sometimes give students the impression that they need to have the "perfect body." Some students are significantly influenced by this and may take actions to keep their weight down by unhealthy means. Students who participate in sports, who are perfectionists, and who experience loss of personal relationships (e.g., family death or breakups) are particularly susceptible to developing some type of eating disorder (Manley, Rickson, & Standeven, 2000).

Bulimia involves binging on food followed by attempts to get rid of the extra food and calories by vomiting, taking medications or laxatives, fasting, or exercising.

Fifteen to 18 percent of high school students show bulimic symptoms (Crago, Shisslak, & Estes, 1996). *Anorexia*, which is less prevalent than bulimia, involves refusal to eat and a disturbed sense of one's body shape or size, which results in thinness and loss of weight that is denied by the individual. Five to 10 percent of cases of anorexia nervosa are males (Crosscope-Happel, Hutchins, Getz, & Hayes, 2000). Both conditions affect one's health, emotional development, and school performance, and can be life-threatening.

You can help these students by being aware of the warning signs of the conditions. Some signs are frequent requests to go to the restroom, dental problems, bad breath, and hair loss (Manley et al., 2000). You also can reflect on your comments, behaviors, and attitudes regarding body image; model healthy attitudes and behaviors; and make sure students are not ridiculed because of their appearance.

Depression and Suicide

Adolescents and young adults often experience stress, confusion, and depression from situations occurring in their families, schools, and communities. Such feelings can overwhelm young people, cause them to be depressed, and lead them to consider suicide as a "solution." About eight percent of adolescents are depressed in any given year and five percent of youth between 9 and 17 years old are depressed, but only a minority of these youth are treated (Stanard, 2000).

According to the Centers for Disease Control and Prevention (2005), suicide is the third leading cause of death among young people ages 15 to 24. In 2001, 3,971 suicides were reported in this group. Of the total number of suicides among ages 15 to 24 in 2001, 86 percent were male and 14 percent were female.

Although most individuals who are depressed do not attempt or commit suicide, there is a high correlation between depression and suicide (Bostic, Rustuccia, & Schlozman, 2001). You should be aware of the warning signs of depression, such as:

- Overwhelming sadness, apathy, irritability, and hopelessness
- Pervasive difficulty in concentrating, remembering, or making decisions
- A sense of inappropriate guilt, worthlessness, or helplessness
- A dramatic drop in school performance
- A radical change in personality
- Noticeable neglect of personal hygiene, dress, and health care

You should be aware of school policies dealing with depressed and suicidal students, make appropriate referrals, provide adequate supervision, and document and report your specific observations and changes in students' behavior.

MAIN POINTS

1. About 13 percent of the school population is enrolled in special education programs. The largest numbers among these students, in descending order, are categorized as having specific learning disabilities, speech impairments, mental retardation, emotional disturbance, health impairments, mobility impairments, hearing impairments, autism, and visual impairments.

2. Regular classroom teachers can make modifications to instruction and management based on the particular disability.

3. About 7.3 percent of all public school students have limited English proficiency, and the great majority spends most or part of their time in English-only classrooms where teachers can make necessary instructional modifications.

4. Some students may have been the victims of circumstances beyond their control, such as having been abused or neglected, living in extreme poverty, or having parents who are abusing alcohol or drugs. Other students may do things that place themselves at risk, such as abusing alcohol or drugs and being prone to violence.

5. Some students face serious and exceptionally challenging situations in their lives that greatly influence their attendance and performance in school, including being homeless, having an eating disorder, and being depressed and considering suicide.

DISCUSSION/REFLECTIVE QUESTIONS

1. Think about your K–12 schooling and recall any classmates who had disabilities. What special provisions did the teacher make for the instructional needs of these students?

2. When making instructional modifications for students with limited English proficiency, how might the other students in the class benefit?

3. If you have a student who is prone to physical behavior and violence, what can you do in your classroom to protect the other students and secure their safety?

4. Do you know anyone who was abused or neglected as a K–12 student? How did that influence the person's conduct and performance in school? What can teachers do to help?

5. If you had a student in your class who was homeless, would you discuss this with the other students in the class? Why or why not?

SUGGESTED ACTIVITIES

1. Students with emotional and behavioral disorders work best in organized, structured environments. Make a list of ways that you can create that structure through your classroom layout and the way you organize and deliver lessons.

2. Select the topic of a daily lesson that you might teach and identify five things that you could plan into the lesson to make appropriate adjustments for limited English proficient students.

3. Seek out and read some resources concerning ways to deal with bullying students.

4. If you teach students who come from low-income families, identify ways that you might provide free learning materials, facilitate after-school programs, and subsidize school expenses.

FURTHER READING

Freiman, Barry B. (2001). *What teachers need to know about children at risk*. New York: McGraw-Hill.
An excellent, concise resource describing the basics about at-risk conditions and how to identify and help students who are at risk. Organized within psychological, physiological, and social conditions. Examples of at-risk conditions covered include children (1) with behavioral problems or chronic medical conditions; (2) who are alienated, gifted, homeless, or raised by grandparents; and (3) influenced by poverty, violence, or abusive parents.

Herrera, Socorro G., & Murry, Kevin G. (2005). *Mastering ESL and bilingual methods: Differentiated instruction for culturally and linguistically diverse (CLD) students*. Boston: Allyn & Bacon.
Provides foundational information about accommodative instruction, discusses issues of readiness, and offers a number of ways to differentiate instruction for culturally and linguistically diverse students.

Payne, Ruby K. (2004). *A framework for understanding poverty* (rev. ed.). Highlands, TX: aha! Process, Inc.

Describes the characteristics and implications for students living in poverty. Provides insight into ways that teachers and students see the world differently and identifies ways to effectively work with students in poverty.

VAUGHN, SHARON; BOS, CANDACE S.; & SCHUMM, JEANNE S. (2003). *Teaching exceptional, diverse, and at-risk students in the general education classroom* (3rd ed.). Boston: Allyn & Bacon.
Provides a comprehensive discussion about diverse student characteristics and thoroughly describes instructional modifications that are suitable. Also examines inclusive instructional approaches for the subject areas and for reading.

Chapter 10

Planning and Conducting Instruction

CHAPTER OBJECTIVES

This chapter provides information that will help you to:
- Select ways to structure lessons and group students.
- Identify ways to hold students academically accountable.
- Identify ways to handle administrative actions that are commonly taken at the start of a lesson.
- Identify actions that can be used at the start of a lesson to capture student interest and focus attention on the learning objectives.
- Identify teacher actions that contribute to effective group management during the middle part of a lesson.
- Identify actions that teachers take at the end of a lesson to provide for lesson summary and enable students to prepare to leave.
- Select ways to manage student work.

Classroom Management: Creating a Successful K-12 Learning Community/Third Edition, by Paul R. Burden
ISBN 0-471-71073-3   Copyright © 2006 John Wiley & Sons, Inc.

CHAPTER OUTLINE

When planning for a vacation trip, you often need to plan ahead. Do you want to stay in one place and relax, or do you want to visit a number of areas? Would you like to schedule several events for each day, or would you like to leave the daily schedule very open? What type of accommodations would you like?

To ensure an enjoyable vacation, you need to give these questions attention. Similarly, you need to give advance thought to the type of classroom you would like to have. How structured do you want your classroom and lessons? How do you want to group your students for instruction? How will you hold the students academically accountable? How will you handle various aspects of lesson delivery? These issues will be explored in this chapter. How you attend to these issues will make a difference in managing instruction and student behavior.

PLANNING DECISIONS AFFECT BEHAVIOR MANAGEMENT

Preparing daily lesson plans is a vital task for effective classroom management and discipline because effective, engaging lessons can keep students on task and can minimize misbehavior. You need to consider the degree of structure that will occur in each lesson. The grouping planned for the instructional activities will also affect student interaction. Furthermore, students are more likely to stay on task and be engaged in instruction when they know that they will be held academically accountable.

The Degree of Structure in Lessons

Many instructional strategies can be used, ranging from teacher-centered, explicit approaches to the presentation of content to student-centered, less explicit approaches. *Teacher-centered approaches* include lectures, demonstrations, questions, recitations, practice and drills, and reviews. *Student-centered approaches* include inquiry approaches, discovery learning and problem solving, role-playing and simulation, gaming, laboratory activities, computer-assisted instruction, and learning or activity centers. Various types of grouping and discussion methods may be student- or teacher-directed, depending on how they are used. Teacher-centered approaches are often more structured than student-centered approaches. As a result, the management issues will vary depending on the approach used.

When deciding on your instructional strategy, you need to weigh the advantages and disadvantages of the various strategies along with the lesson objectives. Effective teachers use several strategies ranging from teacher-directed to student-directed. The lesson objectives may determine what type of approach is most appropriate. Some content may lend itself to inquiry and discovery techniques, whereas other content may be better handled with direct instruction. Over time, students should be given the opportunity to learn through a variety of instructional strategies.

Ways to Group Students for Instruction

Group students in the way most appropriate for the instructional strategies and objectives. Focus on a group as a collection of individuals who learn. Within groups, each individual student observes, listens, responds, takes turns, and so on. Groups can be large or small. Whole-group, small-group, and independent work are options to consider; each affects student conduct and order.

Whole-Group Instruction

In whole-group instruction, the entire class is taught. It allows you to (a) lecture, demonstrate, and explain a topic; (b) ask and answer a question in front of the entire class; (c) provide the same recitation, practice, and drill exercises; (d) work on the same problems; and (e) use the same materials. You can still ask individual students to answer questions, monitor students as they work on assigned activities, and work with individual students. Even with whole-group instruction, however, you need to consider individual student differences.

VOICES FROM THE CLASSROOM   *Shuffling the Seating and Grouping*

Saralee Wittmer, Second-Grade Teacher, Amarillo, Texas

Students in my room are arranged in small groups of four students according to ability. I shuffle the mix every 4–6 weeks. Students get the chance to work with all other students and can sit close to the teacher, at the back of the room, close to the door, and up by the chalkboards.

Students are encouraged to discuss lessons with each other within their groups. It's amazing how much they learn from each other if we will only give them the opportunities. I can tell what the class might not have gotten from my lesson presentations by listening carefully to them when they are in their groups.

Small-Group Instruction

There are times when the objectives can be better met with small groups. In small-group instruction, students tend to be more actively engaged, and teachers can better monitor student progress. If there are more than six in a group, generally not everyone will actively participate. Educators recommend four or five students to a group (Cohen, 1994), with an upper limit of six (Johnson & Johnson, 1999).

Since group work helps develop relationships, it is useful to vary the membership of the groups based on gender and ethnicity. Students with disabilities can be placed in groups with nondisabled students, to integrate them into the mainstream classroom. While there may be good reasons for planning a homogeneous group for certain activities, educators in general recommend the use of heterogeneous groups (Cohen, 1994; Johnson & Johnson, 1999; Slavin, 1991).

Many teachers find that they can divide large classes into groups, committees, or teams, as needed, for their small-group and individualized techniques. Small groups, usually used in elementary school reading and mathematics, can be used in all grade levels and subjects. Small groups can be created based on issues such as student ability, interest, skill, viewpoint, activity, or integration (Cohen, 1994). Groups can be set up arbitrarily. There are three types of groupings: ability grouping, cooperative learning groups, and peer tutoring.

1. *Ability Grouping.* In ability grouping, students judged to be similar in their academic ability are grouped into classes. Within-class grouping involves creating subgroups within a class, with each subgroup being fairly homogeneous in ability. Within-class grouping has been most widely researched in elementary math classes, and results suggest that small numbers of groups are better than large numbers. Group assignments can be flexible, role models for low achievers are available, teacher morale is higher, and the stigmatizing effect is minimized (Slavin, 2006).

2. *Cooperative Learning.* Cooperative learning is a grouping in which students work in small, mixed-ability learning teams. Such groups can be formed at various grade levels and in different subject areas. Through cooperative learning, students understand that they are responsible not only for their own learning but also for the learning of their team members. Cooperative learning approaches are often used to supplement other instructional practices. In spite of renewed interest, class sessions are structured for cooperative learning methods for only 7 to 20 percent of the time (Johnson et al., 1994).

Cooperative learning occurs in three different ways: (a) assignment of individual students to specific responsibilities within a larger group task or project; (b) assignment of students to a shared project or task; or (c) assignment to groups to study and be responsible for group members' learning. There are several common types of cooperative learning techniques. Additional resources on cooperative learning include Slavin (1991, 2006), Johnson and Johnson (2006), and Sharan and Sharan (1992).

3. *Peer Tutoring.* This approach involves students teaching students. The two types of peer tutoring are (a) cross-age tutoring, in which older students work with younger ones; and (b) peer tutoring, in which students within the same class work together. There are several advantages of peer tutoring (Johnson & Johnson, 1999): (a) peer tutors are often effective in teaching students who do not respond well to adults;

(b) peer tutoring can develop a bond of friendship between the tutor and tutored, which is important for integrating slow learners into the group; (c) peer tutoring allows the teacher to teach a large group of students while giving slow learners the individual attention they need; and (d) tutors benefit by learning to teach.

Peer tutoring can be used at all grade levels. Before having students work in pairs, you will need to clarify the purposes of the tutoring, obtain the necessary materials, and provide an appropriate work area where the students can work without disturbing other students. You might offer some guidance about working and studying together.

Independent Work

You might give students opportunities to work on tasks of their own choosing, or you may assign activities that enable students to work alone. Good and Brophy (2003) found that one-third of elementary teachers attempt to individualize instruction and that one-fifth of secondary teachers attempt to do so.

When assigning independent work, you may involve students in any of a number of instructional strategies. In inquiry and discovery instructional approaches, students learn about the process of discovery by collecting data and testing hypotheses. Teachers guide students as they discover new meanings, practice the skills, and undergo the experiences that will shape their learning. These approaches include computer-assisted instruction, learning centers, learning stations, laboratories, discovery techniques, and others.

Not all independent work involves inquiry approaches. *Mastery learning* is an individualized instructional approach that uses a structured curriculum divided into small sets of knowledge and skills to be learned (Bloom, 1981). It is designed to make sure all students achieve the lesson's objectives and to allow each student enough time to do so. Mastery learning is based on traditional group instruction and individual remediation and enrichment.

Planning to Hold Students Academically Accountable

Procedures to help manage student work must be selected. Academic accountability means that the students must complete certain activities related to the instructional objectives. Teacher responsibilities for holding students academically accountable are displayed in Table 10.1, some of which are adapted from Emmer et al. (2006), Evertson et al. (2006), and Jones and Jones (2004).

Consider the following guidelines when holding students academically accountable:

• *Determine a System of Grading (e.g., letter grades or numerical grades, and measures for nonachievement outcomes).* This decision may have been made for you by the school district as reflected in the report card format. Use a variety of evaluation measures (e.g., tests, written or oral reports, homework, ratings, projects) throughout the marking period, and describe the grading system to the students.

• *Make Decisions About Assignments.* Decide on where and how you will post assignments, as well as the requirements and criteria for grading. Students should understand that completed assignments are part of the grading system.

- *Decide on Work and Completion Requirements.* Students need to have guidelines or work requirements for the various assignments. Details about due dates, late work, and missed assignments due to absence should be explained. The relevant procedures will help students understand expectations held of them and should minimize questions on a case by case basis.

- *Monitor Student Progress and Completion of the Assignments.* You may want to use some in class activities as formative exercises for students but not count performance on these in your grading. The activities may be written, oral, or performance demonstrations. Student progress should be monitored. In many cases, the entire class is at work on the designated activity; this enables you to walk around and observe each student carefully to see how the student is progressing.

- *Provide Students with Feedback About Their Progress.* Feedback on in class activities may take the form of statements to the individuals or to the class. Students may exchange papers to evaluate progress on formative exercises. Papers or projects that are to be part of the report card grade should be collected, graded, and returned promptly. In this way, students receive regular feedback about their progress throughout the marking period. Computer programs available for maintaining a grade book can easily generate progress reports for both students and teacher.

VOICES FROM THE CLASSROOM   *Promoting Student Accountability by Posting a Weekly Agenda*

James Roussin, Grades 7–12 English and Literature Teacher, Big Lake, Minnesota

I have found that it is important for students to be aware of the classroom agenda for the week so they can take appropriate actions to prepare for tests or turn in assignments. I post a weekly agenda on the blackboard every Monday morning. I have found this to be extremely useful. In this way, students have a clear idea of what the week will look like and what is expected of them. This weekly agenda also helps if students are absent; they just need to look at the board to see what was missed.

If we cannot get to everything that has been scheduled in the weekly agenda, I collaborate with the class to determine what should be deleted or extended; this allows the students to feel that they are part of the overall planning in the class.

I use various colors on the weekly agenda to emphasize the particular assignments the students will be responsible for. For example, I write in a test with red chalk, a reading assignment in green, and a daily writing assignment in blue. The same colors are used throughout the school year.

The best part of this agenda is that it keeps me organized for the week. I can glance at the board and it will reveal to me if I have a variety of different activities for the lessons that week. One primary "learning goal" is also listed for each day, and this helps me and the students know what is essential in the lesson for that day.

MANAGING LESSON DELIVERY

You've finished your planning. You've selected the instructional strategies. You've prepared and gathered the instructional materials. Now it is the day of your lesson. You're all ready to begin, but wait. You also must recognize that you can take certain

Table 10.1 Holding Students Academically Accountable

Take into account the grade level and subject area when decisions are made on the following issues in an effort to hold students academically accountable.

1. The Grading System
   a. Select a grading system
   b. Select types of evaluation measures
   c. Determine how grades will be assigned
   d. Address nonachievement outcomes
   e. Communicate the grading system to students
   f. Design a grade book
   g. Report grades and communicate to parents
2. Assignments
   a. Post assignments
   b. State requirements and grading criteria for assignments
   c. Long-term assignments
3. Work and Completion Requirements
   a. Identify work requirements
      (1) Use of pencil or pen
      (2) Headings on papers
      (3) Writing on the back of the paper
      (4) Neatness and legibility guidelines
   b. Identify completion requirements
      (1) Due dates
      (2) Late work
      (3) Incomplete work
      (4) Missed work
   c. Make provisions for absent students and make-up work
      (1) Have an assignment list or folder
      (2) Identify a due date
      (3) Select a place to pick up and drop off absent assignments
      (4) Provide a regular time to assist students with make-up work
4. Monitoring Progress and Completion of Assignments
   a. Determine when and how to monitor in-class assignments
   b. Determine when and how to monitor longer assignments, projects, or works in progress
   c. Determine when and how to monitor in-class oral participation or performance
   d. Determine which activities will receive a grade and which will be used only for formative feedback for the student
   e. Select checking procedures that will be used in class
      (1) Students exchanging papers
      (2) Marking and grading papers
      (3) Turning in papers
5. Providing Feedback
   a. Decide what kind of feedback will be provided to students, and when it will be provided
   b. Determine what records students will keep concerning their progress
   c. Select incentives and rewards
   d. Record scores in the grade book
   e. Post selected student work

actions during your instruction that will help students stay on task and achieve the lesson objectives.

There are a number of actions that you can take at certain points in a lesson to manage the group effectively, maintain order and control, and fulfill various administrative and academic objectives. If these actions are not handled appropriately, it is likely that students will be more inclined to be off task and possibly misbehave. As a result, it is important to examine these lesson delivery tasks from the perspective of management and order in the classroom.

The Beginning of a Lesson

A successful lesson beginning can greatly contribute to a meaningful learning experience for students. The beginning of a lesson should be designed to handle various administrative tasks, capture the students' interest, and focus their attention on the learning objectives to be addressed during the lesson. An effective beginning can increase a student's ability to focus on the objectives.

Actions you take at the start of a lesson help establish an atmosphere in which students have the "motivation to learn" (Brophy, 2004). Motivation to learn draws on the meaningfulness, value, and benefits of the academic task to the learner. For example, math problems may be developed relating to student interests, such as selling products for a youth group fundraiser. Thus, the focus is on learning rather than on merely performing. Often students can be motivated at the beginning of a lesson by emphasizing the purpose of the task or the fact that students will be interested in the task.

Prior to beginning the substance of a lesson, take attendance and solicit student attention. At the beginning of the lesson, your actions include providing daily review, providing a set induction, introducing lesson objectives, distributing materials, and giving clear, focused directions.

Taking Attendance

Elementary teachers in self-contained classrooms commonly take attendance first thing in the morning, whereas middle school and high school teachers take attendance at the start of each class. Tardiness also must be noted, and teachers need to follow school policies when recording and responding to tardy students. It is helpful not to hold

---

VOICES FROM THE CLASSROOM   *Getting Students Prepared for Class*

Mary Pat Whiteside, Middle School Teacher, Palm Coast, Florida

Much time is wasted by students who arrive unprepared for class. They take up time asking for materials or returning to their lockers for papers and pencils. I solve this problem by having a pencil and pen jar on my desk. I buy several hundred inexpensive pencils a year, and I collect old pens and pencils left around my room—each of these goes into my jar.

My students know that if they need a pen or pencil, they may borrow one. I also keep a drawer of paper, some of which may have been used on one side. My students know to go to that drawer for paper if they need it. When students come to me and tell me they need materials to write, I smile and point to my supplies.

up the beginning of class to take attendance. You could plan an opening activity for students to do while you take attendance. Some teachers have the first activity posted on the board for the students to do while attendance is taken. It is important to have a seating chart for each class; a substitute teacher would find this to be especially useful.

Getting Attention

Students should understand that they are expected to give full attention to lessons at all times. A lesson should not begin until you gain their full attention. There should be a predictable, standard signal that tells the class, "We are now ready to begin the lesson." The type of signal will vary with teacher preferences. For example, you could raise your hand, ring chimes or a bell, stand in a certain location, or make a statement. After giving the signal, pause briefly to allow it to take effect. Then when you have attention, move quickly into the lesson.

There are a number of ways to solicit attention at the beginning of a lesson. These approaches are designed to secure the students' attention and reduce distractions that might occur at the beginning of a lesson (Jones & Jones, 2004).

1. *Select a Cue for Getting Students' Attention.* Students often need a consistent cue to focus their attention. These cues may include a special phrase that the class has chosen to indicate that you want immediate attention, or it may be a nonverbal cue such as closing the door at the beginning of class.

2. *Do Not Begin Until All Students Are Paying Attention.* It is important that no lesson begin until all students are paying attention to the teacher. Teachers who begin lessons without the attention of all their students spend much more time repeating directions. Also, a teacher who begins a lesson in such a fashion is a poor role model since it indicates that it is all right to talk while others are talking. Teachers sometimes just stand silent, waiting—students soon get the message.

3. *Remove Distractions.* Some students cannot screen out distracting stimuli. You can help remove distractions by closing the door, having the students remove unnecessary materials from the tops of their desks, adjusting the blinds, or taking other appropriate actions.

WHAT WOULD YOU DECIDE? *Getting Attention*

You may use one or more cues or signals to indicate to your students that you are ready to begin the class session.

1. For each of the following—voice, light, sound, and movement—identify a way that you would signal to your students that class is ready to begin.

2. How might the appropriateness of your cues differ for various grade levels?

Providing Daily Review

A lesson can start with a brief review of previously covered material, correction of homework, and review of prior knowledge that is relevant to the day's lesson. The purpose of daily review is to determine if the students have obtained the necessary prerequisite knowledge or skills for the lesson. This review may last from three to eight minutes, and the length will vary according to the attention span of the learners and the nature of the content. Daily review is especially useful for teaching material that will be used in subsequent learning. Examples include math facts, math computation and factoring, grammar, chemical equations, and reading sight words.

You can conduct daily review at the beginning of a lesson (a) to provide additional practice and overlearning for previously learned material and (b) to allow the teacher to provide corrections and reteaching in areas where students are having difficulty. Vary the methods for reviewing material.

Checking homework at the start of class is one form of review. Game formats, such as a trivia game, can be used as a means for review. You can conduct review through discussion, demonstration, questioning, written summaries, short quizzes, individualized approaches, and other methods of instruction (Rosenshine & Stevens, 1986). During reviews, students might answer questions at the chalkboard, in small groups, or as a whole class. Some additional techniques include asking questions about concepts or skills taught in the previous lesson, having students meet in small groups of two to four to review homework, and having students prepare questions about previous lessons or homework and ask them to one another or the teacher can ask them to the class.

In addition to daily review, the learning of new material is also enhanced by weekly and monthly reviews. Weekly reviews may occur each Monday, and monthly reviews every fourth Monday. These reviews provide additional opportunities for you to check for student understanding, ensure that the necessary prior skills are adequately learned, and also check on your pace of instruction (Rosenshine & Stevens, 1986).

VOICES FROM THE CLASSROOM   *Reviewing*

Fred Dahm, High School Social Studies Teacher, Wisconsin Rapids, Wisconsin

Too often students see reviewing as a dull but necessary chore. But it can be much more. At the end of each lesson, I assign a different student the responsibility of preparing a 5- to 10-minute review of the content for class the next day. This review can take several forms—a discussion of major points, a listing of the material covered, a game, a crossword puzzle. The possibilities are endless.

At the beginning of the semester, I also assign pairs of students to a particular unit that we will cover to write a two- or three-page newspaper that would serve as part of the review for that unit. Students can select a title and logo for the newspaper. The articles might include a list of materials covered, related materials available in the library, important points of each lesson, political cartoons, an editorial, a crossword puzzle, and jokes. Each item in the newspaper must be related to the unit content. The student editors then distribute the paper to classmates to begin the review session.

Establishing Set

Set Induction is the initial activity at the beginning of the lesson that is used to induce students to a state of wanting to learn. This activity helps establish the context for the learning that is to follow and helps students engage in the learning. Typically, the set is brief, lasting only long enough to develop student readiness to accomplish the lesson's objective. Set induction helps students see what the topic of the lesson is in a way that is related to their own interests and their own lives. Madeline Hunter (1994) used the term *anticipatory set* to describe this concept, pointing out that the activity is intended to develop a mental readiness (or "set") for the lesson.

For example, a health lesson on the topic of first aid might begin with the reading of a newspaper report about a recent fire or accident. After reading the article, you could ask the students what they would do if they were the first ones to arrive after the accident. A number of ideas are likely to be generated in this discussion. Then you could bring that opening discussion to a close by saying that today's lesson will be about that exact topic—what type of first aid to administer for various conditions. Then you would move into the first part of the lesson. This set induction activity helps create interest in the lesson in a way that students can relate to their own lives.

Effective set induction activities should meet several criteria:

1. *Get the Students Interested in What Is to Be Taught during the Lesson.* This is referred to as an initiating activity. For example, you might begin a lesson on creative writing by turning off the lights in the room and explaining to the students that you will take them on an adventure to a distant planet. As the room remains dark, they are to imagine their trip into outer space.

2. *The Set Induction Activity Must Be Connected to the Lesson.* An activity that is designed to get the students' attention but is not connected to the lesson does not meet this criterion.

3. *Students Must Understand the Material and/or Activity.* The information contained in the initiating activity must be stated in a clear manner so that the students will not only understand the activity but also know how it is connected to later content. Later, the set induction activity can be referred to while teaching the lesson.

4. *The Set Induction and the Content of the Lesson Should Be Related to the Students' Lives or to a Previous Lesson.* Students will be more interested in a lesson if they can relate the material to their own lives. For example, a lesson concerning measurement might include measuring ingredients to bake a cake or some other practical application. Also, you can reduce anxiety by relating the lesson to material already learned by the students.

Introducing Lesson Objectives

At the start of a lesson, you should clearly describe its purpose. In addition, it is helpful to discuss the activities and evaluation process, since these procedures help reduce student anxiety about the lesson. At the beginning, some teachers will clearly explain the objectives, the activities, and evaluation procedures to be used; others will write these elements on the board for the students, or they will wait for an appropriate point in the lesson, such as after the set induction.

By using set induction activities and introducing lesson objectives, a teacher gives students an advance organizer that provides a framework for the new content and helps the students relate it to content they already know. Advance organizers help students by focusing their attention on the subject being considered, informing them where the lesson is going, relating new material to content already understood, and providing structure for the subsequent lesson.

Students learn more, in less time, when they are informed of the lesson objectives (Dubelle, 1986). Furthermore, students are more likely to become involved and derive more satisfaction and enjoyment from an activity that has a definite aim. Roehler, Duffy, and Meloth (1987) reported that after teachers learned to give students specific explanations concerning the purpose of instructional activities, their students demonstrated significantly greater understanding of and appreciation for the purpose of the instruction. For example, when teaching students how to use the *Reader's Guide*, you might explain that the guide could be used to locate information for a research paper assigned by another teacher.

Consider the alternative if you do *not* clearly communicate the learning goals to enable the students to understand the goals. Students may go through the motions of an activity without understanding its purpose or its relationship to other content. Students may be concerned only with completing the assignment, rather than attempting to understand the purposes and objectives behind the assignment. Some students, in fact, may become passive when they see no academic purpose and consider assignments to be busywork with no specific learning objective.

Distributing and Collecting Materials

You often need to distribute materials to students. Their maturity should be considered when determining the most appropriate time and way to do so. Handouts, maps, or student guides can be distributed at the beginning of class to focus student attention on important material and to avoid disruptions during the lesson. Materials could be handed to students as they enter the room to save time during the lesson. You may prefer to distribute materials at the point in the lesson when the materials are actually needed.

Materials should be strategically located in the classroom to provide easy distribution and to minimize disruptions. For example, resource books that are often used should be located where there is sufficient room when the books are needed. Procedures should be established for their distribution. You may have one row at a time get the resource books, have one student in each row get enough copies for that row, have students pick up a copy as soon as they enter the room, or give each student a copy as soon as they enter the room.

Some materials that are distributed need to be collected later in the lesson, and appropriate ways to collect these materials should be selected. The manner of collecting the materials may be the same as or different from the way they were distributed.

Giving Clear, Focused Directions

To give clear and focused directions, you first must carefully plan them. Directions are often given at the beginning of a lesson; of course, directions might also be given for activities throughout a lesson.

When *planning for directions*, you should (a) have no more than three student actions that are required for the activity to be described; (b) describe the directions in the order that students will be required to complete the tasks; (c) clarify what type and quality of product is expected; (d) make the description of each step specific and fairly brief; (e) provide written (on the chalkboard, a transparency, or a handout) and oral directions; (f) give the directions just before the activity; and (g) make provisions for assisting students who have difficulty.

When actually *giving directions*, you need to (a) get student attention; (b) present the directions; (c) check to see if students understand the directions ("Do you have any questions about what you need to do?"); (d) have the students begin the tasks; and (e) remediate if necessary if one or more students are not following directions. Clearly state what books and materials are needed.

It is often helpful to demonstrate the actions expected of the students by doing one problem or activity together. Students then see what is expected of them before they begin to work independently. Once they begin work, you should walk around to see if they are following the directions and to be available to answer student questions. If many questions arise, it may be useful to gain everyone's attention for further explanation.

VOICES FROM THE CLASSROOM   *Giving Directions*

Ron Butler, High School Social Studies Teacher, Gillette, Wyoming

There are several parts of giving directions for class activities. First, I give detailed, step-by-step descriptions for what I want the students to do. This may include mentioning the pages in the textbook and the specific actions that I want the students to take. Second, I seek feedback from the students to see if they understand the directions. Especially when there are several steps in the directions, I ask a randomly selected student to repeat the directions to ensure that the students hear them again. At any time, I can correct any misunderstandings they have. Third, I screen the steps on the overhead projector so the students can refer to them as they move along.

The Middle of the Lesson

A number of teacher behaviors during lesson delivery contribute to effective group management. These include pacing the lesson, providing smooth transitions, avoiding satiation, having a task orientation, ensuring academic learning time, being clear, and exhibiting enthusiasm.

Pacing the Lesson

Pacing is the speed at which the lesson proceeds. It is the rhythm, the ebb and flow, of a lesson. Effective pacing is neither too slow nor too fast. Adjustments in the pace of the lesson are made as the need warrants. To pace a lesson effectively, you should not dwell too long on directions, should distribute papers in a timely and efficient manner, and should move from one activity to another smoothly and without interruption.

Classrooms that lack effective pacing will drag at times or will move along at a pace where the students are unable to grasp the material. You should, however, recognize that it takes more time for students to mentally and physically transition from one activity to another than it does the teacher.

Use the following guidelines to pace a lesson effectively (Good & Brophy, 2003; Jones & Jones, 2004).

1. *Develop Awareness of Your Own Teaching Tempo.* As you gain more experience in the classroom, you will be more aware of your own personal pace in the classroom. A good means of determining your pace is to audio- or videotape your performance. In this way, you are able to determine how fast you talk, how you move around the classroom, and how much wait time you provide your students.

2. *Watch for Nonverbal Cues Indicating That Students Are Becoming Puzzled or Bored.* Monitor student attentiveness and then modify the pacing of the lesson as needed. If high achieving students are looking puzzled, they and perhaps most of the class may be lost. The content may be too complex or it is being covered too quickly. A good indication that your pacing is too slow is if students are becoming restless and inattentive—looking out the window or fiddling with materials on their desks.

Savage (1999) recommends that teachers choose a pace that is appropriate for about 75 percent of the class. While this pace may be a bit slow for some learners, it will keep the lesson moving along and provide success for a majority of the students. You might select several students to notice on a regular basis throughout the lesson as indicators of your pacing.

3. *Break Activities up into Short Segments.* Many teachers go through an entire activity before beginning discussion or review. However, it is more effective to break the activities up into shorter segments and to ask questions or review these shorter segments rather than the entire activity.

4. *Provide Short Breaks for Lessons That Last Longer Than 30 Minutes.* Long lessons can cause inattentiveness and disruptive behavior. A three- to five-minute break can allow the students to return fresh to the activity. These breaks can be short games related to the activity or a stand-up-and-stretch interlude. A brief activity where students can get up to mingle or just stand up and stretch can provide enough of a break.

5. *Vary the Instructional Approach As Well As the Content of the Instruction.* Students often become restless with only a single instructional approach. A lesson plan that incorporates several instructional strategies will result in better attentiveness.

6. *Avoid Interrupting the Flow of the Lesson with Numerous Stops and Starts.* Jerkiness is a term that refers to behaviors that interfere with the smooth flow of the lesson. This occurs when the teacher (a) interrupts an ongoing activity without warning and gives directions to begin another activity; (b) leaves one activity dangling in midair, begins another, only to return to the first; or (c) leaves one activity for another and never returns to the first activity. In such instances, students never experience closure to the activities they were engaged in prior to the switch. Sudden reversals of activities tend to leave students flustered over not completing the previous activity and unprepared to begin the new activity.

7. *Avoid Slowdowns That Interfere with the Pace of the Lesson.* *Slowdowns*, or delays in the momentum or pace of a class, can occur due to overdwelling or fragmentation. *Overdwelling* occurs when too much time is spent on directions or explanations. Overdwelling also is seen when the teacher becomes so enthralled with the details of the lesson or a prop that is being used for a demonstration that the students lose sight of the main idea. For example, an English teacher may get so carried away describing the details of an author's life that the students barely have time to read the author's works. Another example is a science teacher who gets carried away describing the laboratory equipment so that the students have little time to conduct any experiments.

Fragmentation is another form of slowdown in which the lesson is divided into such minute fragments that some of the students are left waiting and become bored. For example, the directions for an experiment may be broken down into such minute, simple parts that the students feel belittled, or an activity is done by one row of students at a time, leaving the rest waiting.

8. *Provide a Summary at the End of a Lesson Segment.* Rather than plan for a single summary at the end of a lesson, it might help the pacing of the lesson to provide a summary after each main point or activity. For example, students might be asked to write a one-sentence summary of each scene as a play is read aloud.

WHAT WOULD YOU DECIDE?   *Pacing Your Lessons*

Pacing is the speed at which the lesson proceeds. The type of instructional activities and the dynamics of the classroom interactions affect the pacing.

1. During a lesson, how will you determine whether adjustments need to be made in the speed at which you are proceeding through the lesson?

2. How will you take pacing into account as you make your instructional plans?

Providing Smooth Transitions

Transitions are movements from one activity to another. A smooth transition allows one activity to flow into another without any breaks in the delivery of the lesson. Transitions that are not smooth create gaps in delivery.

Transition time can occur when (a) students remain at their seats and change from one subject to another; (b) they move from their seats to an activity in another part of the classroom; (c) they move from somewhere else in the classroom back to their seats; (d) they leave the classroom to go outside or to another part of the school building; or (e) they come back into the classroom from outside or another part of the building.

Disorder and misbehavior can arise during transition times. More disruptions occur during transitions (including hitting, yelling, and other inappropriate actions) than during nontransition time. There are several reasons why transitions can be problematic (Gump, 1987). First, you may have difficulty getting the students to finish an activity, especially if they are deeply engaged in it. Second, transitions are more loosely structured than instructional activities, and there typically is more freedom to socialize and move around the room. Third, students may "save up" problems or tensions and deal with them during the transition time. For example, a student may ask to use the restroom, complain to you about another student, or ask permission to get something from a locker. Finally, there may be delays in getting students started in the new activity.

To reduce the potential for disorder during transitions, you should prepare students for upcoming transitions, establish efficient transition routines, and clearly define the boundaries of lessons. Jones and Jones (2004) offer several suggestions for effective transitions:

1. *Arrange the Classroom for Efficient Movement.* Arrange the classroom so that you and the students can move freely without disturbing those who are working.

2. *Create and Post a Daily Schedule and Discuss any Changes Each Morning.* Posting a daily schedule will aid in the elimination of confusion in the students.

3. *Have Material Ready for the Next Lesson.* Prepare and gather materials for the next lesson to ensure that class time is not taken and that activities flow smoothly.

4. *Do Not Relinquish Students' Attention Until You Have Given Clear Instructions for the Following Activity.* All too often, teachers allow the class to become disruptive while they pause between activities or lessons to prepare for the next lesson. It requires considerable time and energy to regain the students' attention.

5. *Do Not Do Tasks That Can Be Done by Students.* Have students take responsibility for their own preparations for the next class session. This will enable you to monitor student actions.

6. *Move Around the Room and Attend to Individual Needs.* By moving around the room, you are able to notice any minor disturbances that might expand into major problems.

7. *Provide Students with Simple, Step-by-Step Directions.* Clearly state exactly what you want your students to do during the time given for the transition.

8. *Remind Students of Key Procedures Associated with the Upcoming Lesson.* Reviewing standard procedures and discussing unique procedures for an upcoming activity help promote smooth transitions because students know what is expected of them.

9. *Develop Transition Activities.* After lunch or physical education, for example, students are excited and may not be ready for quieter work. As a result, you could choose structured transition activities to prepare the students for the next class session. These might include reading to students, discussing the daily schedule, having students write in a journal, or doing some type of activity that may not necessarily deal with the content of the next class session. After this transition time, they will likely be more ready to begin the next class session.

Avoiding Satiation

Satiation means that students have had enough of something, and this may lead to boredom, restlessness, and off-task behavior. For example, students may enjoy seeing a videotape, writing a creative story, or working in pairs on a project. When those activities are used too often or for too much time, however, students will start to lose interest, become bored, and will likely get off task. You need to guard against planning activities that will lead to satiation.

| WHAT WOULD YOU DECIDE? | *Having Smooth Transitions* |

WHAT WOULD YOU DECIDE?   *Having Smooth Transitions*

Assume that you have planned a lesson in which your students viewed a videotape, then had small-group discussions about the videotape, and finally individually outlined some content and answered some questions from the textbook.

1. What arrangements would you need to make to ensure smooth transitions throughout the lesson?
2. How might the directions that you select for the lesson promote smooth transitions?

There are three ways to avoid satiation (Kounin, 1970). First, have students experience progress, which is the feeling they get when steadily moving toward some significant objective. Pacing and group focus help achieve this sense. To promote feelings of progress, you need to avoid dwelling on one topic too long. Second, provide variety as an effective way to avoid satiation. At the same time, classroom routines are necessary to preserve order and organization. You need to sense when enough is enough. Instructional variety helps invite inquisitiveness, excitement, and interest.

Third, select an appropriate degree of challenge in the students' academic work. Students do not tire of success if the success is a genuine test of their abilities and culminates in personally relevant accomplishments. When the challenge is sufficient to court and fortify the best efforts of students, satiation is seldom a problem.

Being Task Oriented

Task orientation has to do with your concern that all relevant material be covered and learned as opposed to being mired in procedural matters or extraneous material. The more time dedicated to the task of teaching a specific topic, the greater the opportunity students have to learn. Task-oriented teachers provide an appropriate amount of time lecturing, asking questions, and engaging the students in activities directly related to the material that is to be learned. Students have higher rates of achievement in classrooms of task-oriented teachers (Berliner & Bittle, 1995).

Task-oriented teachers are goal-oriented, and they plan instructional strategies and activities that support these goals. In addition, task-oriented teachers have a high, but realistic, set of expectations for their students. To be task oriented in the classroom, you should (a) develop unit and lesson plans that reflect the curriculum; (b) handle administrative and clerical interruptions efficiently; (c) stop or prevent misbehavior with a minimum of class disruption; (d) select the most appropriate instructional model for objectives being taught; and (e) establish cycles of review, feedback, and testing (Borich, 2004).

Ensuring Academic Learning Time

Academic learning time is the amount of time students are successfully engaged in learning activities. However, the amount of time that students are actively engaged or on task can vary greatly across and within classrooms. Low achieving students often go off task due to frustrations about not understanding class material. High achieving students, on the other hand, tend to go off task after they have completed their assigned work. Therefore, you should ensure that all students can be successfully engaged in classroom tasks while also ensuring that high achieving students are engaged throughout the lesson. Provide feedback and correctives to students who need assistance, and at the same time monitor the rate of student progress through the lesson.

For new material that students have not yet mastered, expect a lower success rate initially but set a goal of higher success rates as students receive feedback on their performance and gain confidence. As a general rule, students should have a success rate of approximately 80 percent on most initial tasks. The rate of success should be somewhat higher when students are engaged in independent work, such as homework or independent seatwork (Berliner, 1987). The goal is to ensure that students are given meaningful tasks to complete, are given feedback and correctives when needed, and are ultimately able successfully to complete all assigned tasks.

Being Clear

Clarity refers to the precision of your communication to your students regarding the desired behavior. Clarity in teaching helps students understand better, work more accurately, and be more successful. Effective teachers exhibit a high degree of clarity by providing very clear and explicit directions, instructions, questions, and expectations. If you are constantly asked to repeat questions, directions, and explanations, or if your students do not understand your expectations, you are not exhibiting clarity in your instructional behavior.

Clear directions, instructions, and expectations need to be given. Students then know what is expected of them and can act accordingly as they work on classroom activities, assignments, and other tasks. If you are not very clear when giving directions, for example, the student may not complete the assignment in the way you intended, may become confused, and may need additional time and attention later to complete the assignment in the manner intended.

To be clear in the classroom, (a) inform the learners of the objective; (b) provide learners with advance organizers; (c) check for task-relevant prior learning at the beginning of the lesson; (d) give directions slowly and distinctly; (e) know the ability levels of students and teach to those levels; (f) use examples, illustrations, and demonstrations to explain and clarify; and (g) provide a review or summary at the end of each lesson (Borich, 2004).

Exhibiting Enthusiasm

Enthusiasm is an expression of excitement and intensity. It is quite obvious that a teacher who is enthusiastic and vibrant is more entertaining to observe than an unenthusiastic teacher. However, teacher enthusiasm has also been related to higher student achievement (Good & Brophy, 2003). Enthusiasm has two important dimensions: interest and involvement with the subject matter, and vigor and physical dynamism. Enthusiastic teachers are often described as stimulating, dynamic, expressive, and energetic. Their behavior suggests that they are committed to the students and to the subject matter. While teachers often expect students to be interested in *what* they say, students more often react to *how* enthusiastically it is said.

Enthusiasm can be conveyed in a variety of ways. These include the use of animated gestures, eye contact, voice inflection, and movement around the room. A teacher who is enthusiastic in the classroom often manages to develop enthusiastic students. Constant, highly enthusiastic actions are not necessary and, in fact, may be counterproductive. Instead, a variety of enthusiastic actions, ranging from low to high degrees of enthusiasm, would be appropriate.

The Ending of a Lesson

As stated earlier, an effective lesson has three important sections: a beginning, a middle, and an end. All three sections must be planned and implemented effectively if a lesson is to be successful. Simply ending a lesson when the bell rings or when you have covered the planned material is not appropriate. In such cases, students are not given the opportunity to place the lesson in a context with other related lessons or are not permitted to ask questions that might clarify a misunderstood point from the lesson. Providing a summary is imperative for a successful lesson. Furthermore, students need time at the end of the lesson to get ready to leave the classroom.

Providing Closure to Part of a Lesson

Closure refers to actions or statements that are designed to bring a lesson presentation to an appropriate conclusion. Closure has three purposes (Shostak, 2006):

1. *Draw Attention to the End of a Lesson Segment or the Lesson Itself.* Often students need to be cued that they have arrived at an important segment of the lesson or that it is time to wrap things up. They might be cued with a statement that it is time to summarize key concepts.

2. *Help Consolidate Student Learning.* It is the teacher's responsibility to relate the many pieces of the lesson to the whole. Some students are able to see this by themselves while others need assistance. To accomplish this purpose, you might provide a diagram, illustration, outline, or other type of summary indicating how all the content of the lesson is related.

3. *Reinforce the Major Points to Be Learned.* You might emphasize or highlight certain concepts at this point. The major objective is to help the student retain the information presented in the lesson for future use.

Closure is important because students instinctively structure information into patterns that make sense to them. If a learning experience is left with some uncertainties, students may draw inaccurate conclusions as they create their own patterns of understanding from the material, thus detracting from future learning.

The second and third purposes involve summarizing, which is addressed later. The time at the end of a lesson segment or the lesson itself can be used to make homework assignments. Between lesson segments, students may be given 5 to 10 minutes to start the homework assignment while you move around the room to answer questions.

WHAT WOULD YOU DECIDE? *Providing Closure*

Let's assume that you are teaching a history lesson in which a series of significant dates have been identified and related events have been discussed.

1. How might you bring closure to this part of the lesson in a way that helps students see how all the dates and events are related?

2. How might you involve students in this closure?

3. How might you take into account students' varied learning styles?

Summarizing the Lesson

Providing a summary of the main points of a lesson can help students gain a better idea of the content and clarify any misunderstandings. You should plan to stop the lesson several minutes before the bell rings to begin the summation. Make sure that you have the attention of all students before the summary begins. You should avoid merely reiterating the content covered during the lesson. Ask several questions that encourage the students to relate key aspects of the lesson or to evaluate key points. Also ask their opinions about what they believe are the key points.

To add interest and variety, vary the way that the lesson summary is conducted. Some days may involve simply a series of questions for students. On other days, you may ask several students to go to the chalkboard to solve a problem and discuss the thought process involved. A game format could be used as a means of summary, such as questions out of a hat or a "Trivial Pursuit" type of approach. Several creative approaches could offer the desired variety of lesson summaries.

The summary should be used to determine if the students have grasped the main ideas of the lesson. For example, your summary might reveal that several students do not understand the key concepts of a math lesson. It would be foolish to teach the next math lesson as though all students understand the concept. Therefore, you can use the information gathered during the summary to adjust the next day's lesson plan.

Getting Ready to Leave

At the end of the lesson, middle, junior high, or senior high school students usually need to leave the classroom and go to their next class. The bell will ring at the end of the class period and the students will have just a few minutes to get to their next class in another room in the building.

You should plan to complete all instruction and lesson summary by the end of the class period so that students are not delayed in moving to the next class. You should not teach right up to the bell because time needs to be allowed for several other events.

First, you must allow time for students to return any books, supplies, or materials to the appropriate locations. Also, students need time to throw away any scrap paper and to straighten up the classroom. They need time to put away their own books, papers, pencils, or other materials before leaving. You may plan to reserve from one to four minutes at the end of a lesson to allow sufficient time for these final actions to be completed before the bell rings. Students then should be dismissed on time. You need to schedule this time when planning lessons.

MANAGING STUDENT WORK

Students prepare homework and seatwork as a regular part of their instruction. To effectively manage this student work, guidelines are offered here for managing seatwork effectively, collecting assignments and monitoring their completion, maintaining records of student work, managing the paperwork, and giving students feedback.

Managing Seatwork Effectively

Seatwork involves students working on assignments during class that provide practice or review of previously presented material. Students spend hundreds of hours during a school year doing seatwork privately at their desks. It is imperative that you structure seatwork so that it is done effectively while enabling students to experience a high rate of success.

Guidelines for successfully implementing seatwork in the classroom come from a variety of sources (Jones & Jones, 2004; Rosenshine & Stevens, 1986; Weinstein, 2003; Weinstein & Mignano, 2003). The following recommendations represent a synthesis from these sources:

1. Recognize that seatwork is intended to practice or review previously presented material. It is not suited for students to learn new material.

2. Devote no more time to seatwork than is allocated to content development activities.

3. Give clear instruction—explanations, questions, and feedback—and sufficient practice before the students begin their seatwork. Having to provide lengthy explanations during seatwork is troublesome for both you and the student. In addition to procedural directions, explain why the activities are being done and how to do the seatwork.

4. Work through the first few problems of the seatwork together with the students before having them continue independently. This provides a model for completing the work and provides an opportunity for the students to ask questions for clarification about the content or procedures.

5. Decide if you will allow talking during seatwork. It is often desirable to start out with no talking during seatwork to have students work alone. After a month or two, teachers sometimes allow students to talk quietly with others to seek or provide help. Clarify when quiet talking is allowed.

6. Circulate from student to student during seatwork, actively explaining, observing, asking questions, and giving feedback. Monitoring students to provide this positive and corrective feedback is very important.

7. Determine how students will seek help from the teacher. When students are working at their seats and need help, ask them to raise their hands. You can then go to them or signal them to come to you at an appropriate time.

8. Determine when students can get out of their seats. To eliminate unnecessary wandering around the room during seatwork, decide when and for what purpose students can get out of their seats. For example, students may get supplies, sharpen pencils, or turn in papers only when necessary.

9. Have short contacts with individual students (i.e., 30 seconds or less).

10. Break seatwork into short segments rather than one long time slot. Rather than having one lengthy presentation of content followed by an extended period of seatwork, break up instruction into a number of segments followed by brief seatwork after each segment.

11. Arrange seats to facilitate monitoring the students (e.g., face both small groups and independently working students).

12. Establish a routine to use during seatwork activity that prescribes what students will do when they have completed the exercises. Students may complete an additional enrichment assignment for extra credit, or may use the time for free reading or to work on assignments from other classes.

VOICES FROM THE CLASSROOM   *Monitoring During Seatwork*

Edward Gamble, Third-Grade Teacher, Jamestown, Rhode Island

During seatwork, I used to have students come up to my desk to see me if they had any questions or problems. I discovered that students would line up to see me, and they would talk or misbehave while waiting their turn in line. By staying in my seat, I also realized that I wasn't noticing the other students very much. As a result, I decided to have the students stay in their seats during seatwork and raise their hands if they had a question. Overall, this monitoring increased my awareness of what the students were doing and how they were doing.

Collecting Assignments and Monitoring Their Completion

Whether it is homework or seatwork, you need to establish a process for collecting assignments and monitoring their completion.

• *Have a Regular Procedure for Collecting Assignments.* Papers can be collected during class by asking students to pass them in a given direction until you have all papers in your hands. As an alternative, students may be asked to place their completed assignments in certain basket, tray, or drop box at a designated time during class. Once students know this collection procedure, assignments can be gathered quickly and efficiently.

• *Have a Procedure for Grouping Papers by Subject or Class Session.* In an elementary classroom, assignments on a variety of subjects may be submitted during the day. It is useful to have a separate drop box for each subject. In this way, only papers of a certain subject are in a drop box, and you don't need to spend time sorting through all the papers to pick out just the math papers or just the social studies papers. Similarly, middle and secondary classrooms could have a different drop box for each class period. Thus, students in the fourth hour would place their assignments in the box for their class period.

• *Have a Record of Whose Papers Have Been Turned in.* If you evaluate the papers quickly, you will know who has or who has not submitted the assignments when you record the grades in your gradebook. If there is a delay in grading, you may have a checklist to record who has submitted the assignments. In this way, you can follow up with students who did not submit the materials. Some teachers also have students keep an assignment notebook for homework and seatwork to record the items that were due and what was turned in.

Maintaining Records of Student Work

Records of student progress and completion are entered in your gradebook. For elementary classes, you may organize your gradebook by having a separate section for each subject area. The date and description of the assignment can be entered at the top as a subject heading, and student scores can be placed in the appropriate column on the line for their names. Similarly, middle level and secondary teachers can have separate sections of the gradebook for each of their class sections. It is useful to establish a coding system to indicate a student absence or other information related to the assignment.

Gradebook software can be used to record the submission of assignments and the scores that students received. Progress reports for individual students can be easily prepared, and these are useful to show the students and parents.

Developing Your Management Plan: *Planning and Conducting Instruction*

Each grade level and subject has its own characteristics, and each classroom of students you teach will have unique characteristics that will need to be taken into account when planning and conducting instruction. Once you have a specific teaching assignment, you will be more able to describe the details about how you will plan and conduct instruction.

As a starting point, it is useful to provide a general description for ways you intend to plan and conduct instruction. This chapter had several sections, as listed below. For each of the following items, think about and write your general intentions for planning and conducting instruction. This written plan will then provide a framework for your more specific plan when you have a teaching assignment.

The Degree of Structure in My Lessons

Ways to Group Students for Instruction

Planning to Hold Students Academically
   Accountable

Handling the Beginning of a Lesson

Handling the Middle of a Lesson

Handling the Ending of a Lesson

Managing Student Work

Managing the Paperwork

Homework and seatwork involve a lot of paperwork, and it is easy to get overwhelmed by the volume of papers you deal with on a regular basis. Here are some guidelines to effectively manage your handling of the papers.

• *Assess, Record, and Return Assignments Quickly.* Make a commitment to assess and return all assignments in a day or two. Delays in your return of the assignments often lead to a backlog of assignments to be graded. That situation creates a lot of pressure for you, and it is not fair to the students because they need to receive feedback as quickly as possible.

• *Be Realistic About Your Grading Capabilities.* Plan sufficient time in your schedule to assess and record the assignments. If you are making frequent assignments and are getting behind in the grading, it is time to reassess your use of assignments. Strategically space out the assignments that are to be graded. Long assignments take time to assess. Instead, short and specific assignments may be effective in monitoring student learning, and they take less time to assess.

• *Recognize That Every Seatwork Assignment Does Not Need to Have a Grade.* Every subject or every class period does not need an assignment that must be graded by you every day. Therefore, you do not need to receive papers each day. Students can be assessed in class and given feedback in various ways without asking them to submit the paperwork to you to be assessed. For example, you can assign seatwork and then check each student's work and give feedback during class.

• *Have a System for Coding the Papers for Each Subject or Class Section.* As mentioned previously, have a system for collecting assignments from your students. Color coded folders for each subject or each class period can be a helpful technique for organizing the paperwork.

• *Have a Predetermined Way to Return Papers to the Students.* When returning papers to students, keep them in labeled folders by the subject or class period. You could organize the papers by rows or groups to facilitate the return. Plan a certain way to return the papers each time. You may choose to use student helpers in returning the papers.

Giving Students Feedback

You will assign seatwork and homework to help students learn, and it is important that students receive feedback about this work.

• *Provide Frequent and Regular Feedback.* Students need fairly immediate feedback about their performance so they have an opportunity to correct any errors in their knowledge or skills before going ahead to new material. Thus, plan for ways for students to demonstrate their learning and for ways that you can provide frequent and regular feedback about their learning.

• *Develop Ways to Provide Feedback to Students in Class.* To provide prompt feedback and to avoid assigning homework every day, develop ways to provide feedback to students after instruction and practice have taken place in class. For example, you could have students work on problems at the board and give feedback, show answers on an overhead screen, or have students help review one another's work.

• *Take Corrective Actions Promptly with Students Who Do Not Perform Well.* Don't wait until several poor assignments have been turned in or until it is time to submit the report card grade before meeting with a student who is not performing well. Some students may need more assistance to learn the content, and this feedback and assistance should come early without delay.

MAIN POINTS

1. The degree of structure in the lesson and the manner in which students are grouped for instruction need to be taken into account when managing instruction and promoting appropriate behavior.

2. Students are more likely to stay on task when they are held academically accountable for their work.

3. When beginning a lesson, teachers need to take attendance, solicit attention, provide daily review, provide a set induction, introduce lesson objectives, distribute materials, and give clear, focused directions.

4. When conducting a lesson, effective teachers pace the lesson appropriately, provide smooth transitions, avoid satiation, manage seatwork effectively, have a task orientation, ensure academic learning time, and exhibit clarity and enthusiasm.

5. An effective teacher ends a lesson with a summary of important concepts covered in the lesson and allows students time to get ready to leave the room after the lesson.

6. Managing student work involves managing seatwork effectively, collecting assignments and monitoring their completion, maintaining records of student work, managing the paperwork, and giving students feedback.

DISCUSSION/REFLECTIVE QUESTIONS

1. What are the merits of whole-group, small-group, and independent work? What might teachers do to minimize misbehavior with each strategy?

2. In what ways might the selection of the various accountability procedures be affected by differences in grade level and subject areas?

3. From your own school experiences, what approaches to review did you find the most useful? What are the merits of using different approaches for review?

4. Recall several examples when your teachers were not clear in providing directions, instructions, or expectations. What effect did this lack of clarity have on you as a student?

SUGGESTED ACTIVITIES

1. Look at Table 10.1 concerning ways to hold students academically accountable. Then identify ways that you would make assignments and determine work and completion requirements.

2. Talk with several teachers to determine the various ways that they begin and end a lesson. How are these actions affected by the type of instructional strategy they use?

3. Establish some guidelines for yourself in how you assign, monitor, and assess seatwork in your classroom.

4. List a number of approaches that you could use to summarize a lesson. You could direct some of the techniques and some could involve students in an active way.

FURTHER READING

BURDEN, PAUL R., & BYRD, DAVID M. (2007). *Methods for effective teaching* (4th ed.). Boston: Allyn & Bacon. Provides an overview of all aspects of teaching methods including topics such as planning, classroom management, instructional strategies, and assessment. Includes content on lesson delivery.

MARZANO, R.J., PICKERING, D.J., & POLLOCK, J.E. (2005). *Classroom instruction that works: Research-based strategies for increasing student achievement.* Upper Saddle River, NJ: Prentice-Hall/Merrill.

Provides a thorough yet concise review of proven instructional strategies to promote student learning. Examines homework and practice, cooperative learning, cues, questions, advance organizers, summarizing, and other strategies.

Chapter 11

Responding to Inappropriate Behavior

CHAPTER OBJECTIVES

This chapter provides information that will help you:
- Describe the principle of least intervention.
- Identify certain disciplinary practices to avoid.
- Recognize the limitations of punishment and guidelines for its effective use.
- Identify ways that situational assistance can be provided.
- Determine ways to apply mild and moderate responses to misbehavior.
- Identify ways to address chronic misbehaviors.

Classroom Management: Creating a Successful K-12 Learning Community/Third Edition, by Paul R. Burden
ISBN 0-471-71073-3   Copyright © 2006 John Wiley & Sons, Inc.

CHAPTER OUTLINE

Even with an effective management system in place, students may lose interest in the lesson and get off task. You must be prepared to respond with appropriate strategies to restore order. How should you respond to students who are simply off task? What options do you have when a student misbehaves? What are some practices to avoid? This chapter addresses these issues and proposes a three-step response plan to misbehavior.

INTERVENTIONS

The teacher must decide when and how to intervene when students are off task or are misbehaving. An *intervention* is an action taken by the teacher that is intended to stop the disruptive actions and return the student to the academic activities.

Intervention decisions are typically based on the teacher's knowledge of who is misbehaving, what the misbehavior is, and when it occurs. Decisions about the type of the intervention may depend on the student's history of inappropriate behavior. However, you should not automatically jump to conclusions if an incident involves a student with a history of behavior problems. It is helpful to discuss the problem with the student to clarify the problem from both your perspective and the student's before considering the possible interventions.

The Principle of Least Intervention

The *principle of least intervention* states that when dealing with routine classroom behavior, misbehaviors should be corrected with the simplest, least intrusive intervention that will work (Slavin, 2006). If the least intrusive intervention does not work, then you move up to a more intrusive approach. The main goal is to handle the misbehavior in an effective manner that avoids unnecessarily disrupting the lesson. To the extent possible, the lesson should continue while misbehavior is handled.

How do you apply this principle of least intervention? When you notice students starting to lose interest in the lesson or beginning to get off task, you can provide situational assistance—actions to help the student cope with the situation and keep the student on task. If the student then is off task, you can select mild responses to get the student back on task. If mild responses are not effective, you next use moderate responses. Based on the principle of least intervention, this continuum of teacher responses is displayed in Table 11.1 below, and details are provided later in this chapter.

VOICES FROM THE CLASSROOM *Discuss the Problem with the Student*

Claudia Swisher, high school English teacher, Norman, Oklahoma

When I need to correct some specific student behavior or to deal with a problem, I always tell the student to "Meet me in the hall." I have learned that confrontations in class are set up as power plays, and the student has little reason to try to correct the behavior in front of the class. I don't explain the reasons for calling the student into the hall and don't answer any questions in the room. Once the student and I are in the hall, I explain my concern and focus on what needs to be done when we both return to the classroom.

I don't allow the student to change the subject or excuse the behavior. I do listen, and I have often found that I have misunderstood some aspect of the behavior. If more privacy is needed, I will track down a student during my planning period and ask his or her current teacher for a few minutes. The student and I may walk the halls, sit in an empty room, or sit outside. Many misunderstandings can be worked out in this way, and my students know that I respect their feelings.

I know that dealing with these problems in private keeps both the student and me safe from an audience and allows us to be honest. By the end of the year, my students know that "Meet me in the hall" isn't the first step to a confrontation, but an attempt to solve a little problem before it becomes too big for us.

Some Practices to Avoid

Research and practice suggest that some interventions are inappropriate or unsuccessful when trying to restore control. In a comprehensive review of the literature concerning behavior management techniques, Weber and Roff (1983) found that disadvantages outweigh the advantages in the use of harsh reprimands, threats, and physical punishment. Furthermore, practitioners have identified additional approaches that have questionable effectiveness. The message is clear—teachers should avoid the following practices.

1. Harsh and Humiliating Reprimands. A harsh reprimand is very negative verbal feedback. Teachers may be carried away with this verbal thrashing and humiliate the student. Research reports suggest that the use of harsh reprimands is a very ineffective, inefficient, and costly strategy. Harsh reprimands include speaking to the student in an exceptionally stern manner, yelling, and screaming. All of this may progress to the point where the student is humiliated.

2. Threats. A threat is a statement that expresses the intent to punish if the student does not comply with the teacher's wishes. Most practitioners and researchers believe the disadvantages of using threats outweigh any possible benefits. Teachers may warn students to alert them to potential consequences, but a threat often expresses more severe consequences than would normally be expected and may be stated when the teacher has lost emotional control.

3. *Nagging.* Continual or unnecessary scolding only upsets the student and arouses the resentment of other students. The teacher may consider these scoldings as mini-lectures, but they are seen as nagging from the students' point of view.

4. *Forced Apologies.* Forcing a student to express an apology that is not felt is a way of forcing him or her to lie. This approach solves nothing.

5. *Sarcastic Remarks.* Sarcastic remarks are statements that the teacher uses to deride, taunt, or ridicule the student. While the teacher may consider these statements as a means of punishment, they create resentment; they may lower the student's self-esteem, and may lower the esteem of the teacher in the eyes of the students.

6. *Group Punishment.* Group punishment occurs when the entire class or group is punished because of the misbehavior of an individual. Peer pressure is intended to help modify the individual's behavior. Group punishment is difficult to use effectively, and the undesirable side effects are likely to outweigh the advantages. It forces students to choose between the teacher and a classmate. Many students will unite in sullen defiance of the teacher and refuse to blame the classmate if group punishment is used. Even if they go along with the teacher, the punishment engenders unhealthy attitudes.

7. *Assigning Extra Academic Work.* When assigning extra academic work as a punishment, the teacher implies that the work is unpleasant. It is often in the form of homework that is not normally required. The student then associates schoolwork with punishment. This is not the message teachers should convey.

8. *Reducing Grades.* Penalizing a student academically for misbehavior again creates an undesirable association. Students who are penalized for misbehaving may develop an attitude of "What's the use?" toward academic work. Furthermore, reducing grades for misbehavior confounds the grade, which is intended to report only the student's academic progress.

9. *Writing As Punishment.* After students misbehave, teachers may have them copy pages out of a dictionary, encyclopedia, or other book, or have students write a certain statement ("I will not do such and such again.") a number of times. Unfortunately, this approach leads to hostility from the students, gives the impression that writing is a bad thing (English teachers would get upset about the message being conveyed here), and is not logically linked to what the students may have done.

10. *Physical Labor or Exercise.* A teacher may use push-ups or some other physical action as punishment. However, the teacher may not be familiar with the student's physical abilities, and the student could get hurt. In addition to concerns about the student's safety, having students do extra exercises in physical education in response to misbehavior may cause the student to lose interest in the physical activities.

11. *Corporal Punishment.* Corporal punishment is a strategy in which the teacher inflicts physical pain on the student to punish the student for misbehaving. Paddling, spanking, slapping, and pinching are examples. There are many disadvantages to using physical consequences (Hyman, 1990, 1997). Other negative behaviors often emerge, such as escape (running away from the punisher), avoidance (lying, stealing, cheating), anxiety, fear, tension, stress, withdrawal, poor self-concept, resistance, and counter aggression. Many districts have a policy either prohibiting the use of corporal punishment or establishing specific guidelines for its limited use.

WHAT WOULD YOU DECIDE? *Creating a Learning Community*

In *Beyond Discipline: From Compliance to Community* (1996), Alfie Kohn makes an articulate and passionate argument for the reduction of punishment. He challenges educators to ask this question when planning to work with students: "What do they require in order to flourish, and how can we provide those things?" Kohn says teachers should focus on developing caring, supportive classrooms where students participate in problem solving, including problems about behavior. He advises teachers to develop a sense of community in their classrooms.

1. If you were to adopt Kohn's ideas, how would that affect your selection of rules and procedures and your selection of consequences for infractions?

2. To contribute as members of the learning community and participate in decision making, what knowledge and skills would students need to have?

3. How would you justify to parents your classroom approaches where students have so much say in how the class is run?

Cautions and Guidelines for Punishment

The later steps of the principle of least intervention may involve punishment. *Punishment* is the act of imposing a penalty with the intention of suppressing undesirable behavior. There are two procedures for achieving this purpose: (a) withholding positive reinforcers or desirable stimuli through techniques such as logical consequences and behavior modification approaches such as time-out and loss of privileges; and (b) adding aversive stimuli through actions where students receive a penalty for their misbehavior. Withholding positive reinforcers is considered to be less harmful than adding aversive stimuli.

Especially for beginning teachers, dealing with misbehavior that requires moderate or severe responses can be very troubling. It is often helpful to talk with the principal, other teachers, or school counselors to obtain ideas and advice for dealing with students who exhibit more serious misbehavior. In addition, it is often useful to contact the student's parents at any point to inform them of any concerns you might have and to solicit their help in working with the student.

You should express confidence in the students' ability to improve, and punish only as a last resort when students repeatedly fail to respond to more positive treatment. Apply punishment as part of a planned response, not as a means to release your anger or frustration.

The following factors are important to consider when effectively using punishment.

1. *Discuss and Reward Acceptable Behaviors.* Acceptable behaviors should be emphasized when classroom rules are first discussed. Make it clear to students why the rules exist. Discuss the reasons for not engaging in the behavior considered to be inappropriate. Most students will behave appropriately if they know what is expected.

2. *Clearly Specify the Behaviors That Will Lead to Punishment.* Clarifying acceptable behaviors for the students may not be enough. To help the students understand, examples of behaviors that break the rules and lead to punishment should be identified and discussed.

3. *Use Punishment Only When Rewards or Nonpunitive Interventions Have Not Worked, or If the Behavior must be Decreased Quickly Because it is Dangerous.* Punishment should be used as a last resort when other techniques have failed.

4. *Administer Punishment in a Calm, Unemotional Manner.* If you deliver punishment while still emotionally upset, you may select an overly harsh punishment and may also provoke the student into further inappropriate reactions. Punishment should not be an involuntary emotional response, a way to get revenge, or a spontaneous response to provocation.

5. *Deliver a Warning before Punishment Is Applied to Any Behavior.* The warning itself could reduce the need for the punishment. If the student does not correct the behavior after the warning, punishment should be delivered at the next occurrence.

6. *Apply Punishment Fairly to Everyone Who Exhibits the Targeted Behaviors.* You should treat both sexes the same way, and low-achieving and high-achieving students the same way.

7. *Apply Punishment Consistently after Every Occurrence of the Targeted Misbehavior.* Behaviors that reliably receive punishment are less likely to be tried by students than behaviors that occasionally go uncorrected.

8. *Use Punishment of Sufficient Intensity to Suppress the Unwanted Behaviors.* Generally speaking, the greater the intensity, the longer lasting the effect. But this does not mean that you need to resort to extreme measures. For example, the loss of positive reinforcement because of inappropriate behavior is better than shouting "don't do that" with increasing intensity.

9. *Select a Punishment That Is Effective, That Is Not Associated with a Positive or Rewarding Experience, and That Fits the Situation.* Not all aversive consequences that you select may be seen as punishment. Some students, for instance, might think that it is a reward to be placed in a time-out area in the classroom. In that case, a different consequence should be used that is not seen by the student as being positive or rewarding.

10. *Avoid Extended Periods of Punishment.* Lengthy, mild punishment such as missing open study time for a week may have a boomerang effect. Punishment with a short duration is more effective.

A THREE-STEP RESPONSE PLAN

When off-task behavior and misbehavior occurs, a three-step response plan can be followed as a means to restore order and get the students back on task. The three steps described here and shown in Table 11.1 are based on the principle of least intervention discussed earlier. You provide situational assistance as the first approach to get the student back on task, and then sequentially apply mild and moderate responses. If misbehavior continues after moderate responses are applied, other interventions may be needed. In these cases, it is useful to discuss the situation with the principal and school counselor.

Table 11.1 A Three-Step Response Plan to Misbehavior Using the Principle of Least Intervention

Teacher Response	Step 1 Provide Situational Assistance	Step 2 Use Mild Responses	Step 3 Use Moderate Responses
Purpose	To help the student cope with the instructional situation and keep the student on task	To take nonpunitive actions to get the student back on task	To remove desired stimuli to decrease unwanted behavior
Sample Actions	• Remove distracting objects • Provide support with routines • Reinforce appropriate behaviors • Boost student interest • Provide cues • Help student over hurdles • Redirect the behavior • Alter the lesson • Provide nonpunitive time-out • Modify the classroom environment	*Nonverbal Responses* • Ignore the behavior • Use nonverbal signals • Stand near the student • Touch the student *Verbal Responses* • Call on the student during the lesson • Use humor • Send an I-message • Use positive phrasing • Remind students of the rules • Give students choices • Ask "What should you be doing?" • Give a verbal reprimand	*Logical Consequences* • Withdraw privileges • Change the seat assignment • Write reflections on the problem • Place student in time-out • Hold student for detention • Contact the parents • Have student visit the principal

Situational Assistance

Students sometimes pause from the instructional task to look out the window, daydream, fiddle with a comb or other object, or simply take a brief mental break from the work. In these examples, the students are not misbehaving—they are simply off task for a short time. You should take steps to draw the student back into the lesson and to keep the student on task.

To communicate to the student that you have noticed off-task behavior, you should first provide *situational assistance*—actions designed to help the students cope with the instructional situation and to keep them on task or to get them back on task before problems worsen. Problem behaviors thus can be stopped early before they escalate or involve other students.

If students remain off task after situational assistance is provided, move on to *mild responses*. These nonverbal and verbal nonpunitive responses are designed to get the student back on task. The continuum of responses to misbehavior (see Table 11.1) illustrates that situational assistance is the starting point when dealing with off-task behavior. The following techniques can be used to provide situational assistance to help get the students back on task.

1. *Remove Distracting Objects.* Students sometimes bring objects to school that may be distracting, such as combs, key, or magazines. When you see that these objects are keeping the students from the assigned tasks, simply walk over to the student and collect the object. The student should be quietly informed that the object can be picked up after class. Be kind and firm; no discussion is necessary. Inform students that they should store such objects in an appropriate place before school.

2. *Provide Support with Routines.* Students appreciate and often find comfort in knowing what is going to happen during the class period or during the day. They like to know where, when, why, and with whom they will be at various times. It is helpful to announce and post the daily schedule. Changes in the schedule should be announced in advance, if possible. Even for a single lesson, students often appreciate knowing at the start what activities are planned for the lesson. Knowing the schedule provides students with a sense of security and direction. Routines for entering and leaving the classroom, distributing classroom papers and materials, and participating in group work contribute to this sense of security.

3. *Reinforce Appropriate Behaviors.* Students who have followed the directions can be praised. This communicates to the student who is off task what is expected. A statement such as, "I'm pleased to see that Juan has his notebook ready for today's lesson" communicates to others what is expected. Appropriate behavior is reinforced while simultaneously giving a signal to students who are off task. While commonly used in elementary classrooms, this approach may be considered a little juvenile by middle and secondary students.

4. *Boost Student Interest.* Student interest may wane in time as the lesson proceeds. You should express interest in the student's work when the student shows signs of losing interest or being bored. Offer to help, noting how much work has been completed, noting how well done the completed part of the task is, or discussing the task. These actions can help bring the student back on task. Interest boosting is often needed when students do individual or small-group class work.

5. *Provide Cues.* Sometimes all the students are asked to do one thing, such as to prepare their materials or to clean up at the end of class, and cues can be given in these cases. *Cues* are signals that it is time for a selected behavior. For example, you may close the door at the start of class as a cue that instruction is about to begin and that everyone is expected to have all materials ready. The lights could be flipped or a bell sounded to signal time to begin cleanup or to finish small-group work. You can select an appropriate cue and explain its use to the students. This conveys behavioral expectations and encourages constructive, on-task behavior.

WHAT WOULD YOU DECIDE?   *Using Cues or Signals*

Imagine that your students are working in cooperative learning groups on a seven-day project. When the students come into the room, they immediately go to their groups and start work. On some days and during some of the class sessions, you need to give some information to all students.

1. How can you use a cue as a signal for students to stop work at that point and pay attention to you?

2. How can you give a cue that it is time to prepare to leave the class at the end of the class period?

6. *Help Students over Hurdles.* Students who are experiencing difficulty with a specific task need help in overcoming that problem—help over a hurdle—to keep them on task. Hurdle helping may consist of encouraging words from you, an offer to assist with a specific task, or making available additional materials or equipment. For example, in a seatwork activity in which students need to draw several elements, including some straight lines, you might notice that one student is becoming upset that her lines are not straight. You could help her by handing her a ruler. In this way, you help before the student gives up on the assignment or becomes disruptive.

7. *Redirect the Behavior.* When students show signs of losing interest, you can ask them to answer a question, to do a problem, or to read as a means of drawing them back into the lesson. Students should be treated as if they were paying attention and should be reinforced if they respond appropriately. It is important not to embarrass or ridicule students by saying that they would have been able to answer the question if they had been paying attention. Simply by asking a content-related question, students will recognize that you are trying to draw them back into the lesson. Redirecting student behavior back into the lesson discourages off-task behavior.

8. *Alter the Lesson.* Lessons sometimes do not go as well as you would like, and students may lose interest in the lesson for a variety of reasons. The lesson needs to be altered in some way when students are seen daydreaming, writing notes to friends, yawning, stretching, or moving around in their seats. When altering the lesson, select a different type of activity from the one that has proven to be unsuccessful. For example, if a whole-class discussion proves unsuccessful, you might have students work in pairs on a related issue that still deals with the lesson's objectives.

In your initial planning, take student interests and abilities into account and provide a variety of activities in each lesson. The need to alter the lesson once underway is thereby minimized. It is helpful to have several types of activities planned in each lesson, some requiring active student participation. Consider the length of time allocated to each activity by taking into account the students' age and maturity.

9. *Provide Nonpunitive Time-Out.* Students who become frustrated, agitated, or fatigued may get off task and disruptive. When you notice this happening, you could provide a nonpunitive time-out. A *time-out* is a period of time that the student is away from the instructional situation to calm down and reorganize his or her thoughts. The student then returns to the task with a fresh perspective. This time-out is not intended to be punishment for the off-task behavior. When a time-out is needed, you could ask the student to run an errand, help you with something, go get a drink, or do some other task not related to the instructional activity. Be alert to students showing signs of frustration and agitation and be ready to respond quickly.

Sometimes it is useful to have a small area of the room specifically designated for time-outs. This could be a desk placed off in a corner, partially hidden by a filing cabinet. The student could go to this semiprivate area in an effort to calm down and prepare to continue with the lesson. You could suggest that the students be allowed to go to this area when they think they need it. Students who use the corner for nonpunitive time-out should be allowed to decide themselves when they are ready to return.

10. *Modify the Classroom Environment.* The classroom environment itself may contribute to off-task behavior. The arrangement of the desks, tables, instructional materials, and other items in the classroom may give rise to inefficient traffic patterns or limited views of the instructional areas. Other factors include the boundaries between areas for quiet student and group projects and access to supplies. In addition, both your actions and those of your students may affect their behavior. Once misbehavior develops, you may need to separate the students or change the setting in some way. Examine the disturbance and identify the element that contributes to it. Modification in the classroom arrangement may include moving tables, student desks, or the storage area.

Mild Responses

Students may misbehave even after you have developed a system of rules and procedures, provided a supportive instructional environment, and given situational assistance to get misbehaving students back on task. In that case, mild responses should be used to correct the student's behavior. Mild responses are nonpunitive ways to deal with misbehavior while providing guidance for appropriate behavior. Nonverbal and verbal mild responses are meant to stop the off-task behavior and to restore order. The three-step response plan shown in Table 11.1 above illustrates the movement to more directive responses if situational assistance is not successful.

Nonverbal Responses

Even with situational assistance, students may get off task. Nonverbal responses are taken as a nonpunitive means to get the student back on task. Nonverbal responses may include ignoring the behavior, nonverbal signals, standing near the student, and touching the student. These approaches are taken in increasing order of teacher involvement and control.

Shrigley (1985) studied 523 off-task behaviors, and found that 40 percent of the behaviors could be corrected by the nonverbal responses discussed here. Five percent of the behaviors were corrected by ignoring the behavior, 14 percent were corrected by nonverbal signals, 12 percent by standing near the student, and nine percent by touching the student. Nonverbal approaches successfully extinguish many off-task behaviors. If these approaches do not work, higher control approaches such as verbal interventions need to be used.

WHAT WOULD YOU DECIDE?   *Using Nonverbal Responses*

When students are working in small groups on an activity, you notice a group where two students are off task.

1. How could you respond nonverbally to get these two students back on task? What factors might affect your decision on the particular method?

2. At a later time, you are making a presentation to the whole class when you notice two other students off task. What nonverbal responses might you make in that situation?

1. *Ignore the Behavior.* Intentionally ignoring minor misbehavior is sometimes the best course of action as a means to weaken the behavior. This is based on the reinforcement principle called extinction; that is, if you ignore a behavior and withhold reinforcement, the behavior will lessen and ultimately disappear. Minor misbehaviors that might be ignored are pencil tapping, body movements, hand waving, book dropping, calling out an answer instead of raising a hand, interrupting the teacher, whispering, and so on. Behaviors designed to get your attention or that of classmates are likely candidates for extinction, or ignoring the behavior.

Ignoring the behavior is best used to control only behaviors that cause little interference to teaching/learning, and it should be combined with praise for appropriate behavior. Extinction is inappropriate for behaviors (e.g., talking out and aggression) reinforced by consequences that you do not control, or for behaviors (violence) that cannot be tolerated during the time required for extinction to work (Kerr & Nelson, 2006). If the behavior continues after a reasonable period of planned ignoring, you should be more directive.

There are limitations to ignoring the behavior. One risk is that students may conclude that you are not aware of what is happening and may continue the behavior. Although you may ignore the behavior and do not give the student the desired attention, other students may give such attention. Furthermore, the student may continue the behavior for a while after you ignore it, and thus the time taken for correcting the problem is too long.

2. *Use Nonverbal Signals.* A nonverbal signal can be used to communicate to the disrupting student that the behavior is not appropriate. Signals must be directed at the student. They let the student know that the behavior is inappropriate and that it is time to get back to work. Nonverbal signals may include making eye contact with the student who is writing a note, shaking a hand or finger to indicate not to do some inappropriate action, holding a hand up to stop a student's calling out, or giving "the teacher look." These actions should be done in a businesslike manner. You need to move to the next level of intervention if these disruptive behaviors persist.

3. *Stand Near the Student.* Your physical presence near the disruptive student to help the student get back on task is proximity control. This is sometimes warranted when you can't get the student's attention to send a signal because the student is so engrossed in an inappropriate action. For example, a student may be reading something other than class-related material or may be writing a note. While doing this, the student may not even look up at you. As a result, signals will not work. While conducting the lesson, walk around the room and approach the student's desk. It is then likely that the student will notice your presence and put the material away without a word being spoken.

Some proximity control techniques may be somewhat subtle, such as walking toward the student, while other approaches such as standing near the student's desk are more direct. If students do not respond to proximity control, you need to move to a more directive level of intervention.

VOICES FROM THE CLASSROOM   *Using Body Language and "The Teacher Look"*

Lynne Hagar, high school history and English teacher, Mesquite, Texas

I am a small woman, but I can effectively control 30 senior students just by using my voice and my body language. When I want a certain behavior to stop, the first thing I do is to look at the student. Even if that student is not looking at me, he or she eventually becomes aware that I am staring. Then I point at the student and nonverbally indicate that the behavior is to stop. A finger placed on my lips indicates that talking needs to stop.

Often, a questioning or disapproving look or gesture can stop undesirable behaviors right there. I may have to move into a student's personal space or comfort zone to stop a behavior, but a combination of a look and physical proximity are effective about 90 percent of the time. I might even casually rest my hand on the student's desk, never stopping teaching, and stay put for a minute or so until I'm sure the student is back on task.

My advice is to practice "the look" in the mirror until you get it right. It shouldn't be a friendly look, but it doesn't have to be angry either. Learn to say in your manner, "I am in charge here." Also, move around the classroom. Getting close to your students is essential, not only when you are correcting them but also when you want to reassure them or reinforce their positive feelings about you and your classroom. A friendly touch on the shoulder as you are helping a student with a problem or a hug when a student has a big success can go miles toward cementing your positive relationship with that student.

4. *Touch the Student.* Without any verbal exchange, you may place a hand on a student's shoulder in an effort to achieve calm, or take a student's hand and escort the student back to his or her seat. *Touch control* involves mild, nonaggressive physical contact that is used to get the student on task. It communicates that you disapprove of the action. Talk to your principal to be certain you understand the guidelines and legal considerations of appropriate touching.

When deciding whether and how to use touch control, you may take into account the circumstances of the behavior and the characteristics of the students. Students who are angry or visibly upset sometimes do not want to be touched, and some do not want to be touched at any time. How well touch will be received depends on where it occurs and how long it lasts. A touch on the back, hand, arm, or shoulder is acceptable to many students, whereas touch to the face, neck, leg, chest, or other more personal areas are often not acceptable. Brief touch is considered acceptable; the longer the touch, the more it becomes unacceptable.

Verbal Responses

Although nonverbal mild responses may be effective, verbal responses can be used as nonpunitive, mild responses to misbehavior. Their purpose is to get the student back on task with limited disruption and intervention. Various verbal responses are described below.

1. *Call on the Student During the Lesson.* You can recapture a misbehaving student's attention by using his or her name in the lesson, such as, "Now, in this next example, suppose that Kimberly had three polygons that she ....." You could ask a question of the student to recapture the student's attention. Calling on the student in these ways allows you to communicate that you know what is going on and to capture the student's attention without citing the misbehavior. Be cautious—student's dignity should be preserved. If you call on students in these ways only when they misbehave, they will sense that you are just waiting to catch them misbehaving, and this strategy will backfire by creating resentment (Good & Brophy, 2003).

2. *Use Humor.* Humor can be used as a gentle reminder to students to correct their behavior. Humor directed at the situation or even at yourself can defuse tension that might be created due to the misbehavior. It can depersonalize the situation and thus help resolve the problem. You must be careful that the humor is not sarcastic. Sarcasm includes statements that are directed at or make fun of the student; these statements are intended to "put down" or cause pain to the student. Instead, humor is directed at or makes fun of the situation or the teacher. The student may then reconsider his or her actions and then get back on task.

3. *Send an I-Message.* An *I-message* is a statement you make to a misbehaving student that prompts appropriate behavior without giving a direct command (Gordon, 1991). An I-message has three parts: (a) a brief description of the misbehavior; (b) a description of its effects on you or the other students; and (c) a description of your feelings about the effects. For example, you might say, "When you tap your pen on the desk during the test, it makes a lot of noise and I am concerned that it might distract other students." I-messages are intended to help students recognize that their behavior has consequences on other students and that you have genuine feelings about the actions. Since I-messages leave the decision about changing one's behavior up to the student, they are likely to promote a sense of responsibility.

4. *Use Positive Phrasing.* Positive phrasing is used when inappropriate off-task behavior allows you to highlight positive outcomes for appropriate behavior (Shrigley, 1985). This usually takes the form, "When you do X (behave in a particular appropriate way), then you can do Y (a positive outcome)." For example, when a student is out of her seat, you might say, "Renee, when you return to your seat, it will be your turn to participate in the activity." Through the use of positive phrasing, you redirect students from disruptive to appropriate behavior by simply stating the positive outcomes.

5. *Remind Students of the Rules.* Each classroom needs to have a set of rules that govern student behavior, along with a set of consequences for breaking them. When students see that consequences of misbehavior are in fact delivered, reminders of the rules can help them get back on task because they do not want the consequences. When one student is poking another student, for example, you might say, "Delores, the classroom rules state that students must keep their hands and feet to themselves." This reminder often ends the misbehavior because the student does not want the consequence. If the inappropriate behavior continues, you must deliver the consequence; otherwise the reminder will be of little value because students will recognize that there is no follow-through.

6. *Give Students Choices.* Some students feel defensive when confronted about their misbehavior. As a result, you can give them choices about resolving the problem. This allows the student to feel that he or she settled the problem without appearing to back down. All of the choices that you give to the student should lead to resolution of the problem. If a student is talking to another nearby student, you might say, "Harvey, you can turn back in your seat and get back to your project, or you can take the empty seat at the end of the row." In this way, Harvey has a choice, but the result is that he gets back to work in his seat or in the seat at the end of the row.

VOICES FROM THE CLASSROOM | *Giving Students Choices*

Terri Jenkins, Middle School English Teacher, Hephzibah, Georgia

Avoiding conflict is important for classroom survival. This is especially true if the student is trying to seek power or attention. By giving the student a choice in resolving a problem, you defuse the situation and avoid a conflict.

For example, a student may be talking with a neighbor while you are giving instructions. You might say, "Brian, I really need quiet while I am giving directions so that everyone can hear. You have a choice: (1) you may remain where you are and stop talking to Mary, or (2) you may reseat yourself somewhere else in the classroom. Thanks." Then you should walk away.

In this way, students have the power to make a choice. They do not feel challenged and usually respond appropriately. The behavior stops, and little instructional time is lost. Choices should not be punitive or rewarding; they should be designed to stop the misbehavior.

When giving choices, you should be polite and courteous, being careful that the tone of your voice is emotionless. After stating the choices, you should say thank you and then walk away from the student. In this way, it becomes obvious that you expect the student to comply.

---

7. Ask, "What Should You Be Doing?". Glasser (1998a) proposes that teachers ask disruptive students questions in an effort to direct them back to appropriate behavior. When a student is disruptive, you might ask, "What should you be doing?" This question can have a positive effect because it helps redirect the student back to appropriate behavior. Of course, some students may not answer this question honestly or not reply at all. In that case, you should make statements related to the question, for example, "Keith, you were swearing and name calling. That is against our classroom rules. You should not swear or call others names." If the student continues to break the rule, then appropriate consequences should be delivered.

8. Give a Verbal Reprimand. A very straightforward way to have the students stop misbehaving is to simply ask or direct them to do so. This is sometimes called a *desist order* or a *reprimand*, and it is given to decrease unwanted behavior. Verbal reprimands are effective with many mild and moderate behavior problems, but by themselves are less successful with severe behavior disorders (Kerr & Nelson, 2006).

A *direct appeal* involves a courteous request for the student to stop the misbehavior and to get back on task. You might say, "Martina, please put away the comb and continue with the class assignment." A direct appeal often gives the student a sense of ownership for deciding to get back on task and to do as you requested. The student feels a sense of responsibility.

As an alternative, you could use a *direct command* in which you take the responsibility and give a direction in a straightforward manner, such as, "Wayne, stop talking with your friends and get to work on the lab activity." With the direct appeal and the direct command, the student is expected to comply with your directions. If the student defies your request or command, you must be prepared to deliver an appropriate consequence.

Soft reprimands, audible only to the misbehaving student, are more effective than loud reprimands in reducing disruptive classroom behavior (Kerr & Nelson, 2006). Soft, private reprimands do not call the attention of the entire class to the misbehaving student and also may be less likely to trigger emotional reactions.

Moderate Responses

Following situational assistance and mild nonverbal and verbal responses, students might continue to misbehave. In that case, moderate responses should be used to correct the problem. The three-step response plan shown in Table 11.1 illustrates the movement to more directive responses if mild responses are not successful.

Moderate responses are intended to be punitive ways to deal with misbehavior by removing desired stimuli to decrease the occurrence of the inappropriate behavior. Moderate responses include logical consequences and behavior modification techniques. Because student behaviors that warrant moderate responses are more problematic than mild misbehaviors, it is often useful to discuss specific problems with the principal, other teachers, or the school counselor. Parents can be contacted at any point in an effort to inform them of their child's actions and to solicit their help.

A *logical consequence* is an event that is arranged by the teacher that is directly and logically related to the misbehavior (Dreikurs et al., 1982). The consequence should be reasonable, respectful, and related to the student action. For instance, if a student leaves paper on the classroom floor, the student must pick the paper off the floor. If a student breaks the rule of speaking out without raising his or her hand, you would ignore the response and call on a student whose hand is up. If a student marks on the desk, the student is required to clean the marks off. Students are more likely to respond favorably to logical consequences because they do not consider the consequences mean or unfair.

You may tell the student what the consequence is right after the behavior occurs, for example, "Milton, you left the study area a mess. You need to clean it up at the end of class." As an alternative, you may give the student a choice when inappropriate behavior is noticed. This tells the student that the inappropriate behavior must be changed or, if it isn't changed, that a particular consequence will occur. For example, you may say, "Joellen, you have a choice of not bothering students near you or having your seat changed."

When given a choice, students will often stop the inappropriate behavior. This approach can be very effective because the student feels a sense of ownership in solving the problem, and the issue is over quickly. Of course, if the problem behavior continues, you must deliver the consequence that you stated to the student.

At the start of the school year, you should think of two or three logical consequences for each of the classroom rules and inform students of these consequences. Logical, reasonable consequences are preplanned, and you are not under the pressure of thinking up something appropriate at the time the misbehavior occurs. Some examples of logical consequences include the following:

- ***Withdraw Privileges.*** As a regular part of the classroom activities, you may provide your students with a number of special privileges such as a trip to the library, use of a computer, use of special equipment or a game, service as a classroom helper, or other valued privilege. If the misbehavior relates to the type of privilege offered, a logical consequence would be to withdraw the privilege. For example, if a student mishandles some special equipment, then the student would lose the privilege of using the equipment.

- ***Change the Seat Assignment.*** Students may talk, poke, or interact with other students in nearby seats. Sometimes a problem occurs because certain students are seated near each other. Other times, just the placement of the seats enables easy interaction. If inappropriate interaction occurs, a logical consequence would be to relocate the student's seat.

- ***Have the Student Write Reflections on the Problem.*** It is often useful to ask the student to reflect on the situation to help the student recognize the logical connection between the behavior and the consequences. You may ask the student to provide written responses to certain questions; this might be done during a time out.

These questions may include: What is the problem? What did I do to create the problem? What should happen to me? What should I do next time to avoid a problem? Other questions may require the student to describe the rule that was broken, why the student chose to misbehave, who was bothered by the misbehavior, what more appropriate behavior could be chosen next time, and what should happen to the student the next time the misbehavior occurs.

Written responses to these or similar questions help students see their behavior more objectively and promote more self control. You may choose to have the student sign and date the written responses for future reference. The written responses can be useful if the parents need to be contacted at a later time.

VOICES FROM THE CLASSROOM   *Using an Oops Sheet for Reflections*

Lisa Bietau, Fourth-Grade Teacher, Manhattan, Kansas

When my students misbehave, I sometimes ask them to fill out an OOPS sheet to have them reflect on their behavior. OOPS stands for "Outstanding Opportunity for a Personal Stretch." The sheet has a place for their name and date at the top. Then there are several other areas that the student needs to fill in: (1) Describe the problem. (2) What other choices did you have to settle the situation without difficulty? (3) How might you handle this differently if it happens again?

After the student fills out the OOPS sheet, I meet with the student privately to discuss the situation briefly and to review the options and solutions that the student wrote. This reflection and discussion with me helps the students understand my expectations and recognize that they have a responsibility to consider reasonable options when they meet a challenging situation.

I sign the OOPS sheet and make a copy for my files. The original is then sent home with the student to obtain the parent's signature. All of the student's privileges are suspended until the signed sheet is returned. If the sheet is not returned the next day, I call the parents and another copy is sent home if necessary. I have found that students show more self-control after completing the OOPS sheet.

• *Place the Student in a Time Out.* Sometimes a student is talking or disrupting the class in such a way that interferes with the progress of the lesson. In such a case, the student could be excluded from the group; this is called a time out. Removing the student from the group is a logical consequence of interfering with the group. An area of the room should be established as the time out area, such as a desk in a corner or partially behind a filing cabinet. As a general rule, time out should last no longer than 10 minutes.

• *Hold the Student for Detention.* *Detention* means detaining or holding back students when they normally would be free to go and do other things. The student is deprived of free time and perhaps the opportunity to socialize with other students. Detention may include remaining after class or staying after school.

Detention can be a logical consequence for student behaviors that waste class time. A student might be asked to work on the social studies paper that wasn't completed during class due to inappropriate behavior. Students will soon see the logic that time wasted in class will have to be made up later, on their own time in detention.

Make sure the student understands the reasons for the detention. It should logically fit the offense, and the time should not be excessive—20 to 30 minutes after school would be reasonable. Confer with the student and work out a plan to help the student avoid detention in the future and move toward self control.

• *Contact the Parents.* If a student shows a pattern of repeated misbehavior, then you may need to contact the parents or guardians. The logic here is that if all earlier attempts to extinguish the misbehavior do not work, it is appropriate to go to a higher authority. Parents may be notified by a note or a letter to inform them of the problem and to solicit their involvement or support. You may choose to call the parents instead. If the situation is fairly serious, a conference with the parents may be warranted.

• *Have the Student Visit the Principal.* In cases of repeated misbehavior or serious misbehavior, such as fighting, students may be sent to the school office to see the principal. The principal may talk with the student in an effort to use his or her legitimate authority to influence the student to behave properly. Some schools have specific procedures to be followed when students are sent to the principal. When the behavior problems reach this point, additional personnel, including the school counselor or psychologist and the parents, need to be consulted to help the student.

Developing Your Management Plan: *Responding to Inappropriate Behavior*

When planning for the school year, it is important to establish a plan to deal with misbehavior. This chapter provided a number of ways to organize your plan based on the principle of least intervention. Yet, you may want to adapt some these ideas based on your own philosophical perspective, the grade level and/or subject that you teach, or other factors. For each of the following items, think about and write your intentions to deal with student misbehavior.

Your responses will be the basis for your overall plan to deal with misbehavior.

a. Providing situational assistance

b. Using mild responses to misbehavior

c. Using moderate responses to misbehavior

d. Last Dealing with chronic or challenging misbehavior

DEALING WITH CHRONIC MISBEHAVIORS

Chronic misbehaviors are troublesome behaviors that students repeatedly or compulsively perform. They include tattling, clowning, cheating, lying, stealing, profanity, rudeness toward the teacher, defiance or hostility, and failure to do school work. This behavior is recurring and inappropriate, and teachers can take actions to minimize their presence in the classroom (Gootman, 2001). Strategies to address a number of common chronic misbehaviors are presented here.

1. *Tattling.* Tattling occurs when students report minor infractions or perceived injustices to the teacher. Tattling is not disruptive, but it can become a problem when students commonly report minor, petty complaints. To prevent tattling from occurring in the first place, it is important that you let students know what kinds of information they should and should not report to you. You need to know about an incident where a student got hurt, for example, but not when some other student is not doing the school work.

Many teachers, especially in the primary grades, have an explicit lesson about tattling. They describe the difference between reporting important information to the teacher and reports that are tattling about minor infractions. Numerous examples can be provided and discussed for each category. Students can offer example, as well. It is important to convey to students that you will be available to help them with important matters, but that you are not interested in minor complaints.

2. *Clowning.* Students who clown behave in silly or funny ways, or may play practical jokes. This clowning is disruptive to the class. Figuring out the source of the student's clowning can help determine what to do about it (Gootman, 2001). Some students may use clowning to cover up a deficiency; they may clown during a math lesson because they are weak in math. Clowning also may be a vehicle for a student to achieve success—to gain some recognition, fame, and popularity among other students. Still, clowning may be a way of venting frustrations and pressures that students may experience from school, home, or other factors.

Keeping a record of who, what, when, where, and how for clowning incidents can help pinpoint the source of the clowning. Then you can meet privately with the student to discuss the pattern of the clowning behavior and why it is disruptive. Help the student figure out ways to meet his or her needs without being disruptive.

3. *Cheating.* Cheating involves students getting answers or projects from someone else and turning it in as their own. Students may cheat for several reasons. They may cheat if our expectations are too high and they may not be capable of mastering the material. Students then may see cheating as a way out. Other students may simply not be prepared, or they may have test anxiety.

It is best to minimize the temptation to cheat by discussing the difference between helping and cheating, demonstrating expected behaviors for various activities, and having students identify appropriate and inappropriate actions. In addition, it is important to minimize the opportunity to cheat by desk placement during tests and by giving attention to policies, procedures, and submission guidelines for other types of student products.

If you catch a student cheating, you can talk to the student privately, present your reasons for suspecting cheating, express concern and try to find out why the student cheated, explain the consequences, and then discuss the consequences for subsequent cheating (Weinstein & Mignano, 2003). Rather than giving the student a zero on the assignment, you may ask the student to complete the test or assignment again under controlled conditions where cheating cannot occur. Some schools have predetermined consequences for cheating, such as parental notification.

4. *Lying.* Lying involves saying something that is not true in a conscious effort to deceive somebody. Students may have many reasons for lying, such as trying to protect their self-image, to mask their vulnerable points, or to inflate their image in front of others. They may feel afraid, feel insecure, or fear rejection. Students may lie to protect themselves from punishment or if we are too strict with them.

The best response is to express concern about their need to lie by saying "I wonder why you couldn't tell me what really happened?" this approach makes it easier for students to talk about the reason they felt compelled to lie. Stay clam and encourage them to discuss why they felt they needed to tell a lie. In doing so, try not to overreact or get angry with the students. Focus on the student's reasons and feelings that led to the lie. You might encourage the private conversation with a statement such as "If you tell me what really happened, we can figure out what to do about this situation and perhaps I can help you not let this happen again." Encourage students to be honest about their feelings, and use a calm problem-solving approach to help the student address the problem that caused him or her to lie in the first place.

5. *Stealing.* Stealing involves taking something that belongs to somebody else without the owner's permission. Students in early grades may still be learning the difference between sharing and taking what doesn't belong to them. Students may impulsively steal because they may want something, or they may take something from another student because they are angry with the other person.

If an incident of stealing takes place and you know the culprit, you can have a private conversation with the student about what happened. Describe what you saw and have the student return the item, replace it, or make restitution. Help the student figure out options other than stealing. You may need to respond for forcefully depending on the value of the property and the frequency of stealing. In such cases, you may need to contact the principal and the family. Because of legal implications, it is wise to discuss an incident with the principal before conducting a search of backpacks, lockers, or a student's clothing.

6. *Profanity.* Profanity occurs when students use abusive, vulgar, or irreverent language. Age plays a role in the use of profanity. Young children may simply be restating language they heard on television, by family, or by friends with little or no understanding of the meaning. An instructional response is appropriate here, rather than a disciplinary one (e.g., "We don't use words like that in school."). For other students, such language may have become a regular part of their vocabulary, or they may use profanity when they are angry with another person. In such cases, students need to see what is acceptable and unacceptable in school. Stress that using language to hurt others will not be permitted and there are other acceptable ways to express anger.

On three successive quizzes in your class, you notice that four students always get the same score.

1. Under what circumstances would you talk with these four students about their scores?

2. What could you do about the questions and the formatting of the quiz to minimize cheating?

3. What could you do about room arrangement and your monitoring of students during a quiz to minimize cheating?

7. *Rudeness Toward the Teacher.* Students may be rude to the teacher by exhibiting disagreeable or discourteous words or actions that are outside acceptable standards. Rudeness may be expressed in talking back, arguing, making crude remarks, or showing inappropriate gestures. It is best to avoid overreacting, arguing, or getting into a power struggle. A low-key, respectful response is more suitable. When rude behavior first is evident, you should inform the student that the behavior is inappropriate, and you might refer to a classroom rule that relates to respectful behaviors. If the actions continue, you should meet with the student privately to identify the reason for the behavior and to possibly deliver consequences. If the rude behavior continues, you may need to consult with the principal or counselors about additional responses.

8. *Defiance or Hostility Toward the Teacher.* Defiance occurs when a student refuses to obey or conform to teacher directions. These actions may be open, bold, or even hostile, and defiance may be in the form of a confrontation with the teacher during a class session. The best way to deal with defiance is to try to defuse it by keeping it in private and handing it individually with the student. Put the student off by saying that you will discuss the situation in a few minutes when you have time. Avoid a power struggle and remain objective. Listen to the student's point of view but don't engage in an argument. State the consequence clearly and implement it.

Here are some guidelines when students become defiant. First, stay in control of yourself. Direct the rest of the class to work on something while you speak to the student in a private area away from the rest of the students. Stand a few feet away from the defiant student (i.e., don't get in his face). Acknowledge the student's feeling by saying something like, "I can see that you are really angry." Avoid a power struggle in the conversation (e.g., "I am the boss here, and I am telling you what to do."). As a means to defuse the situation, offer the student a choice of actions for what the student needs to do next (Weinstein & Mignano, 2003).

9. *Failure to Do Work in Class or Homework.* You may have some students who regularly do not complete seatwork done in class or homework. You should first examine how you hold students academically accountable in your class (see Chapter 10) and make any needed adjustments to ensure accountability. Next, you should plan to maintain accurate records of the school work and respond early when you recognize students who are regularly not completing their class work.

You also should examine the nature of the assignments and homework. Is the material too difficult to be completed independently? Is it too boring? Is it too long? Could the material be mastered with a shorter assignment? Was there sufficient preparation in class before students were to do the seatwork or homework? Are there other ways to provide practice and to assess student progress without having seatwork and homework everyday? Your reflection on these questions may lead to your adjustment of the assignments and expectations.

When selecting seatwork and homework, it often is helpful to break it up into parts whenever possible. Work on the first few questions in class as a group before asking the students to complete the rest on their own. Monitor students closely to see that they are able to handle the work independently. Be sure to review, collect, and grade all assignments. Many teachers have homework planners where they list the assignments and due dates somewhere in the classroom.

MAIN POINTS

1. The principle of least intervention states that when dealing with routine classroom behavior, misbehavior should be corrected with the simplest, least intrusive intervention that will work. If that doesn't work, then move up to a more intrusive, directive approach.

2. Research and practice suggest that some interventions are inappropriate or unsuccessful when trying to restore order, and these practices should be avoided.

3. Due to inherent problems in the use of punishment, teachers should follow certain guidelines when using punitive responses.

4. Situational assistance is designed to help students cope with the instructional situation and to keep them on task.

5. Mild responses are nonpunitive ways to deal with misbehavior while providing guidance for appropriate behavior. Nonverbal and verbal approaches can be used.

6. Moderate responses deliver punishment by removing desired stimuli as a means of decreasing inappropriate behavior.

DISCUSSION/REFLECTIVE QUESTIONS

1. What are some positive aspects of the principle of least intervention?

2. What inappropriate interventions have you experienced or observed? What were the effects on the students?

3. What are the benefits of providing situational assistance?

4. What student misbehaviors would you be willing to deliberately ignore for a short time? What situations would you not ignore?

5. Can chronic or challenging misbehaviors be adequately addressed in the three-step response plan shown in Table 11.1, which applies the principle of least intervention?

SUGGESTED ACTIVITIES

1. Ask several teachers to describe how they deal with misbehavior. Do they have an overall plan like the principle of least intervention that escalates the interventions?

2. When considering how to apply logical consequences, identify a number of common misbehaviors and the logical consequences that you believe would be appropriate for them.

3. Identify the specific questions that you would have students answer as they write reflections on their misbehavior. Describe how you would use their completed reflections.

4. Prepare a letter that you would send to parents at the start of the school year describing the three-step response plan (or a plan that you develop) to be used in your classroom.

FURTHER READING

BURKE, K. (2000). *What to do with the Kid Who ...: Developing Cooperation, Self-Discipline, and Responsibility in the Classroom* (2nd ed.). Thousand Oaks, CA: Corwin Press. Examines ways to provide positive guidance for students for their behavior. Discusses setting the classroom climate, teaching social skills, teaching responsible behavior, and dealing with students with behavior problems or special needs. Includes useful lists and graphics.

THOMPSON, JULIA G. (2002). *Discipline Survival Guide for the Secondary Teacher*. San Francisco: Jossey-Bass. Provides an excellent, thorough, yet practical guide to all aspects of classroom behavior and discipline. Considers issues such as rules and expectations, class time, cooperation, and preventing and solving discipline problems. Many useful charts and specific guides.

Chapter 12

Dealing with Challenging
or Violent Students

CHAPTER OBJECTIVES

This chapter provides information that will help you:
- Identify characteristics of challenging and violent students.
- Develop a plan for working with challenging students in your classroom.
- Describe ways to teach students alternatives to disruption.
- Develop an action plan for responding to disruption in your classroom.
- Determine when and how to seek outside help.

Classroom Management: Creating a Successful K-12 Learning Community/Third Edition, by Paul R. Burden
ISBN 0-471-71073-3   Copyright © 2006 John Wiley & Sons, Inc.

CHAPTER OUTLINE

It's bound to happen. You have planned an exciting lesson for your students, and two students who often cause disturbances create some problems partway through the lesson. You have to stop what you are doing to deal with these students. Since they don't respond well to some of your usual disciplinary techniques, you know that they will disturb tomorrow's class and that of the day after. Some of the students, in fact, may have a tendency to be physical and violent. What do you do with these challenging students?

The first step is to understand these challenging students—their behaviors and the influences on their behaviors. Next, you need to make a commitment and a plan to work with them. Furthermore, you can teach students alternatives to disruption and violence. Finally, you need to be ready to respond to disruptive or violent behavior if it does occur.

UNDERSTANDING CHALLENGING AND VIOLENT STUDENTS

Challenging students are constantly disruptive, demand attention, openly confront your authority, or do not complete any assigned work. They disrupt learning, interfere with the work of others, and may prompt other students to misbehave. Your regular classroom management system may not work with challenging students. Before considering how to deal with these students, it is helpful to identify the behaviors challenging students actually exhibit, recognize influences that may have contributed to the development of the difficult behaviors, and understand that the behaviors of challenging students may be the early signs of serious problems.

Behaviors

According to Curwin and Mendler (1999), 80 percent of students rarely break classroom rules, 15 percent break rules on a somewhat regular basis, and 5 percent are chronic rule breakers and are generally out of control most of the time. Rhode, Jenson, and Reavis (1992) estimate that about 2 to 5 percent of all students meet their definition of a *tough kid* who has (a) excessive noncompliant and aggressive behavior or (b) behavior deficits in self-management, social, and academic skills. In some school environments, percentages for difficult students may be even higher. Tough kids who persistently break rules and sometimes become involved in serious misbehavior are an ongoing challenge in the classroom.

Characteristic behaviors of challenging and violent students are outlined in Table 12.1. These include *behavior excesses* where students do too much of a behavior. This may include noncompliance and aggression. The behaviors also include

Table 12.1 Characteristic Behaviors of Challenging or Violent Students

1. Behavior Excesses: Too much of a behavior
   a. Noncompliance
      Does not do what is requested
      Breaks rules
      Argues
      Makes excuses
      Delays
      Does the opposite of what is asked
   b. Aggression
      Tantrums
      Fights
      Destroys property
      Teases
      Verbally abuses
      Is cruel to others
2. Behavior Deficits: Inability to adequately perform a behavior
   a. Self-Management Skills
      Cannot delay rewards
      Acts before thinking; impulsive
      Shows little remorse or guilt
      Will not follow rules
      Cannot foresee consequences
   b. Social Skills
      Has few friends
      Goes through friends fast
      Noncooperative; bossy
      Lacks affection
      Has few problem-solving skills
      Constantly seeks attention
   c. Academic Skills
      Generally behind in academics, particularly reading
      Off task
      Fails to finish work
      Truant or frequently tardy
      Forgets acquired information easily

behavior deficits where students are unable to adequately perform a behavior (e.g., self-management, social skills, and academic skills).

These disruptive behaviors can be categorized in different ways. In a study on how teachers perceive and cope with problem students, Brophy and McCaslin (1992) identified 12 problem-student types. At least five of the types relate to challenging students—hostile–aggressive, passive–aggressive, defiant, hyperactive, and distractable.

Many behaviors may be characteristic of challenging or violent students. Let's look at one type of student who expresses these behaviors. A *bully* is a child who oppresses or harasses another child in a physical or psychological way (Germinario, Cervalli, & Ogden, 1992). Bullies are usually male, but some female bullies do exist. They try to control their fellow students with aggressive behavior to relieve their own feelings of low self-esteem. Bullying behaviors may be expressed by physical aggression, social alienation, verbal aggression, or intimidation (Garrity et al., 2000). Their observable behaviors include starting fights, teasing, verbal threats, answering back, and damage to or confiscation of possessions of their victims. Teachers in elementary and middle grades regularly identify about 12 percent of all boys as often harassing or oppressing others in physical or psychological ways (Hoover & Hazlet, 1991). A number of good resources are available for teachers to bully-proof their classrooms (e.g., Bonds & Stoker, 2000; Garrity et al., 2000; Hoover & Oliver, 1996; Rigby, 1998; Stein & Sjostrom, 1996).

Students who are viewed to be at risk also may be considered challenging students. At-risk students may have academic difficulties, a short attention span, low self-esteem, health problems, a narrow range of interests, a lack of social skills, the inability to face pressure, fear of failure, and a lack of motivation. They also may be disorganized, inattentive, distractable, unable to face pressure, and have excessive truancies and absences.

Some students don't simply disturb the classroom; they exhibit violent behaviors. These behaviors range form threats to physical violence to physical assaults and property damage. Some information, however, indicates that the level of violence in schools actually decreased in the 1990s. The Justice Department reported that the number of violent crimes committed by children and teenagers has declined substantially since 1993 and is at the lowest rate since 1986 (Glassner, 1999). During the 1999–2000 school year, 90 percent of the nation's schools reported no serious crime, while 43 percent reported no crime at all (U.S. Department of Education, 2001).

Nevertheless, violent acts take place. In 1997, there were 202,000 serious crimes (e.g., aggravated assault, sexual assault, robbery, and rape) against students 12 to 18 years old in schools and 2.7 million total crimes (Leone, Mayer, Malmgren, & Meisel, 2000). Some statistics about violent behavior include the following:

- More than 525,000 attacks, shakedowns, and robberies occur per month in public secondary schools in the United States (Weinhold & Weinhold, 1998).

- Approximately 14 percent of students reported being in a physical fight at school during the past 12 months (Leone et al., 2000).

- Just over 7 percent reported that they had been threatened or injured with a weapon on school property in the past 12 months (Arnette & Walsleben, 1998).

There are a number of useful Internet Web sites providing information to help understand disruptive and violent student behavior and providing guidance about solutions. Some sites are Safe Schools and Violence Prevention Office (www.cde.ca.gov/spbranch/safety), the Center for the Prevention of School Violence (www.ncsu.edu/cpsv), the National School Safety Center (www.nssc1.org), and the Stop School Violence Clearinghouse (stopschoolviolence.com/links.htm).

Influences

In many of these students, there are underlying influences that may contribute to their persistent misbehavior. Many of these students come from homes where they have been emotionally or physically abused or neglected. Some of them may have had traumatic childhoods as a result of suffering from organic conditions, such as attention deficit-hyperactivity disorder (estimated to affect four percent of school-age children), fetal alcohol syndrome, or the effects of being born to mothers addicted to cocaine. Some of the students may live in a home environment where one or more adults are addicted to alcohol, crack, or other drugs. Many students come from home environments where parents have little influence or control over their children's behavior.

Many students who chronically misbehave come from home environments in which the parents themselves have had a negative school experience. The student then carries this distrust to school with the expectation that school will not be a positive experience. The student also may have limited trust in adults and teachers. Thus, the student enters school with negative influences and expectations. Every failure diminishes his or her self-esteem and often leads to anger and distrust. These are the difficult students, the tough kids who must be reached.

The risk of violent behavior in schools is heightened with the increased occurrence of gangs and weapons. A street gang is a group of people who form an allegiance for a common purpose and engage in violent, unlawful, and criminal activity. Many gang members are of school age, and when they come to school, confrontations often arise.

Schools have struggled over how to address the influence of gangs. Strategies fall into three categories (Webb, 1993): (a) prevention—stopping the problem before it begins by teaching children skills so they will never become violent; (b) intervention—singling out those kids who have shown violent behavior and working one-on-one to change their ways; and (c) suppression—keeping weapons out of schools by using police-style tactics to make schools safe. Deborah Prothrow-Stith (1993), a leading advocate of prevention programs, maintains that we must teach children how to avoid violence—how to keep conflicts from escalating, how to deal with anger, how to recognize dangerous situations, and how to avoid weapons. Resources are available for dealing with gangs (Jensen & Yerington, 1997) and school violence (Lane, Richardson, & VanBerkum, 1996).

The Justice Department estimates that 100,000 children carry guns to school every day. Each year, guns kill nearly 5,000 Americans under the age of 20, according to the National Center for Health Statistics. Getting hold of a handgun is no problem for millions of U.S. children, a Louis Harris survey indicates ("Survey shows," 1993). Among sixth to twelfth graders, more than one in three say they could put their hands on a gun within an hour. Yet the study also shows that these students have anxiety and deep pessimism about their future in a culture of guns and violence.

Early Signs of Serious Problems

Some of the behaviors exhibited by challenging students are troublesome while others are quite serious. Aggressive behaviors such as fighting, throwing tantrums, vandalizing, stealing, and exhibiting abusive behavior very seriously affect the student and the learning environment. Because of the immediacy of the events, you cannot ignore these actions and immediate attention is needed.

Some challenging students, however, exhibit behaviors that may not demand immediate attention, yet they also may be a sign of serious problems. A student who does not comply with directions, has limited self-management skills, or has limited social or academic skills may be considered a challenging student. Whether overtly aggressive or passively noncompliant, challenging students exhibit behaviors that can disrupt their learning and that of others. Some students may show early signs of serious problems through their behavior in the following ways (Levin & Nolan, 2004).

1. *Changes in Physical Appearance.* Students may reveal underlying problems through sudden changes in their physical appearance. This may be evident in deterioration in posture, dress, and grooming habits, or in changes in weight. Bruises and cuts may be signals of abuse, neglect, or even self-mutilation.

2. *Changes in Activity Level.* Excessive tardiness, lethargy, absenteeism, and sleepiness may result from various problems, including depression and substance abuse. Students may also deal with problems by exhibiting hyperactivity, overaggressiveness, impulsivity, or lowered frustration and tolerance levels.

3. *Changes in Personality.* When students experience emotional disturbances, they may express uncharacteristic personality characteristics. These may include sudden expressions of sadness, easy agitation, or anger.

4. *Changes in Achievement.* When students are dealing with problems, they may have a decline in their ability to focus on the school activities, to complete the activities, or to perform at their previous achievement level.

5. *Changes in Health or Physical Abilities.* Complaints about frequent headaches, stomachaches, dizziness, unhealed sores, and frequent bathroom use lead to a concern about a student's health. These changes may be an indication of other difficulties the student is experiencing.

6. *Changes in Socialization.* While students who are suddenly quiet and withdrawn may not cause disruption in the classroom, this change may signal a problem in the student's life that may be later expressed in more outward and potentially disruptive behavior. Contributing factors to these changes may be very serious and beyond your influence to address or remedy. You should be prepared to contact other specialized professionals in an effort to help students who show signs of serious problems. Professionals may include counselors, psychologists, nurses, social workers, or even police officers. It is often helpful to consult with the school principal before making contacts with those outside the school.

Table 12.2 Early and Imminent Warning Signs of Violence

Early Warning Signs

Social withdrawal

Excessive feelings of isolation and being alone

Excessive feelings of rejection

Being a victim of violence

Feelings of being picked on and persecuted

Low school interest and poor academic performance

Expression of violence in writings and drawings

Uncontrolled anger

Patterns of impulsive and chronic hitting, intimidating, and bullying behaviors

History of discipline problems

Past history of violent and aggressive behavior

Intolerance for differences and prejudicial attitudes

Drug use and alcohol use

Affiliation with gangs

Inappropriate access to, possession of, and use of firearms

Serious threats of violence

Imminent Signs of Violence

Serious physical fighting with peers or family members

Severe destruction of property

Severe rage for seemingly minor reasons

Detailed threats of lethal violence

Possession or use of firearms and other weapons

Other self-injurious behaviors or threats of suicide

Students who are prone to violent behaviors often exhibit a number of behaviors prior to any violent acts. The U.S. Department of Education and the Department of Justice published a guide for schools (Dwyer, Osher, & Warger, 1998) that contains a list of early warning signs that can alert teachers to a student's potential to violence, as well as signs that violence is imminent (see Table 12.2).

PLANNING TO WORK WITH CHALLENGING AND VIOLENT STUDENTS

Many schools have taken actions to address violent behavior with formal violence prevention programs, increased school security, zero-tolerance policies, and programs in character development, problem resolution, and anger control. To be successful with challenging and possibly violent students in your own classroom, you must assume responsibility for addressing the situation and take steps to have the student behave within acceptable limits (Jenson, Rhode, & Reavis, 1994; Mendler & Curwin, 1999). There are several things that you could do to meet that challenge.

1. *Establish Rules, Procedures, Consequences, and Reinforcements for the Classroom.* It is vital to develop a comprehensive classroom management and discipline system for all students in the classroom. This is the foundation for any additional actions that you need to take when addressing the special challenges of working with difficult students.

2. *Make a Commitment to Help Challenging Students Succeed.* These students are sometimes accustomed to teachers trying to help them but then later giving up. Actually giving up on the student only reinforces and perpetuates the problem behavior; it will not go away without intervention. The inappropriate behavior will continue unless you make the commitment to help the challenging student.

In doing so, you must clearly communicate your concern to these students. They must know that you will do everything possible to help them succeed. Since you may not be in a position to change any of the underlying contributing factors for the misbehavior, you should focus on the inappropriate classroom behaviors. This commitment is a vital step in overcoming problem behaviors.

3. *Establish a Plan to Deal with Each Challenging Student.* Because there are different types of challenging students, you may need to use a different approach with each type. In addition, each student has his or her own personality, academic history, and circumstances to be considered. For these reasons, it is helpful to establish a plan to deal with the unique characteristics of each challenging student.

Handling each incident as a separate act is not sufficient. Preplanned, sequential actions are needed to address the problem behaviors systematically. Approaches to be used in the classroom as part of this plan are addressed in the next section. Fortunately, some useful guidelines and materials are available (e.g., Garrity et al., 2000; Jenson et al., 1994; Rhode et al., 1992; Young, West, Smith, & Morgan, 2000).

4. *Keep Documentation and Anecdotal Records.* It is important to keep a written record of the incidents of misbehavior and the actions you have taken in a separate folder for each challenging student. This documentation will help you see any patterns in the behavior. If at a later point you need to consult the parents, principal, counselor, psychologist, or others about the student, this documentation will help them better understand the nature and scope of the problems.

There are several types of documentation. First, keep a written *anecdotal record* to document specific events of misbehavior. An anecdote is a brief, narrative description of an incident. Anecdotal records can be quite simple in design and may include a column format on a page. Information that is recorded should include the student's name, the date and time of the incident, the location of the incident, a brief description of the student's behavior, and a brief description of your response.

Second, you might ask the student to fill out an *incident reaction sheet* outlining an incident of misbehavior. Students could write this while in time-out. The incident reaction sheet provides the student with an opportunity to evaluate his or her behavioral choices while calming down. Questions may require the student to describe the rule that was broken, why the student chose to misbehave, who was bothered by the misbehavior, what more appropriate behavior could be chosen next time, and what should happen to the student next time the misbehavior occurs. This reaction sheet should be kept on file as documentation of the incident, and it may be shown to others such as the parents, principal, or counselor as the need warrants.

Third, keep a record of any *one-on-one meetings* with the student as a means to document the series of interactions and decisions that were made in consultation with the student. Fourth, keep a copy of any *behavioral contracts* that were developed with the student or in consultation with others. In addition to these four types of documentation, your folder of documentation might include notes or records of phone conversations concerning the student.

5. *Focus Attention on Preventing Disturbing or Violent Behavior.* Think comprehensively about prevention strategies. These may include teaching students alternatives to disruption and violence, knowing the early warning signs for violent behavior, being attention to student interactions, building a positive classroom community, and taking actions to de-escalate confrontational situations.

6. *Make Plans for Ways to Respond to Disruptive or Violent Behavior.* Decide how you will address aggressive behavior and even how you will respond to physical fights. Thinking about these issues in advance will enable you to make quick, appropriate decisions in the event of an incident.

TEACHING STUDENTS ALTERNATIVES TO DISRUPTION AND VIOLENCE

When confronted with a challenging conflict, students may not have the skills to defuse a situation and thus may resort to disruption and violence as a first step. Students, however, can be taught strategies that emphasize self-control and problem solving. Students can be taught ways to deal with anger, use problem-solving strategies, and use new behavioral skills such as social skills, conflict resolution skills, and self-management skills. By using these skills, students are less likely to exhibit disruptive behaviors or become violent.

Dealing with Anger

Anger is a feeling indicating the person feels frustrated and thwarted. Everybody gets angry at some time or other, and figuring out what to do with anger is the tough part.

Hidden anger often leads a person to a breaking point where they explode with pent-up feelings, but letting anger get out of hand also can lead to many problems. In the classroom, help students manage anger constructively, calm their own anger, and deal with other people's anger.

Managing Anger Constructively

People who are angry may take actions without thinking much about the situation. Here are some ways to manage anger constructively (Johnson & Johnson, 1995b):

1. *Recognize and Acknowledge Your Anger.* Anger is a natural, normal human feeling. It does not need to be feared or rejected. Repressed anger does not vanish: it may erupt suddenly in physical or verbal assaults or as overreactions to minor provocations. Recognize how you get angered and what your responses are.

2. *Decide Whether or Not to Express Your Anger.* You may find something upsetting, but you may or may not want to express your anger. Clarify the situation to be certain someone has done something aggressive or provocative in nature. Then decide whether to express your anger directly or keep it hidden. Detach and let go if you decide not to express your anger.

3. *Express Your Anger Directly and Descriptively When It Is Appropriate to Do So.* Express your anger to the appropriate person and make your point in descriptive, accurate, and brief terms as a means to describe your concerns and to lay the groundwork for settling the difficulty.

4. *When Direct Expression Is Not Appropriate, Express Your Anger Indirectly or React in an Alternative Way.* When not expressing anger openly, you may still have feelings that need to be expressed. This can be done privately by some verbal or physical expression, physical exercise, psychological detachment, or relaxation.

VOICES FROM THE CLASSROOM   *Guidelines for Working with Challenging Students*

Michael Abbott, Teacher in an Alternative High School, Livonia, Michigan

Our alternative high school has a high percentage of students who would be considered at risk and challenging to work with. There is a sign in the school that says, "Soft on people, hard on issues." Probably nothing has helped me in my relationships with my students as much as this simply stated philosophy. To me, it says a great deal about human relationships and provides the following guidance as I work with challenging students:

- Self esteem is easily damaged
- People respond well to gentleness

- It is not necessary to be cruel to be effective
- People respond well if they know the issues
- Expectations must be clear
- Anticipate problems (be proactive rather than reactive)
- State consequences before anything has happened
- Be consistent
- Follow through

5. *When the Other Person Is Angry, Focus on the Task or Issue.* You can control and contain your anger and better manage the situation by staying focused on the goal to be achieved, not on what the other person is saying or doing.

6. *Analyze, Understand, and Reflect on Your Anger.* Get to know yourself so that you recognize the events and behaviors that trigger your behavior and the internal signs that signal you are becoming angry. This will help you understand your anger and stop anger before it develops.

Calming One's Own Anger

There are many easy-to-learn things that make it possible to calm yourself when you are angry (Curwin & Mendler, 1997). These include the following:

1. *Count from 1 to 10.* Plan on this counting before doing anything when you are upset. You may repeat this counting if you are still feeling angry. What did you say or do to the person who upset you? After the counting, how did your feelings change?

2. *Count from 10 to 1.* Counting backwards from 10 to 1 works the same way as counting from 1 to 10, but just in reverse order.

3. *Count Backwards by 5, Starting at 100.* This type of counting requires a little more thinking and thus helps calm the anger.

4. *Breathe in Deeply.* Just breathe in deeply and then let the air out slowly. Repeat this several times. By focusing on your deep breathing for three to five minutes, you can calm your anger.

5. *Breathe in Deeply and Count Together.* This approach combines deep breathing and counting. Silently say the number "one" each time you exhale. Doing this for two minutes or more can slow down and calm the anger.

6. *Count by 5s and Breathe.* This is similar to the exercise in which you say "one" when exhaling. In this exercise, you silently count to five while inhaling, count to five while briefly holding your breath, and count to five while exhaling.

7. *Use Calming Words.* Many students find that they can calm themselves down by silently saying words that make them feel better. This approach could be combined with deep breathing. For example, students might think of words such as calm down, chill out, stay cool, or relax. Students could silently say the first word (e.g., calm) when inhaling and the second word (e.g., down) when exhaling. This can be repeated several times.

Dealing with Another Person's Anger

It is important to not let other people's anger make you angry. There are many things you can do to keep calm when someone is bothering or threatening you (Curwin & Mendler, 1997). Here are some ways to respond to other people's anger constructively (Johnson & Johnson, 1995b):

1. *Let Others Feel Angry.* Remember that anger is a natural human feeling, and that everyone feels angry at some time. It is better for the anger to be expressed than hidden, as long as there is not violence or aggression.

2. *Don't Get Angry Back.* When another person is angry, the first step is to control your own feelings. Losing your temper will only escalate the problem.

3. *Recognize That the use of Aggression By the Other Person Is an Expression of Feeling Weak and Helpless.* The angry person probably does not know what to do when angry and thus may be aggressive. Help the person back off, cool down, and try something else.

4. *Focus Attention on the Task, Not on the Anger.* Focus both your attention and the attention of the angry person on the task to be completed. Don't get sidetracked or baited into a quarrel when the other person is angry.

5. *Explain the Situation.* Your explanation of the situation can help the angry person see the circumstances from a new perspective, understand the cause of his or her anger, and lead to calming of the anger.

VOICES FROM THE CLASSROOM   *Dealing with an Angry Student*

Lynne Hagar, High School History and English Teacher, Mesquite, Texas

John walked into my classroom at the start of the school year ready to fight me all the way. This pugnacious redhead walked, talked, and acted tough as nails, but when I spoke to him sharply, he blushed. John knew that he was going to fail from the beginning; he spoke terrible, redneck grammar, and pushed and shoved his way through the first few weeks.

How should I handle this firecracker of a student? Experience had taught me that a lot of love and consistency would solve many of his problems. I tried to react calmly to John's insulting comments, trusting that once he began to respond to my teaching, he would show more respect. When he became disruptive, I asked him privately to tell me if I had done something to offend him or to lose his respect. I apologized in advance for having done so. John was surprised that a teacher would be concerned about the reasons for his behavior and astonished that I had admitted I was capable of doing something wrong.

Once we had a basis for our relationship, I found something to say to John every day—not necessarily a compliment, just an acknowledgment that I recognized he was there. I tried my best to really listen when John talked to me, making eye contact and coming close to his desk. Sometimes I touched his arm in a friendly way when he entered the room, or laid my hand on his shoulder as I passed his seat. I put long comments on his papers and added stickers when his work began to show improvement.

I soon realized that John attended school every day without fail; it was the best place in his life—the only place where he felt safe enough to express his feelings. I gave John opportunities to let his anger out on paper and to write about his feelings. I found out about things he was proud of and then built writing lessons around subjects such as rodeo-riding and fast cars.

I wish I could say that John became a model student, but he only became an average one, trying hard to please me in all that he did. He still lost his temper at times, blushed when teased, and often spoke without asking. But John began to reveal the intelligent side of his nature, dropped his aggressive pose, and expressed his affection for me and even, once in a great while, his gratitude for my teaching efforts.

There's something about struggling with a difficult student and succeeding in gaining his trust that gives a teacher a special warmth for that student. It's very rewarding in a unique way.

Techniques for Solving Problems

In addition to dealing with anger, students need to be good at figuring out how to solve problems that they have or that others give them. When students confront a conflict, they need problem-solving strategies to help them act effectively without doing damage to themselves or others. Students can use a 10-step process for dealing with problem situations before they do something hurtful to themselves or others (Curwin & Mendler, 1997; Elias & Clabby, 1992).

1. *Stop and Calm Down.* Give yourself time to think and respond when something upsetting occurs. Pay attention to the signs that your body gives you when it feels tense. If angered, use some technique previously discussed to calm your anger.

2. *Identify What the Problem Is.* Clarify your concerns in specific, behavioral terms. Think about the causes of the problem, who was involved, and whether you contributed to the problem in some way. Consider whether you need to talk to others to help come up with a solution.

3. *Decide on Your Goal.* Determine specifically what you want to have happen.

4. *Think of As Many Solutions to the Problem As You Can.* Brainstorm about the many different actions you can choose to take to solve the problem.

5. *For Each Possible Solution, Think of All the Things That Might Happen Next.* Anticipate consequences for these possible solutions.

6. *Choose the Best Solution.* From your list of possible solutions, select one solution that has the most desired consequences.

7. *Choose a Back-Up Solution in Case the First One Doesn't Work Out.* Always have a back-up plan ready. You need to have at least one more possible solution ready in case the first one doesn't work out.

8. *Plan Your Solution and Make a Final Check.* Mentally rehearse when, where, and how a best solution will be implemented. Also anticipate potential obstacles and how to deal with them.

9. *Carry Out Your Solution.* Carry out your decision and see how it works. If it does not work, then try another solution.

10. *Evaluate.* When evaluating your decision making concerning a particular problem, there are three important questions to consider: Did I reach my goal? If the same problem occurs again, what will I do? Are there any people (parents, friends, teacher) who might help me as I figure out the best solution?

WHAT WOULD YOU DECIDE?   *Techniques to Solve Problems*

If students in your class have frequent conflicts, it may be useful to teach them some techniques to solve their own problems.

1. How might you present this idea of learning about problem-solving techniques to your students?

2. How might you provide this training?

Developing New Behavioral Skills

Another way to help students seek alternatives to disruption and violence is to teach them new behavioral skills that help them effectively function in the classroom. A number of authors have developed programs in which students are taught new behavioral skills, such as social skills, conflict resolution skills, and self-management skills. While it is beyond the scope of this book to provide a detailed description of each of these programs, a brief description is provided for a representative sample of the available programs.

• *Social Skills.* Cooperative skills are those that help students get along socially. These skills include communication, cooperation, problem solving, conflict resolution, and team building. Burke (2000) provides comprehensive descriptions and specific activities to teach cooperative social skills to K–12 students. Her program addresses basic interactions, communication skills, team-building skills, and conflict resolution. Separate sections of Burke's book discuss students who have trouble accepting responsibility, students who need help with their interpersonal skills, students with behavior problems, and students with special needs. Activity descriptions, checklists, forms, and related transparency masters are included.

Using a similar approach, Bellanca (1991) offers a series of lessons in a social skills primer that includes detailed lesson plans, overhead masters, and worksheets. The lessons address getting acquainted, friendship, responsibility, working together, problem solving, and conflict resolution. Cooperative skills are also taught through activities or lessons that develop student self-esteem and responsibility. Canfield and Siccone (1995) suggest 101 ways to achieve that purpose. Their book addresses issues such as commitment, role models, empowerment, teaching as a loving and a transforming activity, social responsibility in the classroom, and the classroom as a community.

• *Conflict Resolution and Self-Management Skills.* Some programs provide a set of individual or interactive activities for students to complete to develop self-management and conflict resolution skills (e.g., Cowan, Palomares, & Schilling, 1992; Henley, 2003; Johnson & Johnson, 1995a; Young et al., 2000).

Conflict resolution programs help students develop skills to deal with conflicts they might experience in the classroom. Conflict resolution programs typically involve instruction about the steps in dealing with conflict and the related skills necessary to work through the conflicts. In *Teaching the Skills of Conflict Resolution* (1992), Cowan et al. organize their instruction of the skills into the following units: respecting similarities and differences, understanding and controlling feelings, communicating effectively, cooperation and team building, strategies for resolving conflict, and using the tools of conflict resolution. Their last unit—putting it all together—even includes the development of a classroom bill of rights.

• *Reducing School Violence Through Conflict Resolution.* (Johnson & Johnson, 1995a) also offers specific guidance to help students deal with conflicts in a constructive manner. In *Teaching Students to be Peacemakers* (1995b), Johnson and Johnson examine conflicts in a comprehensive way and then provide guidance in teaching students skills in the following areas: negotiating, conflict strategies, managing anger, mediating conflicts, managing developmental conflicts, and peacemaking.

RESPONDING TO DISRUPTIVE OR VIOLENT BEHAVIOR

Teachers who have a plan to respond to disruptive or violent behavior are often more successful than teachers who do not have a plan. Without a plan, teachers continually feel stressed and ill-equipped to deal with challenging students, and this may contribute to teachers leaving teaching. A number of specific approaches can be used to respond to disruptive behavior. Outside help is available if necessary.

Approaches to Use in the Classroom

The goal is to help challenging students be successful. To achieve that goal, you need to be committed to a preplanned, sequential set of actions to have the student stop misbehaving and get back on task. A set of actions is discussed here to achieve that goal. Communication with parents is vital when dealing with difficult students. One of the following steps is to consult and inform parents, but this contact can occur at any point as the need warrants, even when you are assessing the situation.

Assess the Situation

Before taking any actions to remedy the situation, it is vital to gather information and be reflective about the student, the behaviors, the environment, and yourself.

1. *Find Out about the Characteristics of the Challenging Students and the Influences in Their Lives.* In this way, you will have a better understanding of the students, and this information may help you decide on appropriate actions to help the student succeed. You may obtain this information by talking with the student, through a questionnaire about interests, by asking other teachers who come in contact with the student, or other means.

2. *Examine Your Classroom Management System.* This is a necessary step to see if there are any factors in the classroom contributing to the misbehavior of challenging students. This should include a review of rules and their consequences, procedures, space usage, motivation, lesson delivery, reinforcement, and efforts to monitor students and promote cooperation.

3. *Analyze the Problem Behavior and Your Response.* It is important to identify precisely what the student is doing to create a problem. Some of the student behaviors may be similar to those listed in Table 12.1. Various checklists and observation systems are available to help record the behaviors (Rhode et al., 1992). One useful format is to list the type of student behavior and your related response.

This step of looking at your own actions can be quite enlightening. To borrow from William Glasser (1969), ask, "What am I doing? Is it working?" If it is not working, stop doing it! When asking these questions, your attention is focused on selecting an appropriate, workable response. By looking at the student's behaviors and your related responses, you can often determine the reason for the misbehavior. You then can act in ways not to reinforce the motive behind the student's misbehavior.

This step of self-examination can help determine if your expectations of the student are reasonable. For example, many individual differences may be apparent in students in your class due to factors such as ethnicity, learning styles, academic ability, language, disabling conditions, socioeconomic status, and at-risk status. When considering students who are different from you, it is important to maintain reasonable expectations given their characteristics. Just because a student is different doesn't mean that he or she is a behavioral problem.

Meet with the Student

Some consequences used to stop misbehavior may have only short-term effects with challenging students. These students need help in making better decisions about their behavior. Thus, a one-to-one conference with the student is needed when the behavior is chronic or serious, or if there is a sudden change in behavior. The purpose of the conference is to provide caring and guidance to the student. You should listen to the student's concerns, firmly clarify your own expectations, and then work together to arrive at a practical course of action. There are several guidelines to consider when meeting with the student (Canter & Canter, 1993).

1. *Meet with the Student Privately.* The conference should be confidential, and there should be no other students around to overhear or disrupt the meeting. The conference should also be brief, with a maximum of 10 to 15 minutes.

2. *Show Empathy and Concern.* The conference is intended to help the student explore alternative, more appropriate behaviors. Therefore, you should help the student gain insight into his or her present behavior and choose more responsible behavior. The student should understand that this meeting is to help him or her, rather than punish. The student should also know that you are concerned and that you care.

3. *Question the Student to Find Out Why There Is a Problem.* It is important to listen to the student's point of view rather than assume you know why the student is misbehaving. Question the student about what the problem may be. It might be that the work is too hard or that there is something happening at home or with other students who are contributing to the misbehavior.

Questions should be stated in a caring, nonaccusational manner. Avoid questions such as, "What is your problem?" Instead, use questions such as, "Did something happen today to get you so upset?" or, "Can you tell me what's causing you to be so upset?" After asking the question, listen carefully to the student and don't interrupt. Let the student talk. By doing so, you will have more information and fuller understanding of the student and the circumstances that contribute to the misbehavior.

WHAT WOULD YOU DECIDE?   *Meeting with a Student*

A student has been misbehaving in your class, primarily due to limited self-management and social skills. It has reached the point where you decide that a special, private meeting is warranted to express your concern, provide guidance, clarify your expectations, and seek a practical course of action to overcome the problems.

1. What materials might you need to gather and how might you prepare for this meeting?

2. How might you prepare for and conduct the meeting differently if the student instead showed behavior excesses such as noncompliance and aggression?

4. *Determine What You Can Do to Help.* Based on the answers to your earlier questions, you may discover there is a simple method to get the student back on track, such as moving his or her seat away from another student. In most cases, however, the solution is more difficult to find.

5. *Determine How the Student Can Improve His or Her Behavior.* Part of the meeting should focus on what the student can choose to do differently in that future to avoid problem behaviors. Talk about the situation and listen to the student's input.

At this time, it may be necessary to reteach appropriate behaviors for certain classroom activities. Most students need only a single explanation of procedures for classroom activities such as independent seatwork, discussion, cooperative groups, and entering and leaving the room. Other more difficult students need to be taught how to behave and be reminded often. While you will have previously taught appropriate procedures to the entire class, this one-to-one meeting with the difficult student provides an opportunity to reteach and clarify these procedures and expectations.

6. *State Your Expectations about How the Student Is to Behave.* The student must understand that you are very serious about not allowing the misbehavior to continue. While expressing a caring attitude to work with the student to solve the problem, the student must realize that predetermined consequences will be used if he or she chooses to continue to misbehave. Therefore, near the end of the meeting, you might say something like: "I'm going to work with you to solve this problem. I know that you can behave responsibly. But you must remember that fighting is not acceptable. Anytime you choose to fight, you will be choosing to go to the principal."

7. *Disarm Criticism.* Some difficult students may become argumentative and critical, and may actually blame you for all the problems they have in class. In that case, take steps to disarm the criticism by letting the student speak. Also, ask the student for more information concerning why he or she is upset with you. This approach can help calm the student down, and he or she will see you as being concerned. This additional information will likely help address the problem.

8. *Document the Meeting.* In addition to anecdotal records you keep concerning the student's behavior in class, it is important to keep records of any one-to-one meeting you have with the student. This documentation should include the date of the meeting, a summary of the ideas generated in the meeting, and any conclusions that were drawn.

Consult and Inform Others

You may want to consult with others to get more information or advice about how to deal with the challenging student in the classroom. The principal, school counselor, psychologist, or other teachers who currently or previously came in contact with the student may be consulted for more information. They could also share their experiences in dealing with the student and perhaps offer recommendations for strategies that you could take in the classroom. The student's parents are also a source of information about the student. Consultations are intended to help you deal with the student in the classroom; no referrals for outside services are made at this point.

Rather than wait until the behavior becomes very serious, inform the principal or parents about the problems. They will then know what you are doing and may be able to support you as the situation warrants. If the problems become more serious, the principal and parents will appreciate this earlier contact rather than being surprised by a crisis at a later time. At a later time, the principal and parents may be involved in actions to address the problems if they persist or become more severe.

Provide Positive Support

Students need to receive reinforcement for their appropriate behavior through social reinforcers, activities and privileges, tangible reinforcers, and token reinforcers. Reinforcement encourages the student to continue the rewarded behavior. Challenging students especially need to be reinforced for their appropriate behavior. Even though it may be easy to overlook delivering reinforcement to difficult students, they need to receive their fair share of rewards for their appropriate behavior. You may choose to make notes in your plan book as reminders to reinforce difficult students at regular intervals.

Challenging students need to receive additional positive support beyond what is given to all students in the class (Canter & Canter, 1993; Rhode et al., 1992). One way is to call the student at home before the school year begins. (You will know which students to call based on information you hear from the student's teachers from the previous year.) In this way, you can ask the student for ideas about how the school year could be successful and to express your confidence that you and the student will work together to have a good year.

You could contact the student's parents to express your caring about their child, get the parents' input about the student's experiences the previous year, get input on what the child needs from you this year, emphasize that the student will be most successful if you and the parents work together, and express confidence that by working together the child will have a more successful experience at school. This early contact helps build a positive relationship with the parents before problems arise.

Another approach that can be used with all students but is especially useful with challenging students is to have them fill out a student interest inventory at the start of the school year. Based on the questions you ask and the responses provided, you will have a fuller understanding of the student's interests. Furthermore, personal attention and welcoming words should be given to the challenging child when coming into the classroom. If problems occur during the day, you could call the student at home in the evening to express concern and inquire about the problem.

Relating to the student as an individual is important. Take time to talk with the student or involve yourself with him or her in school activities. The individual attention of a caring adult can make a big difference. Visiting the student at home is another way of showing your concern.

Decrease Inappropriate Behavior

Your rules and consequences for the class should be used for all students, including challenging students. Since the consequences selected may not work for challenging students, you may need to be select alternative consequences for these students only. Some discipline plans include the delivery of a series of consequences based on the number of rule infractions the student has made. Several consequences are discussed below.

1. *Loss of Privileges.* A number of special privileges may be provided for students. Withdrawing privileges can be an effective consequence, but you need to determine which privileges will have the most influence on correcting the student's behavior if the privilege is withdrawn.

2. *Time-Out.* Time-out involves removing the student from the instructional setting. Thus the student is not given the opportunity to obtain reinforcement for the misbehavior. There are several types of time-out. One of the most effective approaches is to remove the student from the instructional situation to be seated apart from the rest of the class; however, the student is expected to continue to do the work or listen to the lesson. In this way, the disruption stops, the rest of the class gets back to work, and the disrupting student is given an opportunity to calm down and get back to the instructional activities. You may ask the student to complete an incident reaction sheet during the time-out.

3. *Time after Class.* Keeping the student for about a minute after class can be an important consequence for students moving on to another classroom after your class. This separates the student from peers, which can be perceived as a big penalty, and provides you with an opportunity to speak to the student about his or her behavior and the better choices that could have been made. At this time, you could give the student an index card on which to write a brief description of what was done in class to warrant staying after class. He or she could then sign and date the card for you to use as documentation in the event that the principal, parents, or others need to be contacted.

4. *Detention.* Detention involves the loss of free time and the opportunity to socialize with other students. Loss of recess time or staying after school are two common types of detention. Students should understand the reasons for the detention, and the time should not be excessive. You may ask the student to complete an incident reaction sheet during detention.

5. *Student Calls a Parent.* Having the student call his or her parent at home or at work in your presence can be a strong deterrent. The student is expected to explain the problem behavior and what will be done to improve. The call should be made as soon as possible after the incident when both you and the student can get to a phone in the building. This may take place at recess, at lunch, or at the end of the class period.

6. *Time-Out in Another Classroom.* If a student is highly disruptive, it may be useful to send him or her to another classroom at the same or higher grade level for a specified amount of time. This approach is useful for students who seek attention, because they are removed from the peers whose attention they seek. It is important that participating teachers discuss and agree to arrangements for sending and receiving disruptive students for a time-out. If students disrupt the classroom where they are sent for the time-out, they should know that the next consequence will be delivered, which may be a trip to the principal's office.

WHAT WOULD YOU DECIDE?   *Decreasing Inappropriate Behavior*

Students in your classroom are working in small groups when you notice that one student argues with others in the group, delays completing expected group work, and does the opposite of what is expected.

1. To decrease the inappropriate behavior, what consequence would you select to deal with this student?

2. Two other students are disruptive in the small groups. One student has a history of disrupting group work, but this is a rare occasion for the other student. How would you address their misbehavior?

Prepare a Behavioral Contract

A *behavioral contract* is a written agreement between you and the student that represents a commitment for the student to behave more appropriately. A contract commonly includes: (a) a statement of the expected, appropriate behavior; (b) a specified time period during which the student is to exhibit such behavior; (c) rewards or positive support for exhibiting the appropriate behavior; and (d) penalties or corrective actions that will be taken if the student does not exhibit the appropriate behavior.

Behavioral contracts are not necessary for all challenging students. Some students may respond favorably to the approaches that have been discussed up to this point. A behavioral contract should be prepared for students who do not respond to the techniques previously described, or if you are delivering more and more consequences for a particular student or are getting frustrated or angry. A behavioral contract should then be drawn up.

Behavior contracting can be used at any grade level, but is often more appropriate and effective with elementary and middle level students, as older students may resent obvious attempts to manipulate their behavior. This contract is also effective with special education students.

Know When to Involve Others

Consultations made earlier with the principal, school counselor, or psychologist were intended to provide information and advice as you deal with the challenging student. Sometimes, however, students do not respond to any of your strategies, and the misbehavior may continue to be chronic and serious. In such cases, it is necessary to involve others in helping the student. Deviant and disruptive behavior warrants referrals to outside help.

Prior informal contacts, telephone calls, and conferences with parents informed them of the student behaviors and your actions. Now, you need formal contact with the principal or counselors to solicit their assistance.

The principal can counsel or intervene in various ways when handling a challenging student. A referral to the school counselor or psychologist is warranted when you recognize that a developing problem is beyond your professional expertise. Remember that you have not been trained to be a psychologist, counselor, or social worker, and you should not view yourself as a failure when referring the student to receive help from someone with appropriate training. Some districts use an intervention assistance team approach. Many district and community agencies work with schools and families, and these agencies also might be contacted.

Be Ready for Urgent Action

It is important to have a thoughtful, deliberate plan to deal with challenging or violent students as outlined earlier. However, unexpected, disturbing events may occur in your classroom that require immediate action. For example, students may become involved in a physical fight, have a tantrum, destroy property, exhibit bullying behavior, tease others in a mean way, show cruel behavior, or carry a weapon.

Give advance thought to disturbing events that might occur and decide on the general ways that you will respond to those events. For example, if there is a physical fight, you may tell students to stop, disperse the other students, do not physically intervene, and get help. You cannot foresee every type of incident, but your advance thought and decision making will enable you to be ready for urgent action if it is needed.

Seeking Outside Help

After deciding to seek outside help, you first need to gather all the documentation that you have prepared up to this time. You then need to select the most appropriate person to contact. When outside help is needed, it is common practice in many schools to first contact the principal, who may take some actions or recommend that you contact the counselor or psychologist. Parents may be involved at any point, depending on the recommendations of the principal, counselor, or psychologist.

Principal

When dealing with chronic or serious misbehavior, the principal has the authority to make certain decisions. The principal may counsel or intervene when dealing with challenging students, including rewarding positive behavior. In consultation with you, the principal may be helpful in giving words of praise or other rewards when the student's behavior has improved. The principal might counsel the student by talking with the student. This additional guidance about the consequences of the student's choices can make a difference in turning the behavior around.

The principal might contact the parents. This keeps the parents informed of actions taken up to that time and they can be asked to support those actions at home. The principal might recommend that the parents come to the school for a conference with the teacher or others. The principal might approve new placements, services, or suspensions. Depending on the circumstances, the principal may take several actions such as changing the classroom placement, arranging for in-school suspension in a separate room, or referring the student to a counselor or psychologist. In more serious cases, the principal has the authority to seek placement in specialized educational settings outside the school, arrange for long-term suspension, or contact the police or other appropriate community agencies.

Counselors and Psychologists

Other than the principal, the school counselor is often one of the first people contacted when outside help is needed for dealing with challenging students. The counselor may explore the student's behavior, the classroom environment, your teaching style, the classroom management plan, or a variety of related issues. The counselor then tries to provide objective feedback and suggestions for new approaches to deal with the problems. By considering the viewpoints of both you and the student, the counselor can serve as an intermediary for any potential conflicts.

Sometimes a student's problems are rooted in deeper and more pervasive personality disturbances or family problems. The school psychologist can provide more intensive evaluation and diagnostic study. The psychologist will use the anecdotal and other records that you have accumulated concerning the student and will supplement them with other tests, interviews, and observations. This analysis can lead to recommendations for actions to be taken by those at the school or may result in referrals to outside agencies or resources.

Developing Your Management Plan: *Preventing and Responding to Violence*

You should be ready for disruptive or violent behavior before it happens, and you should have a plan to prevent and respond to this behavior. Your preparation involves reading chapters such as this one and perhaps other pertinent materials. In the end, you should make plans for how you will address each of the following items as part of your management plan. Think about these items and write how you will accomplish them.

Understanding your challenging students

Planning to work with your challenging students

Teaching students alternatives to disruption

Responding to disruptive or violent behavior

Problem-Solving Teams

Some schools have a committee that assists teachers in dealing with classroom problems. *Problem-solving teams* consist of groups of educational personnel, parents, and other involved parties that meet systematically to discuss problems referred to them by other educational personnel within their school (Short, Short, & Blanton, 1994). The teams provide collegial assistance for teachers with a minimum of bureaucracy. The teams also increase commitment, communication, and morale by involving teachers and parents as expert resources and collaborators in problem solving.

The problem-solving team identifies the needs, receives referrals, and plans and coordinates interventions with teachers, parents, other educational personnel, and community agencies. Some teams become involved in preventive interventions, crisis intervention, and interagency coordination. Teams can provide (a) help for teachers in dealing with educational, behavioral, and discipline problems; (b) early identification and schoolwide prevention of the problems; (c) a means of in-school intervention for the problems; and (d) a mechanism for referral to appropriate educational resources.

Parents

Many teachers, principals, counselors, and psychologists prefer that they be contacted before the parents are contacted. In this way, those at the school can explore all appropriate interventions without prematurely involving the parents. If it becomes necessary to contact the parents, they are often more responsive when they learn that steps have been taken already. Parents may then visit with you or others in the school. This is a more formal meeting than previous informational contacts, and the principal or others at the school may participate.

The initial meeting with the parents gives all parties the opportunity to share information about the student and formulate a common information base. Teachers and counselors, for example, may review the set of documentation about the series of incidents and actions that have taken place. The parents may share information about the child's attitudes and behaviors at home. Together, those present at the meeting can develop a plan of action. Depending on the nature of the problem, they may conclude that some outside agency should be consulted.

The student may be asked to attend this meeting, or will be informed by the teacher, counselor, or principal about the results of this meeting shortly after the meeting occurs. The primary purposes of this meeting are to share information, develop a plan of action to help the child be successful, and gather the support of the parents.

VOICES FROM THE CLASSROOM   *A Meeting with the Parents*

Beth Schmar, Sixth-Grade Teacher, Topeka, Kansas

In the middle of March, my principal and I realized that Brad had taken control of the classroom. The other students hung on his every word and followed each of his actions. Brad was constantly seeking the other students' attention by rotating between being the class clown and the class bully. Either way, he had their admiration or awe.

From the start of the school year, the principal and I tried many behavior management approaches, from a contract to suspension. In an act of desperation, we requested a meeting with Brad and his parents. We decided to include Brad for the entire meeting and to speak to him frankly. The principal and I shared our expectations for Brad's behavior and explained how his current behavior fell below these expectations. With the help of Brad and his parents, we developed a behavior plan that we all could live with.

We expressed to Brad genuine caring and concern about his future along with our own frustrations about his lack of success. Our honesty helped Brad react differently. He even commented to his parents later, "At least now I know the principal and teacher don't hate me." The meeting was the beginning of a new understanding that made our time together more positive.

District or Community Agencies

Community agencies work with schools and families to help each child be successful. For example, Cities in Schools is a national nonprofit organization dedicated to decreasing the dropout rate. Its mission is to assist a targeted group of children to achieve academic and social success by coordinating existing community services to them and their families through the schools. That agency might be contacted to assist in some way.

Many districts or city governments have an office of substance abuse and violence prevention and intervention, and its resources may be useful. Social workers are available in various community agencies. There may be other types of offices and organizations within the district or community that might be contacted for help.

MAIN POINTS

1. Challenging students often have excessive noncompliant and aggressive behavior or behavioral deficits in self-management, social, and academic skills.

2. Underlying influences that may contribute to persistent misbehavior include emotional or physical abuse or neglect, organic conditions, drugs or alcohol, or gangs.

3. A commitment and a plan must be made to help each challenging student succeed.

4. Specific strategies can be used to help students manage their anger constructively, calm their anger, and deal with another person's anger.

5. Students can be taught new behavioral skills, such as social skills, conflict resolution skills, and self-management skills, as a means to help them seek alternatives to disruption and violence.

6. Documentation of the student's behavior and the teacher's actions is needed. This may include anecdotal records, incident reaction sheets, or records of meeting and contracts.

7. The plan of action for the classroom involves assessing the situation, meeting with the student, consulting and informing others, providing positive support for the student, taking steps to decrease inappropriate behavior, preparing a behavioral contract, and knowing when to involve others.

8. The principal, counselor, psychologist, problem-solving teams, or parents may be contacted if actions taken in the classroom are not successful.

DISCUSSION/REFLECTIVE QUESTIONS

1. Should teachers deal only with the student's problem classroom behavior or should they also try to address the underlying influences?

2. Why might teachers sometimes have difficulty in making a commitment to help challenging kids?

3. How might your grade level and the characteristics of your particular students affect how you select and teach strategies to deal with anger, solve problems, and develop new behavioral skills?

4. What might affect the successful implementation of a behavioral contract with a challenging student?

5. How might the principal help or hinder the handling of challenging students?

SUGGESTED ACTIVITIES

1. Ask several teachers about any overall plan or particular strategies they use in dealing with challenging students in their classrooms.

2. Prepare the format for an anecdotal record form and a behavioral contract that you will use in your classroom.

3. Reflect on what makes you upset and angry and also how you respond when you are upset. What guidelines can you establish for yourself when you might get upset about something that happens in your classroom?

4. Obtain and read resource material on teaching students new behavioral skills such as social skills, conflict resolution skills, and self-management skills.

FURTHER READING

BODINE, RICHARD J., & CRAWFORD, DONNA K. (1998). *The handbook of conflict resolution education*. San Francisco: Jossey-Bass.

A comprehensive guidebook for planning, developing, and implementing conflict resolutions programs in K–12 schools.

CANTER, LEE, & CANTER, MARLENE. (1993). *Succeeding with difficult students*. Bloomington, IN: Solution Tree.

A useful, practical guide with content about reaching out to difficult students, meeting their special needs, communicating with them, and using individualized behavior plans.

References and Further Readings

Albert, L. (2003). *A teacher's guide to cooperative discipline: How to manage your classroom and promote self-esteem* (rev. ed.). Circle Pines, MN: American Guidance Service Publishing.

Ames, C. (1992). Classrooms: Goals, structures, and student motivation. *Journal of Educational Psychology*, 84, 261–271.

Arnette, J.L., & Walsleben, M.C. (1998). *Combating fear and restoring safety in schools*. Washington, DC: U.S. Department of Justice, Office of Juvenile Justice and Delinquency Prevention.

Arnold, H. (2001). *Succeeding in the secondary classroom: Strategies for middle and high school teachers*. Thousand Oaks, CA: Corwin Press.

Attention Deficit Disorder Association, Southern Region. (2005). *Behavior management ideas*. www.adda-sr.org/BehaviorManagementIndex.htm.

Baloche, L.A. (1998). *The cooperative classroom: Empowering learning*. Upper Saddle River, NJ: Prentice-Hall/Merrill.

Banks, J.A. (2006). *Cultural diversity and education: Foundations, curriculum, and teaching* (5th ed.). Boston: Allyn & Bacon.

Barbour, C., Barbour, N.H., & Scully, P.A. (2005). *Families, schools, and communities building partnerships for educating children* (3rd ed.). Upper Saddle River, NJ: Prentice-Hall/Merrill.

Bellanca, J. (1991). *Building a caring, cooperative classroom: A social skills primer*. Palatine, IL: Skylight Publishing.

Berger, E.H. (2004). *Parents as partners in education: Families and schools working together* (6th ed.). Upper Saddle River, NJ: Prentice-Hall.

Berliner, D. (1987). Simple views of effective teaching and a simple theory of classroom instruction. In D. Berliner & R. Rosenshine (Eds.), *Talks to teachers* (pp. 93–110). New York: Random House.

Berliner, D., & Bittle, B. (1995). *The manufactured crisis; Myth, fraud, and the attack on America's public schools*. New York: Addison-Wesley.

Bernstein, N. (2000, Feb. 1). Study documents homelessness in American children each year. *The New York Times*, A12.

Bhaerman, R.D., & Kopp, K.A. (1988). *The school's choice: Guidelines for dropout prevention at the middle and junior high school*. Columbus, OH: National Center for Research in Vocational Education, The Ohio State University.

Bloom, B.S. (1981). *All our children learning*. New York: McGraw-Hill.

Bloom, B.S. (1982). *Human interactions and school learning*. New York: McGraw-Hill.

Blumenfeld, P.C., Puro, P., & Mergendoller, J.R. (1992). Translating motivation into thoughtfulness. In H. Marshall (Ed.), *Redefining student learning: Roots of educational change* (pp. 207–239). Norwood, NJ: Ablex Publishing Co.

Bodine, R.J., & Crawford, D.K. (1998). *The handbook of conflict resolution education*. San Francisco: Jossey-Bass.

Bonds, M., & Stoker, S. (2000). *Bully-proofing your school: A comprehensive approach for middle schools*. Longmont, CO: Sopris West.

Borich, G. (2004). *Effective teaching methods* (5th ed.). Columbus, OH: Merrill Publishing.

Bosch, K.A. (1999). *Planning classroom management for change*. Thousand Oaks, CA: Corwin Press.

Bosch, K.A., & Kersey, K.C. (2000). *The first-year teacher: Teaching with confidence (K–8)* (rev. ed.). Washington, DC: National Education Association.

Bostic, J.Q., Rustuccia, C., & Schlozman, S.C. (2001). The suicidal student. *Educational Leadership*, 59 (2), 81–82.

Bosworth, K. (1997). *Drug abuse prevention: School-based strategies that work*. Washington, DC: ERIC Clearinghouse on Teaching and Teacher Education. ED 409316.

Brophy, J.E. (2004). *Motivating students to learn* (2nd ed.). Mahwah, NJ: Lawrence Erlbaum Associates.

Brophy, J.E., & McCaslin, M. (1992). Teachers' reports of how they perceive and cope with problem students. *The Elementary School Journal*, 93 (1), 3–68.

Burden, P.R. (2000). *Powerful classroom management strategies: Motivating students to learn*. Thousand Oaks, CA: Corwin Press.

Burden, P.R., & Byrd, D.M. (2007). *Methods for effective teaching* (4th ed.). Boston: Allyn & Bacon.

Burke, K. (2000). *What to do with the kid who...: Developing cooperation, self-discipline, and responsibility in the classroom* (2nd ed.). Thousand Oaks, CA: Corwin Press.

California Department of Education. (2000). *Classroom management: A California resource guide*. Sacramento, CA: California Department of Education.

Campbell, L., Campbell, B., & Dickinson, D. (2004). *Teaching and learning through multiple intelligences* (3rd ed.). Boston: Allyn & Bacon.

Canfield, J., & Siccone, F. (1995). *101 ways to develop student self-esteem and responsibility*. Boston: Allyn & Bacon.

Canter & Associates. (1998). *First-class teacher: Success strategies for new teachers*. Bloomington, IN: Solution Tree.

Canter, L., & Canter, M. (1993). *Succeeding with difficult students*. Bloomington, IN: Solution Tree.

Canter, L., & Canter, M. (2002). *Assertive discipline: Positive behavior management for today's schools* (3rd ed.). Bloomington, IN: Solution Tree.

Cary, S. (2000). *Working with second language learners: Answers to teachers' top ten questions*. Portsmouth, NH: Heinemann.

Catterall, J., & Cota-Robles, E. (1988). *The educationally at-risk: What the numbers mean*. Palo Alto, CA: Stanford University Press.

Centers for Disease Control and Prevention. (2005). *Suicide: Fact sheet*. (www.cdc.gov)

Chapman, C. (1993). *If the shoe fits: How to develop multiple intelligences in the classroom*. Thousand Oaks, CA: Corwin Press.

Charles, C.M. (2000). *The synergetic classroom: Joyful teaching and gentle discipline*. Boston: Allyn & Bacon.

Charles, C.M. (2005). *Building classroom discipline* (8th ed.). Boston: Allyn & Bacon.

Charles, C.M., & Charles, M.G. (2004). *Classroom management for middle-grades teachers*. Boston: Allyn & Bacon.

Cohen, E.G. (1994). *Designing groupwork: Strategies for the heterogeneous classroom* (2nd ed.). New York: Teachers College Press.

Coloroso, B. (2002). *Kids are worth it! Giving your child the gift of inner discipline* (Rrev. ed.) New York: HarperCollins.

Coughlin, D. (2002). *How to plan for the school year: The elementary teacher's essential guidebook*. Portsmouth, NH: Heinemann.

Council for Exceptional Children. (2003). Exceptional and homeless. *CEC Today*, 9(6), 7, 13, 15.

Cowan, D., Palomares, S., & Schilling, D. (1992). *Teaching the skills of conflict resolution*. Spring Valley, CA: Innerchoice Publishing.

Crago, M., Shisslak, C.M., & Estes, L.S. (1996). Eating disturbances among minority groups: A review. *International Journal of Eating Disorders*, 19, 239–248.

Crosscope-Happel, C., Hutchins, D.E., Getz, H.G., & Hayes, G.L. (2000). Male anorexia nervosa: A new focus. *Journal of Mental Health Counseling*, 22 (4) 365–370.

Curwin, R.L., & Mendler, A.N. (1997). *As tough as necessary: Countering violence, aggression, and hostility in our schools*. Alexandria, VA: Association for Supervision and Curriculum Development.

Curwin, R.L., & Mendler, A.N. (1999). *Discipline with dignity*. Alexandria, VA: Association for Supervision and Curriculum Development.

Cushman, K. (2003). *Fires in the bathroom: Advice for teachers from high school students*. New York: The New Press.

Diffily, D. (2004). *Teachers and families working together*. Boston: Allyn & Bacon.

Dreikurs, R., Grunwald, B.B., & Pepper, F.C. (1982). *Maintaining sanity in the classroom: Classroom management techniques* (2nd ed.). New York: Harper & Row.

Dubelle, S. (1986). *Effective teaching: Critical skills*. Lancaster, PA: Technomic Publishing Co.

Dunn, R., & Dunn, K. (1992a). *Teaching elementary students through their individual learning styles:*

Practical approaches for grades 3–6. Boston: Allyn & Bacon.

Dunn, R., & Dunn, K. (1992b). *Teaching secondary students through their individual learning styles: Practical approaches for grades 7–12.* Boston: Allyn & Bacon.

Dwyer, K., Osher, D., & Warger, C. (1998). *Early warning, timely response: A guide to safe schools.* Washington, DC: U.S. Department of Education.

Edwards, C.H. (2004). *Classroom discipline and management* (4th ed.). New York: John Wiley & Sons.

Eggen, P.D., & Kauchak, D. (2004). *Educational psychology: Windows on classrooms* (6th ed.). Columbus, OH: Merrill.

Elias, M.J., & Clabby, J.F. (1992). *Building social problem-solving skills.* San Francisco: Jossey-Bass.

Emmer, E.T., Evertson, C.M., & Worsham, M.E. (2006). *Classroom management for middle and high school teachers* (7th ed.). Boston: Allyn & Bacon.

Epstein, J.L. (Guest Editor). (1991). Parental involvement [Special issue]. *Phi Delta Kappan*, 72 (5).

Epstein, J.L., Sanders, M.G., Simon, B.S., Salinas, K.C., Jansorn, N.R., & VanVoorhis, F.L. (2003). *School, family, and community partnerships* (2nd ed.). Thousand Oaks, CA: Corwin Press.

Evertson, C.M, Emmer, E.T., & Worsham, M.E. (2006). *Classroom management for elementary teachers* (7th ed.). Boston: Allyn & Bacon.

Fay, J., & Funk, D. (1995). *Teaching with love and logic.* Golden, CO: The Love and Logic Press.

Fogarty, R. (1997). *Problem-based learning and other curriculum models for the multiple intelligences classroom.* Thousand Oaks, CA: Corwin Press.

Frieman, B.B. (2001). *What teachers need to know about children at risk.* New York: McGraw-Hill.

Gardner, H. (1985). *Frames of mind: The theory of multiple intelligences.* New York: Basic Books.

Gardner, H., & Hatch, T. (1989). Multiple intelligences go to school. *Educational Researcher*, 18(8), 6.

Garrity, C., Jens, K., Porter, W., Sager, N., & Short-Camilli, C. (2000). *Bully-proofing your school: A comprehensive approach for elementary schools.* Longmont, CO: Sopris West.

Germinario, V., Cervalli, J., & Ogden, E.H. (1992). *All children successful: Real answers for helping at-risk elementary students.* Lancaster, PA: Technomic Publishing.

Ginott, H.G. (1965). *Between parent and child.* New York: Avon.

Ginott, H.G. (1969). *Between parent and teenager.* New York: Macmillan.

Ginott, H.G. (1972). *Teacher and child.* New York: Macmillan.

Glasser, W. (1965). *Reality therapy.* New York: Harper & Row.

Glasser, W. (1969). *Schools without failure.* New York: Harper & Row.

Glasser, W. (1984). *Control theory: A new explanation of how we control our lives.* New York: Harper & Row.

Glasser, W. (1986). *Control theory in the classroom.* New York: Harper & Row.

Glasser, W. (1998a). *The quality school: Managing students without coercion* (rev. ed.). New York: HarperPerennial.

Glasser, W. (1998b). *The quality school teacher* (rev. ed.). New York: HarperPerennial.

Glasser, W. (2000). *Every student can succeed.* Chatsworth, CA: Black Forest Press.

Glassner, B. (1999, August 13). School violence: The fears, the facts. *New York Times*, A21.

Gollnick, D.M., & Chinn, P.C. (2006). *Multicultural education in a pluralistic society* (7th ed.). Upper Saddle River, NJ: Prentice-Hall/Merrill.

Good, T.L., & Brophy, J.E. (1995). *Contemporary educational psychology* (5th ed.). New York: Longman.

Good, T.L., & Brophy, J.E. (2003). *Looking into classrooms* (9th ed.). Boston: Allyn & Bacon.

Gootman, M.E. (2001). *The caring teacher's guide to discipline: Helping young students learn self-control, responsibility, and respect* (2nd ed.). Thousand Oaks, CA: Corwin Press.

Gordon, T. (1974). *Teacher effectiveness training.* New York: Peter H. Wyden Publishing.

Gordon, T. (1991). *Discipline that works: Promoting self-discipline in children.* New York: Plume (a division of Penguin).

Gregory, G.H., & Chapman, C. (2002). *Differentiated instructional strategies: One size doesn't fit all.* Thousand Oaks, CA: Corwin Press.

Grossman, H., & Grossman, S.H. (1994). *Gender issues in education*. Boston: Allyn & Bacon.

Guillaume, A.M. (2004). *K–12 classroom teaching: A primer for new professionals* (2nd ed.). Upper Saddle River, NJ: Prentice-Hall/Merrill.

Gump, P.V. (1987). School and classroom environments. In D. Stokols & I. Altman (Eds.), *Handbook of environmental psychology* (pp. 691–732). New York: Wiley.

Hargis, C.H. (1997). *Teaching low achieving and disadvantaged students* (2nd ed.). Springfield, IL: Charles C. Thomas Publishers.

Henderson, A.T., & Berla, N. (1995). *A new generation of evidence: The family is critical to student achievement*. Washington, DC: Center for Law and Education.

Henley, M. (2003). *Teaching self-control: A curriculum for responsible behavior* (2nd ed.). Bloomington, IN: Solution Tree.

Herrera, S.G., & Murry, K.G. (2005). *Mastering ESL and bilingual methods: Differentiated instruction for culturally and linguistically diverse (CLD) students*. Boston: Allyn & Bacon.

Hogan, D. (1997). ADHD: A travel guide to success. *Childhood Education*, 73(3), 158–160.

Holloway, J.H. (2003). Addressing the needs of homeless students. *Educational Leadership*, 60 (4), 89–90.

Hoover, J.H., & Hazlet, R.J. (1991). Bullies and victims. *Elementary School Guidance and Counseling*, 25, 212–218.

Hoover, J.H., & Oliver, R. (1996). *The bullying prevention handbook*. Bloomington, IN: Solution Tree.

Hughes, M., Oakes, K., Lenzo, C., & Carpas, J. (2001). *The elementary teacher's guide to conferences and open houses*. Greensboro, NC: Carson-Dellosa Publishing Co.

Hunter, M. (1994). *Enhancing teaching*. New York: Macmillan.

Hyman, I.A. (1990). *Reading, writing, and the hickory stick: The appalling story of physical and psychological abuse in American schools*. Lexington, MA: Lexington Books.

Hyman, I.A. (1997). *School discipline and school violence*. Boston: Allyn & Bacon.

Individuals with Disabilities Education Act. (1997 amendments). Washington, DC: U.S. Government Printing Office.

Jensen, M.M., & Yerington, P. (1997). *Gangs: Straight talk, straight up*. Longmont, CO: Sopris West.

Jenson, W.R., Rhode, G., & Reavis, H.K. (1994). *The tough kid tool box*. Longmont, CO: Sopris West.

Johnson, D.W., & Johnson, R.T. (1995a). *Reducing school violence through conflict resolution*. Alexandria, VA: Association for Supervision and Curriculum Development.

Johnson, D.W., & Johnson, R.T. (1995b). *Teaching students to be peacemakers* (3rd ed.). Edina, MN: Interaction Book Company.

Johnson, D.W., & Johnson, R.T. (1999). *Learning together and alone: Cooperative, competitive, and individualistic learning* (5th ed.). Boston: Allyn & Bacon.

Johnson, D.W., & Johnson, E.P. (2006). *Joining together: Group theory and group skills* (9th ed.). Boston: Allyn & Bacon.

Johnson, D.W., Johnson, R.T., & Holubec, E.J. (1994). *The new circles of learning: Cooperation in the classroom*. Alexandria, VA: Association for Supervision and Curriculum Development.

Johnson, P. (2001). Dimensions of functioning in alcoholic and nonalcoholic families. *Journal of Mental Health*, 23 (2), 127–136.

Jones, F.H. (1987). *Positive classroom discipline*. New York: McGraw-Hill.

Jones, F.H. (2000). *Tools for teaching*. Santa Cruz, CA: Frederic H. Jones & Associates.

Jones, V.F., & Jones, L.S. (2004). *Comprehensive classroom management: Creating communities of support and solving problems* (7th ed.). Boston: Allyn & Bacon.

Jonson, K.F. (2002). *The new elementary teacher's handbook: Flourishing in your first year* (2nd ed.). Thousand Oaks, CA: Corwin Presst.

Kagan, S., Kyle, P., & Scott, S. (2004). *Win–win discipline*. San Clemente, CA: Kagan Publishing.

Keller, J.M. (1983). Motivational design of instruction. In C.M. Reigeluth (Ed.), *Instructional design theories and models: An overview of their current status*. Hillsdale, NJ: Erlbaum.

Kerr, M.M., & Nelson, C.M. (2006). *Strategies for addressing behavior problems in the classroom* (5th ed.). Upper Saddle River, NJ: Prentice-Hall.

Kohn, A. (1996). *Beyond discipline: From compliance to community*. Alexandria, VA: Association for Supervision and Curriculum Development.

Kohn, A. (1999). *Punished by rewards* (rev. ed.). Boston: Houghton Mifflin.

Kottler, E., & Kottler, J.A. (2002). *Children with limited English: Teaching strategies for the regular classroom* (2nd ed.). Thousand Oaks, CA: Corwin Press.

Kottler, J.A., & Kottler, E. (2000). *Counseling skills for teachers*. Thousand Oaks, CA: Corwin Press.

Kounin, J.S. (1970). *Discipline and group management in classrooms*. New York: Holt, Rinehart & Winston.

Kronowitz, E.L. (2004). *Your first year of teaching and beyond* (4th ed.). Boston: Allyn & Bacon.

Landau, B.M. (2004). *The art of classroom management: Building equitable learning communities* (2nd ed.). Upper Saddle River, NJ: Prentice-Hall/Merrill.

Lane, K.E., Richardson, M.D., & VanBerkum, D.W. (1996). *The school safety handbook*. Lancaster, PA: Technomic Publishing.

Lazear, D. (2003). *Eight ways of teaching: The artistry of teaching with multiple intelligences* (4th ed.). Thousand Oaks, CA: Corwin Press.

Lehr, J.B., & Harris, H.W. (1988). *At-risk, low-achieving students in the classroom*. Washington, DC: National Education Association.

Leinhardt, G., Weidman, C., & Hammond, K.M. (1987). Introduction and integration of classroom routines by expert teachers. *Curriculum Inquiry*, 17 (2), 135–176.

Leone, P., Mayer, M.J., Malmgren, K., & Meisel, S.M. (2000). School violence and disruption: Rhetoric, reality, and reasonable balance. *Focus on Exceptional Children*, 33 (1), 1–20.

Lepper, M.R., & Hodell, M. (1989). Intrinsic motivation in the classroom. In C. Ames & R. Ames (Eds.), *Research on motivation in education* (Vol. 3). San Diego: Academic Press.

Levin, J., & Nolan, J.F. (2004). *Principles of classroom management* (4th ed.). Boston: Allyn & Bacon.

Lindberg, J.A., & Swick, A.M. (2002). *Common-sense classroom management: Surviving September and beyond in the elementary classroom*. Thousand Oaks, CA: Corwin Press.

Linn, R.L., & Miller, M. (2005). *Measurement and assessment in teaching* (9th ed.). Upper Saddle River, NJ: Prentice-Hall.

Manley, R.S., Rickson, H., & Standeven, B. (2000). Children and adolescents with eating disorders: Strategies for teachers and counselors. *Intervention in School and Clinic*, 35, 228–231.

Manning, M.L., & Baruth, L.G. (2004). *Multicultural education of children and adolescents* (4th ed.). Boston: Allyn & Bacon.

Manning, M.L., & Bucher, K.T. (2003). *Classroom management: Models, applications, and cases*. Upper Saddle River, NJ: Prentice-Hall/Merrill.

Marshall, P.L. (2002). *Cultural diversity in our schools*. Belmont, CA: Wadsworth.

Marzano, R.J. (2003). *Classroom management that works: Research-based strategies for every teacher*. Alexandria, VA: Association for Supervision and Curriculum Development.

Marzano, R.J., Pickering, D.J., & Pollock, J.E. (2005). *Classroom instruction that works: Research-based strategies for increasing student achievement*. Upper Saddle River, NJ: Prentice-Hall/Merrill.

Mayer, G.R. (1995). Preventing antisocial behavior in the schools. *Journal of Applied Behavior Analysis*, 28, 467–478.

McEwan, E.K. (2005). *How to deal with parents who are angry, troubled, afraid, or just plain crazy* (2nd ed.). Thousand Oaks, CA: Corwin Press.

McFarland, D., Kolstad, R., & Briggs, L. (1995). Educating attention deficit hyperactivity disorder children. *Education*, 115 (4), 597–603.

McGrath, C.E., Watson, A.L., & Chassin, L. (1999). Academic achievement in adolescent children of alcoholics. *Journal of Studies on Alcohol*, 60, 18–26.

Mehan, H., Hertweck, A., Combs, S.E., & Flynn, P.J. (1982). Teachers' interpretations of students' behavior. In L.C. Wilkinson (Ed.), *Communicating in the classroom* (pp. 297–321). New York: Academic Press.

Mendler, A.N., & Curwin, R.L. (1999). *Discipline with dignity for challenging youth*. Bloomington, IN: Solution Tree.

Miltenberger, R.G. (2004). *Behavior modification* (3rd ed.). Belmont, CA: Wadsworth.

Moran, C., Stobbe, J., Baron, W., Miller, J., & Moir, E. (2000). *Keys to the classroom: A teacher's guide to the first month of school* (2nd ed.). Thousand Oaks, CA: Corwin Press.

Murray, B.P. (2002). *The new teacher's complete sourcebook: Grades K–4.* New York: Scholastic Professional Books.

National Center for Children in Poverty. (2005). *Basic facts about low-income children in the United States.* (www.nccp.org)

National Center for Education Statistics. (2004). *Crime and safety in America's public schools.* (www.nces.ed.gov/surveys/ssocs/)

National Clearinghouse on Child Abuse and Neglect Information. (2003). *Recognizing child abuse and neglect: Signs and symptoms.* (www.nccanch.acf. hhs.gov/topics/overview/signs.cfm)

National Coalition for the Homeless. (2001). *Education of homeless children and youth.* NCH fact sheet #10. (www.nationalhomeless.org)

National PTA. (2000). *Building successful partnerships: A guide for developing parent and family involvement programs.* Bloomington, IN: Solution Tree.

National PTA. (2004). *National standards for parent/family involvement programs.* (2nd ed.). Bloomington, IN: Solution Tree.

Nelsen, J. (1996). *Positive discipline* (3rd ed.). New York: Ballantine Books.

Nelsen, J., Lott, L., & Glenn, H.S. (2000). *Positive discipline in the classroom* (3rd ed.). Rocklin, CA: Prima Publishing.

Nieto, S. (2004). *Affirming diversity: The sociopolitical context of multicultural education* (4th ed.). Boston: Allyn & Bacon.

No Child Left Behind (2002). U.S. Department of Education, www.ed.gov/nclb/landing.jhtml.

Payne, R.K. (2001). *A framework for understanding poverty* (rev. ed.). Highlands, TX: aha! Process, Inc.

Post, P., & Robinson, B.E. (1998). School-aged children of alcoholics and non-alcoholics: Their anxiety, self-esteem, and locus of control. *Professional School Counseling*, 1, 36–40.

Prothrow-Stith, D. (1993). *Deadly consequences: How violence is destroying our teenage population and a plan to begin solving the problem.* New York: HarperCollins.

Rafferty, Y. (1998). Meeting the educational needs of homeless children. *Educational Leadership*, 55 (4), 48–52.

Redick, S.S., & Vail, A. (1991). *Motivating youth at risk.* Gainesville, VA: Home Economics Education Association.

Rhode, G., Jenson, W.R., & Reavis, H.K. (1992). *The tough kid book: Practical classroom management strategies.* Longmont, CO: Sopris West.

Rigby, K. (1998). *Bullying in schools and what to do about it.* York, ME: Stenhouse Publishers.

Roberts, M.P. (2001). *Your mentor: A practical guide for first-year teachers in grades 1–3.* Thousand Oaks, CA: Corwin Press.

Roehler, L., Duffy, G., & Meloth, M. (1987). The effects and some distinguishing characteristics of explicit teacher explanation during reading instruction. In J. Niles (Ed.), *Changing perspectives on research in reading/language processing and instruction.* Rochester, NY: National Reading Conference.

Romero, M., Mercado, C., & Vazquez-Raria, J.A. (1987). Students of limited English proficiency. In V. Richardson-Koehler (Ed.), *Educators' handbook: A research perspective.* New York: Longman.

Rosenshine, B., & Stevens, R. (1986). Teacher functions. In M.C. Wittrock (Ed.), *Handbook of research on teaching* (3rd ed.) (pp. 376–391). New York: Macmillan.

Salend, S.J. (2005). *Creating inclusive classrooms: Effective and reflective practices for all students* (5th ed.). Upper Saddle River, NJ: Prentice-Hall/Merrill.

Sapon-Shevin, M. (1999). *Because we can change the world: A practical guide to building cooperative, inclusive classroom communities.* Boston: Allyn & Bacon.

Sarka, P.R., & Shank, M. (1990). *Lee Canter's back to school with assertive discipline.* Santa Monica, CA: Lee Canter & Associates.

Savage, T.V. (1999). *Teaching self-control through management and discipline* (2nd ed.). Boston: Allyn & Bacon.

Schell, L.M., & Burden, P.R. (2000). *Countdown to the first day of school* (2nd ed.). Washington, DC: National Education Association.

Sharan, Y., & Sharan, S. (1992). *Expanding cooperative learning through group investigation.* New York: Teachers College Press.

Short, P.M., Short, R.J., & Blanton, C. (1994). *Rethinking student discipline: Alternatives that work.* Thousand Oaks, CA: Corwin Press.

Shostak, R. (2006). Involving students in learning. In J. Cooper (Ed.), *Classroom teaching skills* (8th ed.) (pp. 77–100). Boston: Houghton Mifflin.

Shrigley, R.L. (1985). Curbing student disruption in the classroom: Teachers need intervention skills. *National Association of Secondary School Principals Bulletin*, 69 (479), 26–32.

Silver, H.F., Strong, R.W., & Perini, M.J. (2000). *So each may learn: Integrating learning styles and multiple intelligences.* Alexandria, VA: Association for Supervision and Curriculum Development.

Skinner, B.F. (1971). *Beyond freedom and dignity.* New York: Knopf.

Slavin, R.E. (1991). *Student team learning: A practical guide for cooperative learning* (3rd ed.). Washington, DC: National Education Association.

Slavin, R.E. (2006). *Educational psychology: Theory and practice* (8th ed.). Boston: Allyn & Bacon.

Sprinthall, N.A., Sprinthall, R.C., & Oja, S.N. (1998). *Educational psychology: A developmental approach* (7th ed.). New York: McGraw-Hill.

Stanard, R.P. (2000). Assessment and treatment of adolescent depression and suicidality. *Journal of Mental Health Counseling*, 22 (3), 204–217.

Stein, N., & Sjostrom, L. (1996). *Bullyproof: A teacher's guide on teasing and bullying for use with fourth and fifth grade students.* Washington, DC: National Education Association.

Sternberg, R.J. (1997). What does it mean to be smart? *Educational Leadership*, 54 (6), 20–24.

Stevens, S. (2000). A teacher looks at the elementary child with ADH D. In B.P. Guyer (Ed.), *ADHD: Achieving success in school and in life* (pp. 67–80). Boston: Allyn & Bacon.

Stipek, D.J. (2002). *Motivation to learn: Integrating theory and practice* (4th ed.). Boston: Allyn & Bacon.

Survey shows kids shadowed by fear of guns and violence. (1993, July 30). *The Wichita Eagle*, p. 3A.

Swap, S.M. (1993). *Developing home-school partnerships: From concepts to practice.* New York: Teachers College Press.

Thompson, J.G. (2002a). *Discipline survival guide for the secondary teacher.* San Francisco: Jossey-Bass.

Thompson, J.G. (2002b). *First-year teacher's survival kit.* San Francisco: Jossey-Bass.

Tomlinson, C.A. (1999). *The differentiated classroom: Responding to the needs of all learners.* Alexandria, VA: Association for Supervision and Curriculum Development.

Tomlinson, C.A. (2001). *How to differentiate instruction in mixed-ability classrooms* (2nd ed.). Alexandria, VA: Association for Supervision and Curriculum Development.

Torrance, E.P., & Sisk, D.A. (1997). *Gifted and talented children in the regular classroom.* Buffalo, NY: Creative Education Foundation Press.

Turnbull, A.P., Turnbull, R., Erwin, E.J., & Soodak, L.C. (2006). *Families, professionals, and exceptionality* (5th ed.). Upper Saddle River, NJ: Prentice-Hall.

Turnbull, A.P., Turnbull, R., Shank, M., & Smith, S.J. (2004). *Exceptional lives: Special education in today's schools* (4th ed.). Upper Saddle River, NJ: Prentice-Hall.

U.S. Department of Education. (2001, Feb./March). Studies report declining rate of school violence. *Community Update*, 85, 1–2

U.S. Department of Health and Human Services. (2005). *Child maltreatment, 2003.* www.acf.hhs.gov/programs/cb/publications/cmreports.htm.

Vaughn, S., Bos, C.S., & Schumm, J.S. (2003). *Teaching exceptional, diverse, and at-risk students in the general education classroom* (3rd ed.). Boston: Allyn & Bacon.

Walker, J.E., Shae, T.M., & Bauer, A. (2004). *Behavior management: A practical approach for educators* (8th ed.). Upper Saddle River, NJ: Prentice-Hall.

Warner, C. (2001). *Promoting your school* (2nd ed.). Thousand Oaks, CA: Corwin Press.

Webb, T. (1993, March 22). Tough-talking programs strip violence of glamorous image. *The Wichita Eagle*, pp. 1, 4.

Weber, W.A., & Roff, L.A. (1983). A review of teacher education literature on classroom management. In W.A. Weber, L.A. Roff, J. Crawford, & C. Robinson (Eds.), *Classroom management: Reviews of the teacher education and research literature* (pp. 7–42). Princeton, NJ: Educational Testing Service.

Weinhold, B., & Weinhold, J. (1998). Conflict resolution: The partnership way in schools. *Counseling and Human Development*, 30(7), 1–12.

Weinstein, C.S. (2003). *Secondary classroom management: Lessons from research and practice* (2nd ed.). New York: McGraw-Hill.

Weinstein, C.S., & Mignano, A.J., Jr. (2003). *Elementary classroom management: Lessons from research and practice* (3rd ed.). New York: McGraw-Hill.

Williamson, B. (1998). *A first-year teacher's guidebook* (2nd ed.). Sacramento, CA: Dynamic Teaching Co.

Wodrich, D.L. (2000). *Attention-deficit/hyperactivity disorder: What every parent wants to know* (2nd ed.). Baltimore: MD: Paul Brookes Publishing Co.

Wolfgang, C.H. (2005). *Solving discipline and classroom management problems* (6th ed.). New York: John Wiley & Sons.

Wong, H.K., & Wong, R.T. (2004). *The first days of school: How to be an effective teacher* (3rd ed.). Mountain View, CA: Harry Wong Publications.

Woolfolk-Hoy, A. (2005). *Educational psychology* (9th ed.). Boston: Allyn & Bacon.

Wyatt, R.L., & White, J.E. (2002). *Making your first year a success: The secondary teacher's survival guide*. Thousand Oaks, CA: Corwin Press.

Yao, E. (1988). Working effectively with Asian immigrant parents. *Phi Delta Kappan*, 70 (3), 223–225.

Young, K.R., West, R.P., Smith, D.J., & Morgan, D.P. (2000). *Teaching self-management strategies to adolescents*. Longmont, CO: Sopris West.

Name Index

Classroom Management: Creating a Successful K-12 Learning Community/Third Edition, by Paul R. Burden
ISBN 0-471-71073-3   Copyright © 2006 John Wiley & Sons, Inc.

Subject Index

Classroom Management: Creating a Successful K-12 Learning Community/Third Edition, by Paul R. Burden
ISBN 0-471-71073-3   Copyright © 2006 John Wiley & Sons, Inc.